UN LLAMADO a la FE

NIVEL C

Harcourt Religion Publishers
www.harcourtreligion.com

Nihil Obstat
Revdo. Dennis J. Colter

Imprimátur
✠ Rvdo. Mayor Jerome Hanus, OSB
Arzobispo de Dubuque
5 de enero de 2004
Día de San John Neumann

La nihil obstat y el imprimátur son declaraciones oficiales de que un libro o folleto no tiene error doctrinal o moral. Lo presente no implica que aquellos a quienes se les otorgó la nihil obstat y el imprimátur están de acuerdo con el contenido, las opiniones o las declaraciones expresadas.

For permission to translate/reprint copyrighted material, grateful acknowledgment is made to the following sources:

Catholic Book Publishing Co., New Jersey: "Oración al Espíritu Santo" from *Libro Católico de Oraciones,* edited by Rev. Maurus Fitzgerald, O.F.M. Text © 1984 by Catholic Book Publishing Co. "Ave María" from *Libro Católico de Oraciones,* edited by Rev. Maurus Fitzgerald, O.F.M. Text © 2003, 1984 by Catholic Book Publishing Co.

Comisión Episcopal Española de Liturgia: "Acto de Contrición" from *Ritual de la Penitencia.* Text © by Comisión Episcopal Española de Liturgia.

Confraternity of Christian Doctrine, Inc., Washington, D.C.: Scriptures from the *New American Bible.* Text copyright © 1991, 1986, 1970 by Confraternity of Christian Doctrine, Inc. All rights reserved. No part of the *New American Bible* may be used or reproduced in any form, without permission in writing from the copyright owner

Editorial Verbo Divino: Scriptures from *La Biblia Latinoamerica,* edited by San Pablo — Editorial Verbo Divino. Text copyright © 1998 by Sociedad Bíblica Católica International (SOBICAIN).

International Commission on English in the Liturgy, Inc.: English translation of "Come, Holy Spirit" (Retitled: "Prayer to the Holy Spirit") from *A Book of Prayers.* Translation © 1982 by International Committee on English in the Liturgy, Inc. (ICEL). English translation of "Act of Contrition" from *Rite of Penance.* Translation © 1974 by International Committee on English in the Liturgy, Inc. (ICEL). From the English translation of *Pastoral Care of the Sick.* Translation © 1982 by International Committee on English in the Liturgy, Inc. (ICEL). From the English translation of *The Roman Missal.* Translation © 1975 by International Committee on English in the Liturgy, Inc. (ICEL). From the English translation of *Rite of Penance.* Translation © 1974 by International Committee on English in the Liturgy, Inc. (ICEL)

International Consultation on English Texts: English translation of Glory to the Father, the Hail Mary, Gloria in Excelsis, The Lord's Prayer, and The Apostles' Creed by the International Consultation on English Texts (ICET).

Obra Nacional de la Buena Prensa, A.C.: Untitled prayers (Titled: "El Credo de los Apóstoles," "Gloria," and "La Oración del Señor") from *Misal Romano.* Text copyright © 1999 by Obra Nacional de la Buena Prensa, A.C.

Additional acknowledgments appear on page 497.

Printed in the United States of America

0-15-901372-0

3 4 5 6 7 8 9 10 030 10 09 08 07 06

Contenido

LECTURAS Y CELEBRACIONES DEL AÑO LITÚRGICO 12

UNIDAD 1
LA FAMILIA DE DIOS

- **Capítulo 1:** El hermoso mundo de Dios 82
- **Capítulo 2:** La comunidad de la Iglesia 98
- **Capítulo 3:** En casa con Dios 114

UNIDAD 2
RESPONDER A DIOS

- **Capítulo 4:** La Santísima Trinidad 134
- **Capítulo 5:** La Iglesia rinde culto 150
- **Capítulo 6:** Orar siempre 166

UNIDAD 3
EL CUERPO DE CRISTO

- **Capítulo 7:** La Buena Nueva 186
- **Capítulo 8:** El sacrificio de Jesús 202
- **Capítulo 9:** La obra de Jesús 218

UNIDAD 4
LA IGLESIA CATÓLICA

- **Capítulo 10:** Los líderes de la Iglesia 238
- **Capítulo 11:** Un pueblo santo 254
- **Capítulo 12:** La misión de la Iglesia 270

UNIDAD 5
LA IGLESIA DIRIGE

- **Capítulo 13:** Decide amar 290
- **Capítulo 14:** Comparte tu luz 306
- **Capítulo 15:** La Iglesia nos guía 322

UNIDAD 6
LOS SIETE SACRAMENTOS

- **Capítulo 16:** Sacramentos de Iniciación 342
- **Capítulo 17:** Sacramentos de Curación 358
- **Capítulo 18:** Sacramentos de Servicio 374

UNIDAD 7
EL REINO DE DIOS

- **Capítulo 19:** Somos de Dios 394
- **Capítulo 20:** La Iglesia hoy 410
- **Capítulo 21:** ¡Vida para siempre! 426

RECURSOS CATÓLICOS 444

AL EMPEZAR EL AÑO 2

- Acerca de tu vida
- Acerca de tu fe
- Acerca de tu libro
- Un llamado a la fe

LECTURAS Y CELEBRACIONES DEL AÑO LITÚRGICO 12

- **Tiempo Ordinario: La Natividad de María** 16
  ACCIÓN RITUAL PARA LA CELEBRACIÓN:
  Letanía de María
- **Adviento: La luz de Dios** 24
  ACCIÓN RITUAL PARA LA CELEBRACIÓN:
  Procesión de alabanza
- **Navidad: Alabemos a Jesús** 32
  ACCIÓN RITUAL PARA LA CELEBRACIÓN:
  La Oración del Señor y la paz
- **Tiempo Ordinario: Comunicar la Palabra de Dios** 40
  ACCIÓN RITUAL PARA LA CELEBRACIÓN:
  La señal sobre la frente
- **Cuaresma: Crecer en la fe** 48
  ACCIÓN RITUAL PARA LA CELEBRACIÓN:
  Oración en silencio
- **Triduo Pascual: ¡Alegrémonos!** 56
  ACCIÓN RITUAL PARA LA CELEBRACIÓN:
  Recordemos el Bautismo
- **Pascua: Santo, Santo, Santo** 64
  ACCIÓN RITUAL PARA LA CELEBRACIÓN:
  Rito del agua bendita
- **Pentecostés: El Espíritu Santo** 72
  ACCIÓN RITUAL PARA LA CELEBRACIÓN:
  Honrar la Sagrada Escritura

UNIDAD 1
LA FAMILIA DE DIOS 80

Capítulo 1 **El hermoso mundo de Dios** .. 82

- Dios creó todas las cosas. Toda la creación muestra la bondad de Dios.
- Dios creó a los seres humanos a su imagen y semejanza.

LA SAGRADA ESCRITURA

La creación de la Tierra
Génesis 1, 1; 2, 3

Capítulo 2 **La comunidad de la Iglesia** 98

- La Biblia es la palabra de Dios escrita en palabras humanas.
- La Iglesia es el Pueblo de Dios unido en el nombre de Jesús.

LA SAGRADA ESCRITURA

Ayudarse los unos a los otros
Hechos 2, 42–47

Capítulo 3 **En casa con Dios** 114

- Los niños descubren primero el amor de Dios por medio de sus familias.
- La familia se conoce como "la Iglesia doméstica".

LA SAGRADA ESCRITURA

María visita a Isabel
Lucas 1, 39-56

Repaso de la Unidad 1 130

UNIDAD 2
RESPONDER A DIOS 132

Capítulo 4 La Santísima Trinidad 134

- La Santísima Trinidad son tres Personas en un solo Dios.
- Jesús, Dios Hijo, enseñó acerca de Dios Padre y Dios Espíritu Santo.

LA SAGRADA ESCRITURA

El Padre y el Espíritu Santo
Juan 14, 6–7 y 16–17

Capítulo 5 La Iglesia rinde culto 150

- La Misa es la forma de rendir culto más importante de la Iglesia.
- En la Misa, la Iglesia recuerda lo que hizo Jesús en la Última Cena.

LA SAGRADA ESCRITURA

La Última Cena
Lucas 22, 14–20

Capítulo 6 Orar siempre 166

- La oración es elevar tu mente y tu corazón a Dios.
- La oración es una parte importante de la vida diaria del cristiano.

LA SAGRADA ESCRITURA

El fariseo y el publicano
Lucas 18, 9–14

Orar bien
Mateo 6, 5–8

Repaso de la Unidad 2 182

UNIDAD 3
EL CUERPO DE CRISTO 184

Capítulo 7 La Buena Nueva 186

- Jesús comunicó la Buena Nueva del Reino de Dios, o el reino de la justicia, el amor y la paz.
- Jesús es el Mesías, el elegido y el Salvador.

LA SAGRADA ESCRITURA

Jesús en la sinagoga
Lucas 4, 16–22

Capítulo 8 El sacrificio de Jesús 202

- Jesús murió y resucitó para salvar a todos del poder del pecado.
- La Iglesia celebra el Misterio Pascual en todos los sacramentos.

LA SAGRADA ESCRITURA

María Magdalena se encuentra con Jesús
Juan 20, 11–18

Capítulo 9 La obra de Jesús 218

- La Iglesia es el Cuerpo de Cristo al que pertenecen todos sus miembros.
- Los miembros de la Iglesia continúan la obra de Jesús ayudando a los demás.

LA SAGRADA ESCRITURA

Los que ayudaron
Mateo 25, 34–40

Repaso de la Unidad 3 234

UNIDAD 4
LA IGLESIA CATÓLICA 236

Capítulo 10 Los líderes de la Iglesia .. 238

- Los obispos son los sucesores de los Apóstoles.
- El Papa, los obispos y los párrocos dirigen y guían a la Iglesia.

LA SAGRADA ESCRITURA

Pedro y Jesús
Mateo 16, 15–19; 26, 69–75; Juan 21, 15–17

Capítulo 11 Un pueblo santo 254

- El Espíritu Santo une y santifica a la Iglesia.
- La unidad de la Iglesia resulta de la fusión de muchas culturas.

LA SAGRADA ESCRITURA

La fiesta de Pentecostés
Hechos 2, 1–12

Capítulo 12 La misión de la Iglesia ... 270

- La misión de la Iglesia es comunicar la Buena Nueva de Jesús a todos los pueblos.
- La Iglesia es católica porque está en todas partes y recibe a todos.

LA SAGRADA ESCRITURA

Hacer la obra de Dios
1 Corintios 3, 5–9

Repaso de la Unidad 4 286

UNIDAD 5
LA IGLESIA DIRIGE 288

Capítulo 13 Decide amar 290

- La ley del amor de Jesús es amar a todas las personas como Él nos ama.
- Jesús nos enseña que debemos amar y perdonar a nuestros enemigos.

LA SAGRADA ESCRITURA

Ama a tu enemigo
Mateo 5, 43–48

Capítulo 14 Comparte tu luz 306

- Los dones que has recibido de Dios de la fe, la esperanza y el amor te ayudan a vivir una vida buena y moral.
- Jesús llama a los cristianos a ser la luz del mundo.

LA SAGRADA ESCRITURA

Deja que brille tu luz
Mateo 5, 14–16

Capítulo 15 La Iglesia nos guía 322

- El Espíritu Santo y las enseñanzas de la Iglesia te ayudan a tomar buenas decisiones.
- Tu conciencia y la gracia también te ayudan a seguir a Dios.

LA SAGRADA ESCRITURA

Saulo y Jesús
Hechos 9, 1–30

Repaso de la Unidad 5 338

UNIDAD 6
LOS SIETE SACRAMENTOS 340

Capítulo 16 Sacramentos de Iniciación 342

- Los sacramentos son signos que provienen de Jesús y que conceden la gracia.
- Los sacramentos de Iniciación son el Bautismo, la Confirmación y la Eucaristía.

LA SAGRADA ESCRITURA

Muchos son bautizados
Hechos 2, 38–41

Capítulo 17 Sacramentos de Curación 358

- Los sacramentos de Curación son la Reconciliación y la Unción de los enfermos.
- En estos sacramentos, la Iglesia ora por la curación espiritual y física.

LA SAGRADA ESCRITURA

Jesús da nueva vida
Lucas 8, 40–42, 49–56

Capítulo 18 Sacramentos de Servicio 374

- Los sacramentos al Servicio de la comunidad son el Orden y el Matrimonio.
- Estos sacramentos celebran el compromiso de las personas ante Dios y la comunidad.

LA SAGRADA ESCRITURA

Servidores y administradores
1 Corintios 4, 1–2

Repaso de la Unidad 6 390

UNIDAD 7
EL REINO DE DIOS 392

Capítulo 19 Somos de Dios 394

- Dios cumplió su promesa de ser fiel para siempre enviándonos a su Hijo, Jesús.
- La Iglesia continúa siendo un signo de la alianza de Dios.

Capítulo 20 La Iglesia hoy 410

- Todos los miembros de la Iglesia comparten su misión de trabajar por la paz y la justicia.
- La Iglesia es un signo del Reino de Dios.

LA SAGRADA ESCRITURA

Los discípulos son enviados
Mateo 10, 5–14

Capítulo 21 ¡Vida para siempre! 426

- Las personas que mueren en amistad con Dios viven para siempre en su presencia.
- Al fin del mundo, Cristo nos juzgará por la forma en que hayamos vivido.

LA SAGRADA ESCRITURA

Una tierra nueva
Apocalipsis 21, 1–4

Alfa y Omega
Apocalipsis 22, 13

Repaso de la Unidad 7 442

Recursos católicos

Sagrada Escritura

- La Biblia ... 444
  - El Antiguo Testamento ... 444
  - El Nuevo Testamento ... 444
  - Los evangelios ... 446
  - Las cartas ... 448
- Los versículos de la Biblia ... 448

Credo

- Dios ... 450
  - Dios Padre ... 450
  - Dios Hijo ... 450
  - Dios Espíritu Santo ... 450
- La Iglesia ... 452
  - La comunión de los santos ... 452
  - Los atributos de la Iglesia ... 454
  - Los doce Apóstoles ... 454
- La vida después de la muerte ... 456
  - Cielo, infierno y purgatorio ... 456
  - El juicio final ... 456
- María ... 458
  - Los títulos de María ... 458
  - Los nombres de María ... 458

Liturgia

- La Misa ... 460
  - Ordinario de la Misa ... 462
- Los sacramentos ... 464
  - Sacramentales ... 464
- Bendiciones ... 464
  - Devociones ... 466
  - Objetos de la Iglesia ... 466

Moral

- Los Diez Mandamientos ... 468
  - El gran mandamiento ... 468
- Las Bienaventuranzas ... 470
- Examen de conciencia ... 472
- La gracia ... 472
  - La solidaridad ... 472
  - La virtud ... 474

Oración

La señal de la cruz ... 476
La Oración del Señor ... 476
Ave María ... 476
Gloria al Padre (Doxología) ... 478
Bendición de los alimentos ... 478
Acto de fe, esperanza y amor ... 478
Oración al Espíritu Santo ... 480
El Credo de los Apóstoles ... 480
Acto de contrición ... 482

Palabras de fe ... 484
Índice ... 492

Contents

SEASONAL LESSONS & CELEBRATIONS 14

UNIT 1
FAMILY OF GOD

Chapter 1: God's Beautiful World 83
Chapter 2: The Church Community 99
Chapter 3: At Home With God 115

UNIT 2
RESPONDING TO GOD

Chapter 4: The Holy Trinity 135
Chapter 5: The Church Worships 151
Chapter 6: Pray Always 167

UNIT 3
THE BODY OF CHRIST

Chapter 7: The Good News 187
Chapter 8: Jesus' Sacrifice 203
Chapter 9: Jesus' Work 219

UNIT 4
THE CATHOLIC CHURCH

Chapter 10: Church Leaders 239
Chapter 11: One Holy People 255
Chapter 12: The Church's Mission 271

UNIT 5
THE CHURCH LEADS

Chapter 13: Choose Love 291
Chapter 14: Share Your Light 307
Chapter 15: The Church Guides 323

UNIT 6
THE SEVEN SACRAMENTS

Chapter 16: Sacraments of Initiation 343
Chapter 17: Sacraments of Healing 359
Chapter 18: Sacraments of Service 375

UNIT 7
KINGDOM OF GOD

Chapter 19: Belonging to God 395
Chapter 20: The Church Today 411
Chapter 21: Life Forever! 427

CATHOLIC SOURCE BOOK 445

BEGINNING THE YEAR 3

- About You
- About Your Faith
- About Your Book
- A Call to Faith

SEASONAL LESSONS & CELEBRATIONS 14

▶ **Ordinary Time: The Birth of Mary** 20
RITUAL ACTION FOR CELEBRATION:
Litany to Mary

▶ **Advent: God's Own Light** 28
RITUAL ACTION FOR CELEBRATION:
Procession of Praise

▶ **Christmas: Praise Jesus** 36
RITUAL ACTION FOR CELEBRATION:
The Lord's Prayer and Sign of Peace

▶ **Ordinary Time: Sharing God's Word** ... 44
RITUAL ACTION FOR CELEBRATION:
Signing of Foreheads

▶ **Lent: Growing in Faith** 52
RITUAL ACTION FOR CELEBRATION:
Silent Prayer

▶ **Triduum: Rejoice!** 60
RITUAL ACTION FOR CELEBRATION:
Remember Baptism

▶ **Easter: Holy, Holy, Holy** 68
RITUAL ACTION FOR CELEBRATION:
Sprinkling Rite

▶ **Pentecost: The Holy Spirit** 76
RITUAL ACTION FOR CELEBRATION:
Honoring the Scriptures

UNIT 1
FAMILY OF GOD 81

Chapter 1 **God's Beautiful World** 83

- God created everything. All creation shows God's goodness.
- God created humans in his image and likeness.

SCRIPTURE

The Creation of the Earth
Genesis 1:1—2:3

Chapter 2 **The Church Community** 99

- The Bible is the word of God written in human words.
- The Church is the People of God gathered in the name of Jesus.

SCRIPTURE

Helping One Another
Acts 2:42–47

Chapter 3 **At Home With God** 115

- Children first learn about God's love through their families.
- The family home is called the "domestic Church."

SCRIPTURE

Mary Visits Elizabeth
Luke 1:39–56

Unit 1 Review 131

UNIT 2
RESPONDING TO GOD 133

4 The Holy Trinity 135
- The Holy Trinity is three Persons in one God.
- Jesus, God the Son, taught about God the Father and God the Spirit.

SCRIPTURE

The Father and the Spirit
John 14:6–7, 16–17

5 The Church Worships 151
- The Mass is the Church's most important form of worship.
- In the Mass the Church remembers what Jesus did at the Last Supper.

SCRIPTURE

The Last Supper
Luke 22:14–20

6 Pray Always 167
- Prayer is the raising of one's mind and heart to God.
- Prayer is an important part of a Christian's daily life.

SCRIPTURE

The Pharisee and the Tax Collector
Luke 18:9–14

Praying Well
Matthew 6:5–8

Unit 2 Review 183

UNIT 3
THE BODY OF CHRIST 185

7 The Good News 187
- Jesus shared the good news about God's kingdom of justice, love, and peace.
- Jesus is the Messiah, the chosen one, and Savior.

SCRIPTURE

Jesus in the Synagogue
Luke 4:16–22

8 Jesus' Sacrifice 203
- Jesus died and rose to new life to save all people from the power of sin.
- The Church celebrates the Paschal mystery in all the sacraments.

SCRIPTURE

Mary Meets Jesus
John 20:11–18

9 Jesus' Work 219
- The Church is the Body of Christ to which all members belong.
- Church members continue Jesus' work when they help others.

SCRIPTURE

Those Who Helped
Matthew 25:34–40

Unit 3 Review 235

UNIT 4
THE CATHOLIC CHURCH 237

Chapter 10 **Church Leaders** 239
- The bishops are the successors of the Apostles.
- The pope, bishops, and pastors lead and guide the Church.

SCRIPTURE

Peter and Jesus
Matthew 16:15–19, 26:69–75; John 21:15–17

Chapter 11 **One Holy People** 255
- The Holy Spirit unites the Church and makes its members holy.
- Many cultures together make up the unity of the Church.

SCRIPTURE

The Feast of Pentecost
Luke 1: 46–50

Chapter 12 **The Church's Mission** 271
- The Church's mission is to share Jesus' good news with the people of all nations.
- The Church is catholic because it is everywhere and welcomes everyone.

SCRIPTURE

Doing God's Work
1 Corinthians 3:5–9

Unit 4 Review 287

UNIT 5
THE CHURCH LEADS 289

Chapter 13 **Choose Love** 291
- Jesus' law of love is to love one another as Jesus loves each of us.
- Jesus teaches that we should love and forgive our enemies.

SCRIPTURE

Love Your Enemy
Matthew 5:43–48

Chapter 14 **Share Your Light** 307
- God's gifts of faith, hope, and love help you live a good and moral life.
- Christians are called by Jesus to be the light of the world.

SCRIPTURE

Your Light Must Shine
Matthew 5:14–16

Chapter 15 **The Church Guides** 323
- The Holy Spirit and the teachings of the Church help you make good choices.
- Your conscience and grace also help you follow God.

SCRIPTURE

Saul and Jesus
Acts 9:1–30

Unit 5 Review 339

UNIT 6
THE SEVEN SACRAMENTS 341

Chapter 16 Sacraments of Initiation 343
- Sacraments are signs that come from Jesus and give grace.
- The Sacraments of Initiation are Baptism, Confirmation, and Eucharist.

SCRIPTURE
Many Are Baptized
Acts 2:38–41

Chapter 17 Sacraments of Healing ... 359
- The Sacraments of Healing are Reconciliation and Anointing of the Sick.
- In these sacraments the Church prays for spiritual and physical healing.

SCRIPTURE
Jesus Gives New Life
Luke 8:40–42, 49–56

Chapter 18 Sacraments of Service ... 375
- The Sacraments of Service are Holy Orders and Matrimony.
- These sacraments celebrate people's commitment to God and the community.

SCRIPTURE
Servants and Stewards
1 Corinthians 4:1–2

Unit 6 Review 391

UNIT 7
KINGDOM OF GOD 393

Chapter 19 Belonging to God 395
- God kept his promise to be forever faithful when he sent his Son, Jesus.
- The Church continues to be a sign of God's covenant.

Chapter 20 The Church Today 411
- All members of the Church share in its mission to work for peace and justice.
- The Church is a sign of the kingdom of God.

SCRIPTURE
Sending Out the Disciples
Matthew 10:5–14

Chapter 21 Life Forever! 427
- People who die in God's friendship live forever in God's presence.
- At the end of the world, Christ will judge all people on the way they lived their lives.

SCRIPTURE
A New Earth
Revelation 21:1–4
Alpha and Omega
Revelation 22:13

Unit 7 Review 443

Catholic Source Book

Scripture

- The Bible . . . 445
  - Old Testament . . . 445
  - New Testament . . . 445
  - Gospels . . . 447
  - Letters . . . 449
- How to Locate Bible Verses . . . 449

Creed

- God . . . 451
  - God the Father . . . 451
  - God the Son . . . 451
  - God the Holy Spirit . . . 451
- The Church . . . 453
  - The Communion of Saints . . . 453
  - Marks of the Church . . . 455
  - The Twelve Apostles . . . 455
- Life After Death . . . 457
  - Heaven, Hell, and Purgatory . . . 457
  - Judgment . . . 457
- Mary . . . 459
  - Titles of Mary . . . 459
  - Mary Names . . . 459

Liturgy

- The Mass . . . 461
  - Order of the Mass . . . 463
- Sacraments . . . 465
- Sacramentals . . . 465
- Blessings . . . 465
- Devotions . . . 467
  - Objects in the Church Building . . . 467

Morality

- The Ten Commandments . . . 469
  - The Great Commandment . . . 469
- The Beatitudes . . . 471
- Examination of Conscience . . . 473
- Grace . . . 473
  - Solidarity . . . 473
  - Virtue . . . 475

Prayer

- The Sign of the Cross . . . 477
- The Lord's Prayer . . . 477
- Hail Mary . . . 477
- Glory to the Father (Doxology) . . . 479
- Blessing Before Meals . . . 479
- Act of Faith, Hope, and Love . . . 479
- Prayer to the Holy Spirit . . . 481
- The Apostles' Creed . . . 481
- Act of Contrition . . . 483

Words of Faith . . . 488

Index . . . 494

Acerca de tu vida

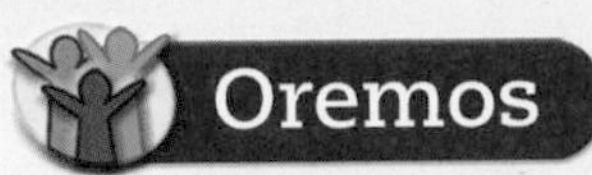
Oremos

Líder: Haznos uno en tu nombre, Señor.
"¡Qué bueno y qué tierno es
ver a esos hermanos vivir juntos!"
Salmo 133, 1

Todos: Haznos uno en tu nombre, Señor. Amén.

Actividad Comencemos

Un año por delante Hoy te unes a un nuevo grupo, tu clase de religión. Este año haremos muchas cosas que te entusiasmarán. Harás nuevos amigos y aprenderás cosas nuevas. Te acercarás más a Jesús y a la Iglesia.

Aprenderás y crecerás junto a tus compañeros. Es posible que haya personas nuevas en tu clase. ¿Qué te gustaría contarles acerca de ti?

¿Cuáles son tus cosas favoritas?

Película

Estación del año

Actividad al aire libre

About You

Let Us Pray

Leader: Make us one in your name, O Lord.
"How good it is, how pleasant
where the people dwell as one."
Psalm 133:1

All: Make us one in your name, O Lord. Amen.

Activity Let's Begin

The Year Ahead Today you are joining a new group—your religion class. You have many exciting things to look forward to this year. You will meet new people and learn new things. You will grow closer to Jesus and the Church.

You will be learning and growing along with your classmates. You may have some new people in your class. What would you want to tell them about yourself?

What are some of your Favorite Things?

Movie

Season

Outside Activity

Acerca de tu fe

Hacer nuevos amigos en tu clase y en tu parroquia forma parte de tu crecimiento en la fe. Tu familia, tus amigos y tu comunidad parroquial te ayudan a seguir a Jesús. Con ellos lees la Biblia y aprendes más acerca de la Iglesia y de cómo compartir el amor de Dios con los demás.

AUTOBÚS ESCOLAR

Actividad

Comparte tu fe

Piensa: ¿Cuál es tu relato favorito de la Biblia?

____

____

____

¿Por qué te parece especial ese relato?

Comunica: Túrnate con un compañero para hablar sobre los relatos favoritos de ambos.

Actúa: Representa uno de los relatos en clase.

About Your Faith

Part of growing in faith is making new friends with people in your class and parish. Your family, friends, and parish community help you follow Jesus. With them you spend time reading from the Bible. You learn more about the Church and how to share God's love with others.

SCHOOL BUS

Activity — Share Your Faith

Think: What is your favorite Bible story?

____

____

____

Why is the story special to you?

Share: With a partner take turns talking about your favorite stories.

Act: Act out one of the stories for the class.

Acerca de tu libro

Tu libro te ayudará a aprender más acerca de tu fe, de siervos de la fe importantes y de las maneras en que los católicos celebran su fe.

Actividad Practica tu fe

Busca y encuentra Al leer el libro encontrarás muchas cosas diferentes. Para familiarizarte con el libro, busca los títulos que aparecen a continuación. Escribe dónde puedes encontrar cada uno.

Página ____________________

UNA BIOGRAFÍA

Página ____________________

Datos de fe

Página ____________________

Palabras de fe

Página ____________________

Siervos de la fe

Página ____________________

Página ____________________

Análisis

Página ____________________

About Your Book

Your book will help you to learn more about your faith, important people of faith, and ways Catholics celebrate faith.

Activity Connect Your Faith

Seek and Find As you read your book, you will find lots of different things. To get to know your book better, look for the features listed below. Write down where you find each of them.

SCRIPTURE

Page ____________

BIOGRAPHY

Page ____________

Faith Fact

Page ____________

Words of Faith

Page ____________

People of Faith

Page ____________

Let Us Pray

Page ____________

Focus

Page ____________

Un llamado a la fe

Juntos

Hagan la señal de la cruz.

Líder:	El Señor esté con vosotros.
Todos:	Y con tu espíritu.
Líder:	Oremos.
	Inclinen la cabeza mientras el líder reza.
Todos:	Amén.

Escucha la Palabra de Dios

Lector:	Lectura del santo Evangelio.
	Lean Marcos 1,16–20.
	Palabra del Señor.
Todos:	Gloria a ti, Señor Jesús.

Reflexiona

¿Cómo crees que se sintieron los primeros discípulos de Jesús?

¿Cómo respondes hoy en día al llamado de Jesús?

A Call to Faith

Gather

Pray the Sign of the Cross together.

Leader: The Lord be with you.

All: And also with you.

Leader: Let us pray.

Bow your head as the leader prays.

All: Amen.

Listen to God's Word

Reader: A reading from the Holy Gospel.

Read Mark 1:16–20.

The Gospel of the Lord.

All: Praise to you, Lord Jesus Christ.

Reflect

How do you think Jesus' first followers felt?

How do you answer Jesus' call today?

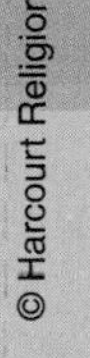

La señal sobre los sentidos

Líder: Oremos.

Jesús, tú nos llamas a creer en ti.

Todos: Creemos en ti.

Hagan la señal de la cruz sobre la frente.

Líder: Jesús, tú nos llamas a amarte.

Todos: Te amamos.

Hagan la señal de la cruz sobre la frente.

Líder: Jesús, tú nos llamas a compartir tu mensaje con los demás.

Todos: Les hablaremos de ti a los demás.

Hagan la señal de la cruz sobre la frente.

Líder: Gloria al Padre, al Hijo, al Espíritu Santo.

Todos: Como era en el principio, ahora y siempre, por los siglos de los siglos. Amén.

¡Evangeliza!

Líder: Compartamos el amor de Dios con los demás.

Todos: Demos gracias a Dios.

Canten juntos.

¡Dios nos llama a obrar con justicia,
Dios nos llama a amar con ternura,
Dios nos llama a servirnos unos a otros;
y a seguirle con humildad!

Signing of the Senses

Leader: Let us pray.

Jesus, you call us to believe in you.

All: We believe in you.

Trace the Sign of the Cross on your forehead.

Leader: Jesus, you call us to love you.

All: We love you.

Trace the Sign of the Cross on your forehead.

Leader: Jesus, you call us to share your message with others.

All: We will tell others about you.

Trace the Sign of the Cross on your forehead.

Leader: Glory to the Father, and to the Son, and to the Holy Spirit,

All: As it was in the beginning, is now, and will be for ever. Amen.

Go Forth!

Leader: Let us go forth to share the love of Christ with one another.

All: Thanks be to God.

Sing together.

We are called to act with justice,
we are called to love tenderly,
we are called to serve one another;
to walk humbly with God!

Días de celebración

Muchas familias se reúnen para celebrar acontecimientos especiales. Los cumpleaños, los aniversarios y los días festivos son momentos importantes de la vida familiar. En esos días las familias cuentan relatos y honran a sus seres queridos.

La Iglesia también se reúne en días y épocas especiales, que se conocen como los tiempos del año litúrgico. En esos días o épocas, la Iglesia recuerda acontecimientos importantes de la vida de Jesús, de María y de los santos.

La Iglesia celebra esos acontecimientos con diferentes palabras y acciones.

Palabras y acciones
Levantamos las manos para orar.
Honramos la Cruz arrodillándonos frente a ella o besándola.
Ofrecemos la paz de Cristo dándonos la mano.
Hacemos la señal de la cruz sobre la frente, el corazón y los labios.

Tu clase usará estas palabras y acciones para celebrar los diferentes tiempos del año litúrgico.

El año litúrgico

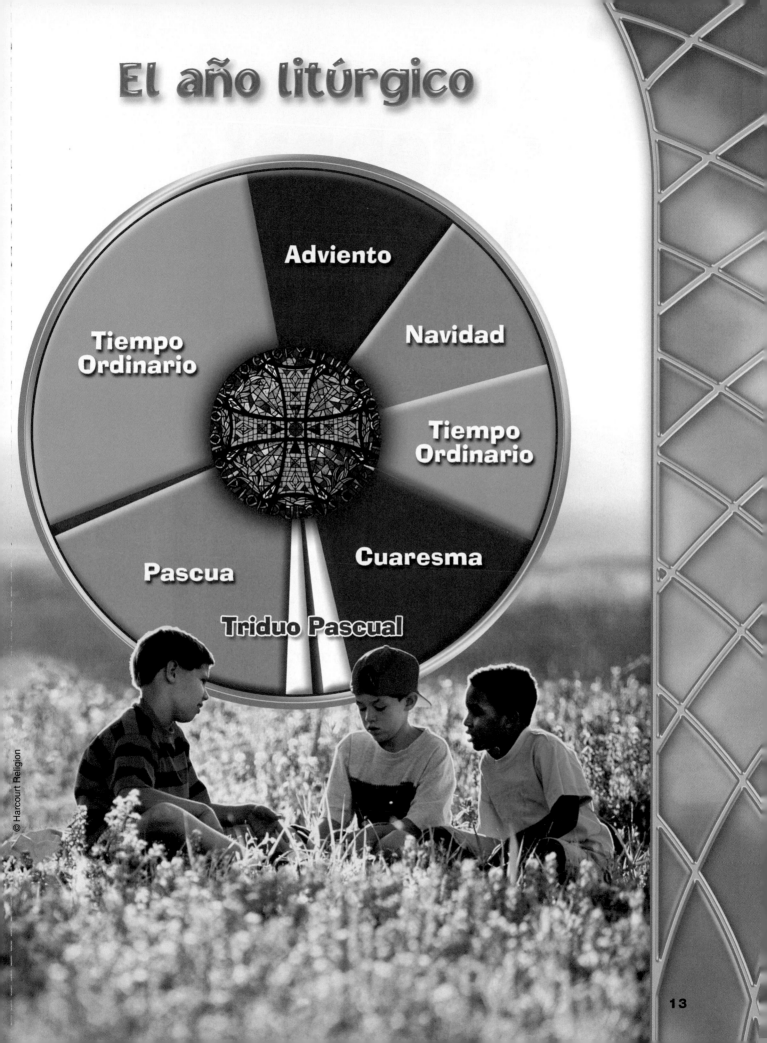

Adviento
Navidad
Tiempo Ordinario
Cuaresma
Triduo Pascual
Pascua
Tiempo Ordinario

Times to Celebrate

Many families gather together for special events. Birthdays, anniversaries, and holidays are important times for families. They share stories and honor loved ones on these days.

The Church gathers for special days and times, too. These special times are called the seasons of the Church year. The Church remembers important events in the lives of Jesus, Mary, and saints.

The Church celebrates with different words and actions.

Words and Actions
Hands are raised in prayer.
The Cross is honored by kneeling in front of it or kissing it.
The sign of Christ's peace is offered with a handshake.
The Sign of the Cross is marked on foreheads, hearts, and lips.

Your class will use these words and actions to celebrate the different seasons.

The Church Year

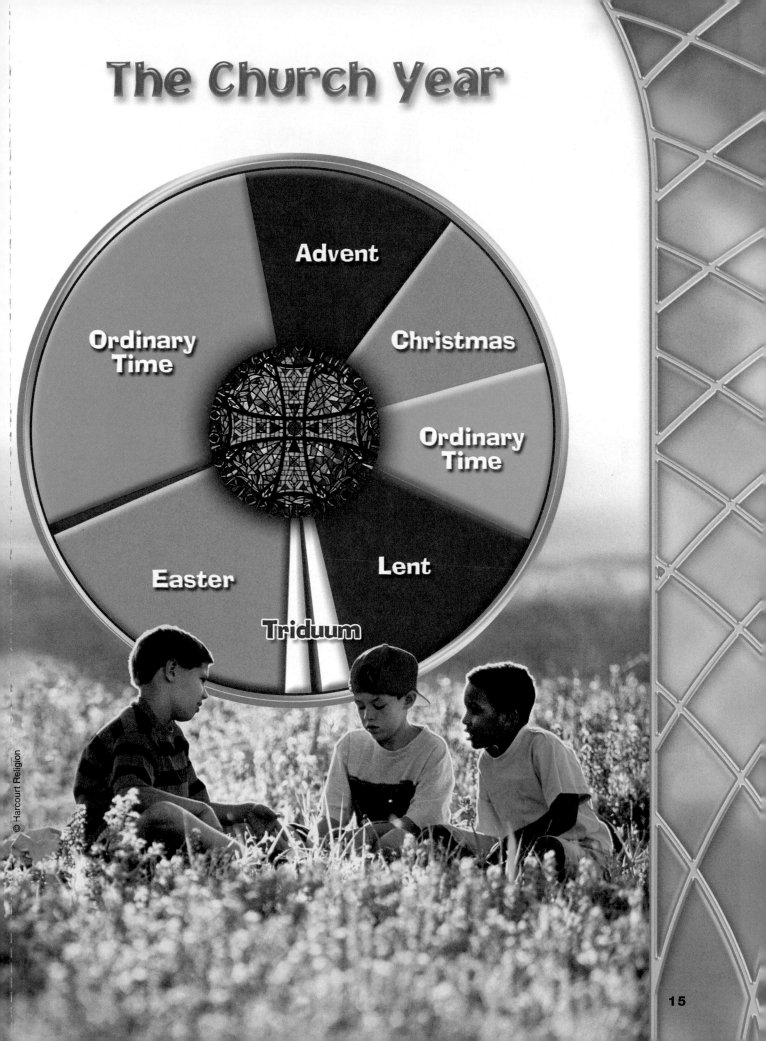

Advent
Christmas
Ordinary Time
Lent
Triduum
Easter
Ordinary Time

La Natividad de María

Durante el Tiempo Ordinario, la Iglesia recuerda muchas de las enseñanzas de Jesús. La Iglesia también honra a María y a los santos. A María se le honra de distintas maneras en días especiales a lo largo del año. Uno de esos días especiales es el 8 de septiembre, la fiesta de la Natividad de María.

El amanecer de la esperanza

En ese día, la Iglesia recuerda que Dios bendijo a María desde el momento en que nació. El nacimiento de María fue el comienzo de nuestra salvación, que nos llegaría por medio de su Hijo.

Dios eligió a María para que fuera la madre de su Hijo. La joven María amaba mucho a Dios, y aceptó hacer lo que Dios le pidió, aunque no entendía totalmente cuál era su plan. María es la más importante de todos los santos porque es la madre del Hijo de Dios.

? ¿De qué maneras honra la Iglesia a María?

Celebremos a María

Juntos

Hagan la señal de la cruz.

Líder: Bendito seas, Señor.

Todos: Bendito seas por siempre, Señor.

Canten juntos.

¡Tu nombre santo es
por toda la eternidad!
También tu misericordia
con el pueblo que elegiste.
Tu nombre santo es.

"Holy Is Your Name" © 1989, GIA Publications, Inc.

Líder: Oremos.

Inclinen la cabeza mientras el líder reza.

Todos: Amén.

Escucha la Palabra de Dios

Líder: Lectura de la carta a los Romanos.

Lean Romanos 8, 28–30.

Palabra de Dios.

Todos: Te alabamos, Señor.

Reflexiona

¿Qué papel tenía María en el plan de Dios?

¿Cómo glorificó Dios a María?

Dedica unos minutos en silencio para pensar cómo te está llamando Dios.

Letanía de María

Arrodíllense cuando el líder comience.

Líder: Dios Padre nuestro

Todos: **ten piedad de nosotros.**

Líder: Dios Hijo

Todos: **ten piedad de nosotros.**

Líder: Dios Espíritu Santo

Todos: **ten piedad de nosotros.**

Líder: Santa María

Todos: **ruega por nosotros.**

Continúen respondiendo "ruega por nosotros" cada vez que el líder lea un título de María.

Líder: Ruega por nosotros, santa Madre de Dios.

Todos: **Para que seamos dignos de alcanzar las promesas de Cristo.**

¡Evangeliza!

Líder: Vayamos confiados en el plan de Dios, como hizo María.

Todos: **Demos gracias a Dios.**

Canten juntos.

¡Tu nombre santo es
por toda la eternidad!
También tu misericordia
con el pueblo que elegiste.
Tu nombre santo es.

Madre de Dios

María amaba mucho a Dios. Siempre hacía lo que Dios le pedía. Él la hizo madre de su propio Hijo. María confiaba en Dios, y Él hizo grandes cosas por ella.

¿Cómo puedes mostrar que confías en Dios?

ACTIVIDAD

Escribe una letanía

Redacta una letanía usando tus propios títulos para María. Reza con tu familia la letanía durante la semana. La respuesta será "Ruega por nosotros".

Ordinary Time

The Birth of Mary

During Ordinary Time, the Church remembers many of the teachings of Jesus. The Church also honors Mary and the saints. Mary is honored in many ways on special days all year long. One special day is September 8, the Feast of the Birth of Mary.

The Dawn of Hope

On this day the Church recalls that God blessed Mary from the very beginning of her life. Her birth was the beginning of our salvation that would be won by the Son born to her.

God chose Mary to be the mother of his Son. The young Mary loved God very much. Mary said yes to what God asked her to do, even though she did not fully understand God's plan. Mary is the greatest of all the saints because she is the mother of the Son of God.

? What are some ways the Church honors Mary?

Celebrate Mary

Gather

Pray the Sign of the Cross together.

Leader: Blessed be God.

All: **Blessed be God forever.**

Sing together.

And holy is your name through
all generations!
Everlasting is your mercy
to the people you have chosen,
and holy is your name.

Leader: Let us pray.

Bow your head as the leader prays.

All: **Amen.**

Listen to God's Word

Leader: A reading from the Letter to the Romans.

Read Romans 8:28–30.

The word of the Lord.

All: **Thanks be to God.**

Reflect

How was Mary part of God's purpose?

How did God glorify Mary?

Take some quiet time to think of ways God is calling you.

Litany of Mary

Kneel as the leader begins.

Leader: God our Father

All: **have mercy on us.**

Leader: God the Son

All: **have mercy on us.**

Leader: God the Holy Spirit

All: **have mercy on us.**

Leader: Holy Mary

All: **pray for us.**

Continue to respond "pray for us" as the leader reads more titles for Mary.

Leader: Pray for us, holy Mother of God.

All: **That we may become worthy of the promises of Christ.**

Go Forth!

Leader: Let us go forth to trust in God's plan as Mary did.

All: **Thanks be to God.**

Sing together.

And holy is your name through all
generations!
Everlasting is your mercy
to the people you have chosen,
and holy is your name.

"Holy Is Your Name" © 1989, GIA Publications, Inc.

Mother of God

Mary loved God very much. She always did what God asked her to do. He made her the mother of his own Son. Mary trusted God, who did great things for her.

❓ **What are some ways you show your trust in God?**

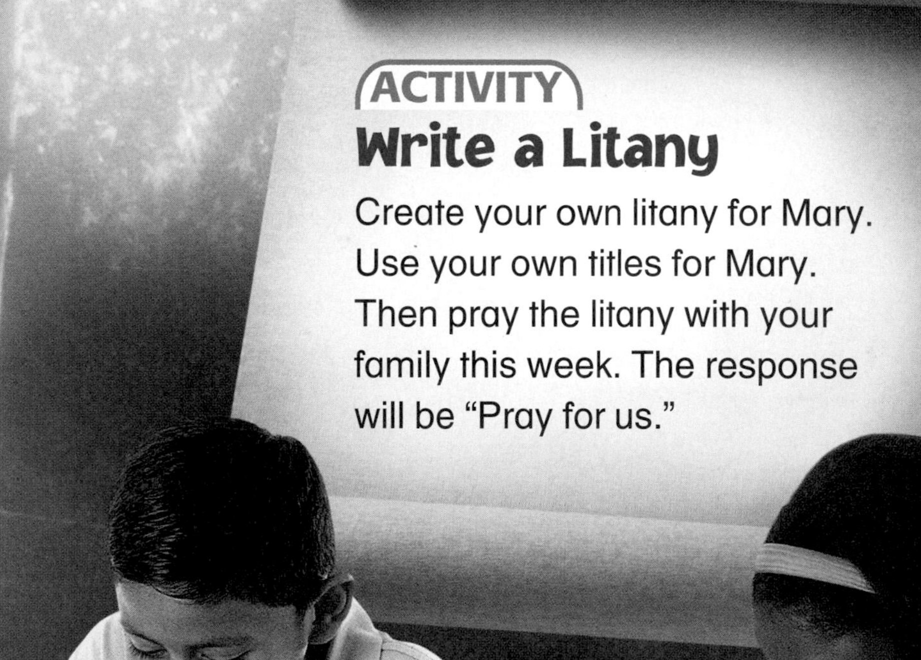

ACTIVITY

Write a Litany

Create your own litany for Mary. Use your own titles for Mary. Then pray the litany with your family this week. The response will be "Pray for us."

La luz de Dios

El primer tiempo del año litúrgico es el Adviento. Es una época muy especial. En el Adviento te preparas para celebrar el nacimiento de Jesús.

Esperando la Luz

Mucho tiempo antes de que naciera Jesús, el Pueblo de Dios esperaba un Salvador que trajera la luz a su vida. "El pueblo que caminaba en la noche" (Isaías 9, 1). Cuando llegó el momento, Dios envió a su Hijo, la Luz de Dios, al mundo.

El Adviento te recuerda que Jesús también es la luz de tu vida. La corona de Adviento te indica que debes preparar tu corazón para recibir a Jesús. La corona tiene cuatro velas. En cada semana de Adviento se enciende una de las velas y se reza una oración especial pidiendo que la luz de Jesús entre en tu vida.

¿Qué cosas hace tu familia durante el Adviento?

Celebremos el Adviento

Juntos

Hagan la señal de la cruz.

Líder: Nuestro auxilio es el nombre del Señor.

Todos: Que hizo el cielo y la tierra.

Canten juntos.

Caminamos en la luz,
en la luz, en la luz.
Caminamos en la luz,
en la luz de Dios.

Líder: Oremos.

Inclinen la cabeza mientras el líder reza.

Todos: Amén.

Escucha la Palabra de Dios

Lector: Lectura del santo Evangelio según san Juan.

Lean Juan 1, 6–9.

Palabra del Señor.

Todos: Gloria a ti, Señor Jesús.

Reflexiona

¿Quién es Jesús?

¿En qué sentido Jesús es una luz para ti?

Oración de los fieles

Líder: Oremos.

Jesús, Luz del Mundo,
te pedimos que lleves tu luz de curación
a aquellos por los que ahora oramos.

Respondan a cada oración con estas palabras.

Todos: **Señor, escucha nuestra oración.**

Procesión de alabanza

Líder: Robustezcan las manos débiles
y afirmen las rodillas que se doblan.

Isaías 35, 3

Caminen en procesión con los brazos en alto alrededor de la sala de oración.

Canten juntos.

Caminamos en la luz,
en la luz, en la luz.
Caminamos en la luz,
en la luz de Dios.

¡Evangeliza!

Líder: En esta semana, preparemos nuestros corazones para recibir a Jesús.

Todos: **Demos gracias a Dios.**

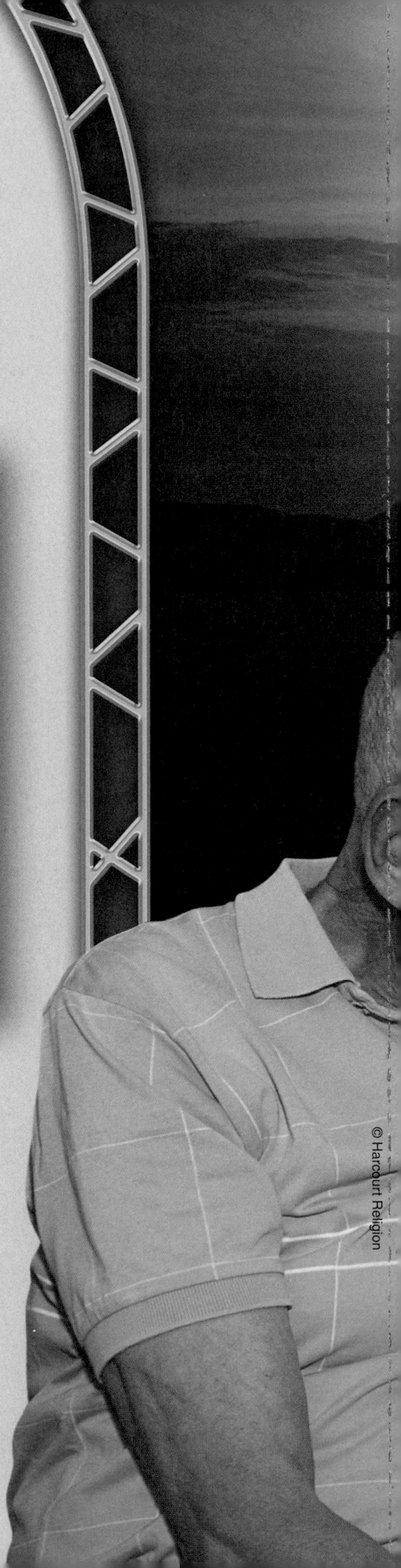

La luz del día

Juan el Bautista, primo de Jesús, ayudó a señalar el camino hacia Jesús, la Luz del Mundo. Dios eligió a Juan para que ayudara a otros a reconocer a Jesús. Jesús ilumina la oscuridad con la luz de Dios.

¿Cómo puedes señalar a los demás el camino hacia Jesús, la Luz de Dios?

ACTIVIDAD

Sé una luz para los demás

Cuando sigues el ejemplo de Jesús, compartes su luz con otros. ¿Cómo puedes iluminar la vida de otros? Escribe una cosa que puedas hacer en tu casa y una cosa que puedas hacer en la escuela.

God's Own Light

The first season of the Church year is Advent. It is a very special time. During Advent you prepare to celebrate the birth of Jesus.

Waiting for the Light

Long before Jesus was born, God's people waited for a Savior to bring light into their lives. They "walked in darkness" (Isaiah 9:1). When the time was right, God sent his Son, God's own Light, into the world.

Advent helps you remember that Jesus is the light in your life, too. The Advent wreath reminds you to prepare your heart to welcome Jesus. The Advent wreath has four candles. A candle is lit each week during Advent. A special prayer is prayed to ask that the light of Jesus come into your life.

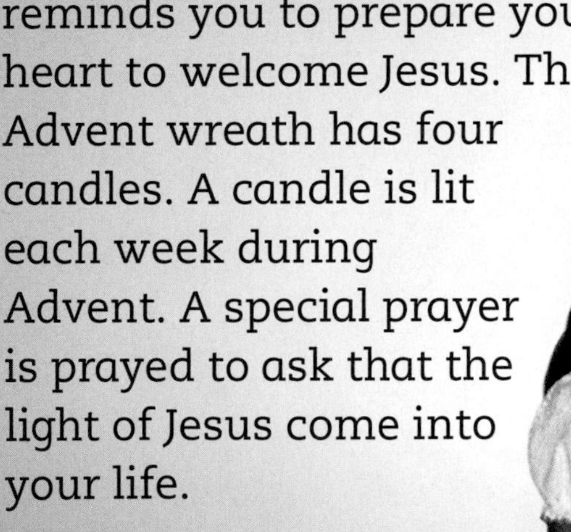

What are some things your family does during Advent?

Celebrate Advent

Gather

Pray the Sign of the Cross together.

Leader: Our help is in the name of the Lord.

All: Who made heaven and earth.

Sing together.

We are walking in the light,
in the light, in the light
We are walking in the light,
in the light of God.

Leader: Let us pray.

Bow your heads as the leader prays.

All: Amen.

Listen to God's Word

Reader: A reading from the holy Gospel according to John.

Read John 1:6–9.

The Gospel of the Lord.

All: Praise to you, Lord Jesus Christ.

Reflect

Who is Jesus?

How is Jesus a light to you?

Intercessions

Leader: Let us pray.

Jesus, Light of the World,
we ask you to bring your healing light
to those for whom we now pray.

Respond to each intercession with these words.

All: **Lord, hear our prayer.**

Procession of Praise

Leader: Strengthen the hands that are feeble,
make firm the knees that are weak.

Isaiah 35:3

Process around the prayer space with arms raised.

Sing together.

We are walking in the light,
in the light, in the light
We are walking in the light,
in the light of God.

Go Forth!

Leader: Let us go forth this week to prepare
our hearts to welcome Jesus.

All: **Thanks be to God.**

The Light of Day

John the Baptist, Jesus' cousin, helped point the way to Jesus, the Light of the World. God chose John to help others recognize Jesus. Jesus comes into the darkness and breaks it open with God's light.

How can you point others to Jesus, God's own Light?

ACTIVITY

Be Light to Others

When you follow Jesus' example, you share his light with others. How can you bring light into someone else's life? Write one thing you can do at home and one thing you do at school.

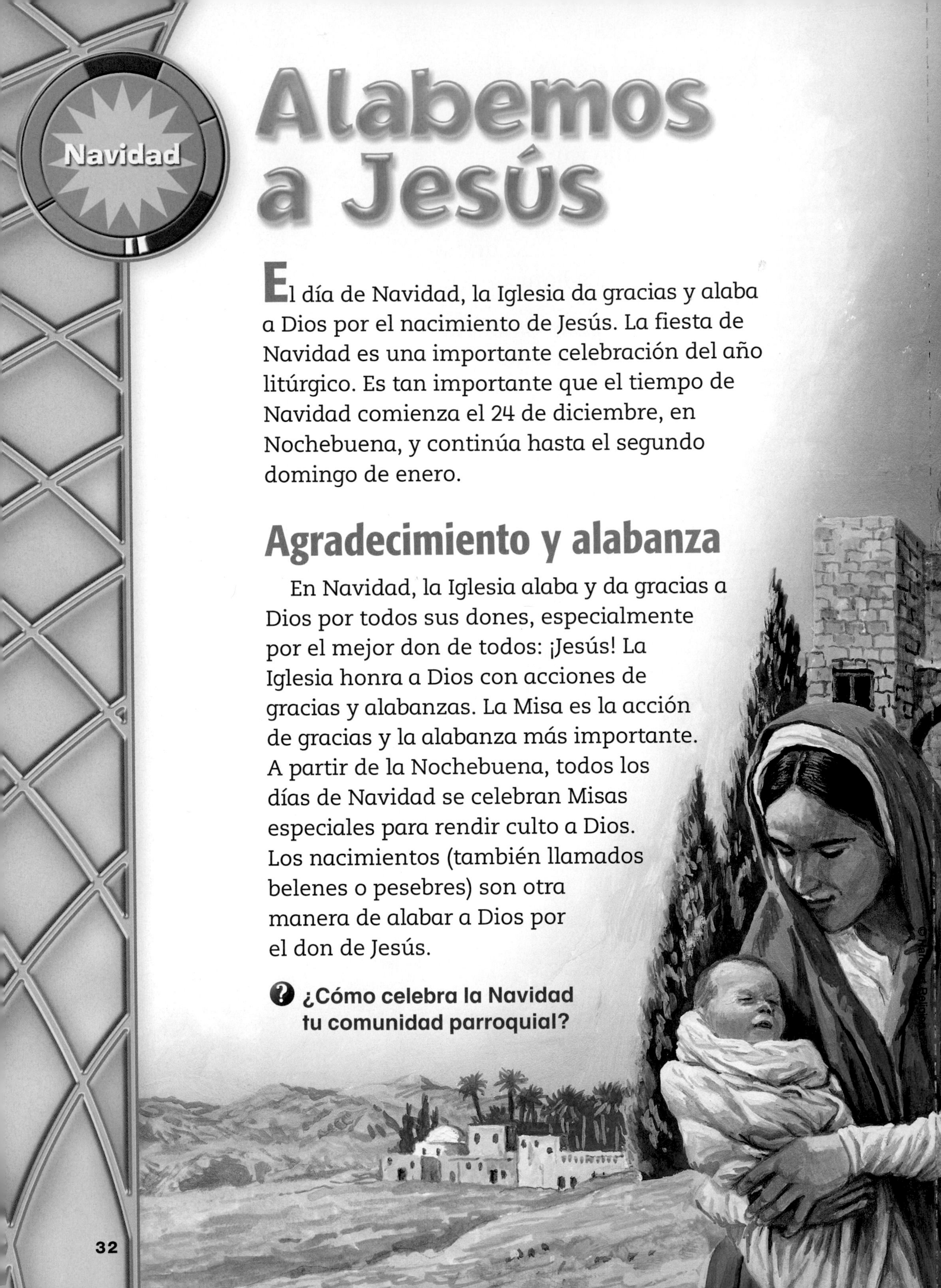

Alabemos a Jesús

El día de Navidad, la Iglesia da gracias y alaba a Dios por el nacimiento de Jesús. La fiesta de Navidad es una importante celebración del año litúrgico. Es tan importante que el tiempo de Navidad comienza el 24 de diciembre, en Nochebuena, y continúa hasta el segundo domingo de enero.

Agradecimiento y alabanza

En Navidad, la Iglesia alaba y da gracias a Dios por todos sus dones, especialmente por el mejor don de todos: ¡Jesús! La Iglesia honra a Dios con acciones de gracias y alabanzas. La Misa es la acción de gracias y la alabanza más importante. A partir de la Nochebuena, todos los días de Navidad se celebran Misas especiales para rendir culto a Dios. Los nacimientos (también llamados belenes o pesebres) son otra manera de alabar a Dios por el don de Jesús.

¿Cómo celebra la Navidad tu comunidad parroquial?

Celebremos a Jesús

Juntos

Canten juntos el estribillo.

Ve, anuncia en las montañas,
en las colinas, por doquier;
Ve, anuncia en las montañas,
que Jesús ya nació.

Hagan la señal de la cruz.

Líder: Bendito sea el nombre del Señor.

Todos: Ahora y por siempre.

Líder: Oremos.

Inclinen la cabeza mientras el líder reza.

Todos: Amén.

Escucha la Palabra de Dios

Líder: Lectura del santo Evangelio según san Lucas.

Lean Lucas 2, 1–14.

Palabra del Señor.

Todos: Gloria a ti, Señor Jesús.

Reflexiona

¿Qué partes de la celebración de la Navidad son especiales para ti?

¿Cómo celebras la Navidad con tu familia?

La Oración del Señor y la paz

Líder: Oremos con las palabras que Jesús nos enseñó.

Todos: **Padre nuestro...**

Líder: Que el Dios de la luz y de la paz llene nuestros corazones y nuestras vidas.

Todos: **Amén.**

Líder: Démonos fraternalmente la paz.

Dense fraternalmente la paz.

¡Evangeliza!

Líder: Esta semana, demos gracias y alabemos a Dios por el don de Jesús que nos dio.

Todos: **Demos gracias a Dios.**

Canten juntos el estribillo.

Ve, anuncia en las montañas,
en las colinas, por doquier;
Ve, anuncia en las montañas,
que Jesús ya nació.

"Go Tell It on the Mountain" © 1995, GIA Publications, Inc.

El gran don de Dios

Dios te ha dado un don especial en Jesús. Tú puedes dar tus propios regalos a Dios: tus oraciones de agradecimiento y alabanza. Puedes orar con palabras, gestos y acciones, durante la Misa o en cualquier otro momento.

¿Cuál es tu manera favorita de dar gracias y alabar a Dios en la oración?

¿Has visto a otras personas orar de manera diferente de la tuya?

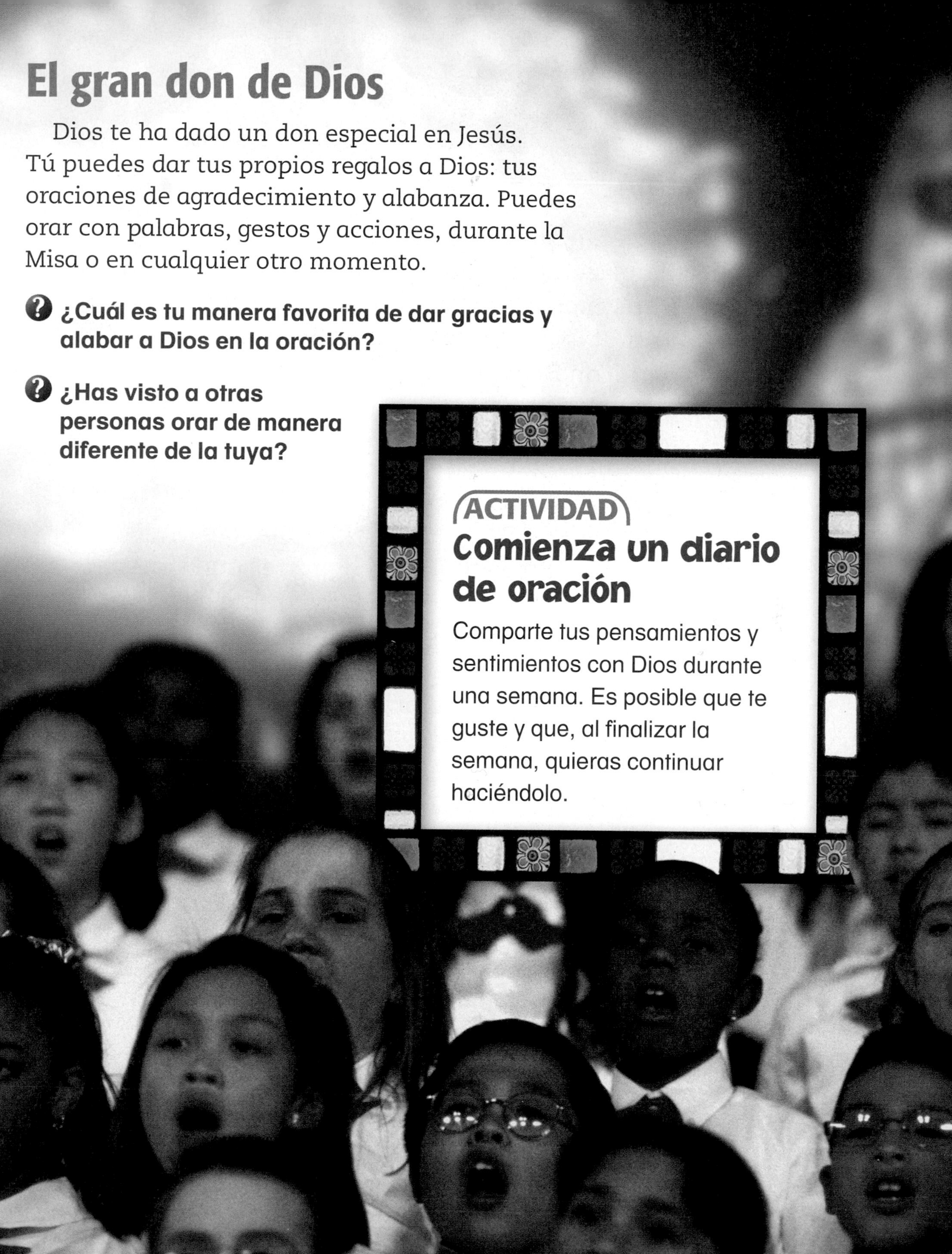

ACTIVIDAD

Comienza un diario de oración

Comparte tus pensamientos y sentimientos con Dios durante una semana. Es posible que te guste y que, al finalizar la semana, quieras continuar haciéndolo.

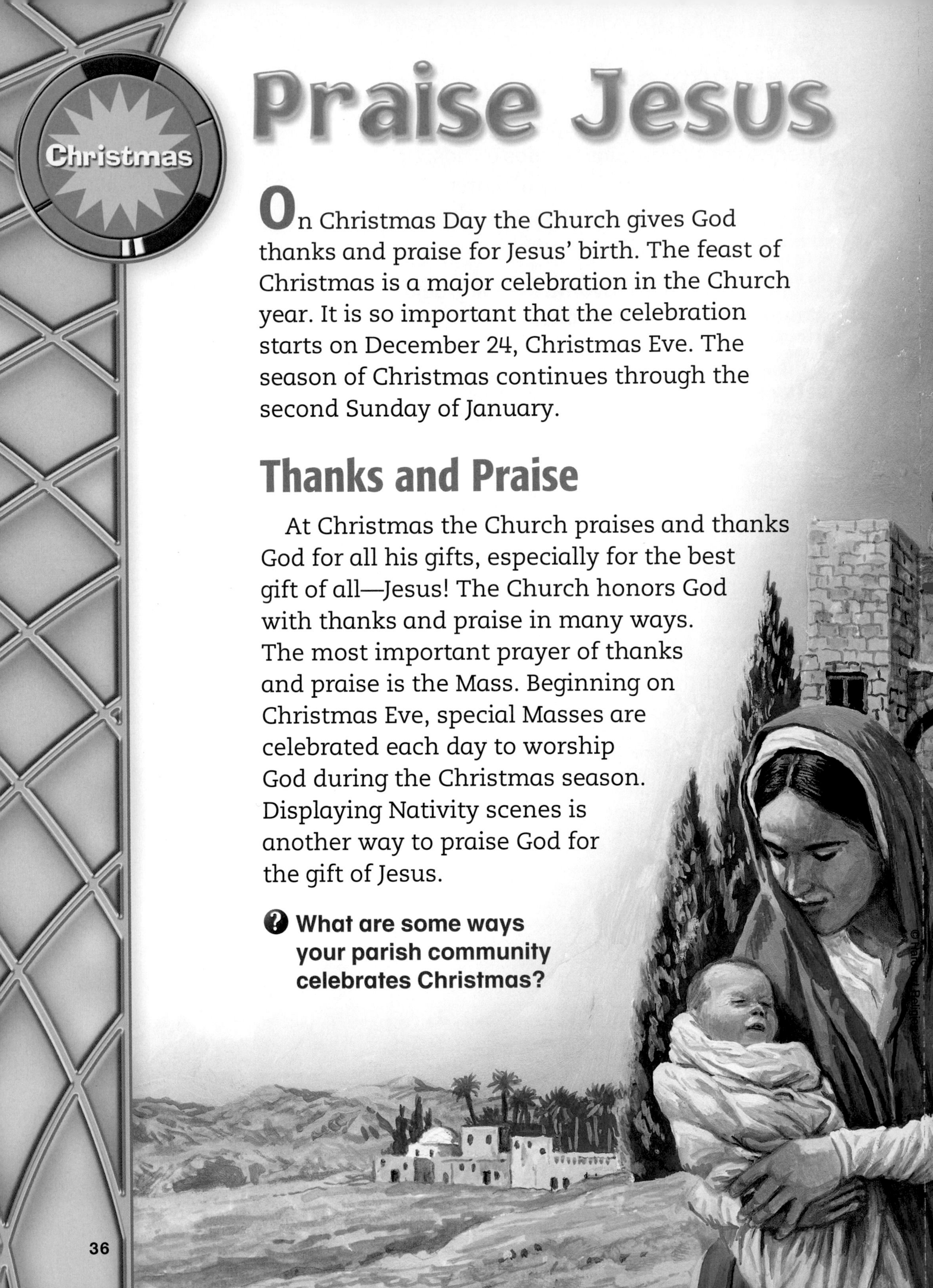

Praise Jesus

On Christmas Day the Church gives God thanks and praise for Jesus' birth. The feast of Christmas is a major celebration in the Church year. It is so important that the celebration starts on December 24, Christmas Eve. The season of Christmas continues through the second Sunday of January.

Thanks and Praise

At Christmas the Church praises and thanks God for all his gifts, especially for the best gift of all—Jesus! The Church honors God with thanks and praise in many ways. The most important prayer of thanks and praise is the Mass. Beginning on Christmas Eve, special Masses are celebrated each day to worship God during the Christmas season. Displaying Nativity scenes is another way to praise God for the gift of Jesus.

What are some ways your parish community celebrates Christmas?

Celebrate Jesus

Gather

Sing together the refrain.

Go tell it on the mountain,
Over the hills and ev'rywhere;
Go tell it on the mountain
That Jesus Christ is born!

Pray the Sign of the Cross together.

Leader: Blessed be the name of the Lord.

All: Now and for ever.

Leader: Let us pray.

Bow your heads as you praise God.

All: Amen.

Listen to God's Word

Leader: A reading from the holy Gospel according to Luke.

Read Luke 2:1–14.

The Gospel of the Lord.

All: Praise to you, Lord Jesus Christ.

Reflect

What parts of the Christmas celebration are special for you?

How do you celebrate Christmas with your family?

The Lord's Prayer and Sign of Peace

Leader: Let us pray in the words that Jesus taught us.

All: **Our Father . . .**

Leader: May the God of light and peace fill our hearts and lives.

All: **Amen.**

Leader: Let us offer to each other a sign of the peace of Christ.

Offer one another a sign of peace.

Go Forth!

Leader: Let us go forth this week to give thanks and praise for God's gift of Jesus.

All: **Thanks be to God.**

Sing together the refrain.

Go tell it on the mountain,
Over the hills and ev'rywhere;
Go tell it on the mountain
That Jesus Christ is born!

God's Great Gift

God gives you a special gift in Jesus. You can give your own gifts to God. Your prayers of thanks and praise are your gifts. You can pray with words, gestures, and actions, during the Mass or at any time.

What is your favorite way to thank and praise God in prayer?

Have you seen other people pray in ways that are different from the way you pray?

ACTIVITY

Start a Prayer Journal

Share your thoughts and feelings with God. Do this for a week. You might find yourself liking it and may even want to continue doing it after the week is up.

Comunicar la Palabra de Dios

Durante el Tiempo Ordinario se celebran muchas fiestas de santos. Una de esas fiestas se celebra el 14 de febrero (11 de mayo en el Oriente). Ese día la iglesia recuerda la vida de los santos Cirilo y Metodio, hermanos que llevaron la Palabra de Dios a los pueblos de Europa del Este.

Los santos Cirilo y Metodio

Cirilo y Metodio vivieron hace cientos de años en Grecia. Cirilo era bibliotecario y Metodio era profesor de una universidad. Dios llamó a Cirilo y a Metodio a ser sacerdotes.

Más tarde, los dos hermanos viajaron a un país de Europa del Este. Allí no había biblias ni ningún otro libro en el idioma local, el eslavo, porque ese idioma no tenía alfabeto escrito.

Cirilo creó un alfabeto para el eslavo, y junto con Metodio tradujeron la Biblia y otros libros que se usaban en la Misa. ¡Al fin, el pueblo pudo leer la Palabra de Dios!

¿Quién te ayuda a leer la Palabra de Dios en la Biblia?

Celebremos la Palabra de Dios

Juntos

Canten juntos.

Como iglesia, de dos en dos,
por todo el mundo vamos a llevar,
la Palabra del Señor,
su Buena Nueva, a proclamar.

Hagan la señal de la cruz.

Líder: Nuestro auxilio es el nombre del Señor.

Todos: Que hizo el cielo y la tierra.

Líder: Oremos.

Inclinen la cabeza mientras el líder reza.

Todos: Amén.

Escucha la Palabra de Dios

Líder: Lectura del profeta Jeremías.

Lean Jeremías 1, 4–9.

Palabra de Dios.

Todos: Te alabamos, Señor.

La señal sobre la frente

Ora en silencio pidiendo al Espíritu Santo que te fortalezca para poder anunciar la Palabra de Dios a todas las personas con las que te encuentres.

Pasa al frente cuando oigas tu nombre. El líder te hará la señal de la cruz sobre la frente.

Líder: (Nombre), que tus palabras y acciones lleven la Buena Nueva de Jesús a los demás.

Todos: Amén.

Oración de los fieles

Líder: Oremos. Estamos llamados a anunciar tu Palabra. Escucha nuestras oraciones pidiéndote fortaleza.

Respondan a cada oración con estas palabras.

Todos: **Señor, envíanos a anunciar tu Palabra.**

Líder: Oremos ahora como Jesús nos enseñó.

Todos: **Padre nuestro...**

¡Evangeliza!

Líder: Anunciemos la Palabra de Dios a todas las personas con las que nos encontremos en esta semana.

Todos: **Demos gracias a Dios.**

La Palabra de Dios para los demás

Es posible que Dios nunca te pida que vayas a un país lejano a anunciar su Palabra, como les pidió a Cirilo y Metodio. Sin embargo, Dios pide a todos los discípulos de Jesús que lleven su Palabra a sus familias, amigos, vecinos y compañeros de clase. Dios también podría llamarte algún día a ser misionero en un lugar lejano.

¿Cómo te han comunicado otras personas la Palabra de Dios?

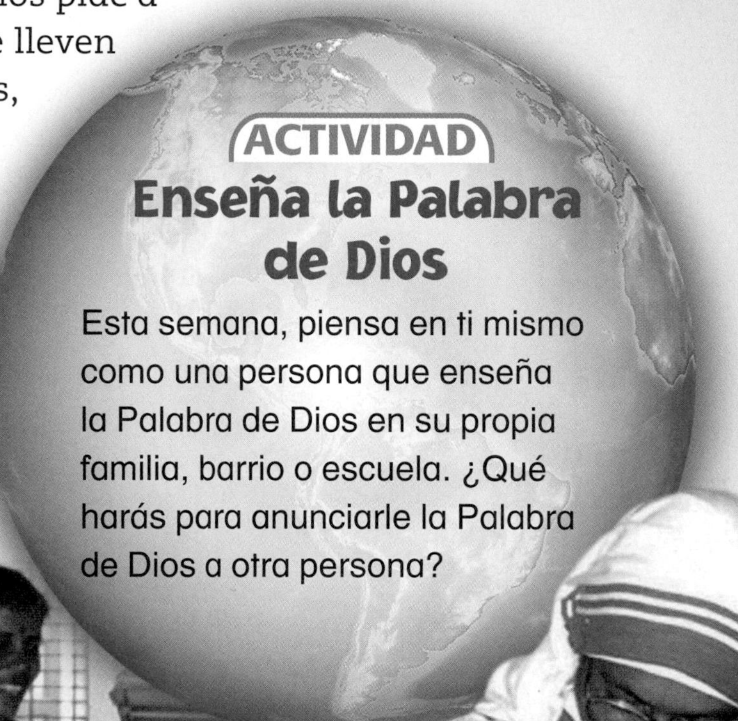

ACTIVIDAD

Enseña la Palabra de Dios

Esta semana, piensa en ti mismo como una persona que enseña la Palabra de Dios en su propia familia, barrio o escuela. ¿Qué harás para anunciarle la Palabra de Dios a otra persona?

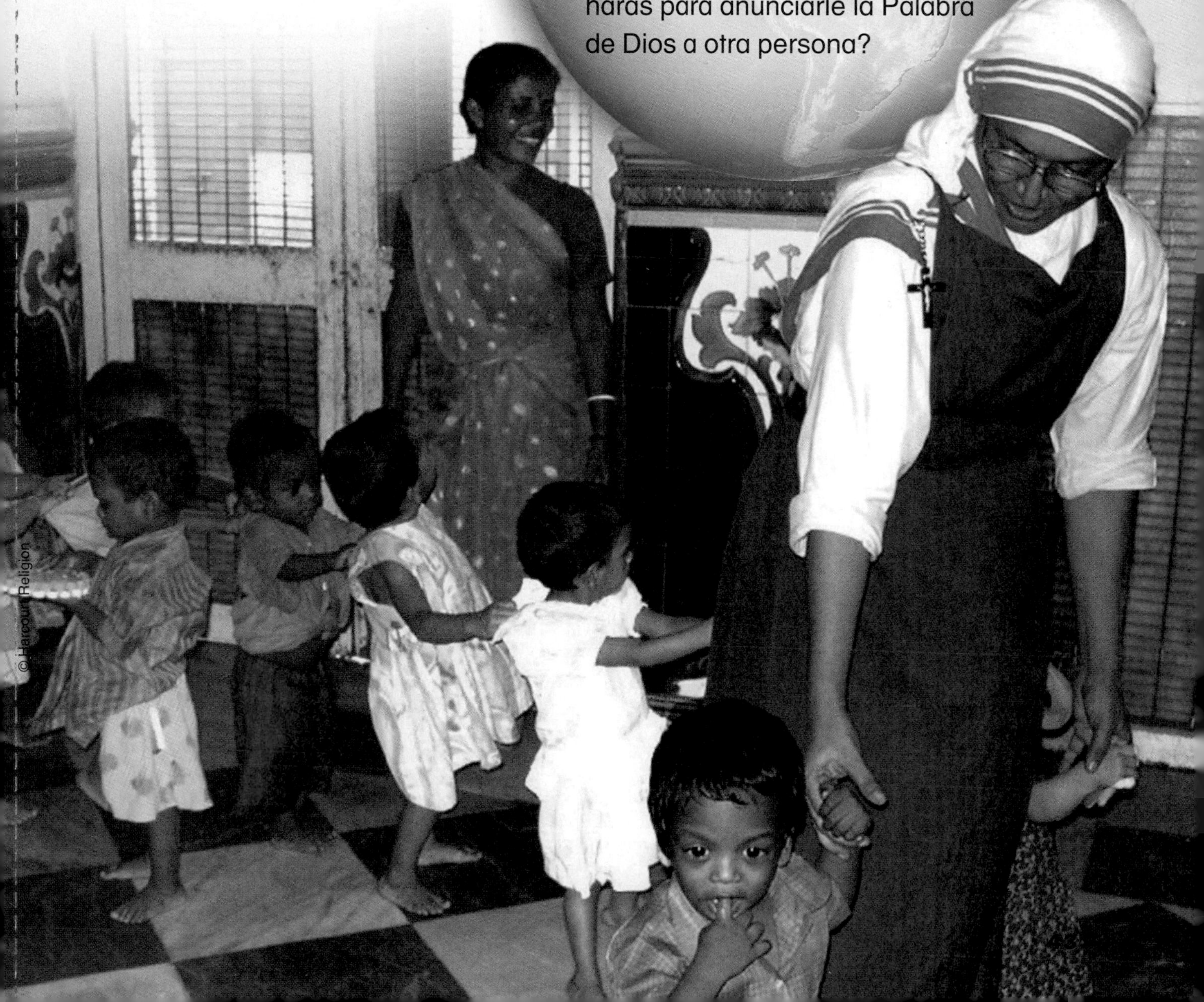

Sharing God's Word

During Ordinary Time, many feasts of saints are celebrated. One such feast is February 14 (May 11 in the East) when the lives of Saints Cyril and Methodius are remembered. The Church recalls how these brothers brought God's word to the people of Eastern Europe.

Saints Cyril and Methodius

Cyril and Methodius lived hundreds of years ago in Greece. Cyril was a librarian. Methodius was a teacher at a university. Then God called Cyril and Methodius to become priests.

Later the brothers went to a country in Eastern Europe. There were no Bibles or other books in Slavonic, the local language. Slavonic had no written alphabet.

Cyril created an alphabet for Slavonic, and together he and Methodius translated the Bible and other books used at Mass. At last the people could read God's word!

? Who helps you read God's word in the Bible?

Celebrate God's Word

Gather

Sing together.

We are sent, two by two.
Sent as church in the world.
Sent to share God's good news,
Sing and tell, spread the Word.

Pray the Sign of the Cross together.

Leader: Our help is in the name of the Lord.

All: **Who made heaven and earth.**

Leader: Let us pray.

Bow your heads as the leader prays.

All: **Amen.**

Listen to God's Word

Leader: A reading from the prophet Jeremiah.

Read Jeremiah 1:4–9.

The word of the Lord.

All: **Thanks be to God.**

Signing of Foreheads

Silently pray asking the Holy Spirit to strengthen you to share God's word with all you meet.

Then come forward as your name is called. The leader will mark your forehead with the Sign of the Cross.

Leader: (Name), may your words and actions bring the good news of Jesus to others.

All: **Amen.**

Intercessions

Leader: Let us pray. We are called to share your word. Hear our prayers for strength.

Respond to each intercession with these words.

All: **Lord, send us to share your word.**

Leader: Let us now pray as Jesus taught us.

All: **Our Father . . .**

Go Forth!

Leader: Let us go forth to share God's word with everyone we meet this week.

All: **Thanks be to God.**

God's Word to Others

God may never ask you to go to a distant country to share his word as he asked Cyril and Methodius to do. But God asks each follower of Jesus to bring his word to their families, friends, neighbors, and classmates. And God may someday call you to be a missionary in a faraway place.

What are ways that others have shared God's word with you?

ACTIVITY

Teach the Word

This week, think of yourself as someone teaching the word of God in your own family, neighborhood, or school. What will you do to share God's word with someone?

Crecer en la fe

Para ayudarte a crecer en la fe como discípulo de Cristo, la Iglesia te da los cuarenta días de Cuaresma. Durante la Cuaresma, preparas tu corazón para el gozo de la Pascua, demostrando que lamentas tus pecados y que quieres ser mejor.

Actos cuaresmales

Para fortalecerte, durante la Cuaresma puedes decidir dejar ciertas cosas que te gusten o alguna actividad favorita. Puedes usar el dinero que ahorras para acordarte de las necesidades de los demás.

Tu práctica cuaresmal puede incluir también acciones positivas. Puedes rezar con más frecuencia, ir a misa más a menudo, o esforzarte mucho y hacer algo bueno por los demás.

¿Qué vas a hacer en esta Cuaresma para acercarte más a Jesús?

© Harcourt Religion

Celebremos la Cuaresma

Juntos

Hagan la señal de la cruz.

Líder: Señor, abre mis labios.

Todos: Y mi boca proclamará tu alabanza.

Líder: Oremos.

Inclinen la cabeza mientras el líder reza.

Todos: Amén.

Escucha la Palabra de Dios

Líder: Lectura de la carta a los Efesios.

Lean Efesios 5, 1–2; 8–10.

Palabra de Dios.

Todos: Te alabamos, Señor.

Reflexiona

¿Qué significa ser hijo de Dios?

¿Cómo puedes ser una luz para los demás?

Oración en silencio

Siéntate en silencio ante la cruz, con la mirada baja o con los ojos cerrados. Pide a Dios que esté contigo. Piensa en lo que puedes hacer durante la Cuaresma para fortalecerte y seguir a Jesús.

Oración de los fieles

Líder: Oremos. Señor Jesús, tú prometes que Dios, nuestro Padre, escuchará nuestras oraciones. Ahora, nosotros rezamos esas oraciones.

Respondan a cada oración con estas palabras.

Todos: **Señor, escucha nuestra oración.**

Líder: Reunamos todas nuestras necesidades y todas nuestras esperanzas, y recemos la oración que Jesús nos enseñó.

Todos: **Padre nuestro...**

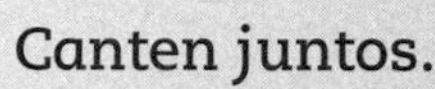

Canten juntos.

Paz ante mí
y paz por detrás,
paz sea a mis pies.
Paz sobre mí
y paz en mí,
paz sea a mi alrededor.

Sigan cantando, cambiando "paz" por "amor" y después por "luz".

¡Evangeliza!

Líder: Evangelicemos esta semana y llevemos la luz y la paz de Cristo a quienes nos rodean.

Todos: **Demos gracias a Dios.**

Parecernos más a Jesús

La cruz es el símbolo de lo que Jesús quería hacer por todas las personas. Hacer la señal de la cruz es un recordatorio de que perteneces a Jesús. Durante la Cuaresma, tú y tu comunidad de fe tratan de parecerse más a Jesús mediante la oración y la ayuda a los demás.

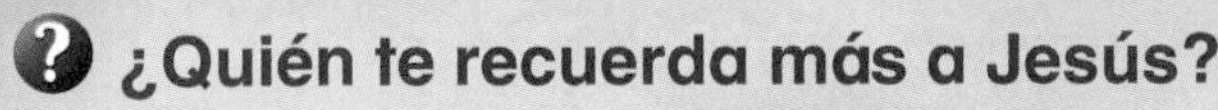

¿Quién te recuerda más a Jesús?

¿Cómo eres cada día "Jesús" para los demás?

ACTIVIDAD

Haz una cruz de Cuaresma

Haz una cruz con materiales sobrantes que encuentres en casa. En ella puedes escribir palabras de Cuaresma, como "oración", "sacrificio personal" o "Jesús". Cuelga tu cruz en un lugar en el que te recuerde a menudo las buenas acciones que estás llevando a cabo durante la Cuaresma.

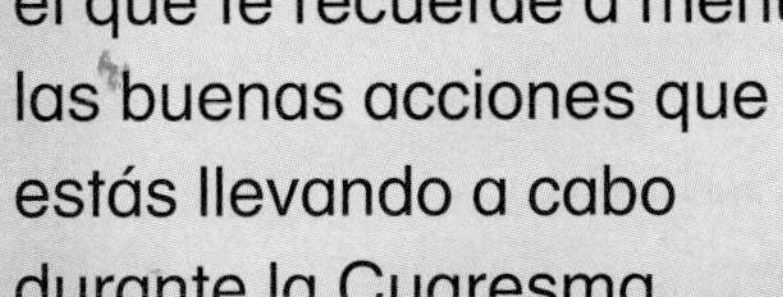

Growing in Faith

To help you grow stronger as a follower of Christ, the Church gives you the forty days of Lent. During Lent you prepare your heart for the joy of Easter by showing that you are sorry for your sins and want to do better.

Lenten Acts

To make yourself stronger, you might decide to give up certain treats or a favorite activity during Lent. You can use any money you save to remember the needs of others.

Your Lenten practice can also include positive actions. You can choose to pray more often, go to Mass more often, or go out of your way to do something good for others.

What will you do this Lent to grow closer to Jesus?

Celebrate Lent

Gather

Pray the Sign of the Cross together.

Leader: O Lord, open my lips.

All: That my mouth shall proclaim your praise.

Leader: Let us pray.

Bow your heads as the leader prays.

All: Amen.

Listen to God's Word

Leader: A reading from the letter to the Ephesians.

Read Ephesians 5:1–2, 8–10.

The word of the Lord.

All: Thanks be to God.

Reflect

What does it mean to be a child of God?

How can you be a light to others?

Silent Prayer

Sit in silence before the cross with your eyes downcast or closed. Ask God to be with you. Think about what you can do during Lent to grow stronger as a follower of Jesus.

Intercessions

Leader: Let us pray. Lord Jesus, you promise that God, our Father, will hear our prayers. We pray those prayers now.

Respond to each intercession with these words.

All: Lord, hear our prayer.

Leader: Let us join all our needs and hopes and pray the prayer Jesus taught us.

All: Our Father . . .

Sing together.

Peace before us, peace behind us,
peace under our feet.
Peace within us, peace over us,
let all around us be peace.

Continue to sing verse beginning with "Love" and then "Light."

Go Forth!

Leader: Let us go forth this week to share Christ's light and peace with those around us.

All: Thanks be to God.

More Like Jesus

The cross is the sign of what Jesus was willing to do for all people. Making the Sign of the Cross is a reminder that you belong to Jesus. During Lent you and your faith community strive to become more like Jesus through prayer and helping others.

Who reminds you most of Jesus?

How are you "Jesus" for others each day?

ACTIVITY

Make a Lenten Cross

Make a cross from scrap materials you find around the house. You may choose to write Lenten words on it, such as prayer, self-giving, or Jesus. Hang your cross in a place where it will remind you often of the extra things you are doing during Lent.

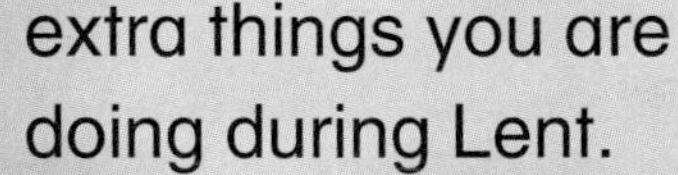

¡Alegrémonos!

Al final de la Cuaresma, la Iglesia recuerda y celebra lo que Jesús hizo por todos. La Iglesia llama a estos tres días especiales el Triduo Pascual. El Triduo Pascual comienza con la Misa del Jueves Santo de la Última Cena y termina con una oración en la noche del Domingo de Pascua.

El Triduo Pascual

El Jueves Santo, la Iglesia recuerda la Última Cena de Jesús con sus discípulos. El Viernes Santo se recuerda el sufrimiento y la muerte de Jesús en la cruz. El Sábado Santo es un día de espera en oración para celebrar la Resurrección de Jesús.

La liturgia de la noche del Sábado Santo se conoce como la Vigilia Pascual. La palabra vigilia significa "hacer guardia durante la noche". En la Vigilia Pascual la comunidad de la Iglesia vela, o hace guardia, con aquellos que esperan ser bautizados.

Para expresar la alegría de la Resurrección de Jesús, el diácono u otro ministro canta el Pregón Pascual.

¿De qué otras maneras expresa la gente alegría por la Resurrección?

Celebremos el Triduo Pascual

Juntos

Canten juntos.

¡Oh, qué bueno es Jesús!
En la cruz por mí murió.
En tres días resucitó.
¡Gloria al Señor!
¡Gloria al Señor! ¡Gloria al Señor!
En tres días resucitó.
¡Gloria al Señor!

Hagan la señal de la cruz.

Líder: Señor, abre mis labios.

Todos: **Y mi boca proclamará tu alabanza.**

Líder: Oremos.

Inclinen la cabeza mientras el líder reza.

Todos: **Amén.**

Escucha la Palabra de Dios

Lector: Lectura de la carta a los Romanos.

Lean Romanos 6, 3–5.

Palabra de Dios.

Todos: **Te alabamos, Señor.**

Reflexiona

¿Cómo te sientes al participar de la nueva vida de Jesús en el Bautismo?

¿Cómo puedes vivir la "nueva vida" que Jesús ganó para ti?

Recordemos el Bautismo

Líder: Renovemos las promesas hechas en el Bautismo.

Respondan "Sí, creo" o "Sí, renuncio" a las preguntas del líder.

¡Evangeliza!

Líder: Recordemos y celebremos en esta semana el gran amor que Jesús nos tiene.

Todos: Demos gracias a Dios.

Canten juntos.

¡Oh, qué bueno es Jesús!
En la cruz por mí murió.
En tres días resucitó.
¡Gloria al Señor!
¡Gloria al Señor! ¡Gloria al Señor!
En tres días resucitó.
¡Gloria al Señor!

Las promesas bautismales

Cuando fuiste bautizado, probablemente tus padres hicieron las promesas bautismales en tu nombre. Ahora que eres mayor, puedes hacer esas mismas promesas por ti mismo. Durante la Vigilia Pascual renovarás las promesas bautismales con toda la comunidad. Estas promesas muestran que eres discípulo de Jesús.

? ¿Cómo muestras que eres discípulo de Jesús?

ACTIVIDAD

Haz promesas

Trabaja con un compañero. Hagan una lista de las cosas que pueden hacer los niños de la clase para mostrar que son discípulos de Jesús. Comiencen cada enunciado con “Prometemos que…”. Luego, hagan un estandarte con las promesas de toda la clase.

Rejoice!

At the end of Lent, the Church remembers and celebrates what Jesus did for all people. The Church calls these three special days the Triduum. The Triduum begins at the Holy Thursday Mass of the Lord's Supper and ends with evening prayer on Easter Sunday.

The Three Days

On Holy Thursday the Church recalls Jesus' Last Supper with his disciples. On Good Friday Jesus' suffering and death on the cross is remembered. Holy Saturday is a day of prayerful waiting to celebrate Jesus' Resurrection.

The liturgy on Holy Saturday evening is called the Easter Vigil. The word vigil means "keeping watch by night." At the Easter Vigil the Church community keeps watch with those waiting to be baptized.

To express the joy of Jesus' Resurrection, the deacon or other minister sings the Easter Proclamation.

? What are some other ways people express joy in the Resurrection?

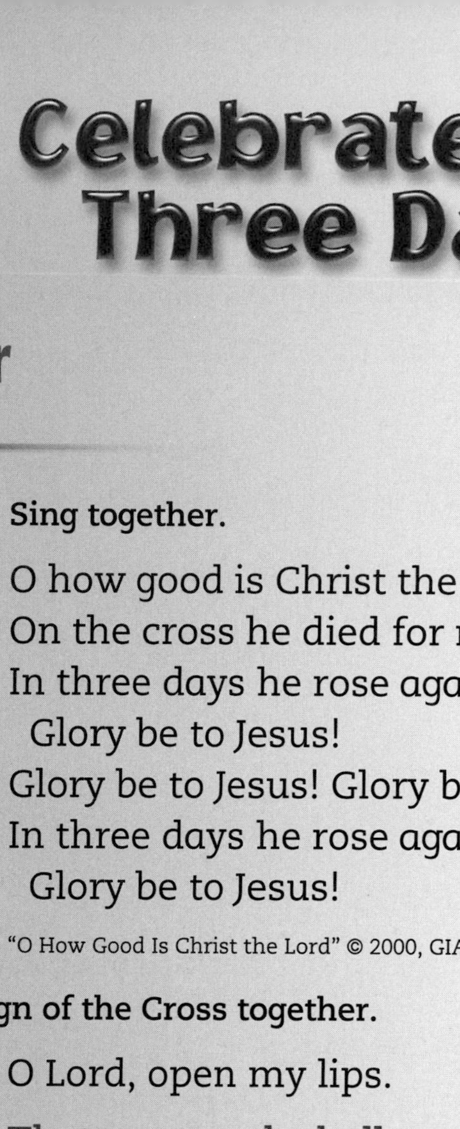

Celebrate the Three Days

Gather

Sing together.

O how good is Christ the Lord!
On the cross he died for me.
In three days he rose again.
  Glory be to Jesus!
Glory be to Jesus! Glory be to Jesus!
In three days he rose again.
  Glory be to Jesus!

Pray the Sign of the Cross together.

Leader: O Lord, open my lips.

All: That my mouth shall proclaim your praise.

Leader: Let us pray.

Bow your heads as the leader prays.

All: Amen.

Listen to God's Word

Reader: A reading from the Letter to the Romans.

Read Romans 6:3–5.

The word of the Lord.

All: Thanks be to God.

Reflect

How do you feel about sharing in Jesus' new life through Baptism?

How can you live the "new life" Jesus won for you?

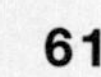

Remember Baptism

Leader: Let us renew the promises made at Baptism.

Respond "I do" to the leader's questions.

Go Forth!

Leader: Let us go forth this week to remember and celebrate Jesus' great love for us.

All: **Thanks be to God.**

Sing together.

O how good is Christ the Lord!
On the cross he died for me.
In three days he rose again.
  Glory be to Jesus!
Glory be to Jesus! Glory be to Jesus!
In three days he rose again.
  Glory be to Jesus!

Baptismal Promises

When you were baptized, your parents probably made the baptismal promises for you. Now that you are older, you can make those same promises for yourself. During the Easter Vigil you will renew your baptismal promises with the whole community. These promises show you are a follower of Jesus.

? How do you show that you are a follower of Jesus?

ACTIVITY

Make Promises

Work with a partner. Make a list of things your class can do to show you are followers of Jesus. Begin each with "We will . . ." Then make a banner of class promises.

Santo, Santo, Santo

El día de Pascua, el día más sagrado del año litúrgico, la Iglesia celebra que Jesús resucitó de entre los muertos. Celebra la vida eterna, que es tuya gracias a la muerte y Resurrección de Jesús. El domingo es el día del Señor porque es el día en que Jesús resucitó de entre los muertos.

Un Pueblo Santo

Ser santo significa ser como Dios. Dios creó a todas las personas para que fueran como Él. Quiere que todos seamos santos. Con su muerte, Jesús santificó a todos los pueblos. Por medio del agua del Bautismo, los cristianos participamos de la vida y la santidad que Jesús conquistó para nosotros.

En la Misa de Pascua, la asamblea renueva las promesas hechas en el Bautismo. El sacerdote camina por la iglesia y rocía a todos con el agua que fue bendecida en la Vigilia Pascual.

¿Dónde está el agua bendita en la iglesia de tu parroquia? ¿Cuándo la usas?

Juntos

Canten juntos.

Un nuevo comienzo vivimos hoy:
¡Aleluya! ¡Aleluya!
Santos, benditos, pueblo de Dios:
¡Aleluya! ¡Aleluya!
¡Cantemos todos con felicidad!
¡Aleluya! ¡Aleluya! ¡Aleluya! ¡Aleluya!

Hagan la señal de la cruz.

Líder: Luz y paz en Jesucristo nuestro Señor, aleluya.

Todos: Demos gracias a Dios, aleluya.

Líder: Oremos.

Inclinen la cabeza mientras el líder reza.

Todos: Amén.

Rito del agua bendita

Líder: Y ustedes sacarán agua con alegría de las vertientes de la salvación.

Isaías 12, 3

Todos: ¡Este es el día que ha hecho el Señor, gocemos y alegrémonos en él!

Salmo 118, 24

Mientras el líder te rocía con agua bendita, haz la señal de la cruz y recuerda que eres hijo de Dios.

Escucha la Palabra de Dios

Lector: Lectura del santo Evangelio según san Lucas.

Lean Lucas 24, 1–12.

Palabra del Señor.

Todos: **Gloria a ti, Señor Jesús.**

Reflexiona

Imagina que estás ante la tumba de Jesús. ¿Qué dirías o harías?

Oración de los fieles

Líder: Oremos. Jesús, tú resucitaste de entre los muertos para que viviéramos como un pueblo santo. Escucha nuestras confiadas oraciones.

Respondan a cada oración con estas palabras.

Todos: **Señor, escucha nuestra oración.**

Líder: Recemos la oración que Jesús nos enseñó.

Todos: **Padre nuestro...**

¡Evangeliza!

Líder: Vivamos como un pueblo santo que pertenece a Jesús Resucitado, aleluya, aleluya.

Todos: **Demos gracias a Dios, aleluya, aleluya.**

Agua viva

Durante la Pascua, se rocía a la asamblea reunida con agua bendita. Esta acción nos recuerda la importancia del Bautismo. En el Bautismo participas de la nueva vida de Jesús, que resucitó para siempre.

¿Qué personas que conoces llevan una vida santa?

ACTIVIDAD

Presenta una obra de teatro sobre la Pascua

Representa con tus compañeros de clase los acontecimientos de la primera mañana de Pascua. Utilicen sus propias palabras y, si lo desean, pueden ponerse disfraces sencillos. Presenten la obra de teatro ante un grupo de niños más pequeños.

Holy, Holy, Holy

On Easter day, the holiest day of the Church year, the Church celebrates Jesus being raised from the dead. It celebrates the everlasting life that is yours because of Jesus' death and Resurrection. Every Sunday is called the Lord's Day because that is the day Jesus rose from the dead.

A Holy People

To be holy means to be like God. God made all people to be like himself. He wants everyone to be holy. By his death, Jesus made people holy, again. Through the waters of Baptism, Christians share in the life and holiness Jesus won for them.

At Easter Mass the assembly renews the promises made when they were baptized. The priest walks throughout the church and sprinkles everyone with the holy water that was blessed at the Easter Vigil.

Where is the holy water in your parish church? When do you use it?

Gather

Sing together.

New beginnings, here in our midst:
Alleluia! Alleluia!
We are God's children, holy and blest:
Alleluia! Alleluia!
People of God, rejoice and sing!
Alleluia! Alleluia! Alleluia! Alleluia!

Pray the Sign of the Cross together.

Leader: Light and peace in Jesus Christ our Lord, alleluia.

All: Thanks be to God, alleluia.

Leader: Let us pray.

Bow your heads as the leader prays.

All: Amen.

Sprinkling Rite

Leader: With joy you will draw water joyfully at the fountain of salvation.

Isaiah 12:3

All: This is the day the Lord has made;
let us rejoice in it and be glad.

Psalm 118:24

As the leader sprinkles you with holy water, make the Sign of the Cross and recall that you are a child of God.

Listen to God's Word

Reader: A reading from the holy Gospel according to Luke.

Read Luke 24:1–12.

The Gospel of the Lord.

All: **Praise to you, Lord Jesus Christ.**

Reflect

Imagine that you are at Jesus' tomb. What might you say or do?

Intercessions

Leader: Let us pray. Jesus, you were raised from the dead so that we might live as a holy people. Listen to our loving prayers.

Respond to each intercession with these words.

All: **Lord, hear our prayer.**

Leader: Let us pray the prayer that Jesus gave us.

All: **Our Father . . .**

Go Forth!

Leader: Let us go to live as holy people who belong to the Risen Jesus, alleluia, alleluia.

All: **Thanks be to God, alleluia, alleluia.**

Living Water

During the Easter season, the assembly gathered is sprinkled with holy water. This is a reminder of the importance of Baptism. Through Baptism you share in the new life of Jesus who is risen forever.

Who are some people in your life who live as holy people?

ACTIVITY

Present an Easter Play

Together with your classmates, act out the events of the first Easter morning. Use your own words, and wear simple costumes if you wish. Your class might like to present this as a play for a group of younger children.

El Espíritu Santo

La Iglesia celebra Pentecostés cincuenta días después de la Pascua. Esta gran fiesta conmemora la venida del Espíritu Santo sobre los primeros discípulos de Jesús. Los fieles oran para que el Espíritu Santo descienda también sobre ellos.

Recibir el Espíritu Santo

Cuando Jesús regresó con el Padre, los discípulos no sabían qué hacer. Más tarde, como Jesús les había prometido, les fue enviado el Espíritu Santo.

El Espíritu Santo fortaleció a los discípulos. Con su ayuda anunciaron la Buena Nueva de Jesús a todas las personas con las que se encontraron.

La Buena Nueva que Jesús anunció fue que todos somos bienvenidos al Reino de su Padre. Jesús también enseñó que el Reino de Dios es un reino de paz, justicia y amor.

El Espíritu Santo nos da la fuerza para anunciar la Buena Nueva del Reino de Dios a todas las personas que conocemos.

¿Qué buena noticia puedes comunicar acerca de Jesús?

Celebremos al Espíritu Santo

Juntos

Canten juntos.

Dios envía a su Espíritu a que nos ayude,
nos recree y nos guíe, es nuestro amigo.
Espíritu que aviva y nos santifica,
libera e ilumina, es nuestro amigo.
Espíritu creador, es nuestro amigo.

Hagan la señal de la cruz.

Líder: Luz y paz en Jesucristo nuestro Señor, aleluya.

Todos: Demos gracias a Dios, aleluya.

Líder: Oremos.

Inclinen la cabeza mientras el líder reza.

Todos: Amén.

Escucha la Palabra de Dios

Honrar la Sagrada Escritura

Líder: Ven, Espíritu Santo, llena los corazones de tus fieles.

Todos: Y enciende en ellos el fuego de tu amor.

Arrodíllense mientras se lleva la Biblia hasta la mesa de oración. Cuando la Biblia sea colocada en su lugar, hagan una reverencia ante ella de uno en uno en señal de respeto.

Líder: Lectura de los Hechos de los Apóstoles.

Lean Hechos 2, 1–11.

Palabra de Dios.

Todos: **Te alabamos, Señor.**

Reflexiona

En el relato del primer Pentecostés, ¿cómo fue la venida del Espíritu Santo?

¿Qué signos del Espíritu Santo están presentes en el mundo hoy en día?

Oración de los fieles

Líder: Oremos. Dios Espíritu Santo, tú nos llenas de tu poder y fortaleza. Escucha las oraciones que ahora te presentamos.

Respondan a cada oración con estas palabras.

Todos: **Señor, escucha nuestra oración.**

Líder: Alabemos a la Santísima Trinidad.

Todos: **Gloria al Padre...**

¡Evangeliza!

Líder: Anunciemos en esta semana la Palabra de Dios a todas las personas con las que nos encontremos.

Todos: **Demos gracias a Dios.**

La fuerza del Espíritu Santo

La fiesta de Pentecostés celebra el don del Espíritu Santo a todos los discípulos de Cristo. Con la guía y la fortaleza del Espíritu Santo, puedes seguir a Cristo y trabajar por el Reino de Dios de justicia, amor y paz.

¿Cómo pueden los jóvenes enseñar a los demás a seguir a Cristo?

ACTIVIDAD

Signos de paz

¿Qué signos de paz y justicia hay en tu parroquia, tu escuela y tu país? Haz una lista de algunos de esos signos con un compañero. Elige una cosa que puedas hacer para difundir la paz y el amor.

The Holy Spirit

The Church celebrates Pentecost fifty days after Easter. This great feast celebrates the coming of the Holy Spirit upon Jesus' first disciples. The assembly prays for the Holy Spirit to come to them, too.

Sharing the Holy Spirit

After Jesus returned to his Father, the disciples did not know what to do. Then, as Jesus had promised, the Holy Spirit was sent to them.

The Holy Spirit strengthened the disciples. With the Holy Spirit's help, they shared the good news of Jesus with everyone they met.

The good news that Jesus shared was that everyone is welcome in his Father's kingdom. Jesus also taught that God's Kingdom is one of peace, justice, and love.

The Holy Spirit gives us the power to share the goods news of God's Kingdom with everyone we meet.

What is some good news about Jesus that you can share?

Celebrate the Holy Spirit

Gather

Sing together.

God sends us his Spirit to befriend
  and help us.
Recreate and guide us, Spirit-Friend
Spirit who enlivens, sanctifies, enlightens,
Sets us free, is now our Spirit-Friend.
Spirit of our Maker, Spirit-Friend.

Pray the Sign of the Cross together.

Leader: Light and peace in Jesus Christ our Lord, alleluia.

All: Thanks be to God, alleluia.

Leader: Let us pray.

Bow your heads as the leader prays.

All: Amen.

Listen to God's Word

Honoring the Scriptures

Leader: Come, Holy Spirit, fill the hearts of your faithful.

All: And kindle in them the fire of your love.

Kneel as the Bible is carried to the prayer table. When the Bible is placed on its stand, take turns respectfully bowing in front of it.

Leader: A reading from the Acts of the Apostles.

Read Acts 2:1–11.

The word of the Lord.

All: Thanks be to God.

Reflect

In the story of the first Pentecost, what was the coming of the Holy Spirit like?

What signs of the Holy Spirit are in the world today?

Intercessions

Leader: Let us pray. God the Holy Spirit, you fill us with your power and strength. Hear the prayers that we bring to you now.

Respond to each intercession with these words.

All: Hear our prayer, O Lord.

Leader: Let us offer praise to the Holy Trinity.

All: Glory to the Father . . .

Go Forth!

Leader: Let us go forth this week to share God's word with everyone we meet.

All: Thanks be to God.

The Power of the Holy Spirit

The Feast of Pentecost celebrates the gift of the Holy Spirit to all Christ's followers. With the Holy Spirit's guidance and strength, you can follow Christ and work for God's kingdom of justice, love, and peace.

How can young people show others how to follow Christ?

ACTIVITY

Signs of Peace

What are some signs of peace and justice in your parish, your school, your country? With a partner make lists of some of these signs. Choose one thing you can do to spread peace and love.

UNIDAD 1

La familia de Dios

Capítulo 1

El hermoso mundo de Dios

¿Qué te enseña la creación sobre Dios?

Capítulo 2

La comunidad de la Iglesia

¿Por qué se reúne la gente para alabar a Dios?

Capítulo 3

En casa con Dios

¿En qué se parece tu familia a la Iglesia?

¿Qué crees que vas a aprender en esta unidad acerca de la familia de Dios?

UNIT 1
Family of God

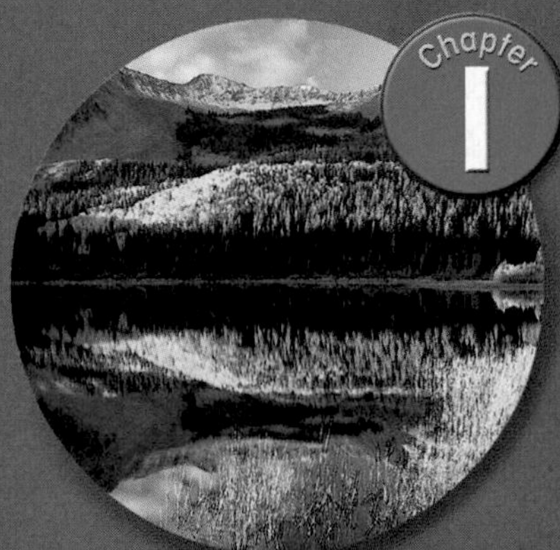

Chapter 1

God's Beautiful World

What does creation teach you about God?

Chapter 2

The Church Community

Why do people gather to worship God?

Chapter 3

At Home with God

How is your family like the Church?

What do you think you will learn in this unit about the family of God?

Capítulo I

El hermoso mundo de Dios

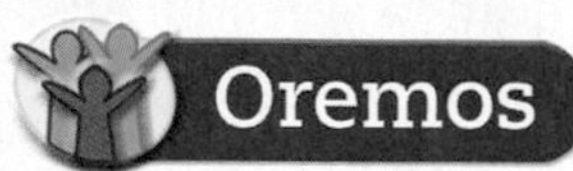

Líder: ¡Dios nuestro Creador, alabamos tu hermosa creación!

“Alaben el nombre del Señor,
pues lo ordenó y
fueron creados”.

Salmo 148, 5

Todos: ¡Dios nuestro Creador, alabamos tu hermosa creación! Amén.

Actividad Comencemos

Canto al mundo que despierta

¡Despierta, mundo; mundo, despierta!
La luz brilla sobre lagos y colinas;
¡Despierta, mundo; mundo, despierta!
Las banderas del viento se despliegan
¡Despierta, mundo; mundo, despierta!
Disfruta de los frutos de la Tierra.

Fragmento de un poema de Countee Cullen

- ¿Qué cosas hermosas has visto en el mundo de Dios hoy?

Chapter 1 God's Beautiful World

Let Us Pray

Leader: God our Creator, we praise your beautiful creation!
"Let them all praise the LORD's name;
for the LORD's commanded and
they were created."

Psalm 148:5

All: God our Creator, we praise your beautiful creation! Amen.

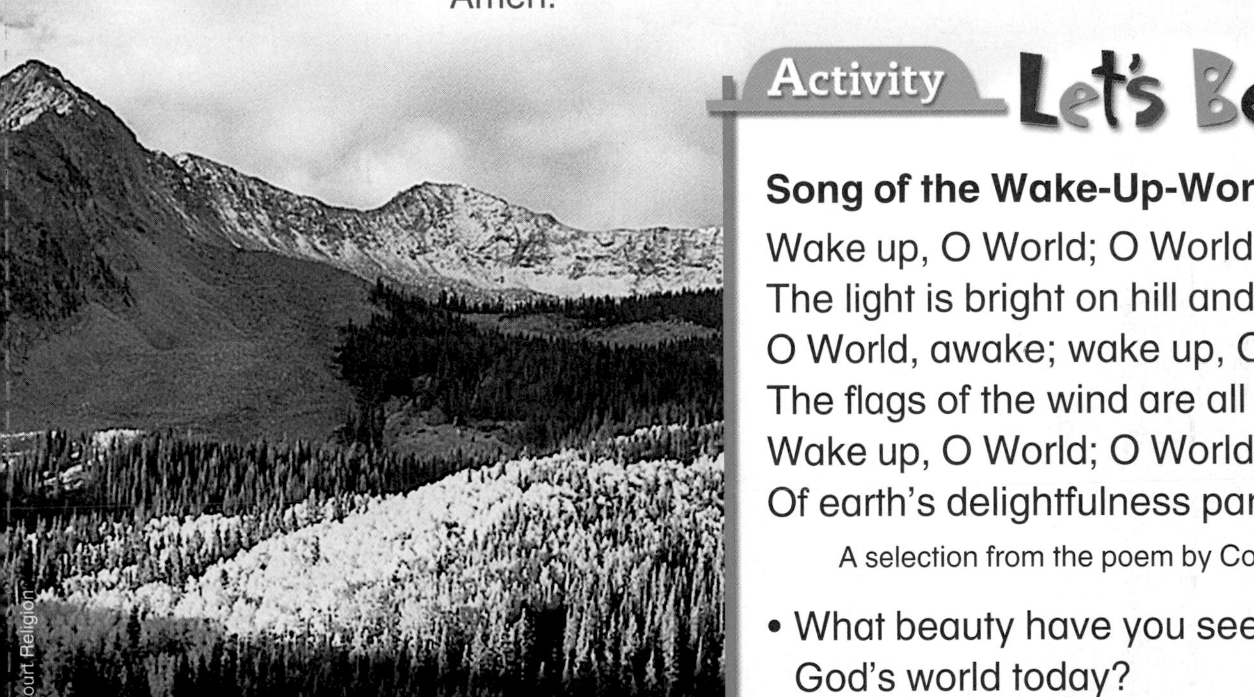

Activity Let's Begin

Song of the Wake-Up-World

Wake up, O World; O World, awake!
The light is bright on hill and lake;
O World, awake; wake up, O World!
The flags of the wind are all unfurled;
Wake up, O World; O World, awake!
Of earth's delightfulness partake.

A selection from the poem by Countee Cullen

- What beauty have you seen in God's world today?

Aprender del pasado

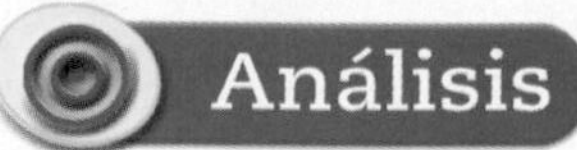

¿Cuáles son algunos de los dones o regalos de Dios?

Este es un relato acerca de cómo una familia descubrió cosas sobre sus familiares que vivieron tiempo atrás.

UN RELATO

Regalos del pasado

"¡Qué casa tan vieja!", dijo Sebastián.

"La construyó mi bisabuelo hace mucho tiempo", dijo mamá. "Mi abuelo y mi papá se criaron aquí".

La tía Marta salió a recibirlos y los invitó a pasar. Mamá miró a su alrededor. "Había olvidado lo hermosas que son las colchas de retazos de la abuela. Con retazos de ropa vieja hacía las colchas más lindas y más calentitas del mundo".

Más tarde, la familia fue al granero. "Mira esas vigas", le dijo papá a mamá. "Todavía se ven las marcas del hacha de tu bisabuelo. Él ponía mucho cariño y empeño en su trabajo".

"Qué interesante", dijo Clara. "Ahora conozco mejor a mis antepasados porque he visto las cosas que hicieron".

¿Qué aprendieron los niños de esta familia sobre sus antepasados?

Learning from the Past

Focus **What are some of God's gifts?**

Here is a story of how one family learned about family members of long ago.

A STORY

Gifts from the Past

"Wow, what an old house!" said Seth.

"My great-grandfather built it long ago," Mom said. "My grandfather and father grew up in it."

Aunt Martha welcomed Seth's family into her home. Mom looked around. "Oh, I had forgotten how beautiful Grandma's quilts are. Grandma used pieces from worn-out clothes to make the prettiest, warmest blankets I can remember."

Later the family walked through the barn. "Look at those beams," Dad said to Mom. "You can still see the marks from your great-grandfather's ax. He put so much love and care into his work."

"This is interesting," Katie said. "I know the people better because I can see what they made."

What did the children in this family learn about their ancestors?

EXPLORACIÓN

Aprender de la creación

Clara y Sebastián aprendieron sobre su familia al ver las cosas que habían hecho otros familiares. Tú puedes aprender sobre Dios a través de su creación. Dios usó su poder para **crear** todo lo que existe.

Palabras de fe

Crear significa hacer algo completamente nuevo. Solamente Dios puede crear algo donde antes no existía nada.

LA SAGRADA ESCRITURA Génesis 1, 1; 2, 3

La creación de la Tierra

El día Primero Dios creó la luz. Separó la luz de las tinieblas y los llamó “Día” y “Noche”.

El día Segundo Dios separó el firmamento de las aguas.

El día Tercero Dios separó la tierra de las aguas. Creó también las plantas y los árboles.

El día Cuarto Dios creó la luna, el sol y las estrellas, y los puso en el cielo.

El día Quinto Dios creó los peces y las aves.

El día Sexto Dios creó los animales terrestres. Y entonces Dios hizo al hombre y a la mujer a su imagen y semejanza. Los bendijo y los puso a cargo de todo lo que había creado. Y Dios vio que su creación era buena.

El día Séptimo Dios descansó.

Basado en *Génesis 1, 1; 2, 3*

Actividad Comparte tu fe

Piensa: ¿Cuál crees que sea la creación más importante de Dios?

Comunica: Habla con tu grupo sobre las cosas que Dios creó.

Actúa: Haz un dibujo de una de las cosas que Dios creó y muéstraselo a la clase.

Learning from Creation

Katie and Seth learned about their family by seeing what family members had made. You can learn about God through his creation. God used his power to **create** everything that exists.

Words of Faith

To **create** means to make something completely new. Only God can create something where nothing existed before.

SCRIPTURE Genesis 1:1-2:3

The Creation of the Earth

On the first day God made light. He separated the light from the darkness and called them day and night.

On the second day God separated the sky from the water below.

On the third day God separated the land from the water. He made plants and trees.

On the fourth day God made the moon, the sun, and the stars and put them in the sky.

On the fifth day God made fish and birds.

On the sixth day God made land animals. Then God made man and woman in his image and likeness. He blessed them and put them in charge of everything he had created. And God saw that his creation was good.

On the seventh day God rested.

Based on *Genesis 1:1, 2:3*

Activity Share Your Faith

Think: What do you think is God's greatest creation?

Share: Talk about God's creations with your group.

Act: Draw a picture of one of God's creations to share with the class.

La belleza del Creador

Análisis **¿Cuál es el propósito de la creación de Dios?**

La Santísima Trinidad (Padre, Hijo y Espíritu Santo) actuó como una sola persona para crear el mundo. La Santísima Trinidad continúa cuidando y manteniendo la creación. Todo lo que Dios creó es bueno y refleja el amor de la Trinidad. A través de la belleza de la creación puedes llegar a conocer a Dios y puedes descubrir la verdad de su bondad.

Todo tiene un propósito en la creación de Dios. Dios quiere que todas las partes de su creación vivan juntas en paz.

Las ballenas y los colibríes, los relámpagos y el viento, el sol y la lluvia, y todas las personas de todas las razas forman parte de la creación de Dios. Todas estas diferencias hacen que el mundo de Dios sea más bello y te muestran su grandeza.

¿Cuáles son algunos signos de la bondad de Dios que ves a tu alrededor?

The Beauty of the Creator

What is the purpose of God's creation?

The Holy Trinity—Father, Son, and Spirit—worked as one to create the world. The Holy Trinity continues to care for and support creation. Everything God created is good and can tell you something about the love of the Trinity. You can come to know God through the beauty of creation. You can learn the truth of his goodness.

Everything in God's creation has a purpose. God wants all parts of his creation to live together in peace.

God's creation includes whales and hummingbirds, lightning and wind, sunshine and rain, and all people of every color. All these differences make God's world more beautiful and teach you more about his greatness.

? What are some signs of God's goodness that you see around you?

A imagen de Dios

Dios creó a los seres humanos a su imagen y semejanza, y les pidió que cuidaran de toda la creación. Dios quiere que seas su amigo durante toda tu vida y que seas feliz con Él. Tú tienes la **responsabilidad** de respetar y amar la creación de Dios.

En el mundo también hay pecado, y por eso la creación de Dios a veces se desequilibra. Dios cuenta con los seres humanos para que contribuyan a restaurar la armonía, o sea el equilibrio y la paz, que Él puso en su creación.

Palabras† de fe

Una **responsabilidad** es un deber o una tarea que se te ha confiado. Dios da a los seres humanos la responsabilidad de cuidar de su creación.

Los bendecidos por Dios

Tu mayor responsabilidad en el cuidado de la creación es hacia la comunidad humana. Los seres humanos son las criaturas más bendecidas por Dios. Dios quiere que respetes y ames a todas las personas porque Él las creó a su imagen y semejanza. En la comunidad de amor de Dios, todos somos hermanos. En esa unidad, tú puedes ser un signo de la bondad y del amor de Dios.

Actividad Practica tu fe

Muestra que eres único Trabaja en grupos de cuatro. Escribe debajo de cada huella dactilar algo en lo que cada uno de ustedes es diferente y algo en lo que todos se parecen.

_______________ _______________ _______________ _______________

_______________ _______________ _______________ _______________

In God's Image

God created humans in his own image and likeness and asked them to care for all creation. God wants you to live in his friendship and to be happy with him. You have a **responsibility** to show respect and love for God's creation.

There is also sin in the world, and because of this God's creation sometimes gets out of balance. God relies on humans to help bring back the harmony, or balance and peacefulness, that he put into his creation.

Words of Faith

A **responsibility** is a duty or a job that you are trusted to do. God gives humans the responsibility of caring for his creation.

Blessed Ones of God

Your most important responsibility in caring for creation is to the human community. Humans are the most blessed of all God's creatures. God wants you to show respect and love for all people because he created each of them in his own image. In God's community of love, everyone is your brother or sister. In your unity you can be a sign of God's goodness and love.

Activity Connect Your Faith

Show Your Uniqueness Work in groups of four. Below each fingerprint shape, write one way in which each of you is different and one way in which you are all similar.

____________ ____________ ____________ ____________

____________ ____________ ____________ ____________

Oración de alabanza

Reúnanse y comiencen con la señal de la cruz.

Canten juntos el estribillo.

Aleluya.

Líder: Dios de amor, ayúdanos a apreciar el maravilloso don de este mundo que has creado.

Todos: **Te damos gracias, Dios, por el don de la creación. Y por eso cantamos.**

Canten el estribillo.

Líder: Nos hiciste a cada uno maravillosamente especiales.

Todos: **Te damos gracias, Dios, por el don de la creación. Y por eso cantamos.**

Canten el estribillo.

Líder: Querido Dios, ayúdanos a amar tu creación.

Todos: **Amén.**

Líder: Oremos.

Inclinen la cabeza mientras el líder reza.

Todos: **Amén.**

Prayer of Praise

Gather and begin with the Sign of the Cross.

Sing together the refrain.

Alleluia.

"Alleluia" © 1987, GIA Publications, Inc.

Leader: Loving God, help us appreciate the marvelous gift of this world that you have created.

All: We thank you, God, for the gift of creation. And so we sing.

Sing the refrain.

Leader: You made each of us wonderfully special.

All: We thank you, God, for the gift of creation. And so we sing.

Sing the refrain.

Leader: Dear God, help us love your creation.

All: Amen.

Leader: Let us pray.

Bow your heads as the leader prays.

All: Amen.

Repasar y aplicar

A Comprueba lo que aprendiste Completa cada enunciado.

1. Crear significa ______________________.
2. Dios ha dado a todos los seres humanos la ______________________ de cuidar de la creación.
3. Todas las personas fueron creadas ______________________ de Dios.
4. Toda la creación es ______________________.
5. Los ______________________ son los más bendecidos de las criaturas de Dios.

B Relaciona ¿Qué podemos hacer para cuidar de la creación de Dios?

____

____

Actividad Vive tu fe

Escribe un poema Este capítulo comenzó con un poema sobre la creación. Escribe un poema con rima sobre la belleza de algo que Dios haya creado. Expresa tus sentimientos sobre esa parte de la creación de Dios. Léele el poema al grupo.

____

____

____

____

____

CHAPTER 1

Review and Apply

A **Check Understanding** Complete each statement.

1. To create means ______________________________ ______________________________.
2. God has given all people the ______________________ to care for creation.
3. All people are made in God's ______________________________.
4. All creation is ______________________.
5. ______________________ are the most blessed of all God's creatures.

B **Make Connections** What are some ways to take care of God's creation?

____

____

Activity Live Your Faith

Write a Poem This chapter began with a poem about creation. Make up a rhyming poem about the beauty of something that God created. Tell your feelings about this part of God's creation. Share your poem with the group.

____

____

____

____

____

CAPÍTULO 1

La fe en familia

Lo que creemos

- Dios creó todas las cosas. Toda la creación muestra la bondad de Dios.
- Dios creó a los seres humanos a su imagen y semejanza.

LA SAGRADA ESCRITURA

El *Salmo 19, 1–7* habla de la gloria de la creación de Dios. Comenta sobre cómo el salmo se relaciona con el relato de la creación.

Visita **www.harcourtreligion.com** para encontrar recursos basados en el año litúrgico y lecturas semanales de la Sagrada Escritura.

Actividad

Vive tu fe

Cuidar de la creación Cuidar de la tierra es una responsabilidad importante que todos compartimos. Comenta con tu familia las cosas que pueden hacer para cuidar de la creación (aire, tierra y agua) y haz una lista. Elijan una de las cosas y pónganla en práctica esta semana.

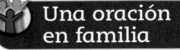

Siervos de la fe

▲ Pierre Teilhard de Chardin 1881–1955

Pierre Teilhard de Chardin nació en Auvernia, Francia. Se hizo sacerdote jesuita. Estudió paleontología, una rama de la ciencia que estudia las formas de vida primitivas. De Chardin utilizó sus conocimientos científicos y sus reflexiones sobre Dios y las personas para ayudar a otros a entender mejor la creación de Dios. De Chardin murió un Domingo de Pascua.

Una oración en familia

Querido Dios, ayúdanos a aprender unos de otros para tratar de comprender la creación. Amén.

 CIC *Consulta el Catecismo de la Iglesia Católica, números 339 y 358, para obtener más información sobre el contenido del capítulo.*

Family Faith

Catholics Believe

- God created everything. All creation shows God's goodness.
- God created humans in his image and likeness.

SCRIPTURE

Psalm 19:1–7 is about the glory of God's creation. Talk about how the psalm connects to the creation story.

www.harcourtreligion.com
For weekly Scripture readings and seasonal resources

Activity

Live Your Faith

Care for Creation Taking care of the earth is an important responsibility that we all share. Discuss and list ways in which you can take care of creation—air, land, and water. Choose one way, and act on it this week.

People of Faith

▲ **Pierre Teilhard de Chardin 1881–1955**

Pierre Teilhard de Chardin was born in Auvergne, France. He became a Jesuit priest. He studied paleontology, a branch of science that explores ancient life forms. De Chardin used what he knew about science and his thoughts about God and people to help others better understand God's creation. De Chardin died on Easter Sunday.

Family Prayer

Dear God, help us learn from one another to try to understand creation. Amen.

CCC *See Catechism of the Catholic Church 339, 358 for further reading on chapter content.*

Capítulo 2 La comunidad de la Iglesia

Líder: Señor, queremos vivir en tu presencia.
"Felices los que habitan en tu casa,
se quedarán allí para alabarte".
Salmo 84, 5

Todos: Señor, queremos vivir en tu presencia. Amén.

Actividad Comencemos

Esta es la Iglesia Mercedes le enseñaba a Emilia, su amiga más joven, unos versos que había aprendido hacía un tiempo, cuando tenía la edad de Emilia. "Es fácil", le dijo. "Tienes que hacer así". Y le mostró cómo poner las manos.

"Esta es la iglesia.
Este, el campanario.
Aquí está la gente
Que entra a diario".

"¡Ahora quiero intentarlo yo!", dijo Emilia.

- ¿Qué personas diferentes ves al abrir las puertas de tu iglesia?

The Church Community

Let Us Pray

Leader: Lord, we want to live in your presence.
"Happy are those who dwell in your house!
They never cease to praise you."

Psalm 84:5

All: Lord, we want to live in your presence. Amen.

Activity Let's Begin

Here's the Church Megan was teaching her younger friend Emily a rhyme she had learned when she was Emily's age. "It's easy," she told Emily. "Just do this." She folded her hands a certain way.

"Here's the church.
Here's the steeple.
Open the doors,
And see all the people."

"Let me try!" said Emily.

- What different people do you see when you open the doors to your church?

Nos necesitamos los unos a los otros

Análisis **¿Dónde puedes aprender lo que Dios quiere que hagas?**

Los edificios no son tan importantes como las personas que los habitan. Hace muchos años, los habitantes de un pueblo de campesinos se habían olvidado de lo importante que era cada persona. También se habían olvidado de cómo llevarse bien con los demás.

UN RELATO

Sopa para todos

¡Talán, talán, talán!, sonó la campana de la plaza del pueblo. Cuando la gente salió a ver qué pasaba, se encontraron con tres soldados.

"Por favor, dennos algo de comer", suplicaron los soldados.

"Me gustaría complacerlos, pero no tengo más que zanahorias", dijo un campesino. "Debo guardarlas para mi familia".

"¡Qué bueno sería poder comer una zanahoria!", dijo otro campesino. "Mi familia no ha comido más que papas durante meses".

"¿Zanahorias? ¿Papas? ¡Ustedes no saben la suerte que tienen! ¡Yo solamente tengo frijoles", dijo un tercero.

Uno de los soldados sonrió y exclamó: "¡Ya sé lo que podemos hacer!".

¿Qué crees que pasó después?

We Need One Another

Where do you learn what God wants you to do?

Buildings are not as important as the people in them. Long ago, the people in a farming town had forgotten how important each person was to the town. They had also forgotten how to get along with one another.

A STORY

Soup for All

Clang, clang, clang! rang the bell in the town square. When the people came out to see why the bell was ringing, they met three soldiers.

"Please give us some food," the soldiers begged.

"I would like to help, but I have only carrots," said one farmer. "I must save them for my family."

"I would love to taste a carrot," said another. "My family has had only potatoes for months!"

"Carrots? Potatoes? How lucky you both are! I have only beans!" said a third farmer.

One of the soldiers clapped his hands. "I know what we can do."

What do you think happened next?

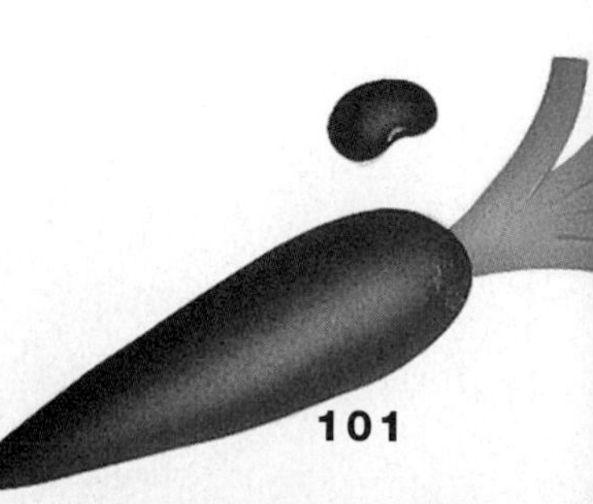

Dios te enseña

El siguiente relato de la **Biblia** cuenta cómo quiere Dios que vivas y lleves a cabo su obra.

Palabras de fe

La **Biblia** es la palabra de Dios escrita en palabras humanas. La Biblia es el libro sagrado de la Iglesia.

LA SAGRADA ESCRITURA — Hechos 2, 42–47

Ayudarse los unos a los otros

Después de la venida del Espíritu Santo, los discípulos de Jesús se reunían frecuentemente para aprender de los Apóstoles, partir el pan y orar. Algunos de ellos vendían lo que tenían y repartían el dinero para ayudar a otros. Muchos de los primeros cristianos compartían sus pertenencias con los necesitados. Estos discípulos de Jesús eran muy felices, y cada día se incorporaban nuevos miembros a la comunidad.

Basado en *Hechos 2, 42–47*

¿Alguna vez has formado parte de un grupo especial? ¿En qué se parece tu grupo al grupo de los discípulos de Jesús?

Actividad — Comparte tu fe

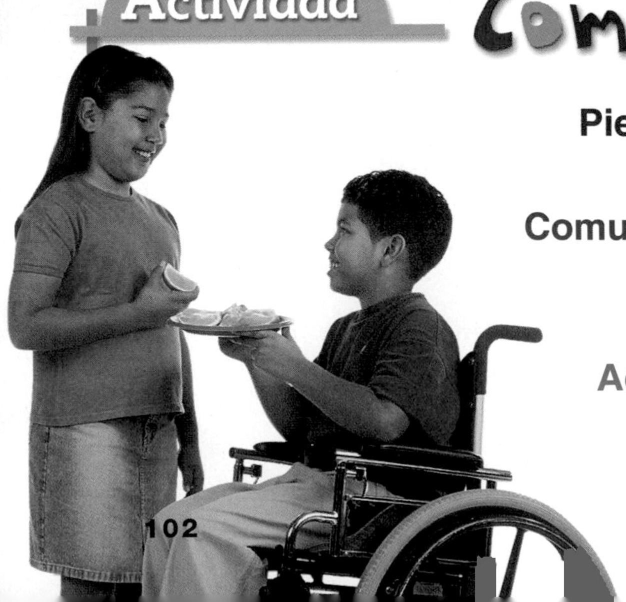

Piensa: ¿Cuándo te ha sido difícil compartir con un amigo o familiar?

Comunica: Conversa con tu grupo sobre cómo en algunas ocasiones compartir puede ser difícil.

Actúa: Representa junto con un compañero una ocasión en la que compartiste aunque te resultara difícil.

God Teaches You

The following **Bible** story tells you how God wants you to live and do his work.

SCRIPTURE **Acts 2:42–47**

Helping One Another

After the Holy Spirit came, Jesus' followers met often to learn from the Apostles, to break bread together, and to pray. Some members of the group sold what they had and gave the money to help the others. Many early Christians shared their belongings with those who were in need. These followers of Jesus were very happy, and new members joined every day.

Based on *Acts 2:42–47*

Have you ever been in a special group? How is your group like Jesus' group of followers?

Words of Faith

The **Bible** is God's word written in human words. The Bible is the holy book of the Church.

Activity Share Your Faith

Think: When have you had trouble sharing with a friend or family member?

Share: Talk to your group about how it can sometimes be difficult to share.

Act: With a partner, act out a time when you shared, even though it was difficult to do so.

Pueblo de Dios

¿Por qué es tan importante la Iglesia?

El relato de la Biblia cuenta que los primeros cristianos aprendieron acerca de Dios a través de Jesús y de sus Apóstoles. Al igual que aquellos cristianos, tú has aprendido que Dios quiere que las personas se amen y trabajen juntas.

Cuando las personas se reúnen con un objetivo común, el grupo que forman se conoce como una *comunidad*. Dios te creó para que formaras parte de una comunidad. Una comunidad puede ayudarte a aprender cosas acerca de Dios que nunca hubieras descubierto por ti mismo.

En las comunidades buenas puedes sentir el amor de Dios y compartir su vida, especialmente en la Iglesia. La **Iglesia** es el Pueblo de Dios reunido en el nombre de Jesucristo. Jesús mostró a todas las personas el amor de su Padre, y envió al Espíritu para que guiara a la Iglesia.

¿Cuándo te reúnes con tu comunidad de la Iglesia?

People of God

Why is the Church so important?

The Bible story shows that the early Christians learned about God from Jesus and from his Apostles. Like these Christians, you have learned that God wants people to love one another and to work together.

When people come together for a shared purpose, the group they form is called a *community*. God created you to be part of a community. A community can help you learn things about God that you might never know if you were learning on your own.

You feel God's love and share God's life in good communities, especially the Church. The **Church** is the People of God gathered in the name of Jesus Christ. Jesus showed all people his Father's love, and he sent the Spirit to guide the Church.

When do you gather with your Church community?

La comunidad de la Iglesia

El término *iglesia* proviene de dos palabras diferentes. Una significa "pueblo convocado" y la otra significa "que pertenece al Señor". Estos significados muestran que la Iglesia es diferente de otras comunidades. Por medio del Bautismo, Dios te llama a formar parte de esta comunidad especial reunida en el nombre de Jesús.

Como miembro de la comunidad de la Iglesia, tú tienes una tarea muy importante que cumplir. Los miembros de la Iglesia se reúnen para honrar a Dios y para ayudar a otras personas. También escuchan las enseñanzas de la Iglesia. La Iglesia te ayuda a comprender la Biblia y el mensaje de Jesús. Y te enseña sobre Dios y su amor.

Palabras de fe

La **Iglesia** es la comunidad del Pueblo de Dios reunida en el nombre de Jesucristo.

Actividad Practica tu fe

La obra de Dios ¿Qué buenas obras están realizando los miembros de tu parroquia? Dibuja a continuación una de las buenas obras de tu parroquia.

The Church Community

The word *church* comes from two different words. One word means "a community called together." The other word means "belonging to the Lord." These meanings tell you that the Church is different from other communities. Through Baptism, God calls you to be part of this special community gathered in Jesus' name.

Words of Faith

The **Church** is the community of the People of God gathered in the name of Jesus Christ.

As a member of the Church community, you have some very important work to do. Church members gather together to honor God and to help other people. They listen to the Church's teaching. The Church helps you understand the Bible and the message of Jesus. It teaches you about God and his love.

Activity Connect Your Faith

God's Work What good works are the people of your parish doing? Draw one of the good works of your parish in the space below.

Oración de agradecimiento

Reúnanse y comiencen con la señal de la cruz.

Lector 1: Jesús, gracias por reunirnos en una comunidad de discípulos tuyos.

Todos: Nos reunimos para darte gracias y alabarte.

Lector 2: Gracias por darnos a otras personas que nos ayudan a llevar a cabo tu obra en el mundo.

Todos: Nos reunimos para darte gracias y alabarte.

Lector 3: Ayúdanos a tener siempre presente que trabajamos mejor cuando trabajamos juntos.

Todos: Nos reunimos para darte gracias y alabarte.

Líder: Oremos.

Inclinen la cabeza mientras el líder reza.

Todos: Amén.

Canten juntos.

¡Yo soy la iglesia!
¡Tú eres la iglesia!
¡Somos la iglesia juntos!
Los que en todo el mundo
a Jesús seguimos.
¡Somos la iglesia juntos!

Prayer of Thanks

Gather and begin with the Sign of the Cross.

Reader 1: Jesus, thank you for bringing us together as a community of your followers.

All: We join together to give you thanks and praise.

Reader 2: Thank you for giving us other people to help us do your work in the world.

All: We join together to give you thanks and praise.

Reader 3: Help us remember that we work best when we work together.

All: We join together to give you thanks and praise.

Leader: Let us pray.

Bow your heads as the leader prays.

All: Amen.

Sing together.

I am the church!
You are the church! We are the church together! All who follow Jesus, all around the world! Yes, we're the church together.

"We Are the Church" © 1972, Hope Publishing Co.

Repasar y aplicar

A **Trabaja con palabras** Completa cada enunciado.

1. Puedes aprender acerca de Dios a través de ______________________, de la Iglesia y de la Biblia.
2. Una ______________________ es un grupo de personas que se reúnen con un objetivo común.
3. Por medio del Bautismo Dios te llamó a formar parte de una comunidad llamada la ______________________.
4. La ______________________ es la palabra de Dios escrita en palabras humanas.
5. La comunidad de la Iglesia también se conoce como ______________________.

B **Comprueba lo que aprendiste** Cómo continuaron siguiendo a Jesús los primeros cristianos?

____

____

Actividad Vive tu fe

Dibuja un cartel Piensa en una buena obra que se pueda realizar en tu comunidad. Diseña en el espacio de abajo un cartel invitando a los miembros de tu parroquia a colaborar. Dibuja a las personas trabajando juntas para llevar a cabo una tarea.

Lavado
de carros
para la
parroquia

CHAPTER 2

Review and Apply

A **Work with Words** Complete each statement.

1. Some ways you learn about God are through ____________________, the Church, and the Bible.
2. A ____________________ is a group of people who come together for a shared purpose.
3. Through Baptism, God called you to be part of a special community called the ____________________.
4. The ____________________ is God's word written in human words.
5. A name for the Church community is ____________________.

B **Check Understanding** How did early Christians continue to follow Jesus?

____

____

Activity Live Your Faith

Draw a Poster Think of good work that needs to be done in your community. Use the space below to design a poster that invites members of your parish to help. Show people working together to get a job done.

CAPÍTULO 2

La fe en familia

Lo que creemos

- La Biblia es la palabra de Dios escrita en palabras humanas.
- La Iglesia es el Pueblo de Dios unido en el nombre de Jesús.

LA SAGRADA ESCRITURA

Juan 15, 12–17 habla sobre el amor y el cuidado a la comunidad de la Iglesia. Lee el pasaje y conversa sobre cómo deberíamos amarnos y cuidarnos los unos a los otros.

Visita **www.harcourtreligion.com** para encontrar recursos basados en el año litúrgico y lecturas semanales de la Sagrada Escritura.

Actividad

Vive tu fe

Haz una tabla Tu parroquia es un lugar para adorar a Dios, aprender acerca de Él, llevar a cabo tareas de servicio, y para pasarla bien en compañía. Haz una tabla con estas cuatro actividades. Escribe una manera en la que tu familia puede realizar cada actividad. Elige una actividad que tú realizarías para hacer de tu parroquia una comunidad más fuerte.

Siervos de la fe

▲ **San Francisco de Asís 1182–1226**

Francisco era hijo de un rico mercader de telas en Asís, Italia. Un día, mientras rezaba, Jesús le pidió que reconstruyera la Iglesia. Francisco ayudó a la gente a ver la belleza del mundo y anunció la Buena Nueva de Jesús. Llevó una vida sencilla y fue bueno con todas las criaturas. El 4 de octubre se celebra su día. Francisco es el santo patrono de la ecología.

Una oración en familia

San Francisco, ruega por nosotros para que trabajemos juntos en la construcción de la Iglesia. Amén.

 CIC *Consulta el Catecismo de la Iglesia Católica, números 781 y 782, para obtener más información sobre el contenido del capítulo.*

CHAPTER 2

Family Faith

Catholics Believe

- The Bible is the word of God written in human words.
- The Church is the People of God gathered in the name of Jesus.

SCRIPTURE

John 15:12–17 is about loving and caring for the Church community. Read the passage and talk about how you should love and care for one another.

www.harcourtreligion.com
For weekly Scripture readings and seasonal resources

Activity

Live Your Faith

Make a Chart Your parish is a place to worship God, to learn about God, to do works of service, and to have a good time together. Make a chart with each of these four activities. Write a way that your family can do each activity. Choose one activity that you will do to make your parish a stronger community.

▲ Saint Francis of Assisi 1182–1226

People of Faith

Francis was the son of a rich cloth merchant in Assisi, Italy. One day while Francis was praying, Jesus asked him to rebuild the Church. Francis helped people see the beauty of the world and preached the good news of Jesus to them. He lived a simple life and was kind to all creatures. His feast day is October 4. Francis is the patron saint of ecology.

Family Prayer

Saint Francis, pray for us that we may work together to build the Church. Amen.

CCC See Catechism of the Catholic Church 781, 782 for further reading on chapter content.

Capítulo 3 En casa con Dios

Oremos

Líder: Dios Padre nuestro, ayúdanos a vivir como tu pueblo.
"¡Qué bueno y qué tierno es
ver a esos hermanos vivir juntos!".

Salmo 133, 1

Todos: Dios Padre nuestro, ayúdanos a vivir como tu pueblo. Amén.

Actividad Comencemos

Una familia

Tengo un hermano al que
le gustan los libros,
una hermana muy divertida,
una mamá que me mima,
y una primita de seis años cumplidos.
Tengo una tía que siempre me visita,
un papá que me alienta en
todos mis partidos,
una abuelita que me llama "querido",
y amigos que vienen a
casa a pasar el día.
Tengo una familia que
me ama y me cuida.

- ¿Quién te cuida a ti? Menciona dos cosas buenas de tu papá, de tu mamá o de alguna otra persona que te cuida.

Chapter 3

At Home with God

Let Us Pray

Leader: God our Father, help us live as your people.
"How good it is, how pleasant,
where the people dwell as one!"

Psalm 133:1

All: God our Father, help us live as your people. Amen.

Activity Let's Begin

A Family

I have a brother who likes to read,
and a sister who makes me laugh,
and a mom who gives me what I need,
and a cousin who is six and a half.

I have an aunt who visits during the year,
and a dad who comes to see me play,
and a grandmother who calls me dear,
and friends who come by my house for the day.

I have a family who loves and takes care of me.

- Who takes good care of you? Tell two good things about your father, your mother, or someone else who cares for you.

Amarse los unos a los otros

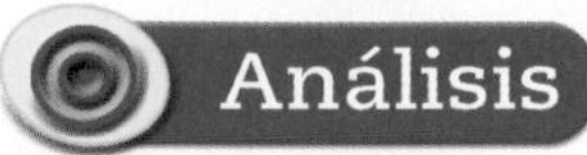

¿Cómo se muestran los familiares que se aman?

Es importante que los familiares participen juntos en momentos especiales. En este relato, un tío enseña una nueva manera de mostrar amor.

UN RELATO

El regalo del tío Daniel

"¡Hola a todo el mundo!", dijo el tío Daniel.

"¡Hola!", dijo Ignacio. "¿Qué me trajiste?".

El tío Daniel parecía confundido. "No traje ningún regalo", respondió.

Ignacio se encerró en su habitación enojado. Al rato, su hermana Cecilia llamó a la puerta. "Mira la casita para pájaros que hice con el tío Daniel", le dijo. "Ahora vamos a hacer pizza. ¿Quieres ayudarnos?".

Ignacio no respondió. Poco después escuchó risas y le llegó el olor de la pizza. Cecilia fue de nuevo a tocar a su puerta.

"El tío Daniel nos quiere enseñar un truco de naipes. ¿Vienes?", le preguntó.

Ignacio preguntó: "¿Cuánto tiempo se va a quedar?".

"Dos días nada más", contestó Cecilia.

¿Qué crees que va a hacer Ignacio?

Loving One Another

How do families show their care for one another?

It is important for family members to share special times. In this story, an uncle teaches a new way to show love for others.

A STORY

Uncle Dan's Present

"Hello, everybody!" Uncle Dan said.

"Hi!" said Nathan. "What did you bring me?"

Uncle Dan looked puzzled. "I didn't bring any presents."

Nathan stomped to his room. Later, his sister Carrie knocked on his door. "Look at the birdhouse Uncle Dan and I made. We're going to make pizza next. Want to help us?"

Nathan didn't say anything. Soon he heard laughter and smelled pizza. Carrie was back at his door.

"Uncle Dan wants to teach us a card trick. Are you coming down?" she asked.

Nathan asked, "How long is he staying?"

"Only two days," Carrie replied.

? What do you think Nathan will do?

EXPLORACIÓN

Cuidarse los unos a los otros

El tío Daniel mostró su amor visitando a Cecilia e Ignacio. La Biblia también cuenta un relato sobre una visita especial: la **Visitación**.

Palabras de fe

La visita de María a Isabel se conoce como la **Visitación**.

LA SAGRADA ESCRITURA **Lucas 1, 39–56**

María visita a Isabel

Isabel, la prima de María, se alegró y se sorprendió cuando María fue a visitarla. Llena del Espíritu Santo, Isabel dijo a María: "¡Bendita tú eres entre las mujeres y bendito el fruto de tu vientre! ¿Cómo he merecido yo que venga a mí la madre de mi Señor?".

El saludo de Isabel alegró a María. "Proclama mi alma la grandeza del Señor, y mi espíritu se alegra en Dios mi Salvador", contestó María.

Basado en *Lucas 1, 39–56*

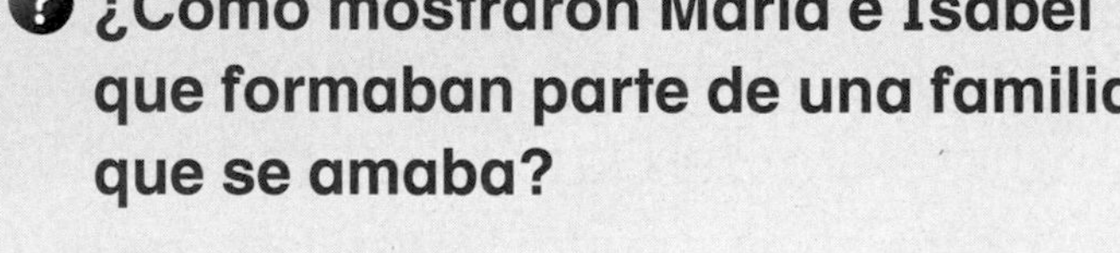

¿Cómo mostraron María e Isabel que formaban parte de una familia que se amaba?

Actividad Comparte tu fe

Piensa: ¿Qué tiene tu familia de especial?

Comunica: Con tu grupo, busca en revistas fotos que muestren cómo los familiares se pueden amar y cuidar entre sí.

Actúa: Recorta y pega las fotos en un cartel.

Caring for One Another

Uncle Dan showed that he cared by visiting with Carrie and Nathan. Another story about a special visit is found in the Bible. This is the story of the **Visitation**.

Words of Faith

The **Visitation** is the name of the visit of Mary to Elizabeth.

SCRIPTURE Luke 1:39–56

Mary Visits Elizabeth

Mary's cousin, Elizabeth, was happy and surprised when Mary visited. Filled with the Holy Spirit, Elizabeth said to Mary, "Most blessed are you among women, and blessed is the fruit of your womb. How does this happen to me, that the mother of my Lord should come to me?"

Elizabeth's greeting made Mary happy. She answered, "My soul proclaims the greatness of the Lord; my spirit rejoices in God my savior."

Based on *Luke 1:39–56*

How did Mary and Elizabeth show that they were caring family members?

Activity Share Your Faith

Think: What is special about your family?

Share: With your group, find pictures in magazines that show ways family members can love and care for one another.

Act: Cut out and glue the pictures to a poster board.

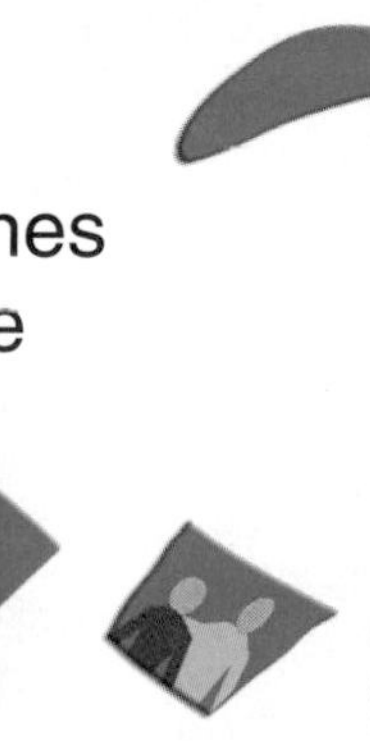

Las familias enseñan a amar

Análisis **¿En qué se parecen la familia y la Iglesia?**

En los dos relatos que acabas de leer, las familias muestran su amor con acciones y con palabras. Tu familia es la que primero te da a conocer el amor que Dios te tiene. Tu familia también te enseña a amar a Dios y a las personas.

Tu familia te muestra cómo llevar una vida saludable. También te enseña medidas de seguridad muy importantes. Con la ayuda de tu familia, puedes aprender a cuidar mascotas o a realizar otras tareas.

Tu familia te ayuda a aprender oraciones, como la bendición de los alimentos, la Oración del Señor y el Ave María. También te da a conocer la Iglesia Católica. Si ya has sido bautizado, formas parte de esta especial familia de Dios. La Iglesia amplía lo que aprendes en tu casa. La familia es el primer lugar en el que los niños aprenden las lecciones que la Iglesia enseña. Por esta razón, a la familia se le conoce como "la Iglesia doméstica" o la iglesia del hogar.

¿Qué aprendiste en tu familia acerca de la Iglesia Católica?

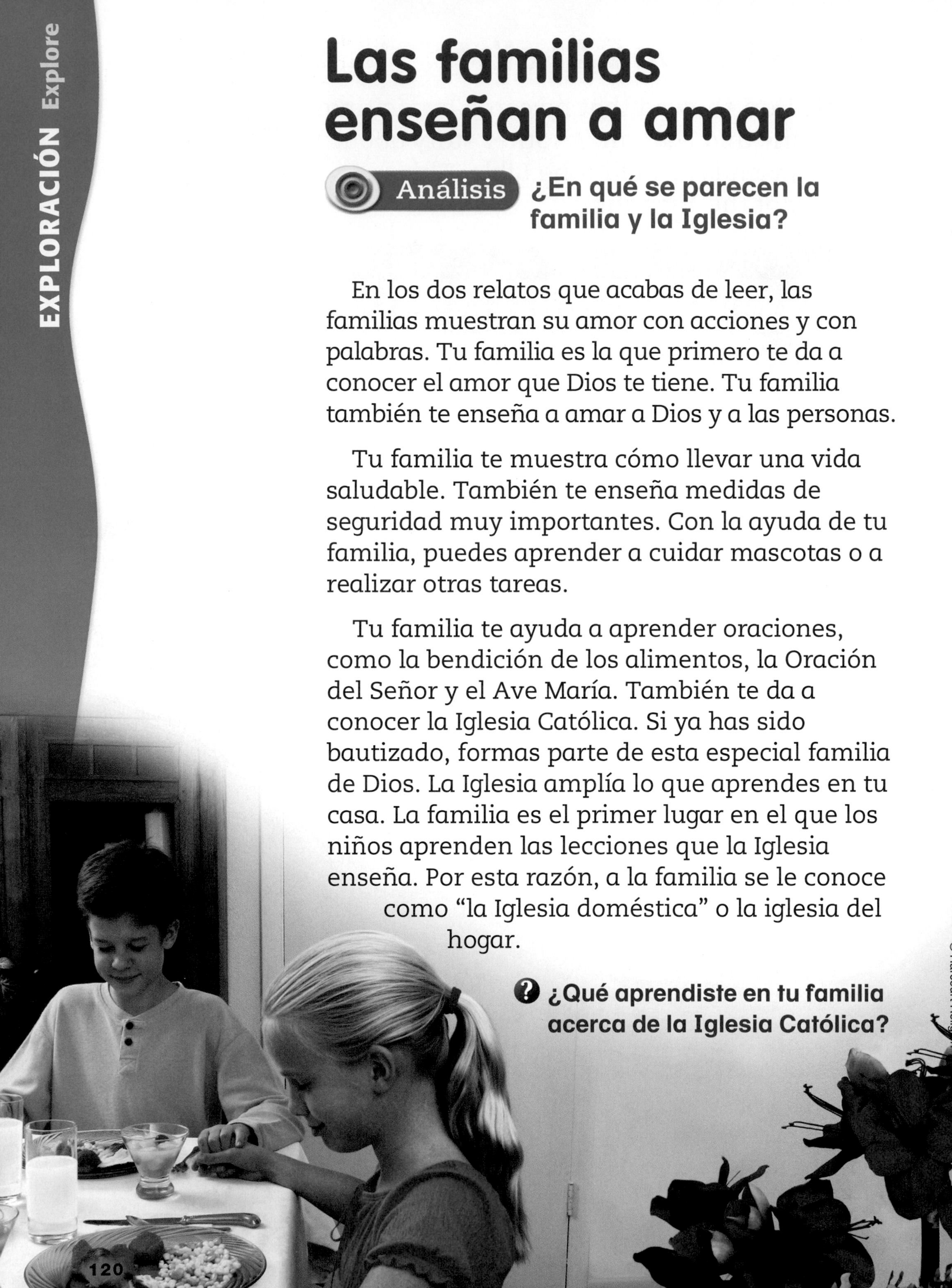

Families Teach Love

How is the family like the Church?

In both of the stories you just read, family members showed their love in actions and in words. You first learn about God's love for you from your family. Your family also teaches you how to love God and others.

You can learn the basics of healthy living from your family. Your family teaches you important safety rules. You may learn how to care for pets or do other chores.

Your family helps you learn prayers, such as the blessing before meals, the Lord's Prayer, and the Hail Mary. Your family introduces you to the Catholic Church. If you are baptized, you are already a member of this special family of God. The Church builds on what you have learned in your home. The family is where children first learn the lessons that the Church teaches. For this reason, the family is called the "domestic Church," or the church of the home.

What is something you have learned about the Catholic Church from your family?

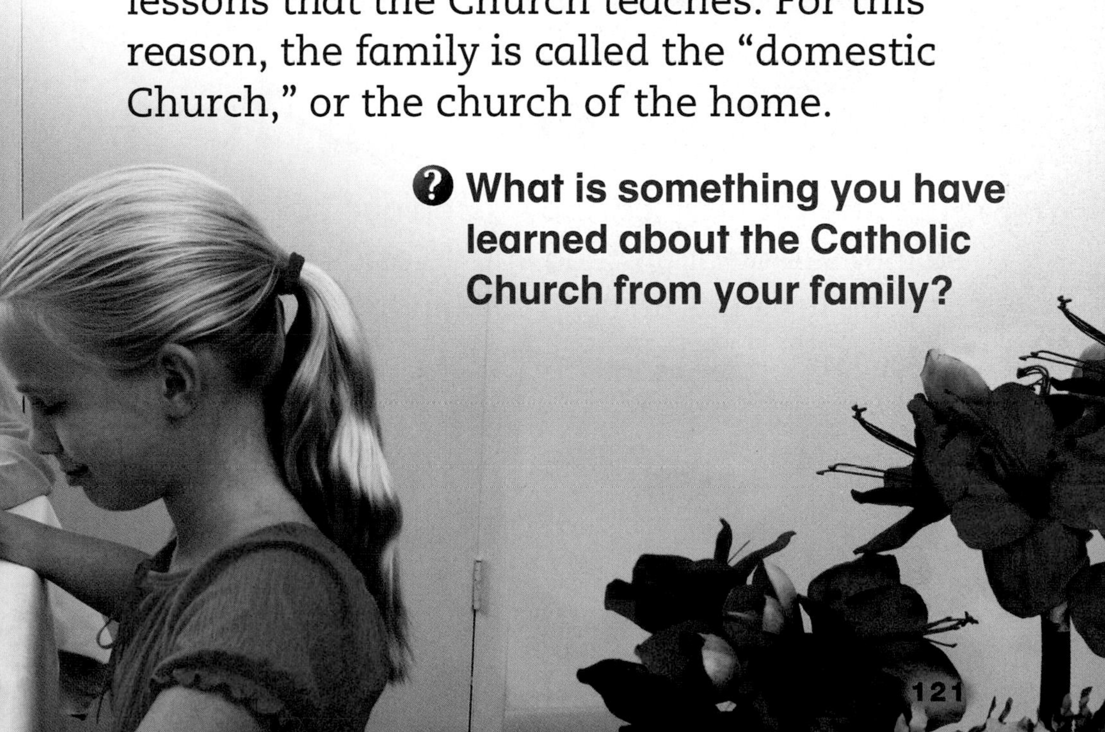

Comunidades de amor

La iglesia del hogar puede ser un signo especial que muestra a otros cómo se aman entre sí las tres personas de la Santísima Trinidad. Tu familia también puede ser un signo de este amor al vivir unida en la fe, en la esperanza y en el amor.

Dios comparte su **autoridad** con los padres, y los invita a amarte y a cuidarte tal como Él lo hace. Dios quiere que respetes la autoridad de tus padres y de las personas que te cuidan, como los maestros y otras personas de la comunidad. Su autoridad también proviene de Dios.

Palabras de fe

Tener **autoridad** significa estar a cargo de algo, y tener el poder para tomar decisiones.

Dios nos ama a todos

Algunas veces tus familiares pueden estar ocupados o cansados. A veces es posible que te decepcionen. Pero aun así, Dios los ama, así como te ama a ti. Es importante que trates a tus familiares con amor y con respeto, y que reces por ellos.

? ¿Cuándo te ha resultado difícil obedecer a alguien que esté a cargo de ti?

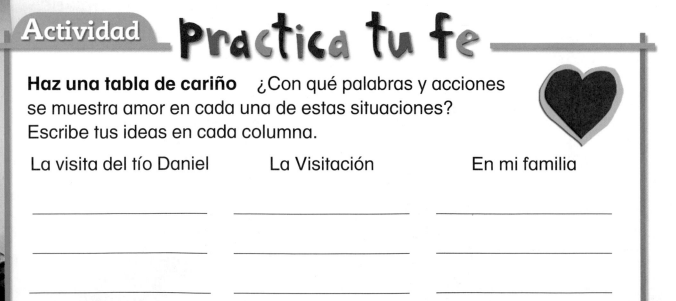

Actividad **Practica tu fe**

Haz una tabla de cariño ¿Con qué palabras y acciones se muestra amor en cada una de estas situaciones? Escribe tus ideas en cada columna.

La visita del tío Daniel	La Visitación	En mi familia
____________	____________	____________
____________	____________	____________
____________	____________	____________

Communities of Love

The church of the home can be a special sign that shows others how the three Persons of the Holy Trinity love one another. Your family can be a sign of this love, too, when you live together in faith, hope, and love.

God shares his **authority** with parents. He invites them to love and care for you just as he does. God wants you to respect the authority of your parents and others who care for you. This includes teachers and community officials. Their authority comes from God, too.

Words of Faith

Having **authority** is being in charge of something and having the power to make decisions.

God Loves Everyone

Sometimes members of families may be busy or tired. They may let you down. They are still loved by God, just as you are. It is important to treat the members of your family with love and respect and to pray for them.

? When has it been hard to obey someone who is responsible for you?

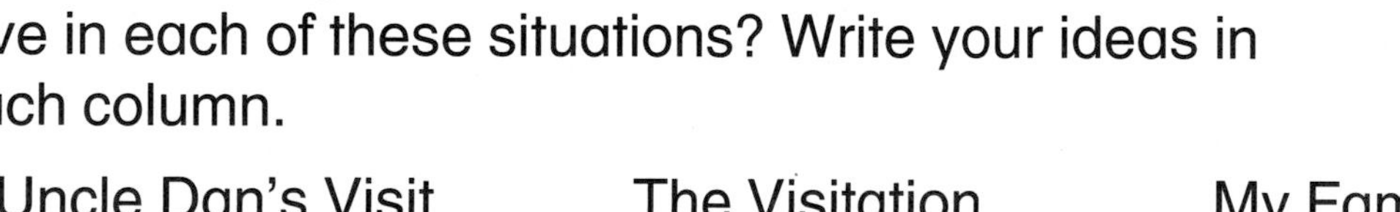

Make a Caring Chart What words and actions show love in each of these situations? Write your ideas in each column.

Uncle Dan's Visit	The Visitation	My Family Life
______________	______________	______________
______________	______________	______________
______________	______________	______________

Oración de agradecimiento

Reúnanse y comiencen con la señal de la cruz.

Líder: Querido Dios, gracias por nuestras familias. Con tu ayuda, les mostraremos nuestro amor y nuestro cariño.

Lector 1: Cuando estemos juntos,

Todos: **Ayúdanos a querernos y a cuidarnos.**

Lector 2: Cuando alguien esté triste,

Todos: **Ayúdanos a querernos y a cuidarnos.**

Lector 3: Cuando tengamos mucha energía e ideas,

Todos: **Ayúdanos a querernos y a cuidarnos.**

Lector 4: Cuando estemos cansados y de mal humor,

Todos: **Ayúdanos a querernos y a cuidarnos.**

Líder: Querido Dios, gracias por el amor en nuestras familias.

Todos: **Amén.**

Líder: Oremos.

Inclinen la cabeza mientras el líder reza.

Todos: **Amén.**

Canten juntos.

Los grandes, los chicos,
las madres, los padres
hermanas y hermanos.
La familia de Dios.

"All Grownups, All Children" © 1977, Patricia Joyce Shelly

Prayer of Thanks

Gather and begin with the Sign of the Cross.

Leader: Dear God, thank you for our families. With your help, we will try to show them our love and care.

Reader 1: When we are together,

All: **Help us show love and care.**

Reader 2: When family members are sad,

All: **Help us show love and care.**

Reader 3: When we are full of energy and ideas,

All: **Help us show love and care.**

Reader 4: When we are tired and grouchy,

All: **Help us show love and care.**

Leader: Dear God, thank you for caring families.

All: **Amen.**

Leader: Let us pray.

Bow your heads as the leader prays.

All: **Amen.**

Sing together.

All grownups, all children, all mothers, all fathers are sisters and brothers in the fam'ly of God.

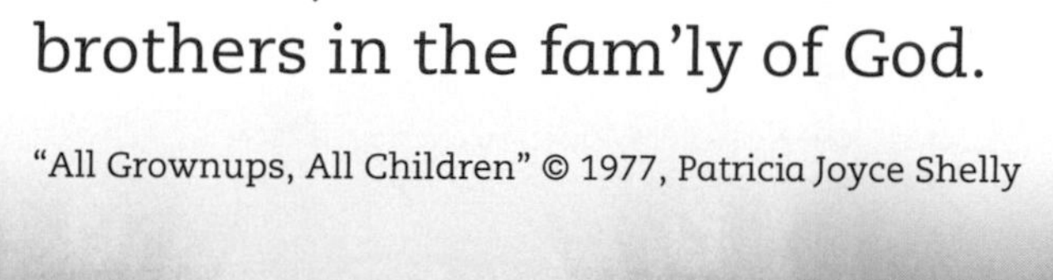

"All Grownups, All Children" © 1977, Patricia Joyce Shelly

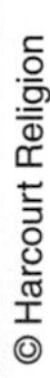

Repasar y aplicar

A Trabaja con palabras Completa cada enunciado.

1. La visita de María a Isabel se conoce como la ______________________________.
2. La familia se conoce a veces como la ______________________________ o la iglesia del hogar.
3. Los familiares deben tratarse unos a otros con ____________________.
4. A los padres y los maestros les ha sido dada ______________________________ para amarte y cuidarte.
5. La "iglesia del hogar" puede mostrar a los demás el amor de la ______________________________.

B Comprueba lo que aprendiste ¿Cuáles son algunas maneras en que puedes mostrar respeto por tus familiares?

____

____

Actividad Vive tu fe

Dibuja una historieta Las historietas sobre familias son muy populares. En estos cuadros, cuenta una historia sobre una familia que muestre su amor mutuo con palabras y con obras. La historieta puede ser cómica o seria.

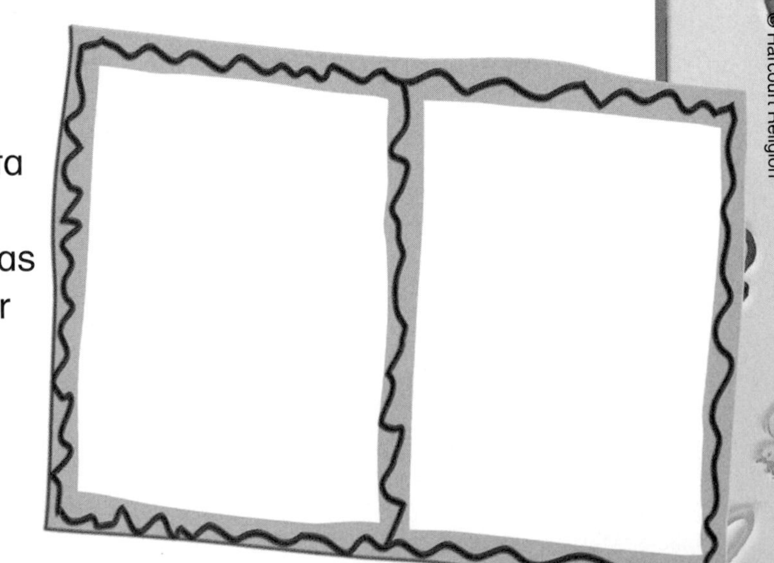

CHAPTER 3

Review and Apply

A Work with Words Complete each statement.

1. Mary's visit to Elizabeth is called the ______________________.
2. The family is sometimes called the ______________________, or the church of the home.
3. Family members should treat one another with ______________.
4. Parents and teachers are given ______________________ to love and care for you.
5. The "church of the home" can show others the love of the ______________________.

B Check Understanding What are some ways to show respect for your family members?

____

____

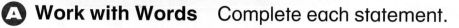

Activity Live Your Faith

Draw a Comic Strip Comic strips are often about families. Use these frames to develop a story about a family whose members use words and actions to show care for one another. The comic strip can be funny or serious.

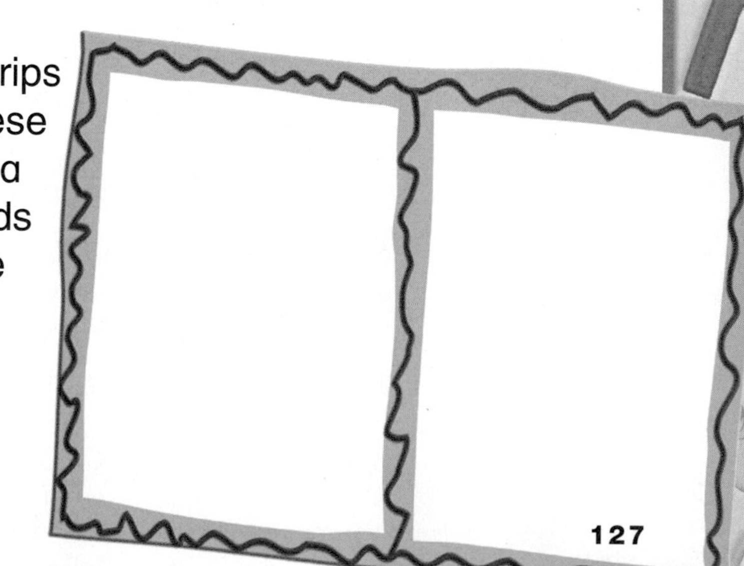

La fe en familia

Lo que creemos

- Los niños descubren primero el amor de Dios por medio de sus familias.
- La familia se conoce como "la Iglesia doméstica".

LA SAGRADA ESCRITURA

Lucas 2, 41–52 habla de cómo Jesús se perdió y María y José lo encontraron. Lee el pasaje y conversa sobre la familia de Jesús.

Visita **www.harcourtreligion.com** para encontrar recursos basados en el año litúrgico y lecturas semanales de la Sagrada Escritura.

Actividad
Vive tu fe

Muestra tu amor Una manera de mostrar amor en las familias es elogiarse entre ellos. Escribe el nombre de cada uno de tus familiares en una tabla dejando mucho espacio para cada persona. Durante la semana, escribe palabras de elogio junto a su nombre cada vez que esa persona muestre amor.

¡Te felicito! ¡Fantástico! ¡Buen trabajo! ¡Así se hace! ¡Muy bien!

▲ Los beatos Luis (1880–1951) y María (1884–1965)

Siervos de la fe

Este matrimonio vivió en Roma. **Luis** era abogado y **María** era escritora y catequista. Luis y María no solo cuidaron a sus hijos sino también a sus vecinos. Fueron un gran ejemplo de cómo los esposos pueden ayudarse mutuamente a vivir una vida santa. Se convirtieron en el primer matrimonio que fue beatificado junto. Su día se celebra el 25 de noviembre.

Una oración en familia

Querido Dios, ayúdanos a servirte a ti y a los demás a través de una vida familiar santa. Amén.

 CIC *Consulta el Catecismo de la Iglesia Católica, números 1657 y 1666, para obtener más información sobre el contenido del capítulo.*

CHAPTER 3

Family Faith

Catholics Believe

- Children first learn about God's love through their families.
- The family home is called the "domestic Church."

SCRIPTURE

Luke 2:41–52 is about Jesus' being lost and then found by Mary and Joseph. Read the passage and talk about Jesus' family.

GO ONLINE **www.harcourtreligion.com** For weekly Scripture readings and seasonal resources

Activity

Live Your Faith

Show Your Love One way that members of a family can show love is to praise one another. Write the name of each person in your family on a chart. Leave a lot of space between the names. During the week, write words of praise next to each person's name when he or she does something that shows love or care.

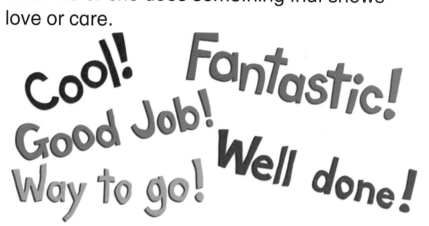

Cool! Fantastic! Good Job! Well done! Way to go!

People of Faith

▲ Blessed Luigi (1880–1951) and Blessed Maria (1884–1965)

This married couple lived in Rome. **Luigi** was a lawyer. **Maria** was a writer and a catechist. Luigi and Maria cared for their own children and for neighbors. Their example shows that married couples can help each other live holy lives. They were the first married couple beatified together. Their memorial day is November 25.

Family Prayer

Dear God, help us serve you and one another through a holy family life. Amen.

CCC See Catechism of the Catholic Church 1657, 1666 for further reading on chapter content.

Repaso de la Unidad 1

Trabaja con palabras Resuelve el crucigrama.

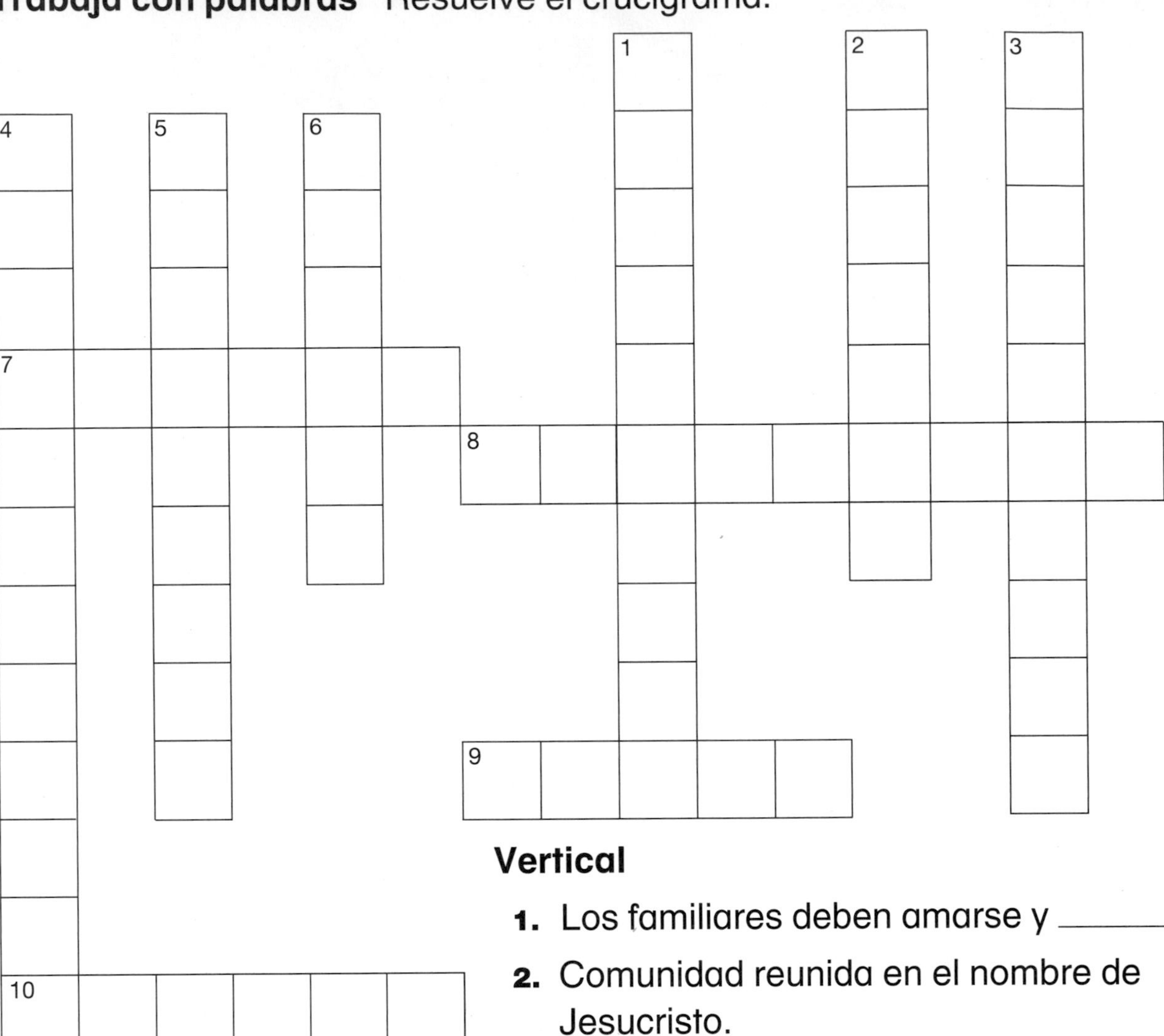

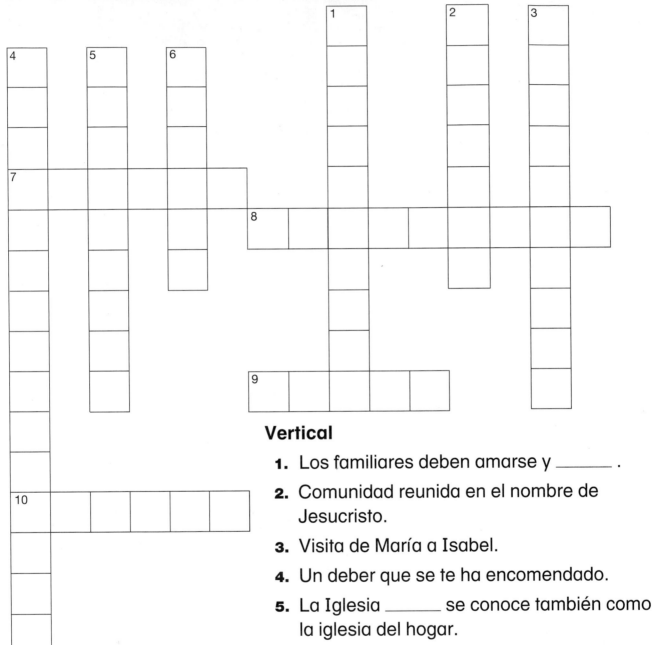

Vertical

1. Los familiares deben amarse y ______ .
2. Comunidad reunida en el nombre de Jesucristo.
3. Visita de María a Isabel.
4. Un deber que se te ha encomendado.
5. La Iglesia ______ se conoce también como la iglesia del hogar.
6. La palabra de Dios escrita en palabras humanas.

Horizontal

7. La comunidad de la Iglesia se conoce como el ______ de Dios.
8. Dios da ______ a los padres y a quienes te cuidan.
9. La Santísima Trinidad actuó como una sola persona para ______ el mundo.
10. Los seres humanos fueron creados a ______ de Dios.

Unit 1 Review

Work with Words Solve the crossword puzzle.

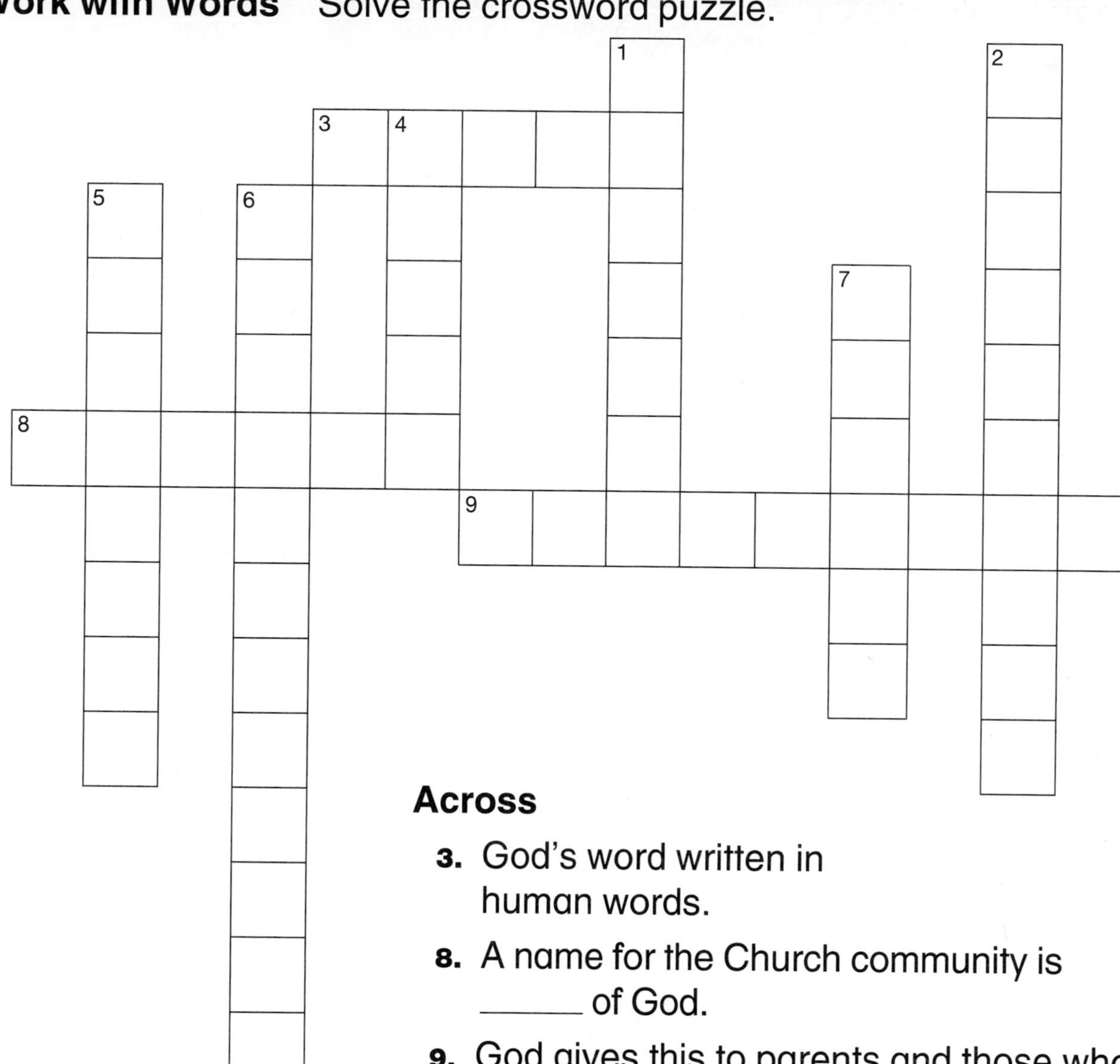

Across

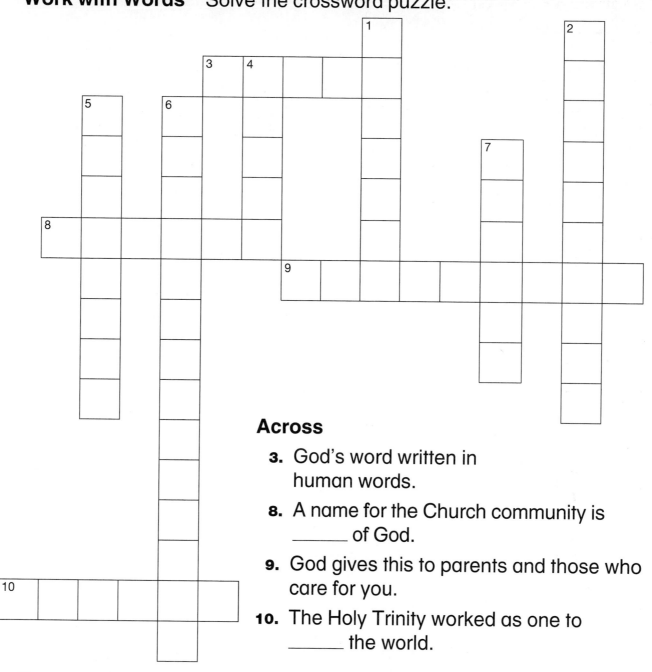

3. God's word written in human words.
8. A name for the Church community is ______ of God.
9. God gives this to parents and those who care for you.
10. The Holy Trinity worked as one to ______ the world.

Down

1. Family members should love and ______ one another.
2. When Mary went to stay with Elizabeth.
4. Humans were created in God's ______.
5. The ______ Church is called the church of the home.
6. A duty or job that you are trusted to do.
7. Community gathered in the name of Jesus Christ.

UNIDAD 2

Responder a Dios

La Santísima Trinidad

¿Cómo puedes entender mejor el misterio de la Santísima Trinidad?

La Iglesia rinde culto

¿Cómo alaban y dan gracias a Dios los católicos?

Orar siempre

¿Cuál es tu manera favorita de orar?

¿Qué crees que vas a aprender en esta unidad acerca de cómo responder a Dios?

UNIT 2
Responding to God

The Holy Trinity

How can you better understand the mystery of the Holy Trinity?

The Church Worships

How do Catholics give praise and thanks to God?

Pray Always

What is your favorite way to pray?

What do you think you will learn in this unit about responding to God?

Capítulo 4 La Santísima Trinidad

Oremos

Líder: ¡Señor Dios, envía al Espíritu Santo para que avive nuestros corazones!

"La gracia de Cristo Jesús, el Señor, el amor de Dios y la comunión del Espíritu Santo sean con todos ustedes".

2 Corintios 13, 14

Todos: ¡Señor Dios, envía al Espíritu Santo para que avive nuestros corazones! Amén.

Actividad Comencemos

Los misterios de la naturaleza

Hay cosas en este mundo que no tienen explicación. Solo Dios entiende totalmente los misterios de su creación.

¿Por qué hizo Dios el cielo azul y la hierba verde?

¿Por qué no es tan lindo el color del barro?

¿Por qué tienen los insectos tantas patas?

¿Por qué no maúllan los perros y ladran los gatos?

- ¿Qué preguntas tienes sobre el misterio de la creación de Dios?

Chapter 4 The Holy Trinity

Leader: Lord God, send forth the Holy Spirit to set our hearts on fire!

"The grace of the Lord Jesus Christ and the love of God and the fellowship of the holy Spirit be with all of you."

2 Corinthians 13:13

All: Lord God, send forth the Holy Spirit to set our hearts on fire! Amen.

Activity Let's Begin

Mysteries of Nature Some things in this world just can't be explained. Only God fully understands the mysteries of his creation.

Why did God make the sky blue and the grass green?

Why can't mud be a prettier color?

Why do insects have so many legs?

Why don't dogs meow and cats bark?

- What questions do you have about the mystery of God's creation?

Aprender acerca del misterio

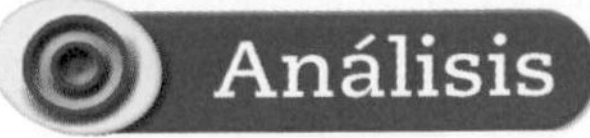

¿Qué enseñó San Patricio acerca de la Santísima Trinidad?

¿Alguna vez aprendiste algo que era difícil de entender? La historia del obispo Patricio relata cómo aprendió el pueblo de Irlanda algo difícil de entender.

UN RELATO

Tres en uno

Hace mucho tiempo, el pueblo de Irlanda tenía dudas acerca de Dios. Cuando el obispo Patricio estaba enseñando sobre las tres Personas en un solo Dios, alguien le preguntó: "¿Cómo puedes decir que hay un solo Dios cuando tú oras al Padre, al Hijo y al Espíritu Santo?".

Para explicar la **Santísima Trinidad** Patricio tomó un trébol del suelo. Lo levantó para que todos lo vieran. "Este trébol que tengo en la mano es una planta, pero tiene tres hojas. El Padre, el Hijo y el Espíritu Santo no son tres dioses, sino tres Personas en un solo Dios. Éste es un misterio que aceptamos por la fe".

¿Qué ayudó al pueblo de Irlanda a entender mejor el misterio de la Santísima Trinidad?

Learning About Mystery

What did Saint Patrick teach about the Holy Trinity?

Have you ever learned something that was hard to understand? The story of Bishop Patrick tells how the people of Ireland learned about something hard to understand.

A STORY

Three in One

Long ago the people of Ireland had questions about God. As Bishop Patrick was teaching about the three Persons in one God, someone asked, "How can you say that there is only one God when you pray to the Father, the Son, and the Holy Spirit?"

Patrick explained the **Holy Trinity** by plucking a shamrock from the ground. He held it up for the people to see. "The shamrock I am holding is one plant, but it has three leaves. The Father, the Son, and the Holy Spirit are not three gods. They are three Persons in one God. This is a mystery that we accept on faith."

What helped the people better understand the mystery of the Holy Trinity ?

Un solo Dios

Patricio ayudó a la gente a entender que hay un solo Dios.

También tú puedes aprender de Jesús, que habló a sus discípulos del Padre y del Espíritu Santo.

La **Santísima Trinidad** es el nombre de las tres Personas en un solo Dios.

LA SAGRADA ESCRITURA Juan 14, 6-7 y 16-17

El Padre y el Espíritu Santo

Un día Jesús estaba hablando con sus discípulos acerca de Dios. Les dijo: "Nadie va al Padre sino por mí. Si me conocen a mí, también conocerán al Padre".

Jesús prometió pedirle al Padre que enviara el Espíritu Santo para enseñar a la gente.

Tomado de *Juan 14, 6–7 y 16–17*

¿Qué dijo Jesús acerca del Padre y del Espíritu Santo?

Comparte tu fe

Piensa: Reflexiona sobre la Santísima Trinidad y el trébol.

Comunica: Conversa con tu grupo acerca del parecido entre el trébol y el Padre, el Hijo y el Espíritu Santo.

Actúa: Dibuja un trébol y escribe en una de las hojas "Padre", en otra "Hijo" y en otra "Espíritu Santo".

One God

Patrick helped the people understand that there is only one God.

You can also learn from Jesus, who told his followers about the Father and the Holy Spirit.

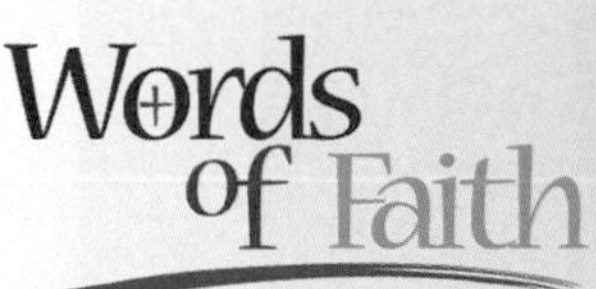

The **Holy Trinity** is the name for the three Persons in one God.

SCRIPTURE John 14:6–7, 16–17

The Father and the Spirit

One day Jesus was talking with his followers about God. Jesus told them, "No one comes to the Father except through me. If you know me, then you will also know my Father."

Jesus promised to ask the Father to send the Holy Spirit to teach the people.

From *John 14:6–7, 16–17*

What did Jesus say about the Father and the Spirit?

Share Your Faith

Think: Think about the Holy Trinity and the shamrock.

Share: Talk to your group about how the shamrock is like the Father, Son, and Holy Spirit.

Act: Draw a shamrock and label one leaf "Father," one leaf "Son," and one leaf "Holy Spirit."

Padre, Hijo y Espíritu Santo

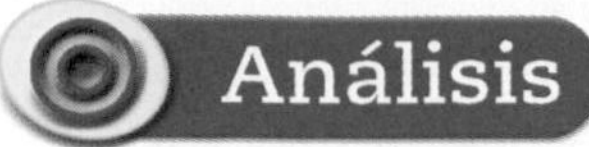

¿Cómo se refleja la obra de la Trinidad?

Jesús llamaba a Dios "Padre", y enseñó a sus discípulos a llamar "Padre" a Dios. Jesús demostró con sus acciones que es Dios Hijo, que se hizo hombre para salvar a todas las personas. Le pidió a su Padre que enviara al Espíritu Santo, que es el amor y la gracia de Dios que te acompañan.

Lo más importante de la Santísima Trinidad es que es una comunión de amor de Personas unidas en una sola por el amor. La Santísima Trinidad es un misterio, una verdad de fe que los católicos creen aunque no puedan entenderla totalmente. Un misterio es una verdad que solo Dios puede entender totalmente.

Mediante la revelación de Dios y con su ayuda puedes entender mejor un misterio como la Santísima Trinidad. Puedes ver a la Santísima Trinidad en acción cuando aprecias el amor en el mundo. También puedes percibir el reflejo de la Santísima Trinidad en la Iglesia. Entenderás mejor a la Santísima Trinidad cuando veas a Dios en el cielo.

¿Cuáles son otros misterios de fe?

Father, Son, and Holy Spirit

What is the work of the Trinity?

Jesus called God "Father," and he taught his followers to call God "Father," too. By his actions Jesus showed that he is God the Son, who became human to save all people. Jesus asked his Father to send the Holy Spirit, who is God's love and grace, present with you.

The most important thing about the Holy Trinity is that it is a loving communion of Persons joined as one in love. The Holy Trinity is a *mystery*, a truth of faith that Catholics believe even though they cannot understand it completely. A mystery is a truth that only God can fully understand.

Through God's revelation and with his help, you can understand more about a mystery like the Trinity. You can see the Trinity at work when you see love in the world. You can see the reflection of the Trinity in the Church. You will better understand the Trinity when you see God in heaven.

What are some other mysteries of faith?

EXPLORACIÓN Explore

Honrar a la Santísima Trinidad

La Iglesia recuerda y honra a las tres Personas en un solo Dios con oraciones como la señal de la cruz y el Gloria al Padre. La Iglesia redactó una serie de resúmenes de la fe denominados **credos**. Uno de los más antiguos es el Credo de los Apóstoles. Es un resumen de la fe en la Santísima Trinidad. Así comienzan sus tres partes:

"Creo en Dios Padre...

Creo en Jesucristo...

Creo en el Espíritu Santo..."

Palabras† de fe

Los **credos** contienen las creencias esenciales acerca de Dios Padre, Dios Hijo y Dios Espíritu Santo, y acerca de otras enseñanzas de la Iglesia.

Trabajar juntos

Dios Padre te creó. Jesús, el Hijo, te salvó y es tu hermano. El Espíritu Santo está contigo ahora, santificándote y ayudándote a llevar el amor y la paz de Dios al mundo. Las tres Personas de la Santísima Trinidad trabajan juntas como un solo Dios.

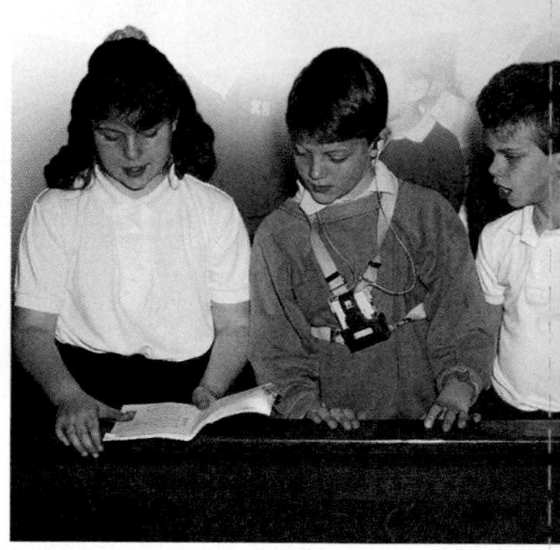

❓ **¿Cuándo puede ayudarte y guiarte el Espíritu Santo?**

Actividad Practica tu fe

Escribe una oración Termina cada oración con tus propias palabras.

Dios Padre nuestro, ________________________________

____

Jesús, Hijo de Dios, ________________________________

____

Espíritu Santo, ayúdanos a ___________________________

____

Honoring the Trinity

The Church remembers and honors the three Persons in one God in such prayers as the Sign of the Cross and the Glory to the Father. The Church has developed summaries of faith called **Creeds**. One of the oldest Creeds is the Apostles' Creed. It is a summary of faith in the Holy Trinity. Here is how the three parts begin.

"I believe in God, the Father . . .

I believe in Jesus Christ . . .

I believe in the Holy Spirit . . ."

Words of Faith

Creeds are statements of the basic beliefs about God the Father, God the Son, and God the Holy Spirit, and about other teachings of the Church.

Working Together

God the Father created you. The Son, Jesus, saved you and is your brother. The Holy Spirit is with you now, making you holy and helping you bring God's love and peace to the world. All three Persons of the Trinity work together as one God.

? When can the Holy Spirit help and guide you?

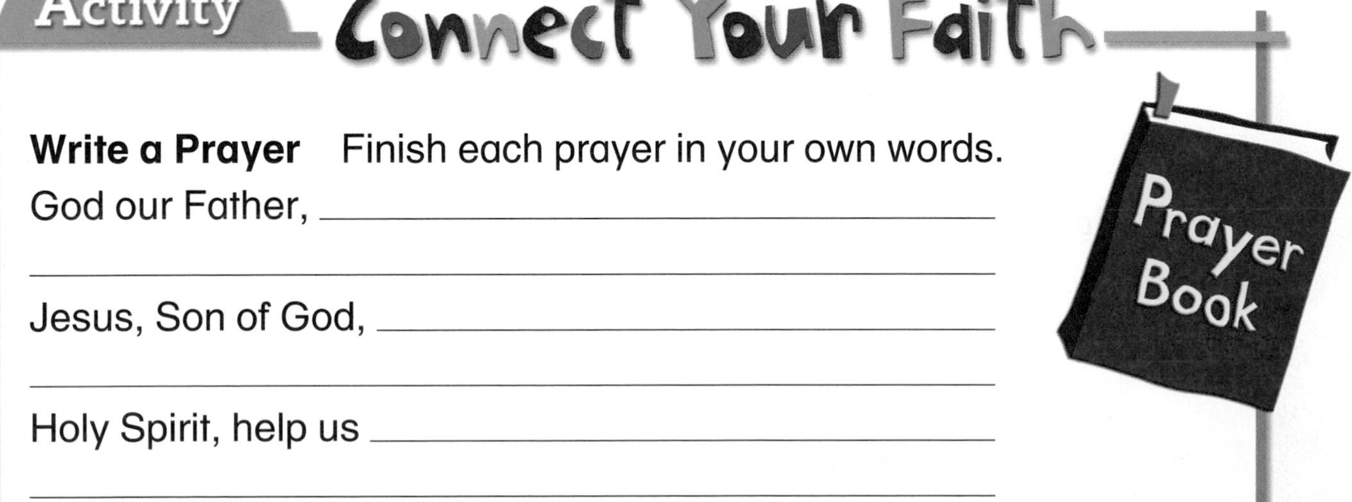

Write a Prayer Finish each prayer in your own words.

God our Father, ______________________________

____

Jesus, Son of God, ______________________________

____

Holy Spirit, help us ______________________________

____

Celebración de la Palabra

Reúnanse y comiencen con la señal de la cruz.

Canten juntos.

Un solo Dios, una fe y un bautismo,

Un solo Señor, de todos Padre.

"There Is One Lord", Taizé Community, © 1984, Les Presses de Taizé, GIA Publications, Inc., agent

Líder: Unidos en comunidad, estamos llamados a una sola fe.

Lector: Lectura de la carta a los Efesios.

Lean Efesios 4, 1–6.

Palabra de Dios.

Todos: Te alabamos, Señor.

Líder: Compartamos nuestra fe en la Trinidad.

¿Creen en Dios Padre?

Todos: Sí, creemos.

Líder: ¿Creen en Jesucristo, su único Hijo?

Todos: Sí, creemos.

Líder: ¿Creen en el Espíritu Santo, Señor y dador de vida?

Todos: Sí, creemos.

Líder: Esta es nuestra fe. Esta es la fe de la Iglesia.

Todos: Amén.

Celebration of the Word

Gather and begin with the Sign of the Cross.

Sing together.

There is one Lord, one faith, one baptism,
There is one God who is Father of all.

"There Is One Lord", Taizé Community, © 1984, Les Presses de Taizé, GIA Publications, Inc., agent

Leader: Joined together as one community, we are called to one faith.

Reader: A reading from the Letter to the Ephesians.

Read Ephesians 4:1–6.

The word of the Lord.

All: **Thanks be to God.**

Leader: Let us share our belief in the Trinity.
Do you believe in God the Father?

All: **We do.**

Leader: Do you believe in Jesus Christ, his only Son?

All: **We do.**

Leader: Do you believe in the Holy Spirit, the Lord and giver of life?

All: **We do.**

Leader: This is our faith. This is the faith of the Church.

All: **Amen.**

Repasar y aplicar

A Trabaja con palabras Completa cada enunciado.

1. Uno de los credos más antiguos de la Iglesia es el ________________.

2. Las tres Personas en un solo Dios se conoce como la ________________.

3. Una verdad que solo Dios puede entender totalmente se llama un ________________.

4. Las tres Personas de la Santísima Trinidad actúan como ________________.

5. Patricio enseñó acerca de la Trinidad utilizando un ________________.

B Comprueba lo que aprendiste Escribe dos maneras de honrar a la Santísima Trinidad.

____

____

Actividad Vive tu fe

Haz un cartel Haz un cartel que muestre con palabras y dibujos cómo la Iglesia transmite al mundo el amor de la Santísima Trinidad.

CHAPTER 4

Review and Apply

A Work with Words Complete each statement.

1. One of the Church's oldest Creeds is the ____________________.
2. The name given to the three Persons in one God is the ____________________.
3. A truth that only God can fully understand is called a ____________________.
4. All three Persons of the Holy Trinity work together as ____________________.
5. Patrick taught about the Trinity by using a ____________________.

B Check Understanding Name two ways to honor the Trinity.

____

____

Activity Live Your Faith

Make a Poster Create a poster that shows in words and pictures how the Church brings the love of the Trinity to the world.

La fe en familia

Lo que creemos

- La Santísima Trinidad son tres Personas en un solo Dios.
- Jesús, Dios Hijo, enseñó acerca de Dios Padre y Dios Espíritu Santo.

LA SAGRADA ESCRITURA

Hechos 2, 1–4 habla de la venida del Espíritu Santo en Pentecostés. Comenta cómo ayudó el Espíritu Santo a los Apóstoles.

Visita **www.harcourtreligion.com** para encontrar recursos basados en el año litúrgico y lecturas semanales de la Sagrada Escritura.

Actividad

Vive tu fe

Muestra amor Hablen sobre la vida de su familia. Menciona distintas maneras de mostrarse unos a otros el amor de la Santísima Trinidad. Pega un trébol de papel en la nevera o en la pared de la cocina. Pon una pegatina en el trébol cada vez que alguien de tu familia muestre amor. Cuando el trébol esté lleno, salgan a celebrar juntos en familia.

Siervos de la fe

Juan nació en Francia y estudió en París. Fue ordenado sacerdote y fundó la Orden de la Santísima Trinidad, conocida como los Trinitarios. La Orden se dedicó a liberar a prisioneros y esclavos cristianos. Los Trinitarios fundaron hospitales y ahora dirigen escuelas. El día de San Juan se celebra el 17 de diciembre.

▲ San Juan de Mata 1160–1213

Una oración en familia

San Juan, ruega por nosotros para que podamos honrar a la Santísima Trinidad trabajando y sirviendo a los demás. Amén.

 CIC *Consulta el Catecismo de la Iglesia Católica, números 237 y 253, para obtener más información sobre el contenido del capítulo.*

CHAPTER 4

Family Faith

Catholics Believe

- The Holy Trinity is three Persons in one God.
- Jesus, God the Son, taught about God the Father and God the Holy Spirit.

Acts 2:1–4 is about the coming of the Holy Spirit at Pentecost. Talk about how the Holy Spirit helped the Apostles.

GO ONLINE **www.harcourtreligion.com** For weekly Scripture readings and seasonal resources

Activity

Live Your Faith

Show Love Talk about your family's life together. List ways that you show the love of the Holy Trinity to one another. Place a paper shamrock on the refrigerator or wall in your kitchen. Each time someone in your family shows love, place a sticker on the shamrock. When the shamrock is filled, go out for a family treat together.

People of Faith

▲ Saint John of Matha 1160–1213

John was born in France, and he studied in Paris. He was ordained a priest and started the Order of the Most Holy Trinity, known as the Trinitarians. The order worked to free Christian prisoners and slaves. The Trinitarians set up hospitals and now run schools. Saint John's feast day is December 17.

Family Prayer

Saint John, pray for us that we may honor the Trinity by working to serve others. Amen.

CCC *See Catechism of the Catholic Church 237, 253 for further reading on chapter content.*

Capítulo 5 La Iglesia rinde culto

Oremos

Líder: Padre Santo, nos regocijamos en tu amor por nosotros.
"Alábenlo con danzas y tamboriles,
alábenlo con mandolinas y flautas".
Salmo 150, 4

Todos: Padre Santo, nos regocijamos en tu amor por nosotros.

Actividad Comencemos

Comparte la alegría La música era fuerte y alegre. Cada bailarín se movía independientemente, pero al mismo tiempo el grupo bailaba en conjunto. Cada bailarín contribuía a la uniformidad de la danza.

Roberto y Lucía imitaban los movimientos del bailarín principal. Les encantaba participar en la danza. Juntos compartían la alegría de la música y se divertían muchísimo.

- Representa un sentimiento mediante la danza u otros movimientos corporales. Pide a tus compañeros de clase que adivinen de qué sentimiento se trata.

Chapter 5

The Church Worships

Let Us Pray

Leader: Holy Father, we celebrate your love for us.
"Give praise with tambourines and dance,
praise him with flutes and strings."
Psalm 150:4

All: Holy Father, we celebrate your love for us.
Amen.

Activity

Let's Begin

Share the Joy The music was loud and lively. Each dancer moved separately, but the group moved together, too. Each dancer helped make the pattern of the dance.

Brendan and Maya imitated the way the dance leader moved. They were glad to be part of the dance. Together they shared the joy of the music and had a lot of fun.

- Act out a feeling by using dance or other body movements. Have classmates guess what you are feeling.

Relatos del amor de Dios

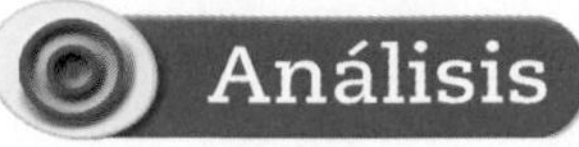

¿Por qué los miembros de la Iglesia celebran juntos?

Los católicos se reúnen para celebrar la Misa. Las fiestas y las comidas especiales son formas excelentes de compartir la alegría de formar parte de la comunidad de Dios.

UN RELATO

La alegría de las celebraciones

En el carro, camino a la fiesta de aniversario de bodas de sus abuelos, Carlos estaba molesto. Se sentía muy acalorado a causa del traje que vestía.

"Mamá", dijo Carlos, "¿por qué tengo que ir a la fiesta si hoy tenía que ir a entrenar?".

"Ya hablamos de eso", dijo la mamá de Carlos. "Este aniversario es una ocasión muy especial, y tú no puedes faltar".

En la fiesta, a Carlos le encantó ver a sus primos. La comida estaba muy rica y la música era divertida. Lo que más le gustó a Carlos fue ver bailar a sus abuelos.

Mientras regresaba a casa, Carlos reflexionó sobre el comportamiento que había tenido cuando iban en camino a la fiesta. "Mamá", dijo, "perdóname porque no quería ir. ¿Cuándo es la próxima fiesta familiar?".

¿Cómo celebra tu familia las ocasiones especiales?

Stories of God's Love

Why do Church members celebrate together?

Catholics come together to celebrate the Mass. Parties or special meals are great ways to celebrate the joy of being part of God's community.

A STORY

The Joy of Celebrations

Kyle was not pleased. He felt far too hot, dressed in a suit and sitting in the car on the way to his grandparents' anniversary party.

"Mom," Kyle said, "why couldn't I have skipped the party and gone to practice?"

"We've been through this," said Kyle's mother. "This anniversary is a very special occasion, and you need to be part of it."

At the party Kyle was happy to see his cousins. There was good food and great music. Kyle especially enjoyed watching his grandparents dance.

On the way home, Kyle thought about how he acted on the way to the party. "Mom," he said, "I'm sorry I didn't want to go. When is the next family party?"

How does your family celebrate special occasions?

Celebrar juntos

Jesús enseñó a sus discípulos cómo celebrar. Les contó relatos y compartió comidas con ellos. La última comida con ellos fue la más memorable de todas.

LA SAGRADA ESCRITURA Lucas 22, 14–20

La Última Cena

Jesús y sus amigos se reunieron para celebrar la fiesta judía de la Pascua.

Al final de la cena, Jesús tomó el pan. Lo bendijo y lo partió. Dio el pan a sus amigos, diciendo: "Esto es mi cuerpo, que es entregado por ustedes. Hagan esto en memoria mía".

Después, Jesús tomó la copa de vino y dijo: "Esta copa es la alianza nueva sellada con mi sangre, que es derramada por ustedes".

Basado en *Lucas 22, 14–20*

Actividad Comparte tu fe

Piensa: Imagina que estás en la Última Cena. ¿Qué crees que quiera decir Jesús con sus palabras?

Comunica: Conversa de esto con tu grupo.

Actúa: Representa con tus compañeros lo que sucedió en la Última Cena.

Celebrating Together

Jesus taught his followers how to celebrate. He told them stories and shared meals with them. His last meal with them was the most memorable one of all.

SCRIPTURE — Luke 22:14–20

The Last Supper

Jesus and his friends were together to celebrate the Jewish feast of Passover.

At the end of the meal, Jesus took some bread. He blessed it and broke it. He gave the bread to his friends, saying, "This is my body, which will be given for you; do this in memory of me."

Jesus then took the cup of wine and said, "This cup is the new covenant in my blood, which will be shed for you."

Based on *Luke 22:14–20*

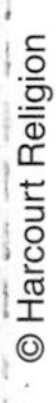

Activity — Share Your Faith

Think: Imagine that you are at the Last Supper. What do you think Jesus means by his words?

Share: Talk about this with a group.

Act: Act out the story of the Last Supper with your classmates.

Rendir culto juntos

Análisis **¿Cómo rinde culto la Iglesia a Dios?**

Cuando rindes **culto**, honras a Dios con la oración y con tus acciones. Puedes adorar a Dios tú solo o también con tu comunidad eclesial. El culto es una manera de corresponder al amor que Dios te demuestra. Puedes adorar a Dios con palabras, con silencio, con música y con acciones.

En la Misa y en los sacramentos, los católicos rinden culto a Dios como comunidad. Este tipo de culto público, comunitario, se conoce como *liturgia*.

Aunque los católicos tienen muchas maneras de orar y rendir culto, la Eucaristía o Misa es la más importante. En la Eucaristía, la comunidad se reúne con Jesús para adorar a Dios Padre en el poder del Espíritu Santo. La comunidad se une en el amor de la Santísima Trinidad.

¿Por qué es importante rendir culto a Dios con otros?

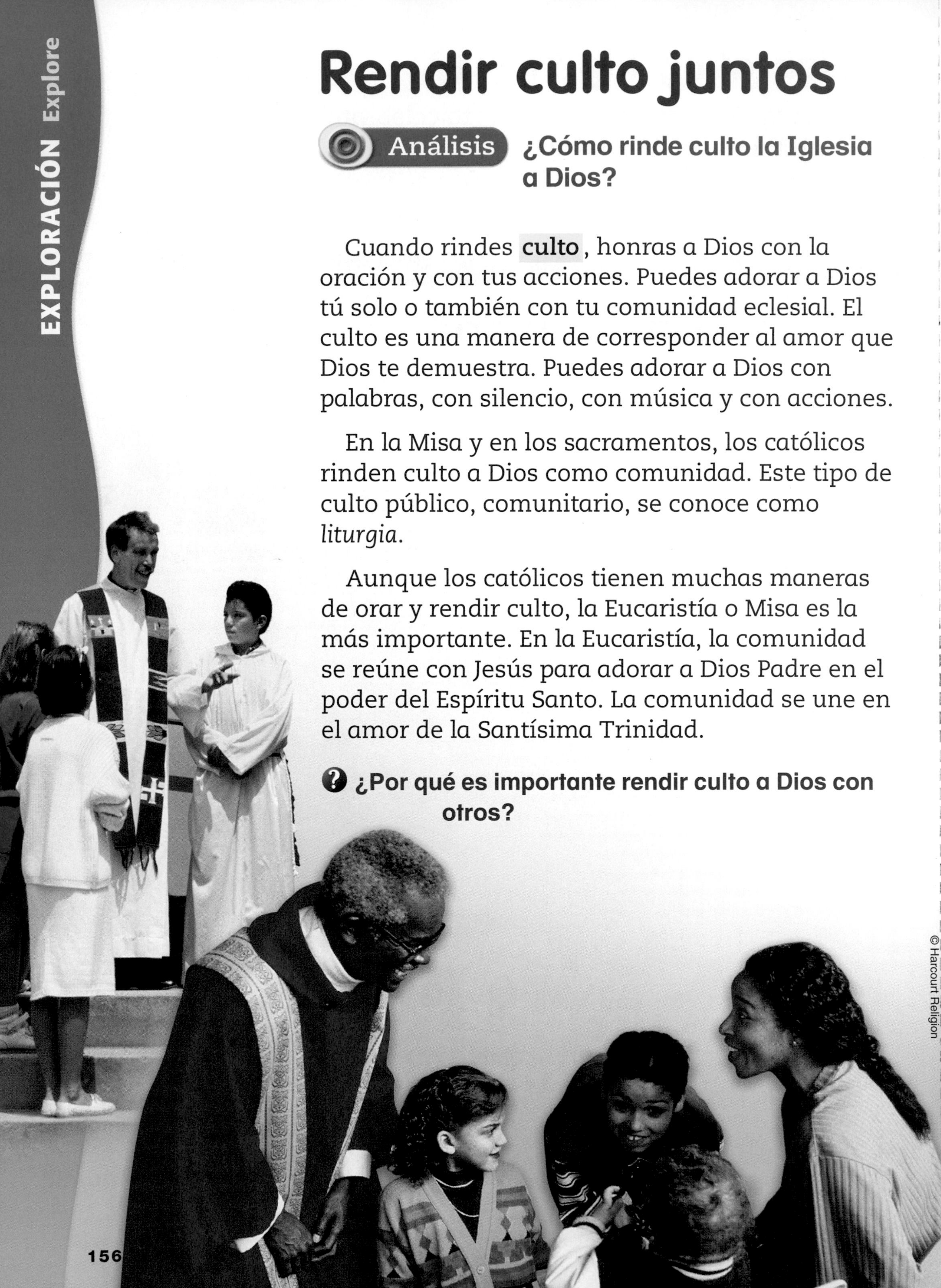

Worship Together

What are some ways in which the Church worships God?

When you **worship**, you honor God in prayer and action. You worship God alone or with your Church community. Worship is a way to return the love that God shows you. You can worship God with words, silence, music, and actions.

At Mass and in the sacraments, Catholics worship as a community. This kind of public, community worship is called *liturgy*. Although Catholics have many ways to pray and worship, the Eucharist, or the Mass, is the most important. In the Eucharist the community joins with Jesus to worship God the Father in the power of the Holy Spirit. The community joins in the love of the Holy Trinity.

? Why is worshiping with others important?

El centro de la Iglesia

En la Misa, los católicos se reúnen para escuchar la Palabra de Dios de la Sagrada Escritura. También recuerdan y celebran lo que Jesús dijo e hizo con sus discípulos en la Última Cena. Cada vez que vas a Misa, te invitan a recibir el Cuerpo y la Sangre de Jesús en la Sagrada Comunión. La Iglesia te pide que hagas esto al menos una vez durante la Pascua.

La Iglesia enseña que los católicos deben asistir a Misa los domingos y días de fiesta de la Iglesia, porque la Misa es el centro de la vida de la Iglesia. Cuando vas cumples con el tercer mandamiento: "Santificarás las fiestas".

Además de demostrar su amor y respeto a Jesús en la Misa, los católicos también lo demuestran en la Eucaristía cuando visitan el **Santísimo Sacramento** en la Iglesia. El pan consagrado en la Misa, una vez transformado en el Cuerpo de Cristo, se guarda en el tabernáculo. Jesucristo está verdaderamente presente en el Santísimo Sacramento.

¿Cómo santifica tu familia el domingo y los días de fiesta?

Palabras de fe

Rendir **culto** es adorar y alabar a Dios.

El **Santísimo Sacramento** es la Sagrada Eucaristía. Este término se refiere especialmente al pan consagrado que se guarda en el tabernáculo.

Actividad Practica tu fe

Una alabanza Escribe un verso que exprese alegría, alabanza o gratitud por el don de la Eucaristía. Frente a la clase, proclama tus palabras en voz alta, cántalas o represéntalas mientras bailas. Escribe tu verso a continuación.

____

____

Center of the Church

At Mass, Catholics gather to hear God's word in Scripture. They also remember and celebrate what Jesus said and did with his disciples at the Last Supper. Every time you go to Mass, you are encouraged to receive Jesus' Body and Blood in Holy Communion. The Church requires that you do this at least once during the Easter Season.

The Church teaches that Catholics must attend Mass on Sundays and holy days because the Mass is the center of the Church's life. When you do this, you follow the third commandment, "Remember to keep holy the Lord's day."

Outside of Mass, Catholics also show love and respect for Jesus in the Eucharist by visiting the **Blessed Sacrament** in church. The blessed Bread from Mass, which has become the Body of Christ, is kept in the tabernacle. Jesus Christ is truly present in the Blessed Sacrament.

How does your family keep holy the Lord's day?

Words of Faith

To **worship** is to adore and honor God.

The **Blessed Sacrament** is the Holy Eucharist. This term especially refers to the blessed Bread that is kept in the tabernacle.

Activity — Connect Your Faith

Give Praise Create a verse of joy, praise, or thanks for the gift of Eucharist. Say your words aloud, sing them, or dance them for your class. Write your verse in the space below.

____

____

Oración de alabanza

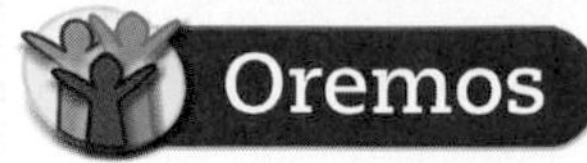

Reúnanse y comiencen con la señal de la cruz.

Canten juntos.

¡Gloria a Dios en el cielo! ¡Cantemos! ¡Gloria a Dios!
¡Gloria a Dios en el cielo y en la tierra paz a los hombres que ama el Señor!

"Gloria (Glory to God)" © 1988, GIA Publications, Inc.

Todos: Gloria a Dios...

Lector: Por tu inmensa gloria te
alabamos, te bendecimos,
te adoramos, te glorificamos,
te damos gracias,
Señor Dios, Rey celestial,
Dios Padre todopoderoso.

Todos: Gloria a Dios...

Lector: Señor, Hijo único, Jesucristo.
Señor Dios, Cordero de Dios,
Hijo del Padre;
tú que quitas el pecado del mundo,
ten piedad de nosotros.

Todos: Gloria a Dios...

Lector: Porque sólo tú eres Santo,
sólo tú Señor,
sólo tú Altísimo, Jesucristo,
con el Espíritu Santo
en la gloria de Dios Padre.

Todos: Gloria a Dios...

Prayer of Praise

Gather and begin with the Sign of the Cross.

Sing together.

Glory to God in the highest, Sing! Glory to God! Glory to God in the highest, and peace to his people on earth!

“Gloria (Glory to God)” © 1988, GIA Publications, Inc.

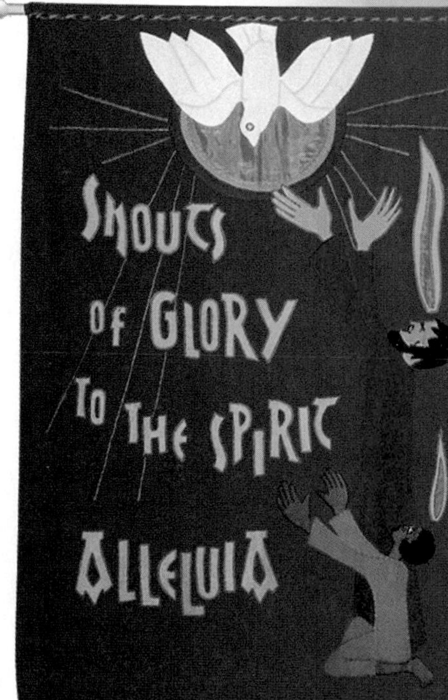

All: **Glory to God . . .**

Reader: Lord God, heavenly King,
almighty God and Father,
we worship you, we give you
thanks, we praise you for
your glory.

All: **Glory to God . . .**

Reader: Lord Jesus Christ, only Son
of the Father, Lord God, Lamb
of God, you take away the sin
of the world, have mercy on us.

All: **Glory to God . . .**

Reader: For you alone are the Holy One,
You alone are the Lord,
You alone are the Most High,
Jesus Christ, with the Holy Spirit
in the glory of God the Father.

All: **Glory to God . . .**

Repasar y aplicar

Comprueba lo que aprendiste Escribe o encierra en un círculo la respuesta correcta.

1. ¿Qué significa rendir culto a Dios?

   ____

2. ¿Cuál es la forma más importante en la que los católicos rinden culto a Dios?

   ____

3. ¿Con qué frecuencia y cuándo deben recibir los católicos la Sagrada Comunión?

   ____

4. ¿Qué es la liturgia?
   a. Una canción que cantamos en la Misa.
   b. Recaudar dinero para las personas pobres.
   c. La Iglesia reunida para rendir culto a Dios en público.

5. ¿Cuándo deben asistir a Misa los católicos?
   a. Los domingos y días de fiesta de la Iglesia.
   b. Solamente en Navidad y en Pascua.
   c. Una vez al mes.

Actividad Vive tu fe

Comparte tu alegría En una hoja de papel, escribe una carta a un amigo que no vaya a la Iglesia los domingos. Cuéntale por qué te reúnes con la comunidad de la Iglesia para rendir culto los domingos. Describe cómo demuestra tu comunidad parroquial su alegría al adorar a Dios. Escribe la primera oración a continuación.

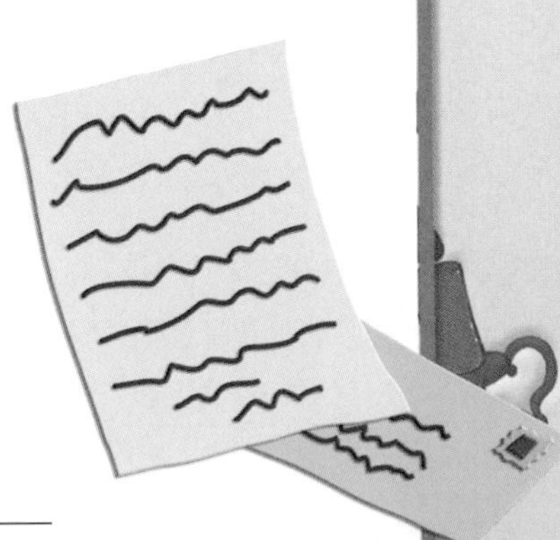

____

____

Review and Apply

Check Understanding Write or circle the correct answers.

1. What does it mean to worship God?

____

2. What is the most important way that Catholics worship God?

____

3. How often and when must Catholics receive Holy Communion?

____

4. What is liturgy?
   a. a song we sing at Mass
   b. collecting money for people who are poor
   c. the Church worshiping together in public
5. When must Catholics attend Mass?
   a. on Sundays and holy days
   b. only on Christmas and Easter
   c. once a month

Activity Live Your Faith

Share Your Joy On another sheet of paper, write a letter to a friend who does not go to church on Sunday. Tell your friend why you gather with the Church community to worship on Sundays. Describe how your parish community shows joy as you worship God. Write your opening sentence below.

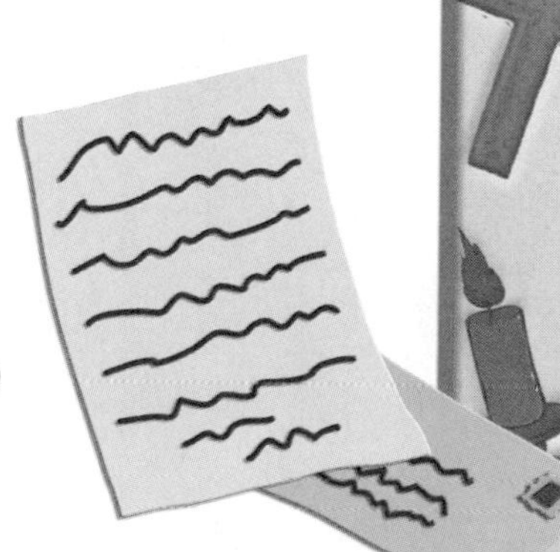

____

____

CAPÍTULO 5

La fe en familia

Lo que creemos

- La Misa es la forma de rendir culto a Dios más importante de la Iglesia.
- En la Misa, la Iglesia recuerda lo que hizo Jesús en la Última Cena.

LA SAGRADA ESCRITURA

Lee *I Corintios 11, 23-26*, y comenta acerca de lo que la Eucaristía significa para ti.

Visita **www.harcourtreligion.com** para encontrar recursos basados en el año litúrgico y lecturas semanales de la Sagrada Escritura.

Actividad

Vive tu fe

Haz una lista Conversa con tu familia sobre cómo pueden prepararse mejor para celebrar la Misa. Escribe una lista de cosas que pueden hacer para participar más plenamente en la Misa. Piensen en algo que puedan hacer para lograr que el domingo sea un día de descanso en familia.

▲ Thea Bowman
1937–1990

Siervos de la fe

Thea Bowman fue tratada injustamente debido al color de su piel. Se sintió llamada a ayudar a la gente a encontrar a Dios. Se hizo hermana franciscana de la Adoración Perpetua y obtuvo títulos universitarios. Enseñó en la escuela elemental, en la superior y en la universidad. Se hizo famosa por utilizar canciones y bailes para comunicar el evangelio. Enfermó de cáncer y vivió con esa enfermedad durante seis años, pero aún así continuó amando y sirviendo a Dios.

Una oración en familia

Querido Dios, ayúdanos a usar nuestros talentos para alabarte y dar testimonio con alegría. Amén.

 CIC *Consulta el Catecismo de la Iglesia Católica, números 61 y 69, para obtener más información sobre el contenido del capítulo.*

CHAPTER 5

Family Faith

Catholics Believe

- The Mass is the Church's most important form of worship.
- In the Mass the Church remembers what Jesus did at the Last Supper.

SCRIPTURE

Read *1 Corinthians 11:23–26,* and talk about what the Eucharist means to you.

GO ONLINE **www.harcourtreligion.com** For weekly Scripture readings and seasonal resources

Activity

Live Your Faith

Make a List As a family, talk about ways you can better prepare yourselves for the celebration of the Mass. List some ways you can participate more fully at Mass. Decide on one way to make Sunday a more restful day for your family.

▲ Thea Bowman 1937–1990

People of Faith

Thea Bowman was treated unfairly because of her color. She felt challenged to help people find God. She became a Franciscan Sister of Perpetual Adoration and earned college degrees. She taught elementary, high school, and college. She was known for using songs and dance to share the gospel. She lived with cancer for six years, but she still kept loving and serving God.

Family Prayer

Dear God, guide us to use our talents to praise you and to be joyful witnesses for you. Amen.

CCC *See Catechism of the Catholic Church 61, 69 for further reading on chapter content.*

Capítulo 6 Orar siempre

Oremos

Líder: Oh Dios, escucha nuestras oraciones.
"Presta oído a mi clamor,
¡oh mi rey y mi Dios!
Pues a ti te imploro, Señor."
Salmo 5, 3

Todos: Oh Dios, escucha nuestras oraciones. Amén.

Actividad Comencemos

Escúchame, Dios mío José está orando a Dios. Imagina lo que Dios podría responderle.

José: "Señor, ¿me oíste cantar en misa el domingo?".

- ¿Qué podría responderle Dios?

José: "Señor, a veces es difícil cantar. No siempre sé toda la letra de las canciones".

- ¿Qué consejo le daría Dios a José?
- ¿Qué dices tú cuando oras? Cuéntaselo a un compañero.

Chapter 6 Pray Always

Leader: O God, listen to our prayers.
"Hear my cry for help,
my king, my God!
To you I pray, O LORD."
Psalm 5:3

All: O God, listen to our prayers. Amen.

Activity Let's Begin

Hear Me, God Joel is praying to God. Imagine what God could be saying to answer him.

Joel: Lord, did you hear me singing at Mass on Sunday?

- What might God say to Joel?

Joel: Lord, sometimes it's hard to sing. I don't always know all the words.

- What advice might God give Joel?
- What do you say when you pray? Tell a partner.

Hablar con Dios

¿Qué te enseña Jesús acerca de la oración?

Jesús contó el siguiente relato sobre dos personas que hablaban con Dios.

LA SAGRADA ESCRITURA **Lucas 18,9–14**

El fariseo y el publicano

Dos hombres subieron al templo a orar. Uno de ellos, fariseo, pasó orgulloso a la parte delantera del templo. Mirando a las otras personas comenzó su oración.

"Oh Dios, te doy gracias porque no soy como los demás hombres, que quieren todo para sí mismos, que son deshonestos", dijo.

"Ni como ese publicano. Ayuno dos veces por semana y doy mi ofrenda al templo", añadió.

A cierta distancia, el publicano oraba con la mirada baja: "Dios mío, ten piedad de mí, que soy un pecador".

Jesús dijo a la gente: "Dios se alegró con la oración del publicano".

Basado en *Lucas 18,9–14*

¿Por qué se alegró Dios con la silenciosa oración de perdón del publicano?

Talking to God

What does Jesus teach you about prayer?

Jesus told this story about two people who talked to God.

SCRIPTURE Luke 18:9–14

The Pharisee and the Tax Collector

Two men went up to the temple to pray. One man, a Pharisee, walked proudly to the front of the temple. He looked at the other people and began his prayer.

"Dear God, I thank you that I am not like others. Other people want everything for themselves. They are not honest," he said.

"I know that I am better than that tax collector. I fast two times a week, and pay money to the temple," he said.

The tax collector stood at a distance. He looked down and prayed, "O God, be merciful to me a sinner."

Jesus told the people, "God was happy with the tax collector's prayer."

Based on *Luke 18:9–14*

Why was God happy with the tax collector's quiet prayer for forgiveness?

Jesús enseña acerca de la oración

Jesús enseñó a sus discípulos que la **oración** es el acto de hablar con Dios y escucharlo. Es elevar tu mente y tu corazón a Dios. Cuando los discípulos de Jesús le pidieron que les enseñara a orar, Él les enseñó la Oración del Señor. Jesús les dijo que buscaran a Dios Padre como lo hacía Él. También les dio el siguiente consejo.

Palabras de fe

La **oración** es el acto de hablar con Dios y escucharlo. Es elevar tu mente y tu corazón a Dios.

LA SAGRADA ESCRITURA — **Mateo 6, 5–8**

Orar bien

Jesús dijo a sus discípulos que no hicieran como los que oran en voz alta y en público para que la gente los vea y los oiga. Ser vistos es su recompensa. Jesús dijo que debes ir a un lugar reservado, cerrar la puerta y orar en silencio al Padre. Dios te oirá.

Algunos piensan que Dios los oye mejor si usan muchas palabras elegantes al orar. No pienses como ellos. El Padre sabe lo que hay en tu corazón incluso antes de que lo digas.

Basado en *Mateo 6,5–8*

¿Dónde sueles orar y qué sueles pedir?

Actividad — Comparte tu fe

Piensa: ¿Tienes un lugar tranquilo donde orar?

Comunica: ¿Dónde sueles orar y qué sueles pedir?

Actúa: Dibuja tu “lugar de oración”.

Jesus Teaches About Prayer

Jesus taught his followers that **prayer** is talking and listening to God. It is raising your mind and heart to God. When Jesus' followers asked him to teach them how to pray, he taught them the Lord's Prayer. Jesus told them to call upon God the Father, as he did. He also gave this advice.

Prayer is talking and listening to God. It is raising your mind and heart to God.

SCRIPTURE Matthew 6:5–8

Praying Well

Jesus told his disciples not to be like the people who pray loudly in public so that others can see and hear them. To be seen is their reward. Jesus said that you should go to a private place, close the door, and pray quietly to the Father. God will hear you.

Some people think that God will hear them better if they use lots of fancy words to pray. Do not be like that. The Father knows what is in your heart even before you say it.

Based on *Matthew 6:5–8*

Where and for what do you pray most often?

Activity Share Your Faith

Think: Do you have a quiet place in which to pray?

Share: Share your ideas for quiet "prayer places."

Act: Draw what your "prayer place" looks like.

Orar es importante

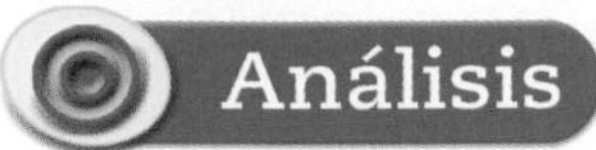

¿Cuáles son algunas maneras de orar?

La oración era una parte importante de la vida de Jesús. A veces madrugaba para orar y otras veces oraba toda la noche. Jesús oraba por otras personas y cuando necesitaba ayuda.

La oración también debe ser una parte importante de tu vida. Puedes orar con tus propias palabras o con oraciones que hayas aprendido de memoria. Incluso puedes orar sin palabras, simplemente en silencio en presencia del amor de Dios. Sea como sea, siempre que ores recuerda que muchos otros cristianos están orando al mismo tiempo que tú.

¿Dónde oras cuando estás en tu casa?

Prayer Is Important

Focus **What are some different ways to pray?**

Prayer was an important part of Jesus' life. Sometimes he got up early to pray. At other times he prayed all night. Jesus prayed for other people. He also prayed when he needed help.

Prayer should be an important part of your day, too. You can use your own words or prayers that you have memorized. You can even pray without words by just being quiet in the presence of God's love. But whenever you pray, you can be sure that many other Christians are praying at the very same time.

? Where do you pray when you are at home?

¿Por qué debemos orar?

Oramos por diferentes razones. Para ayudarte a comprender mejor la oración, aquí tienes cinco tipos:

- **Bendición y adoración:** Con una oración de bendición quieres corresponder al amor y al cariño que Dios te da. Adoras a Dios rindiéndole culto.
- **Alabanza:** La grandeza de Dios te asombra y oras para alabarlo.
- **Petición**: En momentos de necesidad o cuando pecas, pides ayuda o perdón a Dios.
- **Oración de los fieles:** Pides a Dios que ayude a otras personas y a toda la comunidad.
- **Acción de gracias:** Agradeces a Dios todas las cosas buenas que te da.

Palabras de fe

Con una oración de **petición** solicitas algo que quieres o que necesitas.

Actividad Practica tu fe

Identifica las oraciones Busca con un compañero las siguientes citas bíblicas. Escribe qué tipo de oración es cada una.

Salmo 51,3–5	
Salmo 107,1	
Salmo 125,4	

Why Pray?

We pray for different reasons. To help you understand prayer better, here are five types, or forms, of prayer.

- **Blessing and adoration:** In a blessing prayer, you want to return the love and care God gives you. You adore God by worshiping him.
- **Praise:** You are amazed by God's greatness, and you pray to praise God.
- **Petition:** In times of need or when you sin, you ask God for help or forgiveness.
- **Intercession:** You ask for God's help for other people and for the whole community.
- **Thanksgiving:** You thank God for all the good things that he gives you.

A prayer of **petition** is a request for something that you want or need.

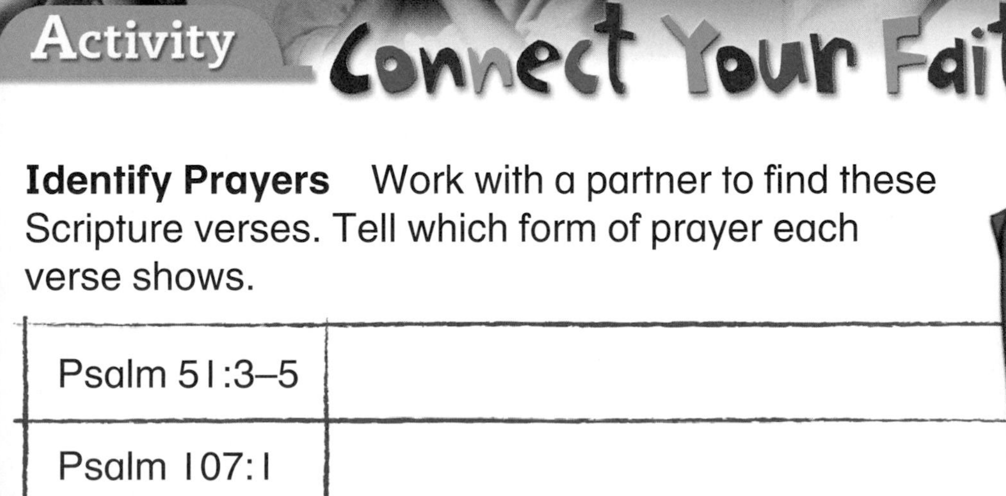

Activity Connect Your Faith

Identify Prayers Work with a partner to find these Scripture verses. Tell which form of prayer each verse shows.

Psalm 51:3–5	
Psalm 107:1	
Psalm 125:4	

Oración de petición

Reúnanse y comiencen con la señal de la cruz.

Canten juntos el estribillo:

Mi socorro viene del Señor,
creador del cielo y la tierra.

"Psalm 121" © 2001, GIA Publications, Inc.

Grupo 1: Ayúdanos a que recordemos bendecirte y adorarte.

Todos: **Canten el estribillo.**

Grupo 2: Ayúdanos a que recordemos alabarte, porque eres grande.

Todos: **Canten el estribillo.**

Grupo 1: Ayúdanos a que recordemos buscarte cuando necesitemos ayuda.

Todos: **Canten el estribillo.**

Grupo 2: Ayúdanos a que recordemos pedirte ayuda para quienes te necesitan.

Todos: **Canten el estribillo.**

Grupo 1: Ayúdanos a que recordemos darte gracias por ser tan bondadoso con nosotros.

Todos: **Canten el estribillo.**

Líder: Oremos.

Inclinen la cabeza mientras el líder reza.

Todos: **Amén.**

Prayer of Petition

Gather and begin with the Sign of the Cross.

Sing together the refrain:

Our help comes from the Lord, the maker of heaven and earth.

"Psalm 121" © 2001, GIA Publications, Inc.

Group 1: Help us remember to bless and adore you.

All: **Sing the refrain.**

Group 2: Help us remember to praise you, for you are wonderful.

All: **Sing the refrain.**

Group 1: Help us remember to turn to you whenever we need help.

All: **Sing the refrain.**

Group 2: Help us remember to ask you to help others who need you.

All: **Sing the refrain.**

Group 1: Help us remember to thank you, for you are so good to us.

All: **Sing the refrain.**

Leader: Let us pray.

Bow your heads as the leader prays.

All: Amen.

Repasar y aplicar

A **Trabaja con palabras** Empareja cada tipo de oración de la columna 1 con su definición de la columna 2. Escribe la letra correcta sobre la línea.

Columna 1	Columna 2
_____ **1.** bendición	**a.** Pedir a Dios que ayude a otras personas.
_____ **2.** alabanza	**b.** Expresar tu agradecimiento a Dios.
_____ **3.** petición	**c.** Responder al amor de Dios.
_____ **4.** oración de los fieles	**d.** Pedir a Dios que te ayude.
_____ **5.** acción de gracias	**e.** Reconocer la grandeza de Dios.

B **Comprueba lo que aprendiste** Escribe una cosa que Jesús enseñó a sus discípulos acerca de la oración.

____

____

Actividad Vive tu fe

Diferentes maneras de orar Imagina que alguien que no supiera español quisiera aprender a orar. ¿Qué le comunicarías si no pudieras usar palabras? Escribe tu idea a continuación.

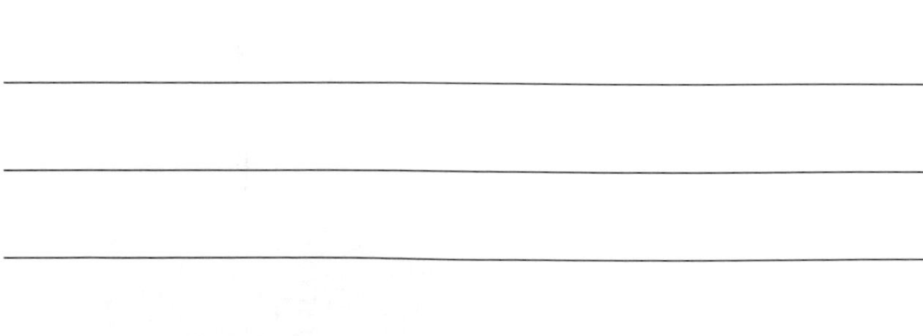

Review and Apply

A Work with Words Match each form of prayer in Column 1 with its definition in Column 2. Write the correct letter on the line provided.

Column 1		Column 2
______	1. blessing	a. asking God to help other people
______	2. praise	b. telling God that you are grateful
______	3. petition	c. responding to God's love
______	4. intercession	d. asking God to help you
______	5. thanksgiving	e. recognizing God's greatness

B Check Understanding Tell one thing Jesus taught his followers about prayer.

____

____

Activity Live Your Faith

Praying in Different Ways Imagine that someone who does not speak your language wants to learn to pray. What will you share with him or her without using words? Write your idea on the lines below.

La fe en familia

Lo que creemos

- La oración es elevar tu mente y tu corazón a Dios.
- La oración es una parte importante de la vida diaria del cristiano.

LA SAGRADA ESCRITURA

Mateo 6,9–13 es la Oración del Señor, también llamada el Padrenuestro. Reza esta oración con tu familia. Conversa acerca de lo que la oración significa para ti.

APRENDE en línea Visita **www.harcourtreligion.com** para encontrar recursos basados en el año litúrgico y lecturas semanales de la Sagrada Escritura.

Actividad

Vive tu fe

Di una oración Escribe una carta a Dios con tu familia. Usa una de las cinco formas de oración para contar a Dios lo que ocurrió en tu familia en el día o en la semana. Si quieres, enciende una vela y pon música suave. Pide a algún familiar que lea la carta en voz alta, como si fuera una oración.

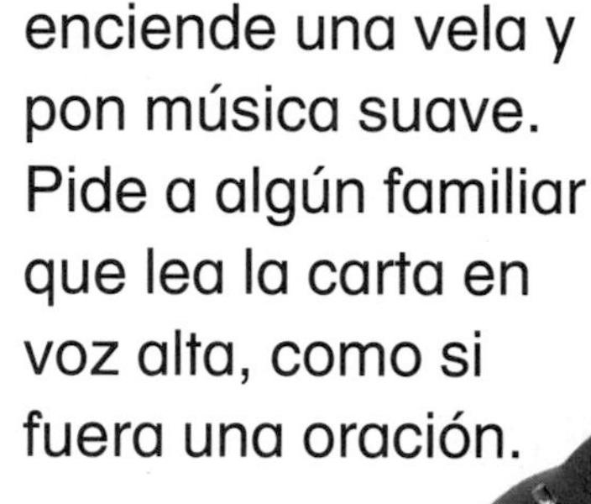

Siervos de la fe

▲ Thomas Merton 1915–1968

Thomas Merton nació en Prades, Francia, y vivió en distintas partes del mundo. Un día, en Louisville, Kentucky, se dio cuenta de que se sentía unido a todas las personas que veía. Decidió hacerse monje. Se convirtió al catolicismo en 1938 e ingresó en un monasterio trapense de Kentucky en 1941. Merton vivió una vida sencilla de oración. Fue poeta y escribió libros acerca de Dios.

Una oración en familia

Querido Dios, ayúdanos a orar y a buscarte en cada momento de nuestra vida, como lo hizo Thomas Merton. Amén.

  *Consulta el Catecismo de la Iglesia Católica, números 2559 y 2659, para obtener más información sobre el contenido del capítulo.*

Family Faith

Catholics Believe

- Prayer is the raising of one's mind and heart to God.
- Prayer is an important part of a Christian's daily life.

SCRIPTURE

Matthew 6:9–13 is the Lord's Prayer, also called the Our Father. Pray the verses with your family. Talk about what the prayer means to you.

GO ONLINE **www.harcourtreligion.com**
For weekly Scripture readings and seasonal resources

Activity

Live Your Faith

Say a Prayer As a family, write a letter to God. Use one of the five forms of prayer to tell God about your family's day or week. If you wish, light a candle and play reflective music. Have one family member prayerfully read the letter aloud.

▲ Thomas Merton 1915–1968

People of Faith

Thomas Merton was born in Prades, France and lived all over the world. One day, in Louisville, Kentucky, he realized that he felt connected to every person he saw. He decided to become a monk. He became a Catholic in 1938 and joined a Trappist monastery in Kentucky in 1941. Merton lived a simple life of prayer. He was a poet and wrote books about God.

Family Prayer

Dear God, help us pray every moment of our lives and find you, as Thomas Merton did. Amen.

CCC *See Catechism of the Catholic Church 2559, 2659 for further reading on chapter content.*

Repaso de la Unidad 2

A **Trabaja con palabras** Responde a cada pregunta con el término correcto del vocabulario.

VOCABULARIO

bendición
alabanza
petición
oración de los fieles
acción de gracias

1. ¿Qué tipo de oración pide perdón a Dios? ____________________
2. ¿Qué tipo de oración pide a Dios que ayude a otras personas? ____________________
3. ¿Qué tipo de oración da gracias a Dios por todas las cosas buenas de tu vida? ____________________
4. ¿Qué tipo de oración reconoce la grandeza de Dios? ____________________
5. ¿Qué tipo de oración corresponde al amor de Dios? ____________________

B **Comprueba lo que aprendiste** Completa cada enunciado encerrando en un círculo la palabra correcta.

6. La Santísima Trinidad son las (tres/dos) Personas en un solo Dios.
7. Los católicos creen en (las preguntas/los misterios) de fe sin comprenderlos por completo.
8. La Iglesia te pide que recibas la Sagrada Comunión al menos una vez al año durante el tiempo litúrgico de la (Pascua/Navidad).
9. Los católicos deben asistir a (reuniones/Misa) los domingos y días de fiesta de la Iglesia.
10. En (la rectoría/el tabernáculo) se guarda la Sagrada Eucaristía.

Unit 2 Review

A Work with Words Answer each question with the correct word from the Word Bank.

WORD BANK
blessing
praise
petition
intercession
thanksgiving

1. Which form of prayer asks God for forgiveness? ____________________

2. Which form of prayer asks God to help other people? ____________________

3. Which form of prayer thanks God for all the good things in your life? ____________________

4. Which form of prayer recognizes God's greatness? ____________________

5. Which form of prayer returns God's love? ____________________

B Check Understanding Complete each sentence by circling the correct word.

6. The Holy Trinity is the (three/two) Persons in one God.

7. Catholics believe in the (questions/mysteries) of faith without completely understanding them.

8. The Church requires that you receive Holy Communion at least once each year during (Easter/Christmas) Season.

9. Catholics must attend (meetings/Mass) on Sundays and holy days.

10. The (rectory/tabernacle) holds the Holy Eucharist.

UNIDAD 3

El Cuerpo de Cristo

La Buena Nueva

¿Cuál es la Buena Nueva que nos comunica la Iglesia?

El sacrificio de Jesús

¿Qué sacrificio hizo Jesús por ti?

La obra de Jesús

¿Por qué decimos que la Iglesia es el Cuerpo de Cristo?

¿Qué crees que vas a aprender en esta unidad acerca del Cuerpo de Cristo?

UNIT 3

The Body of Christ

The Good News

What good news does the Church share?

Jesus' Sacrifice

What sacrifice did Jesus make for you?

Jesus' Work

How is the Church the Body of Christ?

What do you think you will learn in this unit about the Body of Christ?

Capítulo 7 La Buena Nueva

Oremos

Líder: Querido Dios, ayúdanos a seguirte siempre.
"Me enseñarás la senda de la vida,
gozos y plenitud en tu presencia,
delicias para siempre a tu derecha".

Salmo 16, 11

Todos: Querido Dios, ayúdanos a seguirte siempre. Amén.

Actividad Comencemos

La mejor noticia del mundo En el libro de religión de Mariana aparecían estas preguntas:

¿Cuál es la mejor noticia que te han dado?

"¡Mi papá me compró un gatito!", escribió Mariana.

¿Qué hiciste cuando te enteraste de la noticia?

"Se la conté a todos mis amigos", contestó Mariana.

¿Por qué lo hiciste?

"¡Porque sabía que también se alegrarían!".

- ¿Cómo comunicas las buenas noticias a otros? Escribe tres maneras.

The Good News

Leader: Dear God, help us follow you always.
"You will show me the path to life,
abounding joy in your presence,
the delights at your right hand forever."
Psalm 16:11

All: Dear God, help us follow you always. Amen.

Activity Let's Begin

The Best News Ever Taleshia's religion book had these questions:

What's the best news you have ever heard?

"My dad got me a new kitten!" she wrote.

What did you do when you heard the news?

"I told all my friends," wrote Taleshia.

Why did you do that?

"I knew it would make them happy, too!"

- How do you share good news with others? Name three ways.

Comunicar noticias

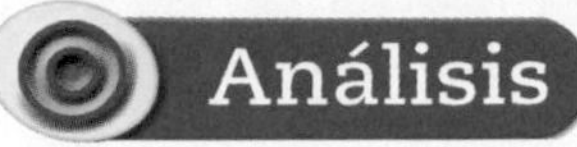

¿Cuál es la Buena Nueva que nos comunica Jesús?

A todos nos gusta comunicar una buena noticia. Jesús comunicó su Buena Nueva mediante palabras y acciones. A veces, comunicamos una buena noticia mediante dibujos o con ciertos objetos.

UN RELATO

La cometa de Andrés

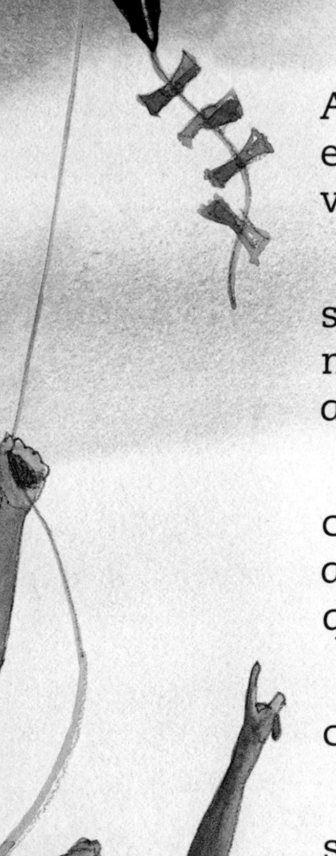

El señor Gómez era un anciano amigo de Andrés que vivía junto al parque, cerca de su escuela. Siempre estaba sentado junto a la ventana mirando a los niños jugar.

Un día, Andrés se detuvo a hablar con el señor Gómez. El señor Gómez le dijo: “Siempre me han gustado los arco iris. Me recuerdan el amor de Dios, pero casi nunca veo ninguno”.

Andrés se acordó de una cometa con los colores del arco iris que estaba guardada en su armario. Fue a buscar a su amigo Diego para que lo ayudara a volarla.

Andrés y Diego fueron al parque, junto a la casa del señor Gómez, e hicieron volar la cometa.

Al día siguiente, cuando los niños vieron al señor Gómez, este les gritó: “Recibí su mensaje, niños. ¡Gracias por mandarme un arco iris!”.

? ¿Qué mensaje enviaron los niños al señor Gómez mediante la cometa que tenía los colores del arco iris?

Sharing News

What good news does Jesus share?

Everyone wants to share good news. Jesus shared his good news through words and actions. Sometimes you share good news with pictures or through certain objects.

A STORY

Andrew's Kite

Andrew's friend, old Mr. Levy, lived by the park near Andrew's school. He always sat at his window and watched the kids playing.

One day Andrew stopped to talk to Mr. Levy. Mr. Levy said, "I have always liked rainbows. They remind me of God's love, but I hardly ever see rainbows."

Andrew thought of a rainbow kite in his closet. He got his friend Diego to help him.

The boys went to the park near Mr. Levy's house and flew the kite.

The next day, the boys saw Mr. Levy. He called out, "I got your message, boys. Thank you for sending me a rainbow!"

? What message did the boys send Mr. Levy with the rainbow kite?

Jesús comunica la Buena Nueva

Andrés y Diego comunicaron un mensaje de alegría al señor Gómez. El arco iris era una señal de que pensaban en él y de que querían que estuviera contento. La Buena Nueva que nos comunica Jesús es que Dios Padre ama a su pueblo y lo salva del poder del pecado y de la muerte eterna.

Así como Jesús te comunica la Buena Nueva del amor de Dios, tú la comunicas a los demás. La misión de la Iglesia Católica es comunicar la Buena Nueva de Jesús mediante palabras y acciones.

La Buena Nueva también se conoce como el *Evangelio*. La Iglesia llama así a los cuatro libros de la Biblia que hablan de la vida de Jesús y de sus enseñanzas. Los **evangelios** llevan los nombres de Mateo, Marcos, Lucas y Juan. La Iglesia pide que se lean los evangelios en Misa.

¿Cómo puedes comunicar la Buena Nueva de Jesús?

Palabras de fe

Los **evangelios** son los cuatro libros del Nuevo Testamento que cuentan relatos de la vida, la muerte y la Resurrección de Jesús. Son los libros más importantes para la Iglesia, porque se centran en Jesús.

Actividad Comparte tu fe

Piensa: ¿Cuándo has comunicado la Buena Nueva de Jesús?

Comunica: Haz una lista de palabras que describan la Buena Nueva.

Actúa: Escribe en tus propias palabras un comercial de radio acerca de la Buena Nueva de Jesús y léelo en voz alta a tus compañeros.

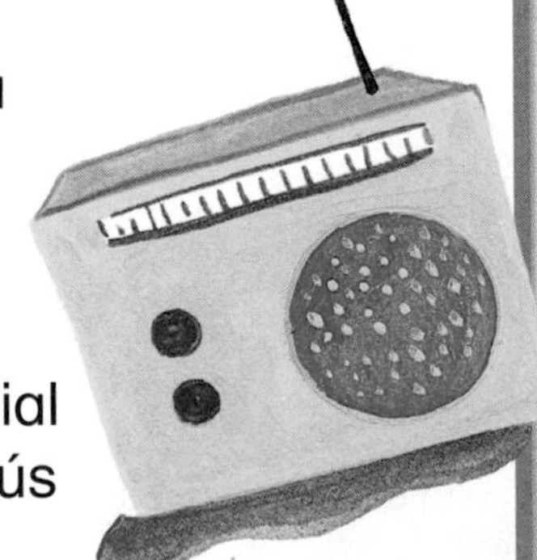

Jesus Shares Good News

Andrew and Diego shared a happy message with Mr. Levy. The rainbow was a sign that they were thinking of him and wanted him to be happy. The good news Jesus shares is that God the Father loves his people and saves them from the power of sin and everlasting death.

Just as Jesus shares the good news of God's love with you, you pass it on to others. The work of the Catholic Church is to share the good news of Jesus in words and actions.

Another word for good news is *gospel.* The Church gives this name to the four books of the Bible that tell about Jesus' life and teachings. The **Gospels** are named for Matthew, Mark, Luke, and John. The Church reads from the Gospels at every Mass.

How can you share Jesus' good news?

Words of Faith

The **Gospels** are the four books in the New Testament that tell the stories of Jesus' life, death, and Resurrection. They are the most important books for the Church because they focus on Jesus.

Activity Share Your Faith

Think: When have you spread the good news about Jesus?

Share: List words that would help describe the good news.

Act: Write a radio commercial that uses your words about the good news of Jesus, and read it to the class.

El mensaje de Jesús

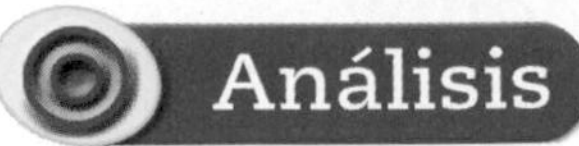

¿Cuál es la Buena Nueva del Reino de Dios?

Las lecturas de la Biblia, también llamada *Sagrada Escritura*, se utilizan cada vez que la comunidad de la Iglesia se reúne para rendir culto a Dios. Estas lecturas también se utilizaban para rendir culto a Dios en la época de Jesús.

LA SAGRADA ESCRITURA Lucas 4, 16 –22

Jesús en la sinagoga

Un día Jesús volvió a Nazaret, donde se había criado. Todos estaban reunidos para el culto. Jesús abrió el libro de Isaías y leyó las palabras que describían a una persona que Dios había prometido enviar.

"El Espíritu del Señor está sobre mí.
Él me ha ungido para llevar buenas
nuevas a los pobres".

Jesús continuó diciendo que había venido a liberar a los cautivos, hacer ver a los ciegos y proclamar las bendiciones del Señor.

Entonces Jesús sorprendió a todos con estas palabras: "Hoy les han llegado noticias de cómo se cumplen estas palabras proféticas".

Basado en *Lucas 4,16–22*

La gente se sorprendió con el mensaje de Jesús. Estaban esperando a un **mesías**, o *salvador*. Pero no esperaban que fuera un hombre de Nazaret.

¿Por qué se sorprendió la gente con el mensaje de Jesús?

Jesus' Message

What is the good news of God's kingdom?

Readings from the Bible, also called *Scripture*, are used every time the Church community gathers to worship. These readings were used to worship in Jesus' day, too.

SCRIPTURE — Luke 4:16–22

Jesus in the Synagogue

One day, Jesus came back to his hometown of Nazareth. Everyone had gathered for worship. Jesus opened the Book of Isaiah and read words that described a person God promised to send.

> "The Spirit of the Lord is upon me,
> because He has anointed me
> to bring glad tidings to the poor."

Jesus then said he had come to set people free and to make people who are blind see. He had come to announce a time of blessings from God.

Then Jesus surprised everyone. He said, "Today, this scripture passage has been fulfilled in your hearing."

Based on *Luke 4:16–22*

The people were surprised by Jesus' message. They were waiting for a **messiah**, or *savior*. They did not expect him to be a man from Nazareth.

? Why were people surprised by Jesus' message?

EXPLORACIÓN Explore

El Reino de Dios

Las palabras de la Sagrada Escritura que Jesús leyó hablaban del **Reino de Dios**, o el reino de la justicia y la paz. En el Reino de Dios los pobres reciben noticias de alegría, y nadie es prisionero del pecado y la tristeza. Los enfermos son curados.

Jesús contaba parábolas para describir el Reino de Dios. Por ejemplo, dijo que el Reino de Dios era como un grano de mostaza. Esta pequeña semilla se convierte en un árbol grande y hermoso. Jesús estaba plantando la semilla del reino. Jesús mostró a la gente cómo vivir. Curó a quienes estaban enfermos. Liberó a quienes sufrían de soledad y de dolor y eran prisioneros del pecado. Jesús le pide a su Iglesia que invite a todos a formar parte del Reino de Dios.

¿Cómo puedes ayudar a que el Reino de Dios continúe creciendo como el grano de mostaza?

Palabras de fe

Mesías es una palabra hebrea que significa *ungido.* Los cristianos creen que Jesús es el Mesías, el que ha sido ungido o elegido.

El **Reino de Dios** es el reino de la verdadera justicia, el verdadero amor y la verdadera paz de Dios.

Actividad Practica tu fe

Escribe un titular Imagina que eres periodista y estás en Nazaret el día en que Jesús lee el libro de Isaías. ¿Qué titular utilizarías para relatar este acontecimiento en el periódico local? Escríbelo aquí.

La Gaceta de Nazaret

____

____

God's Kingdom

The words Jesus read from Scripture tell about the **kingdom of God**, or the rule of justice and peace. In God's kingdom, those who are poor hear joyful news. No one is a prisoner of sin and sadness. People who are sick are healed.

Jesus told parables to describe the kingdom of God. For example, he said that the kingdom of God was like a mustard seed. This seed grows from a tiny seed into a large, beautiful tree. Jesus was planting the seed of the kingdom. Jesus showed people how to live. He healed people who were sick. He set people free from loneliness, sorrow, and sin. Jesus sends his Church to invite everyone into God's kingdom.

How can you help the kingdom of God keep growing like the mustard seed?

Words of Faith

Messiah is a Hebrew word that means *anointed*. Christians believe that Jesus is the Messiah—the one who has been anointed, or chosen.

The **kingdom of God** is God's rule of true justice, love, and peace.

Activity Connect Your Faith

Write a Headline Imagine yourself as a newspaper reporter in Nazareth on the day that Jesus read from the Book of Isaiah. What headline would you use for a story about this event in the local newspaper? Write it here.

Nazareth Times

____

____

Oración de petición

Reúnanse y comiencen con la señal de la cruz.

Líder: Querido Jesús, tú nos enseñaste de muchas maneras. Nos contaste relatos acerca de Dios.

Todos: **Ayúdanos a entender tus enseñanzas.**

Líder: Tú nos mostraste cómo actuar bondadosamente.

Todos: **Ayúdanos a actuar como tú lo hiciste.**

Líder: Tú viniste a darnos el amor de tu Padre.

Todos: **Ayúdanos a amar más a nuestra familia y amigos.**

Líder: Tú viniste a sanar a los enfermos y a perdonar.

Todos: **Ayúdanos a consolar a los que están enfermos y solos, y a perdonar a los que nos ofenden.**

Líder: Oremos.

Inclinen la cabeza mientras el líder reza.

Todos: Amén.

Canten juntos.

Como iglesia, de dos en dos,
por todo el mundo vamos a llevar,
la Palabra del Señor,
su Buena Nueva, a proclamar.

"Two by Two" © 2000, GIA Publications, Inc.

Asking Prayer

Gather and begin with the Sign of the Cross.

Leader: Dear Jesus, you taught us in so many ways. You told us stories about God.

All: **Help us understand your lessons.**

Leader: You showed us how to act with kindness.

All: **Help us act as you did.**

Leader: You came to share your Father's love.

All: **Help us be more loving with our families and friends.**

Leader: You came to heal the sick and to forgive.

All: **Help us comfort those who are sick and lonely and forgive those who have hurt us.**

Leader: Let us pray.

Bow your heads as the leader prays.

All: Amen.

Sing together.

We are sent two by two.
Sent as church in the world.
Sent to share God's good
news, Sing and tell, spread
the Word.

Repasar y aplicar

Comprueba lo que aprendiste Escribe o encierra en un círculo la respuesta correcta.

1. La misión de la Iglesia es ______________________ ______________________________________.
2. Los cristianos creen que Jesús es el ____________________, el que ha sido ungido o elegido.
3. Jesús usó ____________________ para enseñar a la gente sobre Dios y su Reino.
4. La palabra *Evangelio* significa ______.
   a. relato
   b. Buena Nueva
   c. religión
5. El Reino de Dios es ______.
   a. un país de Oriente Medio
   b. algo que existió solamente en los tiempos de la Biblia
   c. el reino de paz y justicia de Dios

Actividad Vive tu fe

Comunica la Buena Nueva En el siguiente recuadro, diseña una pegatina para el carro que comunique el mensaje de Jesús. Usa palabras y dibujos para tu pegatina.

Review and Apply

Check Understanding Write or circle the correct responses.

1. The work of the Church is to ________________ ________________________________.
2. Christians believe that Jesus is the ________________ who has been anointed, or chosen.
3. Jesus used ________________ to teach people something about God and his kingdom.
4. The word *gospel* means _____.
   a. storytelling
   b. good news
   c. religion
5. God's kingdom is _____.
   a. a country in the Middle East
   b. something that existed only in Bible times
   c. God's rule of peace and justice

Activity Live Your Faith

Spread Good News Design a bumper sticker that shares Jesus' message. Use the space below to combine words and art for your bumper sticker.

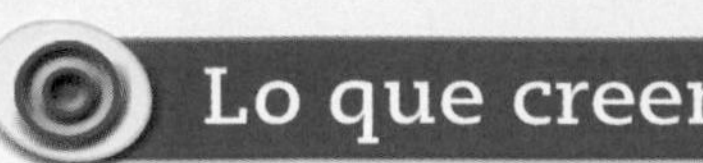

CAPÍTULO 7

La fe en familia

Lo que creemos

- Jesús comunicó la Buena Nueva del Reino de Dios, o el reino de la justicia, el amor y la paz.
- Jesús es el Mesías, el elegido y el Salvador.

LA SAGRADA ESCRITURA

Lee *Marcos 8,27–30.* Comenta acerca de lo que estos versículos significan para ti.

Visita **www.harcourtreligion.com** para encontrar recursos basados en el año litúrgico y lecturas semanales de la Sagrada Escritura.

Actividad

Vive tu fe

Leer la Biblia Comiencen a leer regularmente fragmentos de la Biblia con toda la familia. Lean la parábola del sembrador que plantó semilla de trigo buena (ver *Mateo 13, 24 –30*). Hablen acerca de lo que significa esta parábola. Si necesitan ayuda, lean *Mateo 13, 36–43.* Allí encontrarán cómo Jesús explicó la parábola.

▲ San Pedro Canisio 1521–1597

Siervos de la fe

Pedro Canisio nació en Nimega, una ciudad que hoy día forma parte de los Países Bajos. Pedro encontró muchas maneras de comunicar la Buena Nueva de Dios. Enseñó a la gente acerca de la Iglesia Católica. Mientras viajaba, predicaba y celebraba los sacramentos. Se hizo famoso por fundar diversas escuelas. El día de San Pedro Canisio se celebra el 21 de diciembre.

Una oración en familia

San Pedro, ruega por nosotros para que utilicemos nuestros recursos para difundir la Palabra de Dios. Amén.

 CIC *Consulta el Catecismo de la Iglesia Católica, números 546 y 1154, para obtener más información sobre el contenido del capítulo.*

CHAPTER 7

Family Faith

Catholics Believe

- Jesus shared the good news about God's kingdom of justice, love, and peace.
- Jesus is the Messiah, the chosen one and Savior.

SCRIPTURE

Read *Mark 8:27–30.* Talk about what these verses mean to you.

www.harcourtreligion.com
For weekly Scripture readings and seasonal resources

Activity

Live Your Faith

Read the Bible Begin to share stories from the Bible at a regular time. Read together the parable of the farmer who planted good wheat seed. (See *Matthew 13:24–30.*) Talk about what this parable means. If you need help, read *Matthew 13:36–43.* You will find out how Jesus explained the parable.

▲ Saint Peter Canisius 1521–1597

People of Faith

Peter Canisius was born in Nijmegen, a city which is now part of the Netherlands. He found many ways to share God's good news. He taught people about the Catholic Church. Peter Canisius preached and celebrated the sacraments as he traveled. He is known for starting schools. Saint Peter Canisius's feast day is December 21.

Family Prayer

Saint Peter, pray for us that we may use our resources to share the word of God. Amen.

See Catechism of the Catholic Church 546, 1154 for further reading on chapter content.

Capítulo 8 El sacrificio de Jesús

Líder: Dios de amor, ayúdanos a entregarnos a los demás.

"Pero dale gracias a Dios con sacrificios,
y cumple tus mandas al Altísimo".

Salmo 50, 14

Todos: Dios de amor, ayúdanos a entregarnos a los demás. Amén.

Actividad Comencemos

Cambio

Egoísta
tacaño, avaro
quita, toma, quiere
desconsiderado, indiferente
cariñoso, amable
comparte, ayuda, da
generoso, sin fin
Abnegado

Este poema en forma de diamante muestra el cambio del egoísmo a la generosidad. Al igual que en el poema, las personas también pueden cambiar de ser egoístas a ser generosas.

- ¿Cómo puedes transformar un acto de egoísmo en un acto de amabilidad?

Chapter 8 Jesus' Sacrifice

Let Us Pray

Leader: Loving God, help us give of ourselves.

"Offer praise as your sacrifice to
God;
fulfill your vows to the Most High."

Psalm 50:14

All: Loving God, help us give of ourselves. Amen.

Activity Let's Begin

Change

Selfish
stingy, greedy
grab, take, want
thoughtless, uncaring, loving, kind
share, help, give
generous, endless
Selfless

This diamante poem shows a change from selfish to selfless. Like the poem, people can change from being selfish to being selfless, too.

- How do you turn a selfish act into one of kindness?

Tomar decisiones

¿Qué significa hacer un sacrificio?

Jesús le hizo una promesa a su Padre. Una promesa puede ser fácil o difícil de cumplir. A veces hay que renunciar a algo para cumplir una promesa. Lee el siguiente relato acerca de la importancia de cumplir las promesas.

UN RELATO

La promesa de Tina

Un día Tina tuvo que tomar una decisión difícil. Estaba divirtiéndose con sus amigos cuando, de repente, se detuvo y miró el reloj.

"Es tarde. Me tengo que ir", dijo Tina.

"Llama y di que estás jugando", le sugirió Martina.

"Hice una promesa. Tengo que irme", respondió Tina.

En el hogar de ancianos, a la tía Margarita se le iluminó la cara. "¡Tina, qué alegría verte!".

"Te prometí que saldríamos a pasear juntas".

La tía Margarita sonrió y dijo: "¡Qué bien! Entonces vámonos".

¿A qué renunció Tina?

Making Choices

What does it mean to make a sacrifice?

Jesus made a promise to his Father. A promise can be easy or difficult to keep. You may need to give something up to keep a promise. Read this story about keeping promises.

A STORY

Gina's Promise

One day Gina was faced with a difficult choice. She was having fun with her friends when suddenly she stopped and looked at her watch.

"It's late. I have to go," Gina said.

"Call and say you're playing," Martina said.

"I made a promise. I have to go," Gina said.

At the care center, Aunt Margaret smiled brightly. "Hello, Gina. I am so glad to see you!"

"I promised to go for a walk with you."

Aunt Margaret smiled and said, "Great! Let's go!"

What did Gina give up?

Los sacrificios muestran amor

Tina renunció a pasar la tarde con sus amigos porque había hecho una promesa. Un **sacrificio** es cuando renuncias a algo o haces algo difícil por amor. Hacer un sacrificio no es fácil. Requiere mucho amor y valentía. Para hacer un sacrificio, tienes que ser generoso.

El sacrificio de Jesús

Jesús eligió hacer el sacrificio más grande de todos. Hizo algo que nadie más podía hacer. Él renunció a su vida para que todos pudiéramos ser salvados del poder del pecado y de la muerte eterna. Jesús entregó su propia vida voluntariamente para que nosotros tuviéramos una vida nueva y eterna con Dios.

¿Cuándo hiciste algún sacrificio por alguien? ¿Cómo muestran amor los sacrificios?

Palabras de fe

Un **sacrificio** es renunciar a algo por un bien mayor.

Actividad Comparte tu fe

Piensa: ¿Renunciarías a jugar con tus amigos para ayudar a un familiar?

Comunica: Conversa con tu grupo sobre un sacrificio que hayas hecho.

Actúa: Escribe cómo te sentiste al hacer ese sacrificio.

____

____

____

Sacrifices Show Love

Gina gave up an afternoon with friends because she made a promise. When you give up something or do something difficult out of love, it is called a **sacrifice**. It is not easy to make a sacrifice. It takes a lot of love and courage. You have to be unselfish when you make a sacrifice.

Jesus' Sacrifice

Jesus chose to make the greatest sacrifice of all. He did something that no one else could do. Jesus gave up his life so that people could be saved from the power of sin and everlasting death. He freely gave up his life so that all people could have new life with God forever.

When have you made a sacrifice for someone? How do sacrifices show love?

Words of Faith

To **sacrifice** is to give up something for a greater good.

Activity — Share Your Faith

Think: Would you give up playtime with your friends to help a family member?

Share: Talk to your group about a time when you made a sacrifice.

Act: Write about how this sacrifice made you feel.

____

____

____

La Resurrección de Jesús

Análisis **¿Qué significa el Misterio Pascual?**

La elección que hizo Jesús por amor cumplió el plan de Dios para salvar a su pueblo. A través de la obra del Espíritu Santo, el Padre pasó a Jesús de la muerte a una nueva vida. Esto se conoce como la **Resurrección**. La Resurrección mostró que el poder de Dios es más fuerte que la muerte.

LA SAGRADA ESCRITURA **Juan 20,11–18**

María Magdalena se encuentra con Jesús

María Magdalena fue al sepulcro de Jesús, pero lo encontró vacío. Pensó que alguien se había llevado el cuerpo de Jesús. Entonces los ángeles le hablaron y oyó que alguien la llamaba por su nombre. Cuando se dio la vuelta, ¡Jesús estaba allí!

Al principio, no reconoció a Jesús. Creyó que era el cuidador del huerto y le preguntó dónde estaba Jesús. Él le dijo: "¡María!".

Entonces María se dio cuenta de que era Jesús. Lo llamó *Maestro*. Jesús le pidió que dijera a sus amigos que volvía al Padre.

Basado en *Juan 20,11–18*

¿Cómo se comunica hoy la noticia de la Resurrección de Jesús?

Jesus' Resurrection

What does the Paschal mystery mean?

Jesus' loving choice fulfilled God's plan to save his people. Through the work of the Holy Spirit, the Father raised Jesus from death to new life. This is called the **Resurrection**. The Resurrection showed that God's power is stronger than death.

SCRIPTURE John 20:11–18

Mary Meets Jesus

Mary Magdalene went to Jesus' tomb, but she found it empty. She thought that people had taken Jesus' body away. Then angels spoke to her, and she heard someone call her name. When she turned, Jesus was there!

When Mary first saw Jesus, she didn't recognize him. Thinking that he was the gardener, she asked where Jesus was. He said, "Mary!"

Then she knew it was Jesus. She called him *Teacher*. He told her to tell his friends that he was returning to the Father.

Based on *John 20:11–18*

How is the news of Jesus' Resurrection shared today?

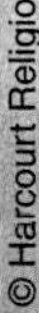

El Misterio Pascual

El sufrimiento, la muerte, la Resurrección y la Ascensión de Jesús se conocen como el **Misterio Pascual**. La palabra *Pascual* proviene de una palabra que significa "paso". Jesús murió para salvar a todas las personas de sus pecados en la época del año en que los judíos celebran la Pascua. Jesús resucitó de entre los muertos y ascendió al cielo. Él "pasó" de la muerte a la vida para que todos podamos tener una nueva vida con Dios en el cielo.

La Misa y los sacramentos son maneras que tiene la Iglesia de vivir este gran misterio. Cuando participas de la celebración de la Eucaristía, compartes el poder de salvación del Misterio Pascual.

Palabras de fe

La **Resurreccón** es el acontecimiento en el que Dios Padre hizo que Jesús pasara de la muerte a la nueva vida, mediante la fuerza del Espíritu Santo.

El **Misterio Pascual** es el misterio del sufrimiento, la muerte, la Resurrección y la Ascensión de Jesús.

Actividad Practica tu fe

Crea un crucifijo El sufrimiento, la muerte, la Resurrección y la Ascensión de Jesús pueden darte esperanza en tiempos difíciles o tristes. Dibuja un crucifijo o haz uno de arcilla, de madera o de otro material. Cuando estés pasando por un momento difícil, míralo y recuerda las acciones de salvación de Jesús.

The Paschal Mystery

Jesus' suffering, death, Resurrection, and Ascension are called the **Paschal mystery**. The word *Paschal* comes from a word that means "passover." Jesus died to save people from their sins at the time of year when Jews celebrate Passover. Jesus was raised from the dead and ascended into heaven. He "passed over" from death to life so that all people can have new life with God in heaven.

The Mass and the sacraments are ways that the Church lives out this great mystery. When you take part in the celebration of the Eucharist, you share in the saving power of the Paschal mystery.

Words of Faith

The **Resurrection** is the event of Jesus' being raised from death to new life by God the Father through the power of the Holy Spirit.

The **Paschal mystery** is the mystery of Jesus' suffering, death, Resurrection, and Ascension.

Activity — Connect Your Faith

Create a Crucifix Jesus' suffering, death, Resurrection, and Ascension can give you hope during hard or sad times. Draw a picture of a crucifix, or create one from clay, wood, or some other material. Look at it during difficult times, and remember Jesus' saving actions.

Oración de alabanza

Reúnanse y comiencen con la señal de la cruz.

Canten juntos el estribillo.

Canta un nuevo canto,
canta a Cristo, quien resucitó.

¡Aleluya! ¡Aleluya!
Canta un nuevo canto.

"Sing a New Song" © 2001, GIA Publications, Inc.

Líder: Estamos reunidos para dar gracias y alabar a Dios. Le damos gracias por el sacrificio de su Hijo, Jesús. Proclamemos el misterio de nuestra fe.

Todos: **¡Cristo ha muerto, aleluya!**
¡Cristo ha resucitado, aleluya!
¡Cristo de nuevo vendrá, aleluya!

Canten el estribillo.

Líder: Proclamemos el misterio de nuestra fe.

Todos: **Anunciamos tu muerte, proclamamos tu resurrección. ¡Ven, Señor Jesús!**

Canten el estribillo.

Líder: Oremos.

Inclinen la cabeza mientras el líder reza.

Todos: **Amén.**

Prayer of Praise

Let Us Pray

Gather and begin with the Sign of the Cross.

Sing together the refrain.

Sing a new song. Sing of Christ who rose from the dead.

Alleluia! Alleluia! Sing a new song.

Leader: We gather to give God thanks and praise. We are grateful to him for the sacrifice of his Son, Jesus. Let us proclaim the mystery of our faith.

All: **Christ has died, Alleluia!**
Christ is risen, Alleluia!
Christ will come again, Alleluia!

Sing the refrain.

Leader: Let us proclaim the mystery of our faith.

All: **Dying you destroyed our death,**
rising you restored our life.
Lord Jesus, come in glory.

Sing the refrain.

Leader: Let us pray.

Bow your heads as the leader prays.

All: **Amen.**

Repasar y aplicar

Comprueba lo que aprendiste Escribe o encierra en un círculo la respuesta correcta.

1. Un ______________________ es renunciar a algo por un bien mayor.
2. Jesús ______________________ para salvarnos del poder del pecado y de la muerte eterna.
3. ______________________ comunicó a los Apóstoles la noticia de la Resurrección de Jesús.
4. El sufrimiento, la muerte, la Resurrección y la Ascensión de Jesús se conocen como _____.
   a. el misterio de la Santísima Trinidad
   b. el Misterio Pascual
   c. la señal de la cruz
5. Compartes el misterio del sufrimiento, la muerte, la Resurrección y la Ascensión de Jesús cuando _____.
   a. participas en la celebración de la Eucaristía
   b. decoras el árbol de Navidad
   c. contemplas un amanecer

Actividad Vive tu fe

Recuerda un sacrificio Escribe una nota de agradecimiento a alguien que haya hecho un sacrificio por ti.

CHAPTER 8

Review and Apply

Check Understanding Write or circle the correct response.

1. A ____________________ is giving up something for a greater good.
2. Jesus ____________________ to save people from the power of sin and everlasting death.
3. ____________________ shared with the Apostles the news of Jesus' Resurrection.
4. The suffering, death, Resurrection, and Ascension of Jesus are called the _____.
   - a. mystery of the Trinity
   - b. Paschal mystery
   - c. Sign of the Cross
5. You share in the mystery of Jesus' suffering, death, Resurrection, and Ascension when you _____.
   - a. take part in the celebration of the Eucharist
   - b. decorate the Christmas tree
   - c. look at a sunrise

Activity Live Your Faith

Remember a Sacrifice Write a thank-you note to someone who has made a sacrifice for you.

____

____

____

____

La fe en familia

Lo que creemos

- Jesús murió y resucitó para salvar a todos del poder del pecado.
- La Iglesia celebra el Misterio Pascual en todos los sacramentos.

LA SAGRADA ESCRITURA

Marcos 15,33–41 habla de la muerte de Jesús. Lee este relato y comenta con tu familia sobre su significado.

Visita **www.harcourtreligion.com** para encontrar recursos basados en el año litúrgico y lecturas semanales de la Sagrada Escritura.

Actividad

Vive tu fe

Da gracias Tu familia es una escuela de fe. En tu casa aprendes el significado del sacrificio cuando otros se sacrifican por ti y tú te sacrificas por ellos. Compartan juntos una comida especial. En la comida, túrnense para agradecerle a cada uno algún sacrificio que haya hecho por la familia.

▲ Santa María Magdalena, Siglo I d.C.

Siervos de la fe

María Magdalena fue discípula de Jesús. Estuvo a los pies de la cruz mientras Jesús sufría y lo acompañó en el momento de su muerte. Visitó el sepulcro de Jesús la primera mañana de Pascua y fue la primera en anunciar a la gente la Resurrección de Jesús. Su día se celebra el 22 de julio.

Una oración en familia

Santa María, ruega por nosotros para que apreciemos el sacrificio de Jesús y sintamos la alegría de su Resurrección. Amén.

 CIC *Consulta el Catecismo de la Iglesia Católica, números 613 y 1085, para obtener más información sobre el contenido del capítulo.*

CHAPTER 8

Family Faith

Catholics Believe

- Jesus died and rose to new life to save all people from the power of sin.
- The Church celebrates the Paschal mystery in all of the sacraments.

SCRIPTURE

Mark 15:33–41 is about Jesus' death. Read this story and talk with your family about its meaning.

GO ONLINE **www.harcourtreligion.com** For weekly Scripture readings and seasonal resources

Activity

Live Your Faith

Give Thanks Your family is a school of faith. You learn the meaning of sacrifice at home as others sacrifice for you and you sacrifice for them. Share a special meal together. At the meal, take turns thanking each member of the family for a sacrifice that he or she has made for the family.

▲ **Saint Mary Magdalene first century A.D.**

People of Faith

Mary Magdalene was a follower of Jesus. She stood at the foot of Jesus' cross as he suffered and died. She went to Jesus' tomb on the first Easter morning. She was the first to tell others about Jesus' Resurrection. Her feast day is July 22.

Family Prayer

Saint Mary, pray for us that we may appreciate Jesus' sacrifice and feel the joy of his Resurrection. Amen.

Capítulo 9 La obra de Jesús

Oremos

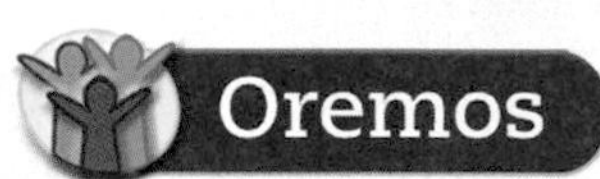

Líder: Dios de amor, danos esperanza y consuelo.
"Denle el favor al débil y al huérfano,
hagan justicia al que sufre y al pobre".
Salmo 82, 3

Todos: Dios de amor, danos esperanza y consuelo. Amén.

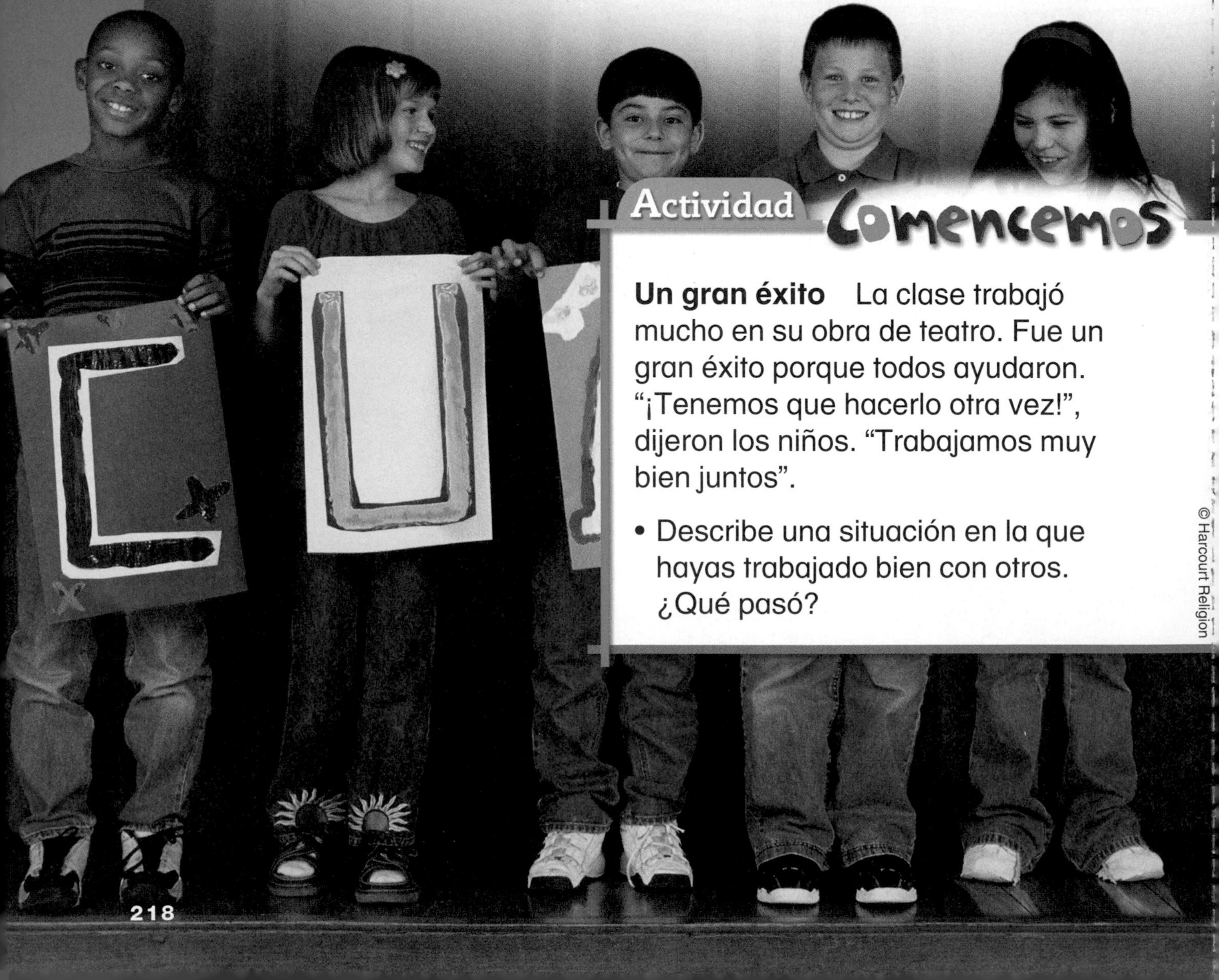

Actividad Comencemos

Un gran éxito La clase trabajó mucho en su obra de teatro. Fue un gran éxito porque todos ayudaron. "¡Tenemos que hacerlo otra vez!", dijeron los niños. "Trabajamos muy bien juntos".

- Describe una situación en la que hayas trabajado bien con otros. ¿Qué pasó?

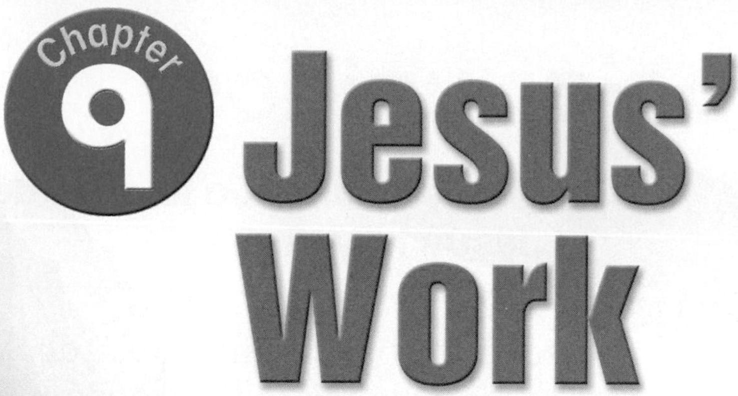

Chapter 9 Jesus' Work

Let Us Pray

Leader: Loving God, bring hope and comfort to all people.
"Defend the lowly and fatherless;
render justice to the afflicted and needy."
Psalm 82:3

All: Loving God, bring hope and comfort to all people.
Amen.

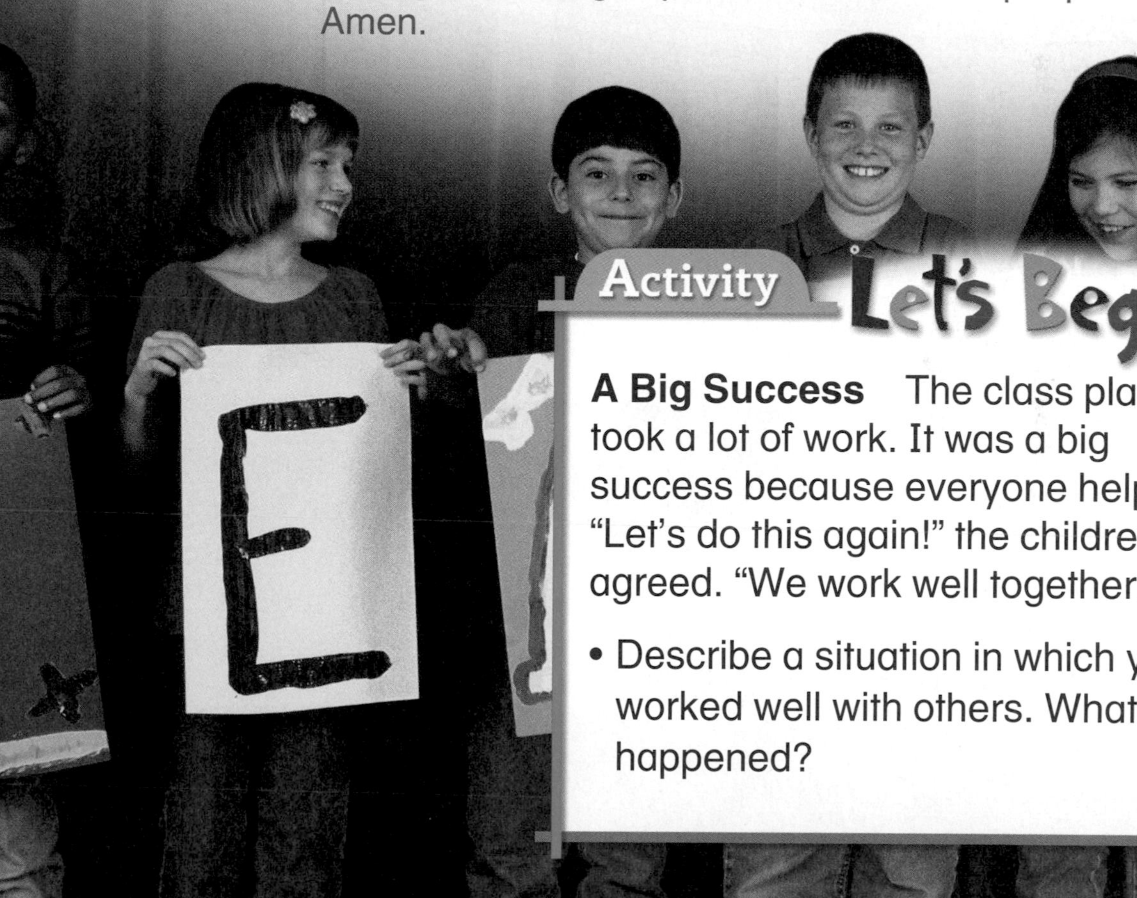

Activity Let's Begin

A Big Success The class play took a lot of work. It was a big success because everyone helped. "Let's do this again!" the children all agreed. "We work well together."

- Describe a situation in which you worked well with others. What happened?

Trabajar unidos

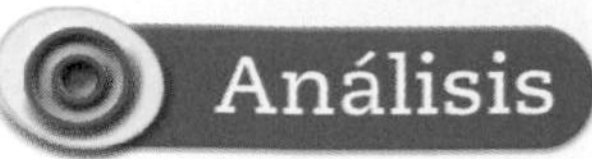

¿Quién continúa la obra de Jesús hoy día?

Cuando las personas trabajan unidas, el trabajo es más fácil para todos. Este relato trata de lo importante que puede ser trabajar unidos.

UN RELATO

Los amigos de Carla

"¿Qué te pasa?", preguntó Carla al ver a su hermana Elena sentada a la mesa, llorando.

"Me ofrecí a enviar estas cartas para ayudar a la oficina de la iglesia, pero estoy atrasada. Tengo que llevarlas hoy al correo y todavía me faltan cincuenta para terminar", sollozó Elena.

"No te preocupes, conseguiré ayuda", contestó Carla.

Poco después llegaron los amigos de Carla para ayudar. Joaquín organizó los sobres y Florencia los cerró. Carla y Raquel pegaron las estampillas. Cuando las cartas estuvieron listas, Elena y su mamá las llevaron rápidamente a la oficina de correos.

"Muchas gracias por ayudarme", dijo Elena cuando volvió a casa. "Es increíble lo rápido que se puede terminar un trabajo cuando todos trabajan unidos".

¿Cuándo has trabajado con otros para solucionar un problema?

Working Together

Focus **Who continues Jesus' work today?**

When people work together, the job is easier for everyone. This story tells how important working together can be.

A STORY

Kerry's Friends

"What's wrong?" asked Kerry when she saw her sister Erin crying at the table.

"I offered to help the church office send out these letters, but I am running out of time. They need to go in the mail today, and I still have fifty more to do," cried Erin.

"Don't worry, I'll find help," replied Kerry.

Soon, Kerry's friends came to help. Curtis stuffed the envelopes and Felicia sealed them. Kerry and Rachel put on the stamps. Then Erin and her mom rushed the letters to the post office.

"Thank you so much for your help," said Erin when she returned home. "It's amazing how quickly a job can be completed when everyone works together."

When have you worked with others to help solve a problem?

EXPLORACIÓN Explore

La Iglesia

Al igual que los niños del relato, la comunidad de la Iglesia trabaja unida. Cuando Jesús vivió en la tierra, realizó la obra de su Padre. El Espíritu Santo estaba con Jesús. Con su Ascensión, Jesús regresó al cielo con su Padre. Entonces Jesús envió al Espíritu para que acompañara a su Iglesia. El Espíritu Santo hace posible que la Iglesia continúe la obra de Jesús hoy día.

Palabras† de fe

La Iglesia se conoce también como el **Cuerpo de Cristo**, y Cristo es su cabeza. Todos los bautizados son miembros del Cuerpo de Cristo.

Como miembro bautizado de la familia de la Iglesia, tú eres Jesús para los demás. Tú usas las manos y los pies, la boca y los oídos, la mente y el corazón para llevar a cabo la obra de Jesús. La Iglesia se conoce también como el **Cuerpo de Cristo**. Este nombre te indica que todos los miembros de la Iglesia son uno solo, así como las partes de un cuerpo forman un solo cuerpo. También te dice que perteneces a Jesús.

¿Por qué el Cuerpo de Cristo es un buen nombre para la Iglesia?

Actividad Comparte tu fe

Piensa: ¿Cuándo es la Iglesia una comunidad que ayuda a los demás?

Comunica: Escribe con tu grupo una canción corta acerca de trabajar unidos para ayudar a los demás.

Actúa: Canten la canción al resto de la clase.

The Church

Like the children in the story, the people of the Church work together. When Jesus lived on earth, he did his Father's work. The Holy Spirit was with Jesus. At his Ascension, Jesus returned to his Father in heaven. Then Jesus sent the Spirit to be with his Church. The Holy Spirit makes it possible for the Church to continue Jesus' work today.

As a baptized member of the Church family, you are Jesus to other people. You use your hands and feet, your mouth and ears, and your mind and heart to do Jesus' work. One name for the Church is the **Body of Christ**. This name tells you that all Church members are one, as the parts of a body are one. It also says that you belong to Jesus.

Why is the Body of Christ a good name for the Church?

Words of Faith

The **Body of Christ** is a name for the Church, of which Christ is the head. All of the baptized are members of the Body of Christ.

Activity — Share Your Faith

Think: When is the Church a community that helps others?

Share: With a group, write a short song about working together to help others.

Act: Sing your song to the class.

Llevar a cabo la obra de Jesús

¿Cómo lleva a cabo la Iglesia la obra de Jesús?

La Iglesia continúa la obra de Jesús en la tierra. Pero, ¿qué debemos hacer exactamente los discípulos de Jesús? Jesús explicó cómo cuidar de los que necesitan ayuda. Dijo que quienes aman a Dios y a los demás realizan su obra. Jesús contó a sus discípulos este relato, en el que les dice que Él es el rey.

LA SAGRADA ESCRITURA **Mateo 25, 34–40**

Los que ayudaron

Al final de los tiempos, el rey llamará a todos ante su presencia. A algunos les dirá: "¡Entren en el reino y alégrense! Porque tuve hambre y ustedes me dieron de comer; tuve sed y ustedes me dieron de beber. Anduve sin ropas y me vistieron; estuve en la cárcel y me fueron a ver".

Ellos dirán: "¿Cuándo hicimos esto por ti?".

Y el rey contestará: "Cada vez que ayudaron a los necesitados, me ayudaron a mí".

Basado en *Mateo 25, 34–40*

¿Cómo puedes ayudar a Jesús ayudando a los demás?

Doing Jesus' Work

Focus **How does the Church do Jesus' work?**

The Church continues to do Jesus' work on earth. But what exactly should Jesus' followers do? Jesus explained how to care for people who need help. He said that people who loved God and others were doing his work. Jesus told his followers this story. In it, Jesus speaks of himself as a king.

SCRIPTURE — Matthew 25:34–40

Those Who Helped

At the end of time, the king will call all people before him. To some people, the king will say, "Enter into the kingdom and be joyful! When I was hungry, you fed me. You gave me water when I was thirsty and clothes when I needed them. When I was in prison, you visited me."

The people will say, "When did we do these things for you?"

The king will say, "Whenever you helped anyone in need, you helped me."

Based on *Matthew 25:34–40*

How can you help Jesus by helping someone else?

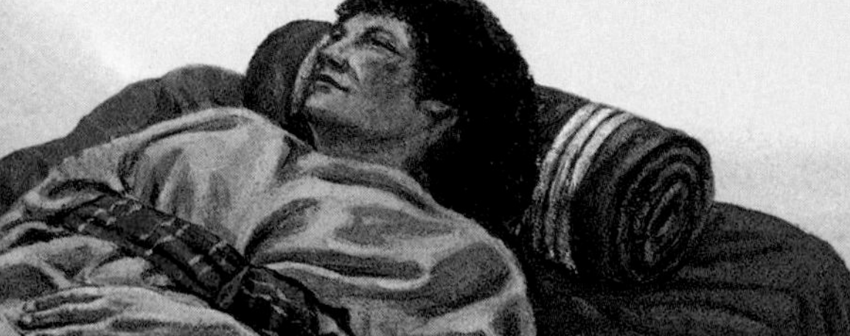

Usa tus dones

Dios le ha dado a cada persona dones especiales, o *talentos*. Un talento es algo que te gusta hacer y que haces bien. Dios te hace un llamado para que uses tus talentos en el servicio a los demás. La Iglesia es una, pero tiene muchos miembros diferentes con muchos dones diferentes.

Todos tenemos talentos diferentes. Cuando unimos nuestros talentos y trabajamos en conjunto como el Cuerpo de Cristo, podemos hacer mucho más que si trabajamos por separado.

Al final de la Misa nos vamos con la misión de realizar la obra de Jesús en el mundo. El sacerdote o el diácono dice: "¡Podéis ir en paz!". La manera de amar y servir al Señor es amar y servir a todo el pueblo de Dios.

¿Cuántos talentos diferentes puedes contar entre los niños de tu clase?

Actividad Practica tu fe

Usa tus talentos Haz un cartel que represente algunos de tus talentos y cómo los puedes usar para ayudar a los demás.

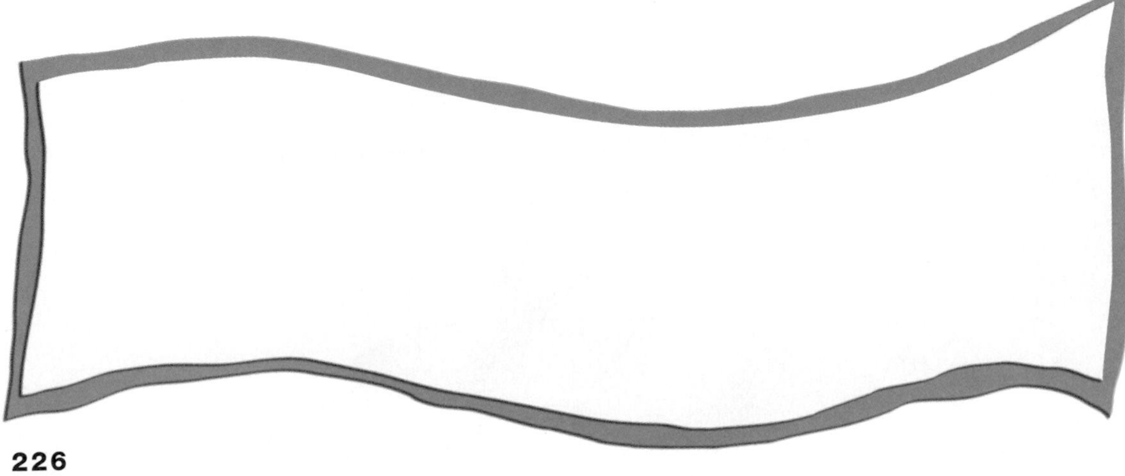

Share Your Gifts

God gave each person special gifts, or *talents*. A talent is something you enjoy doing and can do well. You are called to use your talents to serve others. The Church is one, but it has many kinds of members with many kinds of gifts.

Everyone has different talents. When people put their talents together and work as the Body of Christ, they can do more than any one person can do alone.

At the end of Mass, you go forth to do Jesus' work in the world. The priest or deacon says, "Go in peace to love and serve the Lord!" You love and serve the Lord by loving and serving all of God's people.

How many different talents can you count among the people in your classroom?

Activity Connect Your Faith

Share Your Talents Design a banner that shows what some of your talents are and how you can use them to help others.

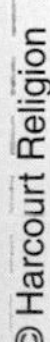

Oración de petición

Reúnanse y comiencen con la señal de la cruz.

Líder: Dios Padre nuestro, estamos ante ti como el Cuerpo de Cristo.

Lector 1: Ayuda a nuestros ojos a ver la obra que hay que realizar,

Todos: Para que podamos ayudarnos los unos a los otros.

Lector 2: Ayuda a nuestros oídos a oír a los que piden ayuda,

Todos: Para que podamos ayudarnos los unos a los otros.

Lector 1: Ayuda a que nuestras manos y pies sean fuertes,

Todos: Para que podamos ayudarnos los unos a los otros.

Lector 2: Ayuda a que nuestros corazones estén llenos de amor,

Todos: Para que podamos ayudarnos los unos a los otros.

Líder: Oremos.

Inclinen la cabeza mientras el líder reza.

Todos: Amén.

Canten juntos.

Somos muchas partes, pero un solo cuerpo,
y los dones que tenemos, los debemos compartir.
Que el Espíritu de amor nos haga uno:
uno en el amor,
uno en la esperanza,
uno en la cruz.

Asking Prayer

Gather and begin with the Sign of the Cross.

Leader: God our Father, we stand before you as the Body of Christ.

Reader 1: Help our eyes see work that needs to be done,

All: **So that we can help one another.**

Reader 2: Help our ears hear those who ask for help,

All: **So that we can help one another.**

Reader 1: Help our hands and feet be strong,

All: **So that we can help one another.**

Reader 2: Help our hearts be full of love,

All: **So that we can help one another.**

Leader: Let us pray.

Bow your heads as the leader prays.

All: Amen.

Sing together.

We are many parts, we are all one body,
and the gifts we have we are given to share.
May the Spirit of love make us one indeed;
one, the love we share, one, our hope in
despair, one, the cross that we bear.

Repasar y aplicar

Comprueba lo que aprendiste Escribe o encierra en un círculo la respuesta correcta.

1. La Iglesia se conoce también como ______ porque está formada por muchos miembros que trabajan unidos en nombre de Jesús.

   a. el cielo en la tierra

   b. la guardiana de las llaves

   c. el Cuerpo de Cristo

2. ¿Cómo amas y sirves al Señor?

   ____

   ____

3. Desde que Jesús volvió al Padre, ¿quién realiza la obra de Jesús en la tierra?

   ____

4. Cuando Jesús volvió al cielo, ¿a quién envió a acompañar a la Iglesia?

   ____

5. Menciona tres maneras en las que puedes continuar la obra de Jesús ayudando a los demás.

   ____

   ____

Actividad Vive tu fe

Usa tus talentos Diseña un cartel que invite a los demás a usar sus talentos para ayudarse unos a otros como miembros del Cuerpo de Cristo. Si es posible, haz un cartel grande y preséntalo a tu clase.

Alimenta
a los
que pasan
hambre

CHAPTER 9

Review and Apply

Check Understanding Write or circle the correct answer.

1. The Church is sometimes called _____ because it is made up of many members who work together in Jesus' name.
   a. heaven on earth
   b. the keeper of the keys
   c. the Body of Christ
2. How do you love and serve the Lord?

   ____

   ____
3. Since Jesus returned to his Father, who does Jesus' work on earth?

   ____
4. When Jesus returned to heaven, whom did he send to be with the Church?

   ____
5. Name three ways you can continue Jesus' work by helping others.

   ____

   ____

Activity Live Your Faith

Use Your Talents Design a poster to encourage people to use their talents to help one another as members of the Body of Christ. If possible, enlarge your design, and put it on poster board to display it.

CAPÍTULO 9

La fe en familia

Lo que creemos

- La Iglesia es el Cuerpo de Cristo al que pertenecen todos sus miembros.
- Los miembros de la Iglesia continúan la obra de Jesús ayudando a los demás.

LA SAGRADA ESCRITURA

Juan 15, 1–5 y 7–10 habla acerca de formar parte del Cuerpo de Cristo. Comenta por qué piensas que tu familia forma parte del Cuerpo de Cristo.

Visita **www.harcourtreligion.com** para encontrar recursos basados en el año litúrgico y lecturas semanales de la Sagrada Escritura.

Actividad

Vive tu fe

Usa tus talentos Como miembros del Cuerpo de Cristo, decidan cómo pueden usar la combinación de talentos única que poseen, en un proyecto para ayudar a alguien que lo necesite. Lleva a cabo el proyecto con tu familia, o pide ayuda a otros que tengan talentos necesarios para el proyecto.

▲ Santa Mariana de Jesús - Quito 1618–1645

Siervos de la fe

Mariana nació en Quito, una ciudad de Ecuador, en América del Sur. Su familia pertenecía a la nobleza. Siendo muy joven prometió vivir una vida santa en la pobreza. Dedicaba mucho tiempo a orar y a actos de penitencia. Solo salía de casa para asistir a Misa. Alimentaba a los pobres y enseñaba a los niños en su casa. Poseía el don de sanación. El día de Santa Mariana de Jesús es el 26 de mayo.

Una oración en familia

Santa Mariana de Jesús, ruega por nosotros para que sirvamos a Dios sirviendo a quienes nos piden ayuda. Amén.

 CIC *Consulta el Catecismo de la Iglesia Católica, números 521 y 1267, para obtener más información sobre el contenido del capítulo.*

CHAPTER 9

Family Faith

Catholics Believe

- The Church is the Body of Christ, to which all members belong.
- Church members continue Jesus' work when they help others.

SCRIPTURE

John 15:1–5, 7–10 is about being a member of the Body of Christ. Talk about how your family is part of the Body of Christ.

www.harcourtreligion.com
For weekly Scripture readings and seasonal resources

Activity

Live Your Faith

Share Your Talents As members of the Body of Christ, decide how your unique combination of talents could be used in a project to help someone in need. Do the project with your family, or join with others who may have useful talents.

People of Faith

▲ Saint Mary Ann of Quito 1618–1645

Mary Ann was born in Quito, a city in Ecuador, South America. She was from a noble family. At an early age, she promised to live a holy life in poverty. She spent much time in prayer and acts of penance. She left home only to attend Mass. She gave food to people and taught children in her home. She was blessed with the gift of healing. Saint Mary Ann's feast day is May 26.

Family Prayer

Saint Mary Ann, pray for us that we may serve God by serving those who ask us for help. Amen.

See Catechism of the Catholic Church 521, 1267 for further reading on chapter content.

Repaso de la Unidad 3

A Trabaja con palabras Empareja cada descripción de la columna 1 con el término correcto de la columna 2.

Columna 1		Columna 2
______	1. Relatos que contaba Jesús para enseñar.	a. Mesías
______	2. Jesús hizo un gran ______ por nosotros.	b. Misterio Pascual
______	3. Otra manera de nombrar a la Iglesia, con Cristo a la cabeza.	c. parábolas
______	4. Palabra hebrea que significa "ungido".	d. Cuerpo de Cristo
______	5. Sufrimiento, muerte, Resurrección y Ascensión de Jesús.	e. sacrificio

B Comprueba lo que aprendiste Encierra en un círculo la letra de la opción que mejor complete el enunciado o responda la pregunta.

6. Los cuatro libros sobre Jesús en el Nuevo Testamento son ______.
   a. las parábolas b. los evangelios c. las biblias

7. El Reino de Dios también se conoce como ______ de Dios.
   a. el reino de la justicia y la paz b. la promesa c. la justicia

8. ¿Qué sucedió tres días después de la muerte de Jesús?
   a. la Visitación b. la Resurrección c. la Ascensión

9. Los evangelios llevan el nombre de Mateo, Marcos, Lucas y ______.
   a. Santiago b. José c. Juan

10. ¿A quién nos envió Jesús cuando regresó al cielo?
    a. al Espíritu Santo b. a los Apóstoles c. a María

Unit 3 Review

A Work with Words Match each description in Column 1 with the correct term in Column 2.

Column 1

_____ 1. Teaching stories that Jesus told

_____ 2. Jesus made a great _____ for us.

_____ 3. A name for the Church, of which Christ is the head

_____ 4. A Hebrew word that means "anointed"

_____ 5. Jesus' suffering, death, Resurrection, and Ascension

Column 2

a. Messiah

b. Paschal mystery

c. parables

d. Body of Christ

e. sacrifice

B Check Understanding Circle the letter of the choice that best completes the sentence or answers the question.

6. The four books about Jesus in the New Testament are the _____.

   a. parables b. Gospels c. Bibles

7. The kingdom of God is also called God's _____.

   a. reign b. promise c. justice

8. What happened three days after Jesus' death?

   a. Visitation b. Resurrection c. Ascension

9. The Gospels are named for Matthew, Mark, Luke, and _____.

   a. James b. Joseph c. John

10. Whom did Jesus send to us after he returned to heaven?

   a. Holy Spirit b. Apostles c. Mary

UNIDAD 4

La Iglesia Católica

Capítulo 10

Los líderes de la Iglesia

¿Quiénes son los líderes de la Iglesia?

Capítulo 11

Un pueblo santo

¿Cómo están unidos los miembros de la Iglesia?

Capítulo 12

La misión de la Iglesia

¿Cuál es la misión de la Iglesia?

¿Qué crees que vas a aprender en esta unidad acerca de la Iglesia Católica?

UNIT 4

The Catholic Church

Chapter 10

Church Leaders

Who are the leaders of the Church?

Chapter 11

One Holy People

How are members of the Church united?

Chapter 12

The Church's Mission

What is the Church's mission?

What do you think you will learn in this unit about the Catholic Church?

Capítulo 10 Los líderes de la Iglesia

Oremos

Líder: Dios bondadoso, ayúdanos a seguir tu voluntad en nuestras vidas.

"Me guías conforme a tus designios
y me llevas de la mano tras de ti".

Salmo 73, 24

Todos: Dios bondadoso, ayúdanos a seguir tu voluntad en nuestras vidas. Amén.

Actividad Comencemos

Todos necesitamos líderes
Los líderes ayudan a la gente a saber qué hacer. Los buenos líderes saben enseñar y guiar. Saben qué hay que hacer. También saben cómo hacer para que cada persona dé lo mejor de sí. Para ser un buen líder, hay que ser una persona especial.

- ¿Qué clase de líder quieres ser? ¿Cuándo y cómo eres un líder hoy en día?

Chapter 10 Church Leaders

Let Us Pray

Leader: Caring God, help us follow your will for our lives.

"With your counsel you guide me,
and at the end receive me with
honor."

Psalm 73:24

All: Caring God, help us follow your will for our lives. Amen.

Activity Let's Begin

Everyone Needs Leaders
Leaders help people know what to do. Good leaders know how to teach and guide. They know what needs to be done. They can figure out how to get each person to do the best job possible. It takes a special person to be a good leader.

- What kind of leader do you hope to be? When and how are you a leader now?

El primer líder

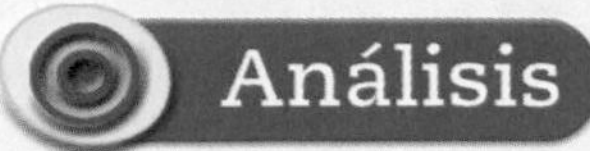

¿Qué misión especial le dio Jesús a Pedro en su Iglesia?

Este es un relato sobre el primer líder de la Iglesia Católica.

LA SAGRADA ESCRITURA **Mateo 16, 15–19; 26, 69–75; Juan 21,15–17**

Pedro y Jesús

ESCENA 1

Jesús: Y ustedes, ¿quién dicen que soy yo?

Simón: Tú eres el Mesías, el Hijo de Dios.

Jesús: Simón, ninguna persona de carne y hueso te ha dicho que digas eso. Te lo ha dicho Dios. Y ahora tu nombre es Pedro.

Narrador: *Pedro* significa "piedra".

Jesús: Sobre ti, Pedro, edificaré mi Iglesia. Yo te daré las llaves del Reino de los Cielos. El mal nunca te vencerá.

ESCENA 2

Narrador: La noche en que Jesús fue traicionado, Pedro lo siguió hasta la casa del sumo sacerdote.

Sirvienta 1: Tú estabas con Jesús esta noche, ¿no?

Pedro: Yo no conozco a ese hombre.

Sirvienta 2: Este hombre andaba con Jesús.

Pedro: No, ¡ni siquiera sé quién es Jesús!

The First Leader

What did Jesus choose Peter to do for his Church?

Here is a story about the first leader of the Catholic Church.

SCRIPTURE Matthew 16:15–19, 26:69–75; John 21:15–17

Peter and Jesus

SCENE 1

Jesus: Who do you say that I am?

Simon: You are the Christ, the Son of God.

Jesus: Simon, no human told you to say that. God told you to say that. Your name is now Peter.

Narrator: *Peter* means "rock."

Jesus: Upon you, Peter, I will build my church. I will give you the keys to the kingdom of heaven. Evil will never overpower you.

SCENE 2

Narrator: On the night Jesus was betrayed, Peter followed him to the high priest's house.

Servant 1: You were with Jesus tonight, weren't you?

Peter: No, no, I don't know him.

Servant 2: This man was with Jesus.

Peter: No, I don't even know who Jesus is!

Sirvienta 3: ¡Yo te vi con él!

Pedro: ¡No! ¡Yo no conozco a Jesús!

[Se oye el canto de un gallo.]

Narrador: Pedro recuerda. Jesús dijo que Pedro lo negaría tres veces antes de que cantara el gallo.

Pedro: ¿Qué he hecho? [Llora.]

ESCENA **3**

Narrador: Después de su Resurrección, Jesús se apareció ante sus discípulos.

Jesús: Simón Pedro, ¿me amas?

Pedro: Sí, Señor, tú sabes que te quiero.

Jesús: Apacienta mis corderos. ¿Me amas?

Pedro: Sí, Señor, tú sabes que te quiero.

Jesús: Cuida de mis ovejas. ¿Me amas?

Pedro: Tú tienes que saber que te quiero.

Jesús: Apacienta mis ovejas.

Basado en *Mateo 16, 15–19, Mateo 26, 69–75 y Juan 21, 15–17*

¿Por qué crees que Jesús le hizo a Pedro la misma pregunta tres veces?

Comparte tu fe

Piensa: ¿Alguna vez te pidieron que fueras líder?

Comunica: Habla acerca de tu experiencia cuando dirigiste un grupo al que pertenezcas. ¿Fue fácil o difícil?

Actúa: Dirige a la clase para que unas veces recen y otras veces canten.

Servant 3: I saw you with him!

Peter: No! I don't know Jesus!

[Sound of a rooster crowing.]

Narrator: Peter remembers. Jesus said that Peter would deny him three times before the rooster crowed.

Peter: What have I done? [Cries.]

SCENE 3

Narrator: After his Resurrection, Jesus showed himself to his followers.

Jesus: Simon Peter, do you love me?

Peter: Jesus, you know that I love you.

Jesus: Feed my lambs. Do you love me?

Peter: Yes, you know that I love you.

Jesus: Take care of my sheep. Do you love me?

Peter: You must know that I love you.

Jesus: Feed my sheep.

Based on *Matthew 16:15–19, Matthew 26:69–75, John 21:15–17*

? Why do you think Jesus asked Peter the same question three times?

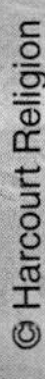

Activity — Share Your Faith

Think: Have you ever been asked to be a leader?

Share: Talk about your experience in leading a group to which you belong. Was leading easy or difficult?

Act: Take turns leading your class in prayer or song.

Dirigir y servir

Análisis **¿Cómo dirigen la Iglesia el Papa y los obispos?**

Los **Apóstoles** fueron elegidos por Jesús para ser los primeros líderes de la Iglesia. Realizaron la misión de Jesús de predicar la Buena Nueva y salvar al pueblo. Jesús escogió a Pedro para que dirigiera a los Apóstoles.

Pedro se convirtió en la cabeza de la Iglesia en la tierra porque Jesús lo eligió como primer líder de los Apóstoles. Hoy en día, la persona que ocupa ese cargo se denomina *Papa*. El Papa es el encargado de cuidar al pueblo de Dios. La palabra *papa* proviene de una palabra italiana que significa "padre".

El Papa es también el obispo de Roma. La palabra *obispo* significa "inspector". Los **obispos** dirigen a la Iglesia. Cada obispo dirige y sirve a una diócesis. El Papa y los obispos continúan el trabajo de los Apóstoles dirigiendo, guiando y cuidando al pueblo de Dios.

El magisterio y la autoridad de los Apóstoles se han transmitido a los obispos, que son los líderes de la Iglesia en la actualidad. Los obispos ocupan hoy en día el lugar de los Apóstoles en la tierra.

¿Cuáles crees que son las responsabilidades de un obispo?

Lead and Serve

How do the pope and bishops lead the Church?

The **Apostles** were chosen by Jesus to be the first leaders of the Church. They carried out Jesus' mission of preaching the good news and saving people. Jesus chose Peter to be the leader of the Apostles.

Peter became the head of the Church on earth because Jesus chose Peter to be the first leader of the Apostles. The person in this position is now called the *pope*. The pope is in charge of caring for all of God's people. The word *pope* comes from an Italian word that means "father."

The pope is also the Bishop of Rome. The word *bishop* means "overseer." The **bishops** lead the whole Church. Each bishop leads and serves a diocese. The pope and bishops carry on the work of the Apostles in leading, guiding, and caring for God's people.

The Apostles' teaching and authority have been handed down to the bishops, who are the leaders of the Church today. They are the people who now take the place of the Apostles on earth.

What do you think the responsibilities of a bishop are?

Líderes de la parroquia

Las diócesis están formadas por muchas parroquias. Cada parroquia también tiene sus propios líderes. El párroco es un sacerdote que ha recibido autoridad para dirigir una comunidad parroquial. Es quien celebra los sacramentos y trabaja con otros para servir a la gente de la parroquia. Los diáconos son ordenados para que celebren algunos sacramentos y hagan obras de caridad.

Palabras de fe

Los **Apóstoles** fueron los primeros doce líderes que eligió Jesús.

Los **obispos** son ordenados para trabajar con el papa, enseñando y guiando a la Iglesia. Son los sucesores de los Apóstoles.

Los miembros de la Iglesia sirven

En las parroquias hay también otras personas que están llamadas a servir y dirigir. Estos hombres y mujeres no están ordenados, pero ayudan en muchos de los ministerios parroquiales. Tu catequista es una de esas personas. Otros ejemplos son los ministros de la liturgia, los miembros del consejo parroquial, los directores de educación religiosa y los miembros del ministerio con los jóvenes.

Actividad Practica tu fe

Mi comunidad de la Iglesia Completa los espacios en blanco para mostrar cómo perteneces a la comunidad de la Iglesia.

Me llamo ______________________.

Pertenezco a la parroquia de ______________________

de la arquidiócesis/diócesis de ______________________.

Nuestro párroco es ______________________.

Nuestro arzobispo/obispo es ______________________.

El papa ______________________ y los obispos dirigen la Iglesia Católica.

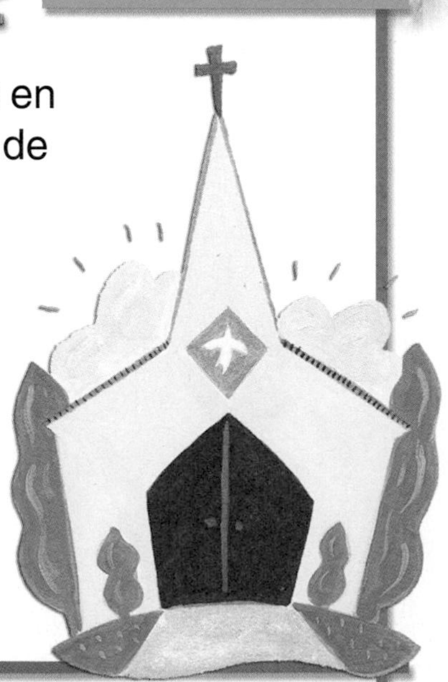

Leaders of the Parish

Dioceses are made up of many parishes. Each parish has leaders, too. The pastor is a priest who has been given the authority to lead a parish community. He celebrates the sacraments and works with others to serve the people of the parish. Deacons are ordained to celebrate some of the sacraments and to do works of charity.

Church Members Serve

There are other people in a parish who are called to serve and lead. These men and women are not ordained, but they help with many parish ministries. Your catechist is one of these people. Other examples include liturgical ministers, parish committee members, and directors of religious education and youth ministry.

Words of Faith

The **Apostles** were the first twelve leaders called by Jesus.

Bishops are ordained to work with the pope in teaching and guiding the Church. They are the successors of the Apostles.

Activity Connect Your Faith

My Church Community Fill in the blanks to show how you belong to the community of the Church.

My name is ____________________.

I belong to ____________________ parish in the (Arch)diocese of ____________________.

Our pastor is ____________________.

Our (arch)bishop is ____________________.

Pope ____________________ and the bishops lead the Catholic Church.

Oración de petición

Reúnanse y comiencen con la señal de la cruz.

Líder: Nos hemos reunido hoy para orar por nuestros líderes y por las necesidades de la Iglesia.

Lector 1: Por el papa, los obispos, los sacerdotes y demás líderes de la Iglesia, para que actúen con sabiduría y justicia, roguemos al Señor.

Todos: **Señor, escucha nuestra oración.**

Lector 2: Por nuestros maestros y catequistas, para que nos ayuden a entender tu plan para nosotros, roguemos al Señor.

Todos: **Señor, escucha nuestra oración.**

Lector 3: Por todos los miembros de la Iglesia, para que podamos usar nuestros dones para servir, roguemos al Señor.

Todos: **Señor, escucha nuestra oración.**

Líder: Oremos.

Inclinen la cabeza mientras el líder reza.

Todos: **Amén.**

Canten juntos.

Dios siempre fiel,
misericordioso,

Dios de tu pueblo,
escucha nuestra oración.

"General Intercessions" © 1990, GIA Publications, Inc.

Asking Prayer

Let Us Pray

Gather and begin with the Sign of the Cross.

Leader: We gather today to pray for our leaders and for the needs of the Church.

Reader 1: For the pope, the bishops, the priests, and other Church leaders, that they may act with wisdom and justice, we pray to the Lord.

All: **Lord, hear our prayer.**

Reader 2: For our teachers and catechists, that they may help us understand your plan for us, we pray to the Lord.

All: **Lord, hear our prayer.**

Reader 3: For all members of the Church, that we may use our gifts to serve, we pray to the Lord.

All: **Lord, hear our prayer.**

Leader: Let us pray.

Bow your heads as the leader prays.

All: **Amen.**

Sing together.

God ever faithful,
God ever merciful,
God of your people,
hear our prayer.

Repasar y aplicar

Trabaja con palabras Empareja cada descripción de la columna 1 con el término correcto de la columna 2.

Columna 1

_______ 1. Dirige la Iglesia en la tierra.

_______ 2. Eligió a los Apóstoles para liderar la Iglesia.

_______ 3. Fue el primer líder de los Apóstoles.

_______ 4. Dirige una diócesis.

_______ 5. Dirige una parroquia.

Columna 2

a. Jesús

b. Papa

c. obispo

d. Pedro

e. párroco

Actividad Vive tu fe

Reflexiona sobre el liderazgo Escribe una descripción de las tareas que realiza un obispo, sacerdote, diácono o catequista parroquial. Menciona tres buenas cualidades que necesita para su trabajo.

____

____

____

____

____

____

____

CHAPTER 10

Review and Apply

Work with Words Match each description in Column 1 with the correct term in Column 2.

Column 1

_____ 1. leads the whole Church on earth

_____ 2. chose the Apostles to lead the Church

_____ 3. was the first leader of the Apostles

_____ 4. leads a diocese

_____ 5. leads a parish

Column 2

a. Jesus

b. pope

c. bishop

d. Peter

e. pastor

Activity Live Your Faith

Think About Leadership Write a description of what a bishop, priest, deacon, or parish catechist does. List three good qualities that such a person needs in his or her work.

____

____

____

____

____

____

____

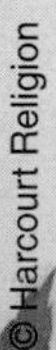

CAPÍTULO 10

La fe en familia

Lo que creemos

- Los obispos son los sucesores de los Apóstoles.
- El Papa, los obispos y los párrocos dirigen y guían a la Iglesia.

LA SAGRADA ESCRITURA

1 Corintios 3, 10–11 habla acerca de la construcción de los cimientos. Comenta cómo puedes construir la Iglesia.

Visita **www.harcourtreligion.com** para encontrar recursos basados en el año litúrgico y lecturas semanales de la Sagrada Escritura.

Actividad

Vive tu fe

Investiga De vez en cuando, los obispos escriben cartas a todos los fieles de su diócesis. Estas cartas guían a las personas en cuestiones de fe. Busca información sobre la última carta que tu obispo escribió a la comunidad de tu diócesis. Probablemente encuentres la carta en la página de Internet de tu diócesis, o tu párroco puede ayudarte a buscarla.

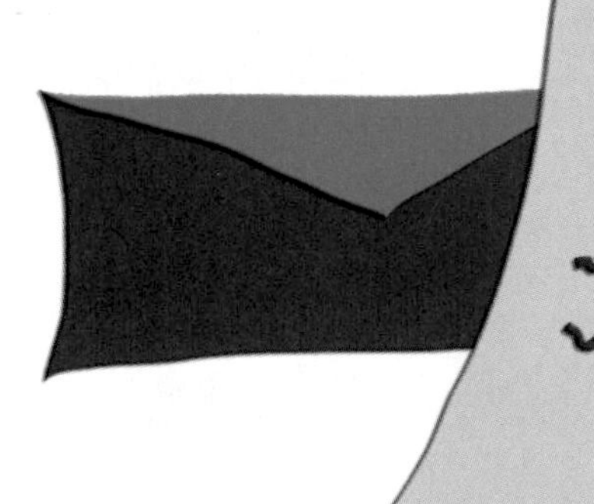

Siervos de la fe

▲ San Gregorio Magno c. 540–604

Gregorio nació en Roma. Vendió todo lo que tenía para ayudar a los pobres. Cuando se convirtió en papa, preparó a misioneros, que viajaron a Inglaterra y trabajaron para liberar a los esclavos y predicar el Evangelio. Sus escritos ayudaron a la gente a aprender acerca de Dios. La música llamada canto gregoriano lleva su nombre. El día de San Gregorio se celebra el 3 de septiembre.

Una oración en familia

San Gregorio, ruega por nosotros para que usemos nuestros talentos para servir a los demás. Amén.

 CIC Consulta el Catecismo de la Iglesia Católica, números 816 y 939, para obtener más información sobre el contenido del capítulo.

CHAPTER 10

Family Faith

Catholics Believe

- The bishops are the successors of the Apostles.
- The pope, bishops, and pastors lead and guide the Church.

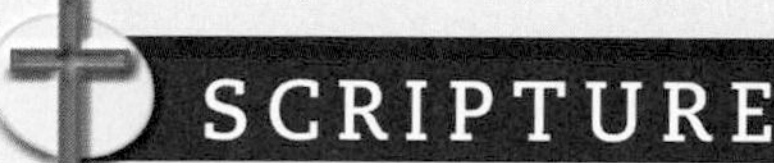

SCRIPTURE

1 Corinthians 3:10–11 is about building a foundation. Talk about how you can build up the Church.

www.harcourtreligion.com
For weekly Scripture readings and seasonal resources

Activity
Live Your Faith

Do Research Bishops write letters to all the faithful of their dioceses from time to time. These letters guide the people on matters of faith. Find out about the last letter your bishop wrote to the people of your diocese. You can probably find the letter on the Web site for your diocese, or your pastor can help you find it.

▲ Saint Gregory the Great c. 540–604

People of Faith

Gregory was born in Rome. He sold what he owned to help the poor. After he became pope, he trained missionaries, who traveled to England and worked to free slaves and preach the Gospel. Gregory's writings helped people learn about God. Music called Gregorian chant is named for him. Saint Gregory's feast day is September 3.

Family Prayer

Saint Gregory, pray for us that we may use our talents to serve others. Amen.

CCC See Catechism of the Catholic Church 816, 939 for further reading on chapter content.

Capítulo 11 Un pueblo santo

Oremos

Líder: Señor Dios, ayúdanos a realizar tu obra.
"Si el Señor no construye la casa,
en vano trabajan los albañiles".
Salmo 127, 1

Todos: Señor Dios, ayúdanos a realizar tu obra. Amén.

Actividad Comencemos

De muchos, uno

Un hilo delgado y luego otro
entretejidos con firmeza en su lugar.
Seis hilos más de otro color
un diseño en el espacio ayudan a formar.
Cuando la obra de la Tejedora queda terminada,
hay un todo donde antes no había nada.

- ¿Qué es más fuerte, un hilo o todo un tejido? ¿Por qué?

Chapter 11 One Holy People

Let Us Pray

Leader: Lord God, help us do your work.
"Unless the LORD build the house,
they labor in vain who build."
Psalm 127:1

All: Lord God, help us do your work. Amen.

Activity Let's Begin

One from Many

One tiny thread and then another
Woven tightly into place.
Six more threads, another color
Build the pattern, shape the space.
When Weaver Woman's work is done
There is a whole where once was none.

- Which is stronger, a single thread or a whole piece of cloth? Why?

Juntos en la Iglesia

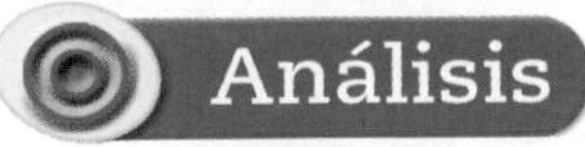

¿De qué manera es una la Iglesia Católica?

Esta carta muestra que, aunque las comunidades religiosas pueden ser diferentes, son todas una en Jesús.

UNA CARTA

La visita de Juanita

Querida mamá:

Estoy disfrutando mucho de mi visita al tío Miguel y a la tía Teresa. Ayer fuimos a su parroquia. ¡El edificio era circular! El altar estaba en el centro. Podía mirar hacia el otro lado del altar y ver a las personas que estaban enfrente. Había gente de todas las razas.

A pesar de que todo parecía diferente, cuando la misa comenzó me sentí como en casa. Yo conocía las oraciones del sacerdote. Luego hubo una lectura de las Escrituras, tal como lo hacemos nosotros. El libro de cánticos era diferente, pero yo me sabía los cánticos.

Ahora entiendo que las creencias de la gente y la forma como honran a Dios es lo que conforma nuestra Iglesia.

Cariños, Juanita

¿En qué se parece tu iglesia a la iglesia que visitó Juanita? ¿En qué se diferencia?

Together in the Church

Focus **How is the Catholic Church one?**

This letter explores how Church communities are sometimes different, but all are one in Jesus.

A LETTER

Jackie's Visit

Dear Mom,

I'm having fun visiting Uncle Mike and Aunt Theresa. Yesterday we went to their parish church. The building was round! I could look past the altar and see people facing me! There were people of all different colors.

Then Mass started and I felt right at home. The priest was praying words I knew. There were Scripture readings, just like at home. The songbook was different, but I knew the songs.

I can see that what makes our Church is what people believe and how they honor God.

Love, Jackie

How is your church the same as the one Jackie visited? How is it different?

En todo el mundo

En otras culturas, se pueden ver algunas diferencias en la celebración de la Misa.

- En África, por ejemplo, los niños avanzan en procesión hacia el altar mientras bailan al ritmo de tambores.
- En India, el diácono honra el libro de los evangelios pasando sobre él una bandeja de flores fragantes.
- Lo mismo sucede en muchos otros países, donde el lenguaje y la música de la liturgia varían.

En todos ellos se celebra el mismo misterio de fe y Cristo se hace presente para unir a la gente. Las principales partes de la Misa son iguales en todos lados porque la Iglesia Católica es una.

Comparte tu fe

Piensa: ¿Cómo crees que se celebra la Misa en otras partes del mundo?

Comunica: Elige un país en un mapa o globo terráqueo. Conversa con tu grupo sobre las diferencias que pueden haber entre la Misa en ese país y la Misa en Estados Unidos.

Actúa: ¿Cómo te imaginas que se celebra la Misa en ese país? Haz un dibujo.

Around the World

In other cultures, you would see some differences in the Mass celebration.

- In Africa, children might dance up the aisle in procession to the rhythm of drums.
- In India, the deacon might honor the Book of the Gospels by passing a tray of fragrant flowers over it.
- In many other countries, the language and music of the liturgy would be different.

The same mystery of faith is being celebrated in all these places. Christ is present, uniting the people. The main parts of the Mass are the same everywhere because the Catholic Church is one.

Activity Share Your Faith

Think: How do you think Mass is celebrated in different parts of the world?

Share: Using a map or a globe, choose a country. Discuss with your group how Mass in that country might be different from Mass in the United States.

Act: Draw a picture of how Mass might look in the country you chose.

Una Iglesia

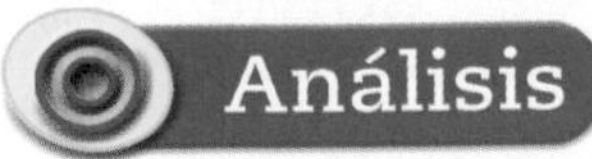

¿Qué hace santa a la Iglesia Católica?

Muchas personas de diversos países quedaron unidas el día en que el Espíritu Santo descendió sobre los discípulos de Jesús. Ese día se conoce como el día de **Pentecostés** y marca el comienzo de la Iglesia. Desde entonces, los discípulos de Jesús comprendieron más claramente que eran un cuerpo de creyentes que había sido santificado.

LA SAGRADA ESCRITURA — Hechos 2, 1–12

La fiesta de Pentecostés

Cincuenta días después de la Resurrección de Jesús, sus discípulos estaban reunidos en una casa de Jerusalén. De pronto, la casa se llenó de un ruido como el del viento. Lenguas de fuego se posaron sobre cada uno de ellos. Todos quedaron llenos del Espíritu Santo y comenzaron a hablar en lenguas que no conocían.

Ese día había muchos judíos en Jerusalén provenientes de todas partes del mundo. Escucharon predicar a los Apóstoles y se asombraron porque las personas de Galilea hablaban en su lengua natal y ellos podían entender lo que decían.

Basado en *Hechos 2, 1–12*

¿Qué ocurrió después de que el Espíritu Santo descendió sobre los Apóstoles el día de Pentecostés?

One Church

Focus **What makes the Catholic Church holy?**

People from many different countries were united when the Holy Spirit came to followers of Jesus on **Pentecost**. Pentecost is the beginning of the Church. From that day on, the people understood more clearly that they were one body of believers who had been made holy.

SCRIPTURE Acts 2:1–12

The Feast of Pentecost

Fifty days after Jesus was raised from the dead, his followers were together in a house in Jerusalem. Suddenly the house was filled with a noise like wind. Tongues of fire came to rest on each person in the room. All were filled with the Holy Spirit. They began speaking languages that they did not know.

Jerusalem was filled with Jews from all over the world that day. They heard the Apostles preaching. They were amazed that they could understand people from Galilee in their own languages.

Based on *Acts 2:1–12*

What happened after the Holy Spirit came to the Apostles at Pentecost?

Unidos en la fe

Hoy día, el Espíritu Santo aún mantiene unida a la Iglesia y la santifica. El Espíritu Santo también guía a los líderes de la Iglesia y te guía a ti para que estés más cerca de Jesús.

Los católicos de todo el mundo están unidos por su fe en Cristo. La Iglesia también está unida con los santos, personas consagradas a Dios que están con Él en el cielo. La Iglesia honra a los santos, especialmente a María, la madre de Jesús, por su santidad. Los cristianos pueden aprender del ejemplo de los santos.

La Iglesia también es conocida como la **comunión de los santos**. Esto significa que todos los miembros de la Iglesia, en la tierra, en el purgatorio y en el cielo, están unidos. Los santos te acompañan en la adoración al Padre, al Hijo y al Espíritu Santo.

¿A quién conoces que pertenezca a la comunión de los santos?

Palabras de fe

Pentecostés celebra la venida del Espíritu Santo cincuenta días después de la Pascua.

La **comunión de los santos** está formada por todos los que han sido redimidos por Jesús: personas que están en la tierra, personas que han muerto y están en el purgatorio, y los santos, que están en el cielo.

Anuncia la Buena Nueva El Espíritu Santo dio a los discípulos el valor suficiente para que comunicaran la Buena Nueva de Jesús. Escribe alguna de las noticias que conforman la Buena Nueva. Coméntala con tu clase.

____

____

United in Faith

The Holy Spirit continues to unify the Church today and make it holy. The Spirit guides the leaders of the Church. The Spirit guides you to follow Jesus more closely.

Catholics all over the world are united by their faith in Christ. The Church is even united with the saints, holy people of faith who are with God in heaven. The Church honors the saints, especially Mary, the Mother of Jesus, for their holiness. Christians can learn from the examples of the saints.

The Church is sometimes called the **communion of saints**. This means that the members of the Church on earth, in purgatory, and in heaven are all united. The saints join you in worshiping the Father, the Son, and the Holy Spirit.

? Whom do you know who belongs to the communion of saints?

Words of Faith

Pentecost celebrates the coming of the Holy Spirit fifty days after Easter.

The **communion of saints** is made up of everyone who has been redeemed by Jesus—people on earth, people who have died and are in purgatory, and the saints in heaven.

Connect Your Faith

Tell the Good News The Holy Spirit made the disciples brave enough to share the good news of Jesus. Write some good news of Jesus that you think they may have shared. Tell your class.

____

____

Oración de petición

Oremos

Reúnanse y comiencen con la señal de la cruz.

Líder: Ven, Espíritu Santo, llena los corazones de tus fieles.

Todos: Y enciende en ellos el fuego de tu amor.

Líder: Envía, Señor, tu Espíritu y todo será de nuevo creado.

Todos: Y renovarás la faz de la tierra.

Líder: Oh Dios, que has iluminado los corazones de los fieles con la luz del Espíritu Santo; haznos dóciles a las inspiraciones del mismo Espíritu para gustar siempre del bien y gozar de su consuelo.

Todos: Te lo pedimos en nombre de Cristo nuestro Señor. Amén.

Líder: Oremos.

Inclinen la cabeza mientras el líder reza.

Todos: Amén.

Canten juntos.

Veni Sancte Spiritus;
Veni Sancte Spiritus;
Veni, veni, Sancte Spiritus;
Veni Sancte Spiritus.

Prayer of Petition

Let Us Pray

Gather and begin with the Sign of the Cross.

Leader: Come, Holy Spirit, fill the hearts of your faithful.

All: **And kindle in them the fire of your love.**

Leader: Send forth your Spirit and they shall be created.

All: **And you will renew the face of the earth.**

Leader: Lord, by the light of the Holy Spirit you have taught the hearts of your faithful. In the same Spirit, help us choose what is right and always rejoice in your consolation.

All: **We ask this through Christ our Lord. Amen.**

Leader: Let us pray.

Bow your heads as the leader prays.

All: **Amen.**

Sing together.

Veni Sancte Spiritus;
Veni Sancte Spiritus;
Veni, veni, Sancte Spiritus;
Veni Sancte Spiritus.

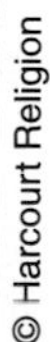

Repasar y aplicar

Comprueba lo que aprendiste Encierra en un círculo la palabra Verdadero si el enunciado es verdadero o la palabra Falso si el enunciado es falso. Corrige los enunciados falsos.

1. Hoy día, el Espíritu Santo une a la Iglesia.
   Verdadero Falso ______________________________
2. Los santos son personas consagradas a Dios.
   Verdadero Falso ______________________________
3. La Iglesia se conoce como la comunión de los santos porque solo los santos pueden recibir la Comunión.
   Verdadero Falso ______________________________
4. La comunión de los santos está conformada solo por personas que han muerto.
   Verdadero Falso ______________________________
5. La fiesta de Pentecostés se celebra cincuenta días después de la Pascua.
   Verdadero Falso ______________________________

Actividad Vive tu fe

Diseña un estandarte Usa palabras y acciones que describan al Espíritu Santo. Piensa primero en lo que hace el Espíritu Santo.

Palabras	Acciones
____________________	____________________
____________________	____________________
____________________	____________________

Review and Apply

Check Understanding Circle True if a statement is true, and circle False if a statement is false. Correct any false statements.

1. The Holy Spirit unifies the Church today.

   True False ____________________

2. Saints are holy people of faith.

   True False ____________________

3. The Church is called the communion of saints because only saints can receive Communion.

   True False ____________________

4. The communion of saints is made up entirely of people who have died.

   True False ____________________

5. Pentecost is celebrated fifty days after Easter.

   True False ____________________

Activity Live Your Faith

Design a Banner Use words and actions that describe the Holy Spirit. Think first of what the Holy Spirit does.

Words	Actions
____________________	____________________
____________________	____________________
____________________	____________________

CAPÍTULO 11

La fe en familia

Lo que creemos

- El Espíritu Santo une y santifica a la Iglesia.
- La unidad de la Iglesia resulta de la fusión de muchas culturas.

LA SAGRADA ESCRITURA

Juan 20, 21–23 narra que Jesús concedió el don del Espíritu Santo a sus discípulos para que los guiara en la tierra.

Visita **www.harcourtreligion.com** para encontrar recursos basados en el año litúrgico y lecturas semanales de la Sagrada Escritura.

Actividad

Vive tu fe

La santidad en el hogar La familia es la iglesia del hogar. Esto significa que debe ser una y santa. Comenta cuál es la mejor muestra de unidad que existe en tu familia y cómo puedes hacerla más fuerte. Pide al Espíritu Santo que te ayude. El Espíritu es tu fuente de santidad.

Siervos de la fe

▲ Santa Perpetua y Santa Felícitas murieron c. 202–203 d.C.

Perpetua y **Felícitas** murieron juntas a causa de su fe, en África del Norte. Perpetua era una mujer de origen noble que se convirtió al cristianismo. En su diario íntimo relató sus sufrimientos en prisión debido a su fe. Felícitas era una mujer esclava y cristiana. Ambas eran madres jóvenes. Mientras estaban en prisión se ayudaron y consolaron mutuamente. Su día se celebra el 7 de marzo.

Una oración en familia

Santa Perpetua y Santa Felícitas, rueguen por nosotros para que podamos estar unidos con otros creyentes en una Iglesia santa. Amén.

 CIC *Consulta el catecismo de la Iglesia Católica, números 813 y 814, para obtener más información sobre el contenido del capítulo.*

CHAPTER 11

Family Faith

Catholics Believe

- The Holy Spirit unites the Church and makes it holy.
- Many cultures together make up the unity of the Church.

SCRIPTURE

John 20:21–23 tells of Jesus' gift of the Holy Spirit to guide his followers on earth.

GO ONLINE **www.harcourtreligion.com** For weekly Scripture readings and seasonal resources

Activity

Live Your Faith

Holy at Home The family is the church of the home. That means that you are called to be one and holy. Discuss the best way that your family shows unity and one thing that would make your family a stronger unit. Ask the Holy Spirit to help you. The Spirit is the source of your holiness.

People of Faith

▲ Saints Perpetua and Felicity died c. A.D. 202–203

Perpetua and **Felicity** died together for their faith in northern Africa. Perpetua was a noblewoman who became a Christian. She kept a journal recording what happened to her in prison because of her faith. Felicity was a slave and a Christian. Both women were young mothers. They helped and comforted each other during their time in prison. Their feast day is March 7.

Family Prayer

Saints Perpetua and Felicity, pray for us to unite with other believers into a holy Church. Amen.

CCC *See Catechism of the Catholic Church 813, 814 for further reading on chapter content.*

Capítulo 12 La misión de la Iglesia

Oremos

Líder: Jesús, ayúdanos a comunicar tu mensaje.
"Mas por todo el orbe se capta su ritmo,
y el mensaje llega hasta el
fin del mundo".

Salmo 19,5

Todos: Jesús, ayúdanos a comunicar tu mensaje. Amén.

Actividad Comencemos

Cumplir una misión Una misión es un trabajo o tarea especial que alguien realiza.

Había una vez un niño campesino que se propuso como misión encontrar un tesoro. Por el camino tenía que atravesar un bosque peligroso, pero un duende valiente le ofreció ayuda.

- ¿Qué crees que pasó después? Piensa en un final para el relato.

Chapter 12

The Church's Mission

Let Us Pray

Leader: Jesus, help us share your message.

"Yet their report goes forth through
all the earth,
their message, to the ends of
the world."

Psalm 19:5

All: Jesus, help us share your message. Amen.

Activity Let's Begin

On a Mission A mission is a particular job or duty that someone undertakes.

Once there was a farm boy who set off on a mission to find a treasure. The farm boy had to pass through a dangerous forest along the way, but a brave elf offered to help.

- What happens next in the story? Think of an ending to complete the story.

Plantar las semillas

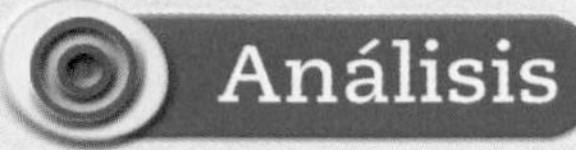

¿Qué semillas siembran los cristianos?

El relato anterior trata sobre un niño que fue a cumplir una misión. Lee este otro relato sobre un hombre que descubrió su verdadera misión.

UN RELATO

El trabajo de Juanito

"¿Quién está durmiendo bajo nuestro manzano?".

"No lo despiertes", le dijo su mamá.

El anciano abrió los ojos y dijo: "Me encanta ver las flores de los manzanos. Me recuerdan que pronto vendrán cosas buenas".

"Usted es Juanito Manzano. ¡Usted fue el que plantó semillas de manzano por todos lados! Papá dice que plantó algunas aquí".

"Sí. Llevo más de treinta años viajando y sembrando. Planté estos árboles hace mucho tiempo. ¡Deben de dar muchas manzanas!".

"Dan muchísimas. ¿Le gustaría tomar algunas?", preguntó Guille.

"Pues sí, muchas gracias. Por eso planto árboles: para que nadie pase hambre".

¿En qué se parece este relato a las enseñanzas de Jesús?

Planting the Seeds

Focus What seeds do Christians plant?

The opening story was about someone on a mission. Here is another story about a man who discovered his true mission.

A STORY

Johnny's Job

"Who's asleep under our apple tree?"

"Don't wake him," said Willie's mom.

The old man's eyes opened. He said, "I love to see apple blossoms. They remind me that good things are coming soon."

"You're Johnny Appleseed. You planted apple seeds everywhere! Dad said you planted some here."

"Yes. I've traveled and planted for over thirty years. I planted these trees long ago. They must give lots of apples!"

"They do. Would you like some?" Willie asked.

"I would love some. That's why I plant trees—so no one will be hungry."

? How does this story remind you of Jesus' teachings?

Comunicar la Buena Nueva de Dios

Juanito Manzano viajaba de un lado a otro con la misión de llevar a todos las cosas buenas de la tierra. Así, el apóstol Pablo viajaba con la misión de fundar nuevas comunidades cristianas. Después escribía cartas a esas comunidades para seguir comunicando la Buena Nueva de Dios.

LA SAGRADA ESCRITURA — I Corintios 3, 5–9

Hacer la obra de Dios

¿Quién es Pablo? ¿Quién es Apolo? Somos ministros mediante los cuales ustedes se hicieron creyentes. Yo planté la semilla. Mi ayudante Apolo la regó. Después, Dios la hizo crecer. El que planta y el que riega no son tan importantes como Dios, porque es Dios quien hace que las cosas crezcan. Apolo y yo somos ayudantes de Dios, y ustedes son el campo de Dios.

Basado en *I Corintios 3, 5–9*

¿Qué semilla plantó el apóstol Pablo?

Actividad — Comparte tu fe

Piensa: Recuerda alguna de las buenas obras que hayas hecho para fortalecer a la Iglesia.

Comunica: En un grupo pequeño, habla acerca de algunas de esas obras.

Actúa: Dibuja un manzano en una hoja. Agrégale una manzana cada vez que hagas una buena obra.

Sharing God's Good News

Johnny Appleseed traveled on a mission to share the good things of the earth. The Apostle Paul traveled on a mission to start new Christian communities. He wrote letters back to these communities, continuing to share the good news about God.

SCRIPTURE I Corinthians 3:5–9

Doing God's Work

Who is Paul? Who is Apollos? We are ministers through whom you became believers. I planted the seed. My helper Apollos watered the seed. Then God made the seed grow. The planter and the waterer are not nearly as important as God is, because it is God who makes things grow. Apollos and I are God's coworkers. You are God's field.

Based on *I Corinthians 3:5–9*

What was the seed that the Apostle Paul planted?

Activity Share Your Faith

Think: Remember some of the good works you have done to make the Church stronger.

Share: In a small group, tell about some of these works.

Act: Draw an apple tree on a separate sheet of paper. Add a new apple each time you do a good work.

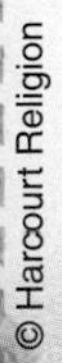

La Iglesia es católica

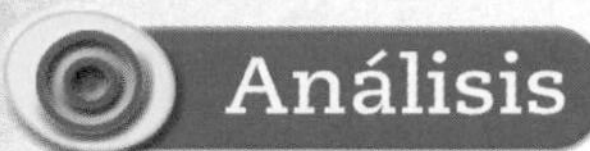

¿Cómo cumple la Iglesia su misión?

Pablo ayudó a los primeros cristianos a entender que la Iglesia es para todos. La Iglesia es católica porque es para todas las personas de todas las épocas y lugares. La palabra *católica* significa "universal" o "en todas partes".

La Iglesia es apostólica porque Jesús dio a sus Apóstoles la **misión** de comunicar su Buena Nueva a las personas de todos los lugares del mundo.

La palabra *misión* también significa una comunidad de la Iglesia en otro país o en un lugar remoto en el que las personas necesitan oír la palabra de Dios. A veces, el término se utiliza también para describir una iglesia poco numerosa.

Los **misioneros** son personas que viajan para comunicar la Buena Nueva de Jesús, tal como hizo Pablo. Tú puedes ayudar a los misioneros de la Iglesia orando por ellos y por las personas con las que trabajan. Puedes también escribirles cartas y ayudar a recaudar dinero para las cosas que necesiten.

¿Qué pueden hacer los católicos para continuar la misión de la Iglesia?

The Church Is Catholic

How does the Church fulfill its mission?

Paul helped the early Christians know that the Church was for everyone. The Church is catholic because it is for all people in all times and places. The word *catholic* means "universal" or "everywhere."

The Church is apostolic because Jesus gave his Apostles the **mission** of sharing his good news with people all over the world.

The word *mission* also means a church community in another country or in a remote place where people need to hear the word of God. The term is sometimes used to describe a church with few members.

Missionaries are people who travel to share Jesus' good news, just as Paul did. You can help the Church's missionaries by praying for them and the people with whom they work. You can write letters to them and help raise money for things that the missionaries need.

? What can Catholics do to continue the Church's mission?

Compartir con los demás

Al mismo tiempo que comunican la Buena Nueva de Jesús, los misioneros comparten comida, refugio y medicamentos, entre otras cosas, con las personas que necesitan su ayuda. Es algo importante, porque de este modo cubren las necesidades básicas de esas personas. Los cristianos siempre han compartido sus bienes y se han preocupado por las necesidades de los demás.

Dios no solo quiere que compartas cosas materiales, como la comida, sino también cosas espirituales o sagradas. Por eso, los misioneros cristianos enseñan acerca de Jesús y construyen iglesias, hospitales y escuelas. Quieren que todas las personas de todos los lugares oigan la Buena Nueva de Dios.

¿Cómo puedes comunicar la Buena Nueva a los demás?

Palabras de fe

Una **misión** es un trabajo o tarea de la que una persona se hace responsable. La misión de la Iglesia es anunciar la Buena Nueva del Reino de Dios.

Los **misioneros** son personas que viajan para comunicar la Buena Nueva de Jesús.

Actividad Practica tu fe

Haz la obra de Dios Investiga qué persona de tu parroquia o diócesis está sirviendo a Dios como misionero o misionera en otro país o en un lugar lejano de este país. En una hoja, dibuja una tarjeta para esa persona y escríbele un mensaje de agradecimiento.

Sharing with Others

Along with spreading the good news of Jesus, missionaries also share food, shelter, medical supplies, and other things with the people who need their help. These things are important because they provide for people's basic needs. Christians have always shared with others and been concerned for their needs.

God wants you to share not only physical things, such as food, but also spiritual, or holy, things. That is why Christian missionaries teach the people about Jesus and build churches, hospitals, and schools. They want to be sure that people everywhere hear God's good news.

How can you share the good news with other people?

Words of Faith

A **mission** is a job or duty that someone takes responsibility for. The Church's mission is to announce the good news of God's kingdom.

Missionaries are people who travel to share Jesus' good news.

Activity Connect Your Faith

Do God's Work Find out who in your parish or diocese is serving God as a missionary in another country or in a faraway place in this country. On a separate sheet of paper, design a card for him or her and add a note of thanks.

Oración de petición

Reúnanse y comiencen con la señal de la cruz.

Líder: Querido Jesús, ayúdanos a ser como san Pablo.

Grupo 1: Ayúdanos a escucharte como lo hizo Pablo.

Todos: Ayúdanos, Señor.

Grupo 2: Ayúdanos a hablar a los demás de tu amor.

Todos: Ayúdanos, Señor.

Grupo 1: Ayúdanos a ser signos de tu amor para los demás.

Todos: Ayúdanos, Señor.

Líder: Señor Jesús, gracias por darnos a tus misioneros como regalo.

Todos: Gracias, Señor. Amén.

Líder: Oremos.

Inclinen la cabeza mientras el líder reza.

Todos: Amén.

Canten juntos.

El mensaje del Señor llega a toda la tierra.

Salmo 18 (19) Leccionario III © 1998 OBRA NACIONAL DE LA BUENA PRENSA, A.C.

Asking Prayer

Gather and begin with the Sign of the Cross.

Leader: Dear Jesus, help us be like Saint Paul.

Group 1: Help us listen to you as Paul did.

All: **Help us, O Lord.**

Group 2: Help us tell people about your love.

All: **Help us, O Lord.**

Group 1: Help us be signs of your love to others.

All: **Help us, O Lord.**

Leader: Lord Jesus, thank you for the gift of your missionaries.

All: **Thank you, Lord. Amen.**

Leader: Let us pray.

Bow your heads as the leader prays.

All: **Amen.**

Sing together.

Their message goes out through all the earth.

"Psalm 19: Their Message Goes Out"
© 1969, 1981, and 1997, ICEL

Repasar y aplicar

A **Comprueba lo que aprendiste** Encierra en un círculo o escribe la respuesta correcta.

1. ¿Cómo comunicó Pablo la Buena Nueva?
   - **a.** Visitando a los nuevos cristianos y escribiéndoles cartas.
   - **b.** Escribiendo en un periódico.
   - **c.** Entregando biblias a todos sus amigos.
2. ¿Cuál es la tarea de los misioneros?
   - **a.** Recaudar dinero.
   - **b.** Plantar manzanos.
   - **c.** Comunicar el mensaje de Dios a todo el mundo.
3. ¿Cómo participas de la misión de la Iglesia?

   ____

   ____
4. ¿Por qué la Iglesia se llama *católica?*

   ____

   ____
5. ¿En qué se parecen la misión de Juanito Manzano y la de Pablo? ______________________________

   ____

Actividad Vive tu fe

Comunica la Buena Nueva Escribe una nota a un amigo en la que le hables de la Buena Nueva de Jesús.

____

____

____

Review and Apply

A Check Understanding Circle or write the correct response.

1. How did Paul share the good news?
   - a. by visiting and writing letters to new Christians
   - b. by writing for a newspaper
   - c. by giving Bibles to all of his friends
2. What is the job of missionaries?
   - a. to take up collections
   - b. to plant apples
   - c. to share God's message around the world
3. How do you share in the mission of the Church?

   ____

   ____
4. Why is the Church called *catholic*?

   ____

   ____
5. How were the missions of Johnny Appleseed and Paul alike? ______________________________

   ____

Activity Live Your Faith

Share Good News Write a note to a friend telling good news about Jesus.

____

____

____

La fe en familia

Lo que creemos

- La misión de la Iglesia es comunicar la Buena Nueva de Jesús a todos los pueblos.
- La Iglesia es católica porque está en todas partes y recibe a todos.

LA SAGRADA ESCRITURA

Lee *Mateo 28, 19–20*, los versículos con las instrucciones que dio Jesús a sus discípulos después de su Resurrección.

APRENDE en línea

Visita **www.harcourtreligion.com** para encontrar recursos basados en el año litúrgico y lecturas semanales de la Sagrada Escritura.

Actividad

Vive tu fe

Recibe a los demás La Iglesia muestra que es católica, o universal, al recibir a todos como miembros. Al igual que la Iglesia, puedes recibir a todos como hermanos y hermanas en la familia de Dios. En familia, trabajen en un proyecto de bienvenida para alguien que sea nuevo en la parroquia o que haya llegado de visita desde otro país.

▲ **Beato José Vaz 1651–1711**

Siervos de la fe

José Vaz nació en India. Fue sacerdote misionero en Ceilán, donde no se permitía a los católicos practicar su fe. Vestía como un campesino y celebraba los sacramentos. Cuando estuvo en la cárcel, llevó la palabra de Dios a los otros presos. Más adelante animó a otros misioneros a ir a Ceilán. Su día se celebra el 16 de enero.

Una oración en familia

Querido Dios, ayúdanos a difundir la Buena Nueva de Jesús y apoyar a quienes llevan nuestra fe a otras personas. Amén.

CIC *Consulta el Catecismo de la Iglesia Católica, números 830 y 831, para obtener más información sobre el contenido del capítulo.*

CHAPTER 12

Family Faith

Catholics Believe

- The Church's mission is to share Jesus' good news with the people of all nations.
- The Church is catholic because it is everywhere and welcomes everyone.

SCRIPTURE

Read *Matthew 28:19–20,* verses that contain Jesus' instructions to his disciples after his Resurrection.

www.harcourtreligion.com
For weekly Scripture readings and seasonal resources

Activity

Live Your Faith

Welcome Others The Church shows that it is catholic, or universal, by welcoming all people as members. Like the Church, you can welcome all people as brothers and sisters in God's family. As a family, work on a welcome project for a parishioner who is new to the parish or who is visiting from another country.

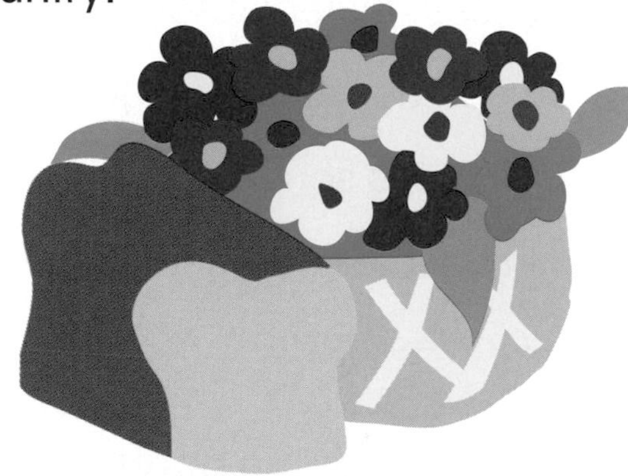

People of Faith

▲ Blessed Joseph Vaz 1651–1711

Joseph Vaz was born in India. He became a missionary priest to Ceylon, where Catholics were not allowed to practice their faith. He dressed as a peasant and celebrated the sacraments. He brought the word of God to his fellow prisoners. Later he brought more missionaries to Ceylon. His feast day is January 16.

Family Prayer

Dear God, help us spread the good news of Jesus and support those who share the faith. Amen.

CCC *See Catechism of the Catholic Church 830, 831 for further reading on chapter content.*

Repaso de la Unidad 4

A Trabaja con palabras Responde a cada pregunta con la palabra correcta del vocabulario.

VOCABULARIO

misioneros
Apóstoles
obispos
Pentecostés
misión

1. Viajamos para comunicar la Buena Nueva de Jesús. ¿Quiénes somos?

   ____

2. En esta fiesta se celebra la venida del Espíritu Santo. ¿Cuál es?

   ____

3. Somos los primeros doce discípulos de Jesús. ¿Quiénes somos? ____________________

4. Ayudamos al papa a guiar a la Iglesia. ¿Quiénes somos? ____________________

5. Un trabajo o tarea de la que una persona se hace responsable. ¿Qué es? ____________________

B Comprueba lo que aprendiste Empareja cada descripción de la columna 1 con el término correcto de la columna 2.

Columna 1		Columna 2
______	6. Está formada por todos los redimidos por Jesús.	a. papa
______	7. Se celebra cincuenta días después de la Pascua.	b. comunión de los santos
______	8. Dirige una parroquia.	c. Pedro
______	9. Proviene de una palabra italiana que significa "padre".	d. párroco
______	10. Es el nuevo nombre que Jesús dio a Simón.	e. Pentecostés

Unit 4 Review

A Work with Words Answer each question with the correct word from the Word Bank.

WORD BANK
missionaries
Apostles
bishops
Pentecost
mission

1. We travel to share Jesus' good news. Who are we? ____________

2. This feast celebrates the coming of the Holy Spirit. What is it?

   ____

3. We are the first twelve followers of Jesus. Who are we? ____________

4. We work with the pope in guiding the Church. Who are we? ____________

5. This is a job or duty for which someone is responsible.

   What is it? ____________

B Check Understanding Match each description in Column 1 with the correct term in Column 2.

Column 1

_____ 6. made up of everyone redeemed by Jesus

_____ 7. celebrated fifty days after Easter

_____ 8. leads a parish

_____ 9. comes from an Italian word meaning "father"

_____ 10. new name that Jesus gave to Simon

Column 2

a. pope

b. communion of saints

c. Peter

d. pastor

e. Pentecost

UNIDAD 5

La Iglesia dirige

Capítulo 13

Decide amar

¿Cuál es la ley del amor de Jesús?

Capítulo 14

Comparte tu luz

¿Cómo te da Dios fe, esperanza y amor?

Capítulo 15

La Iglesia nos guía

¿Cómo te ayuda la Iglesia a tomar buenas decisiones?

¿Qué crees que vas a aprender en esta unidad acerca de cómo dirige la Iglesia?

UNIT 5
The Church Leads

Choose Love
What is Jesus' law of love?

Share Your Light
How does God give you faith, hope, and love?

The Church Guides
How does the Church help you make right choices?

What do you think you will learn in this unit about how the Church leads?

Capítulo 13 Decide amar

Líder: Dios bondadoso, guíanos con tu ley del amor.
"La ley del Señor es perfecta,
es remedio para el alma".
Salmo 19, 8

Todos: Dios bondadoso, guíanos con tu ley del amor.
Amén.

Actividad Comencemos

¿Cuál de todas?

Lindas cajas envueltas en papel.
Elige una para abrirla después.
¿Cuál elegir? ¿Cuál dejar?
¿Cuál crees que te va a gustar?

- ¿Qué regalo elegirías? Explica el motivo de tu decisión.

Chapter 13 Choose Love

Let Us Pray

Leader: Loving God, guide us with your law of love.
"The law of the LORD is perfect,
refreshing the soul."

Psalm 19:8

All: Loving God, guide us with your law of love.
Amen.

Activity Let's Begin

Which One?

Pretty boxes wrapped in paper.
Pick one box to open later.
Which to choose? Which to leave?
Can you guess which one will please?

- Tell which present you would choose. Give a reason for your choice.

Aprender a perdonar

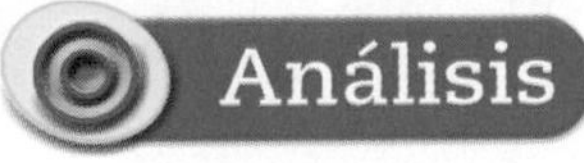

¿Cómo demostró José que podía perdonar?

Decidir qué regalo abrir es fácil. A lo largo de tu vida, tendrás que tomar decisiones mucho más difíciles. Esta carta cuenta la historia de un hombre que tomó una decisión difícil después de haber sido separado de su familia. Está basada en un relato del Antiguo Testamento.

UNA CARTA

El padre y los hermanos de José

Querido padre:

Espero que te encuentres bien. Tengo buenas noticias para ti. ¡Soy tu hijo, José, y estoy vivo!

Hace mucho tiempo, tú me enviaste a ayudar a mis hermanos a cuidar tus ovejas. Ellos estaban celosos porque tú me amabas mucho, y por eso me vendieron como esclavo. Después te dijeron que yo había muerto.

Fui esclavo en Egipto. Estuve a cargo del almacenamiento y la distribución de comida porque era muy trabajador y sabía interpretar los sueños. Un día, cuando la familia necesitaba alimentos, enviaste a mis hermanos a pedirlos en Egipto. Ellos no me reconocieron porque habían pasado muchos años.

Al principio no les dije quién era yo, pues todavía estaba enojado con ellos. Entonces me dijeron que tú estabas vivo.

Learning to Forgive

How did Joseph show forgiveness?

Choosing which present to open is easy. During your life you will have to make much harder choices. This letter tells the story of a man who made a difficult choice after he was separated from his family. It is based on a story from the Old Testament.

A LETTER

Joseph's Father and Brothers

Dear Father,

I hope this letter finds you well. I have great news for you. I am your son Joseph, and I am alive!

Long ago, you sent me to help my brothers tend your sheep. They were jealous because you loved me so much, so my brothers sold me as a slave. Then they told you that I was dead.

I was a slave in Egypt. I was put in charge of storing and giving out food because I worked hard and could explain dreams. One day, when the family needed food, you sent my brothers to Egypt to ask for it. They did not recognize me because so many years had passed.

At first, I did not tell them who I was. I was still angry with them. Then they told me that you were alive. I left the room

Salí de la habitación porque no quería que me vieran llorar. ¡Te he extrañado tanto!

Al final, les dije quién era. Se sorprendieron y se pusieron contentos. Los perdoné, y espero que tú hagas lo mismo.

Con cariño,
José

¿Cómo crees que se sintió José cuando volvió a ver a sus hermanos?

¿Qué otras decisiones podría haber tomado José?

Actividad Comparte tu fe

Piensa: ¿Cómo crees que se sintieron los hermanos de José cuando les dijo quién era?

Comunica: Habla con tu grupo acerca de lo que los hermanos podrían haberle dicho a José.

Actúa: Representa la escena en clase.

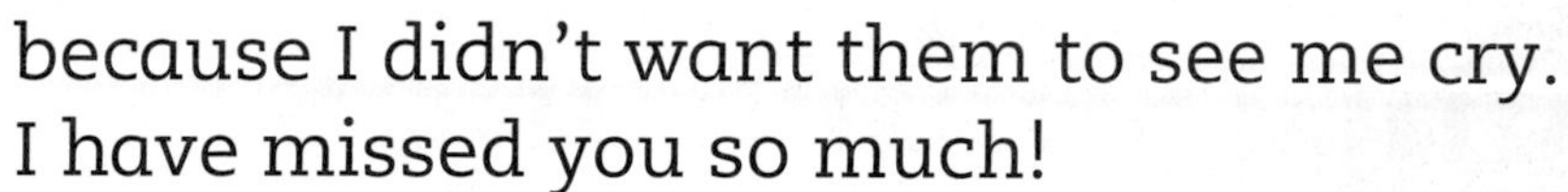

because I didn't want them to see me cry. I have missed you so much!

Finally, I told them who I was. They were surprised and happy. I have forgiven them, and I hope that you will, too.

Love,
Joseph

How do you think Joseph felt when he saw his brothers again?

What other choices could Joseph have made?

Activity Share Your Faith

Think: How do you think Joseph's brothers felt when Joseph told them who he was?

Share: Talk with your group about what the brothers might have said to Joseph.

Act: Act out this scene for your class.

Amarse los unos a los otros

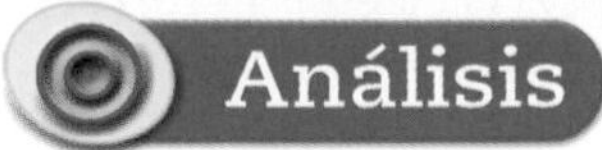

¿Por qué es necesario que ames y perdones?

José eligió perdonar a sus hermanos porque los amaba. Mucho antes de la época de Jesús, José mostró cómo amar a quienes nos ofenden. Un día, Jesús estaba hablando con sus discípulos sobre cómo tratar a las personas.

LA SAGRADA ESCRITURA — Mateo 5, 43–48

Ama a tu enemigo

A ustedes les han enseñado a amar a los amigos y odiar a los enemigos. Pero ahora yo les digo: Amen a sus enemigos y recen por quienes los ofenden. Si hacen eso, serán hijos de Dios. Dios no quiere que hagan solamente lo que es fácil. Si solo son amables con las personas que son amables con ustedes, ¿qué tiene eso de especial? Así se comportan las personas que no conocen a Dios. Ustedes deben ser perfectos, como Dios es perfecto.

Basado en *Mateo 5,43–48*

Jesús dijo que es más fácil amar a quienes nos aman. ¡También dijo que debemos amar a nuestros enemigos! Eso nos puede resultar tan difícil como fue para José perdonar a sus hermanos.

¿Alguna vez lastimaste a alguien con tus actos?

¿De qué maneras puedes vivir las enseñanzas de Jesús?

Love One Another

Focus **Why do you need to be loving and forgiving?**

Joseph chose to forgive his brothers because he loved them. Long before the time of Jesus, Joseph showed how to love those who hurt you. One day, Jesus was talking with his followers about how to treat people. This is what he told them.

SCRIPTURE **Matthew 5:43–48**

Love Your Enemy

You have been told to love your friends and hate your enemies. But now I am telling you: Love your enemies, and pray for people who hurt you. This will make you children of God. God doesn't want you to do only what is easy. If you are friendly only to people who are friendly to you, why is that special? People who know nothing about God do that. You must be perfect as God is perfect.

Based on *Matthew 5:43–48*

Jesus said that it is easier to love those who love you. He also said that you must love your enemies! That can be as difficult for people as it was for Joseph to forgive his brothers.

- **Have you ever acted in a hurtful way towards others?**
- **What are some ways that you can live out Jesus' teaching?**

La ley del amor

Las principales enseñanzas de Jesús se refieren al amor y la atención que estás llamado a mostrar a los demás. En una enseñanza llamada las **Bienaventuranzas**, Jesús dijo que los que trabajan por la paz y son compasivos son bendecidos por Dios. La **ley del amor** de Jesús resume los Diez Mandamientos y las Bienaventuranzas en un solo enunciado: "Que se amen los unos a los otros. Ustedes deben amarse unos a otros como yo los he amado" (*Juan 13, 34*).

Palabras de fe

Las **Bienaventuranzas** son enseñanzas de Jesús que muestran el camino de la verdadera felicidad y te dicen cómo vivir en el Reino de Dios.

La **ley del amor** de Jesús resume los Diez Mandamientos y las Bienaventuranzas en un solo enunciado.

Vivir la ley del amor

Los miembros de tu parroquia también tratan de vivir según la ley del amor de Jesús. Probablemente, en tu parroquia hay voluntarios que construyen casas, enseñan a leer o dan de comer a quienes están hambrientos. Ellos trabajan por la paz y la justicia allí donde hace falta, y se esfuerzan mucho para mostrar su amor.

¿Cómo puede ayudarte la ley del amor de Jesús a tomar buenas decisiones?

Practica tu fe

Busca la respuesta Resuelve este acertijo para aprender una lección sobre el amor. Usa el código para poner la letra correcta en cada espacio en blanco y responder a la pregunta.

¿Qué tienen en común estas tres palabras?

D	I	O	S		P	R	Ó	J	I	M	O		E	N	E	M	I	G	O
1	2	3	4		5	6	7	8	9	10	11		12	13	14	15	16	17	18

___ ___ TA ___ ___ ___ LLA ___ A ___ ___ ___
12 4 10 3 4 15 1 11 4

A A ___ A ___ L ___ ___.
15 6 18 4

The Law of Love

Jesus' main teachings are about the love and care you are called to show to others. In a teaching called the **Beatitudes**, Jesus said that those who make peace and show mercy are blessed by God. Jesus' **law of love** sums up the Ten Commandments and the Beatitudes in one statement: "Love one another. As I have loved you, so you also should love one another" *(John 13:34)*.

Words of Faith

The **Beatitudes** are teachings of Jesus that show the way to true happiness and tell how to live in God's kingdom.

Jesus' **law of love** sums up the Ten Commandments and the Beatitudes in one statement.

Living the Law of Love

People in your parish try to live by Jesus' law of love, too. There are probably volunteers who build houses, teach people to read, or give food to people who are hungry. They work for peace and justice wherever there is need. They go out of their way to show their love.

? How can Jesus' law of love help you make good decisions?

Activity Connect Your Faith

Find the Answer Solve this puzzle to learn a lesson about love. Put the correct code letter in each blank to answer the question.

G	O	D	N	E	I	G	H	B	O	R	E	N	E	M	Y
1	2	3	4	5	6	7	8	9	10	11	12	13	14	15	16

What do these three words have in common?

W ___ (5)   A ___ ___ (11 14)   CALL ___ ___ (12 3)

T ___ (2)   L ___ V ___ (10 12)   T ___ ___ ___ (8 14 15).

CELEBRACIÓN Celebrate

Oración de petición

Reúnanse y comiencen con la señal de la cruz.

Líder: Dios Padre nuestro, ayúdanos a amar como hizo Jesús.

Lector: Cuando alguien nos hace algo malo, como los hermanos hicieron con José,

Todos: Ayúdanos a perdonar como hizo José.

Lector: Cuando nos resulta difícil amar,

Todos: Ayúdanos a amar como hizo Jesús.

Líder: Recemos juntos una oración de amor.

Todos: Oh Dios, te amamos sobre todas las cosas, con todo nuestro corazón y con toda nuestra alma, porque eres bueno y mereces todo el amor. Amamos a nuestro prójimo como a nosotros mismos por amor a ti. Perdonamos a quienes nos ofenden y pedimos perdón a quienes hemos ofendido.

Líder: Oremos.

Inclinen la cabeza mientras el líder reza.

Todos: Amén.

Canten juntos.

Ámense uno al otro,
ámense uno al otro
como los he amado yo.

Cuídense uno al otro,
cuídense uno al otro
como los he cuidado yo.

Prayer of Petition

Gather and begin with the Sign of the Cross.

Leader: God our Father, help us love as Jesus did.

Reader: When someone is mean to us, as Joseph's brothers were to him,

All: **Help us forgive as Joseph did.**

Reader: When we find it difficult to love,

All: **Help us love as Jesus did.**

Leader: We pray together an Act of Love.

All: **O God, we love you above all things, with our whole heart and soul, because you are all-good and worthy of all love. We love our neighbor as ourselves for love of you. We forgive all who have injured us and ask pardon of all whom we have injured.**

Leader: Let us pray.

Bow your heads as the leader prays.

All: **Amen.**

Sing together.

Love one another. Love one another, as I have loved you.

Care for each other. Care for each other, as I care for you.

"Love One Another" © 2000, GIA Publications, Inc.

Repasar y aplicar

A Comprueba lo que aprendiste Ordena estos acontecimientos del relato de José escribiendo el número correcto junto a cada enunciado.

_____ José reconoce a sus hermanos y les dice quién es.

_____ Los hermanos venden a José como esclavo.

_____ José es el preferido de su padre. Sus hermanos están celosos.

_____ José perdona a sus hermanos.

_____ A José le va muy bien en Egipto. Llegan sus hermanos a pedirle comida.

B Relaciona ¿Cómo cumples la ley del amor de Jesús?

____

____

____

Actividad Vive tu fe

Da consejos Escribe una sección de consejos para un periódico. En una hoja aparte, inventa un problema que un lector pueda tener en su escuela o en su barrio. Dile cómo la ley del amor de Jesús ayudaría a solucionar las cosas.

Review and Apply

A Check Understanding Put these events from the story of Joseph in order by numbering the sentences correctly.

_____ Joseph recognizes his brothers and tells them who he is.

_____ The brothers sell Joseph as a slave.

_____ Joseph is loved by his father. His brothers are jealous.

_____ Joseph forgives his brothers.

_____ Joseph does well in Egypt. His brothers come to him for food.

B Make Connections How do you follow Jesus' law of love?

____

____

____

Activity Live Your Faith

Give Advice Write an advice column for a newspaper. On a separate sheet of paper, make up a problem that a reader might have in your school or neighborhood. Tell how Jesus' law of love would help make things better.

CAPÍTULO 13

La fe en familia

Lo que creemos

- La ley del amor de Jesús es amar a todas las personas como Él nos ama.
- Jesús nos enseña que debemos amar y perdonar a nuestros enemigos.

LA SAGRADA ESCRITURA

I Corintios 13, 1–7 habla acerca del significado del amor. Piensa en las diferentes maneras en que puedes mostrar tu amor a cada uno de tus familiares.

Visita **www.harcourtreligion.com** para encontrar recursos basados en el año litúrgico y lecturas semanales de la Sagrada Escritura.

Actividad

Vive tu fe

Haz un recordatorio Copia la ley del amor de Jesús en una placa decorativa y cuélgala en un lugar donde tu familia la vea todos los días. Cada semana, dedica un momento con tus padres para hablar sobre la semana que pasó y preguntarse cómo cumplieron con la más importante de las enseñanzas de Jesús.

Que se amen los unos a los otros como yo los he amado.

▲ Beato Bartolomé Osypiuk 1844–1874

Siervos de la fe

Bartolomé Osypiuk fue un mártir católico del rito oriental asesinado en Pratulin, Polonia. Bartolomé estaba casado y tenía dos hijos. Él y sus amigos fueron asesinados por soldados rusos porque se negaron a cumplir las órdenes del emperador sobre religión. Los soldados dispararon a Bartolomé, pero él los perdonó antes de morir.

Una oración en familia

Querido Dios, ayúdanos a perdonar a nuestros enemigos, como hizo Bartolomé Osypiuk. Amén.

 CIC *Consulta el Catecismo de la Iglesia Católica, números 1933 y 1970, para obtener más información sobre el contenido del capítulo.*

Family Faith

Catholics Believe

- Jesus' law of love is to love one another as Jesus loves each of us.
- Jesus teaches that we should love and forgive our enemies.

SCRIPTURE

1 Corinthians 13:1–7 is about the meaning of loving. Think about different ways you can show your love for each family member.

www.harcourtreligion.com
For weekly Scripture readings and seasonal resources

Activity
Live Your Faith

Make a Reminder Copy Jesus' law of love onto a decorative plaque, and hang it in your home where all will see it every day. Each week, sit down and review the past week, asking yourselves how well you have lived up to this central teaching of Jesus.

Love One Another As I Have Loved You

People of Faith

▲ Blessed Bartholomew Osypiuk 1844–1874

Bartholomew Osypiuk was an Eastern Catholic martyr killed in Pratulin, Poland. Bartholomew was married and the father of two children. He and his friends were killed by Russian soldiers because they refused to follow the ruler's commands about religion. The soldiers shot Bartholomew, but he forgave them before he died.

Family Prayer

Dear God, help us learn to forgive our enemies as Bartholomew Osypiuk did. Amen.

CCC See Catechism of the Catholic Church 1933, 1970 for further reading on chapter content.

Capítulo 14 Comparte tu luz

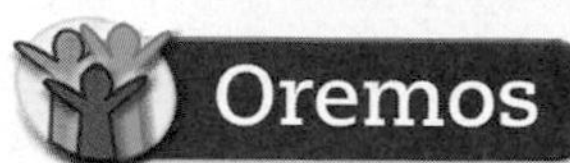

Oremos

Líder: Dios Creador nuestro, ayúdanos a ser una luz en la oscuridad.

"Envíame tu luz y tu verdad:
que ellas sean mi guía".

Salmo 43, 3

Todos: Dios Creador nuestro, ayúdanos a ser una luz en la oscuridad. Amén.

Actividad Comencemos

Vela

Brillante, pequeña
Resplandece, parpadea, danza
Amiga que da consuelo
En la oscuridad de la noche

- ¿En qué sentido puedes ser como una vela para los demás?

Chapter 14 Share Your Light

Let Us Pray

Leader: God our Creator, help us be a light in the darkness.

"Send your light and fidelity,
that they may be my guide."

Psalm 43:3

All: God our Creator, help us be a light in the darkness. Amen.

Activity Let's Begin

Candle

Brilliant, small
Flaming, flickering, dancing
Gives comfort
Friend in the night

- How can you be like a candle for others?

Ser una luz

¿Cómo puedes ser una luz para los demás?

Una vela da luz y aliento. Este es un relato verdadero sobre una joven que, con su luz, animó a los demás.

UN RELATO

La luz de Abbie

"Hija, tengo que ir a buscar provisiones. ¿Crees que tendrás problemas con el faro hasta que yo regrese?", preguntó el padre de Abbie.

"No, pero hay algo que me preocupa: ¿Podré mantener la luz encendida si viene una tormenta?", dijo Abbie.

"Haz todo lo que puedas. Yo tengo fe en ti", le respondió su padre antes de irse.

Esa tarde se desató una tormenta que duró varias semanas. Todos los días, Abbie mantenía la luz encendida para que los barcos pudieran encontrar su rumbo.

Al fin, paró de llover. El padre de Abbie volvió a su casa y abrazó a su hija. "Sabía que podías hacer este trabajo. ¡Estoy muy orgulloso de ti!", exclamó.

? ¿A qué se refería el padre de Abbie cuando le dijo que tenía fe en ella?

Be a Light

How can you be a light to others?

A candle brings light and comfort. This is a true story about a young girl who was a comforting light for others.

A STORY

Abbie's Light

"I have to go get supplies. Do you have any questions about the lighthouse?" asked Abbie's father.

"No. But I worry about keeping the light on in a storm," Abbie said.

"Just do your best. I have faith in you," said her father as he left.

That afternoon, a storm came, and it lasted for weeks. Every day Abbie made sure that the light was shining so that ships could find their way through the storm.

Finally, the storm ended. Her father returned. The two hugged each other. "I knew you could do this job well. I am so proud of you!" Abbie's father said.

What did Abbie's father mean when he said he had faith in her?

La luz del mundo

La luz de Abbie ayudó a los marineros a encontrar su camino hacia la costa. Jesús dijo que debemos ayudar a los demás a encontrar su camino. Un día, Jesús les dijo a sus discípulos lo que el mundo necesitaba de ellos.

LA SAGRADA ESCRITURA **Mateo 5, 14–16**

Deja que brille tu luz

"Ustedes son la luz del mundo", dijo Jesús. "¿Cómo se puede esconder una ciudad asentada sobre un monte?".

Jesús continuó: "Nadie enciende una lámpara para taparla con un cajón; la ponen más bien sobre un candelero, y alumbra a todos los que están en la casa".

Por último dijo: "Hagan, pues, que brille su luz ante los hombres; que vean estas buenas obras, y por ello den gloria al Padre de ustedes que está en los Cielos".

Basado en *Mateo 5, 14–16*

¿Quién ha compartido contigo la luz de Cristo?

Actividad Comparte tu fe

Piensa: ¿Qué buenas acciones has realizado últimamente?

Comunica: Conversa con tu grupo sobre las maneras en que compartiste la luz de Cristo con otras personas.

Actúa: Recorta llamas de papel y escribe una de tus buenas acciones en cada llama. Pega las llamas en un cartel.

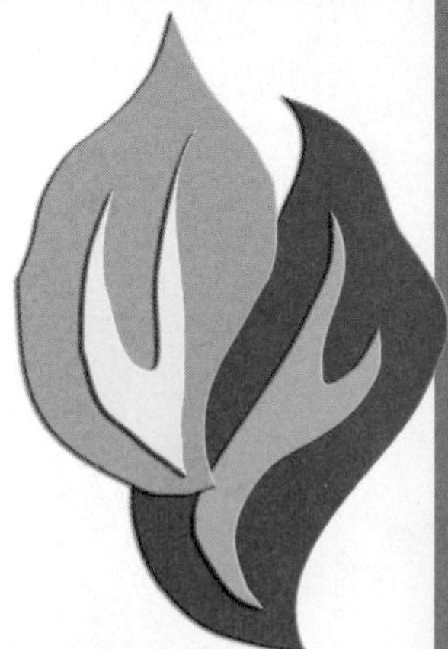

The Light of the World

Abbie's light helped people at sea find their way to shore. Jesus talked about how people should help others find their way. One day Jesus told his followers what the world needed from them.

SCRIPTURE Matthew 5:14–16

Your Light Must Shine

"You are the light of the world," Jesus said. "A city on a mountaintop cannot be hidden."

He went on, "Nor do you light a lamp and then put it under a bushel basket; it is set on a lampstand, where it gives light to all in the house."

Finally he said, "Your light must shine before others, that they may see your good deeds and glorify your heavenly Father."

Based on *Matthew 5:14–16*

? Who has shared the light of Christ with you?

Activity Share Your Faith

Think: What good deeds have you performed lately?

Share: With your group, discuss ways you have shared the light of Christ with someone.

Act: Cut out paper flames and write one of your good deeds on each flame. Glue the flames to a piece of poster board.

Las virtudes

Análisis ¿Cuál es tu guía en la vida?

En algunos aspectos, el relato de Abbie se refiere a las **virtudes** es decir, los hábitos de fe, esperanza y amor.

Tener fe en alguien es creer en esa persona. El padre de Abbie creyó que ella iba a ser capaz de mantener la luz encendida.

Como discípulo de Jesús, tú crees en Él. La verdadera fe es creer en Dios y en todo lo que Dios ha dicho y ha hecho, aunque no lo entiendas totalmente.

Durante la tormenta, Abbie nunca perdió la esperanza de que su padre regresaría. La esperanza es la virtud que te ayuda a confiar en lo que Dios ha revelado. La Iglesia tiene la esperanza de que el mundo se parezca cada vez más al Reino de Dios.

¿Qué te ayuda a mantener la esperanza en momentos difíciles?

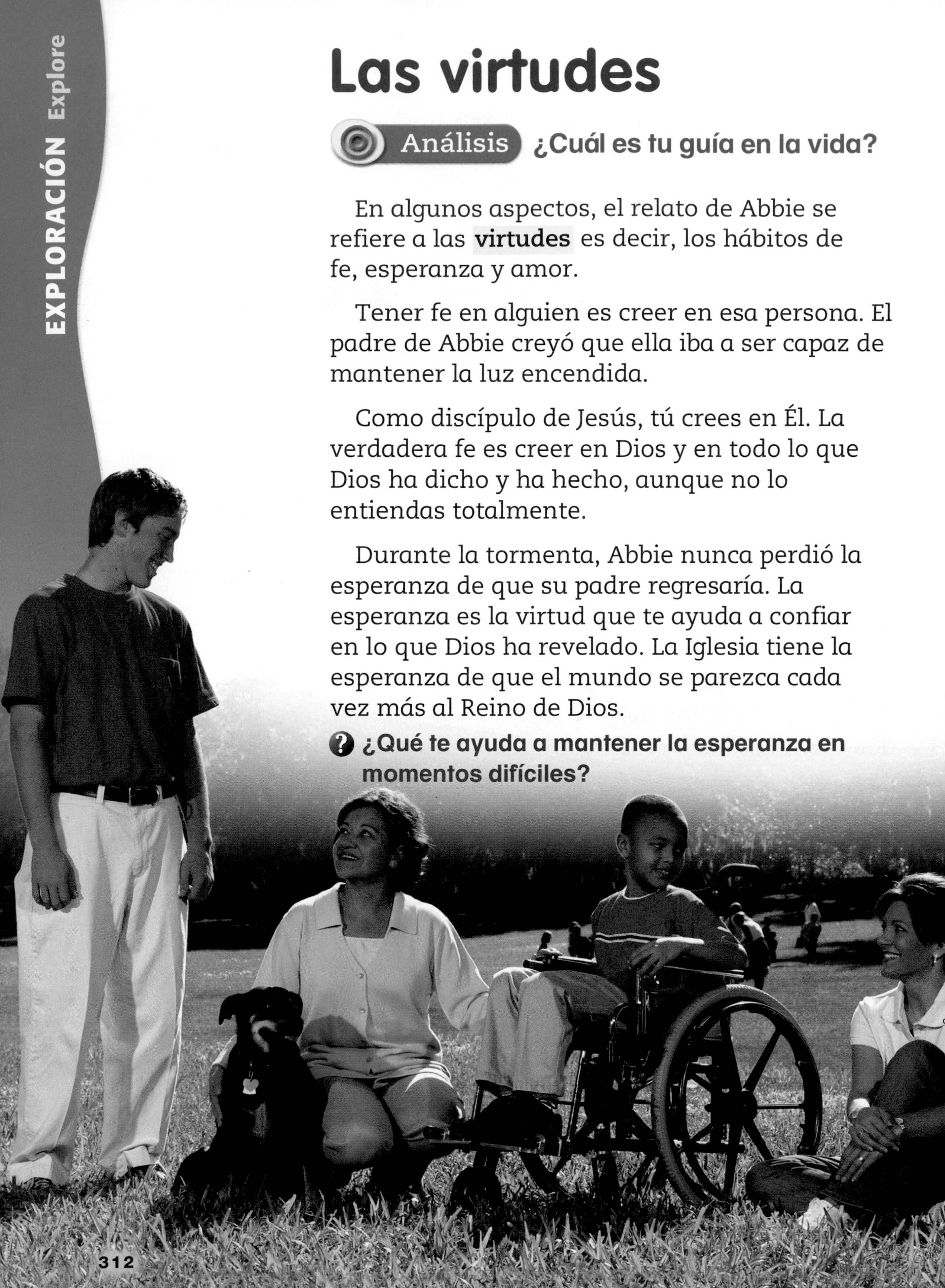

The Virtues

What guides you through life?

In some ways, Abbie's story is about the **virtues**—the habits of faith, hope, and love.

To have faith in someone is to believe in that person. Abbie's father believed that she could keep the light burning.

As a follower of Jesus, you believe in him. True faith is believing in God and all that God has said and done, even though you do not understand completely.

All through the storm, Abbie hoped that her father would come home. Hope is the virtue that helps you trust in what God has revealed. The Church hopes for a world that is more like God's kingdom.

? What helps you stay hopeful during difficult times?

Amar

Cuando Abbie mantuvo encendida la luz del faro, realizó un acto de amor hacia los marineros que estaban en el mar. Tú muestras amor a Dios amando a los demás. Ayudas a los demás y escuchas a tus amigos cuando tienen problemas. Para que puedas mostrar amor a Dios, la Iglesia te enseña a tratar a todos con bondad y respeto.

Palabras de fe

Las **virtudes** son buenas cualidades, o hábitos de bondad. Las virtudes teologales de la fe, la esperanza y el amor son dones de Dios.

Practicar las virtudes

Para progresar en cualquier actividad, tienes que practicar. Con las virtudes sucede lo mismo: tienes que practicarlas hasta que se conviertan en hábitos. Cada vez que pones en práctica la fe, la esperanza y el amor, esos tres dones de Dios se fortalecen en tu interior.

? ¿Cómo mostraste fe, esperanza o amor esta semana?

Actividad Practica tu fe

Crea un recordatorio En una hoja aparte, diseña un señalador que ilustre la práctica de una de las virtudes al compartir la luz de Cristo con los demás. Cada vez que veas el señalador, recordarás que debes practicar las virtudes.

Love

When Abbie kept the light burning, she did a loving thing for the people at sea. You show your love for God by loving others. You help people. You listen to friends who have problems. The Church helps you show love for God by teaching you how to treat everyone with kindness and respect.

Words of Faith

Virtues are good qualities, or habits of goodness. The theological virtues of faith, hope, and love are gifts from God.

Practicing Virtues

In order to get better at something, you need to practice. You have to practice virtues until they become habits. When you do, these gifts from God—faith, hope, and love—grow strong in you.

How have you shown faith, hope, or love this week?

Activity — Connect Your Faith

Create a Reminder On a separate sheet of paper, design a bookmark about practicing one of the virtues as you share the light of Christ with others. Use the bookmark to remind yourself about practicing the virtues.

Oración de petición

Reúnanse y comiencen con la señal de la cruz.

Líder: Oremos juntos, y pidamos a Jesús que nos ayude a crecer en la fe, la esperanza y el amor.

Todos: **Te conocemos y tenemos fe en ti, ¡oh Jesús!**

Lector 1: Ayúdanos a obrar con amor hacia los demás.

Lector 2: Ayúdanos a compartir la luz de tu amor.

Lector 3: Danos la esperanza de vivir contigo en el cielo.

Todos: **Amén.**

Líder: Oremos.

Inclinen la cabeza mientras el líder reza.

Todos: **Amén.**

Canten juntos.

Esta es la luz de Cristo, yo la haré brillar,
Esta es la luz de Cristo, yo la haré brillar;
Esta es la luz de Cristo, yo la haré brillar.
Brillará, brillará, brillará.

"This Little Light of Mine": African-American spiritual

Prayer of Petition

Gather and begin with the Sign of the Cross.

Leader: We pray together, asking Jesus to help us grow in faith, hope, and love.

All: **We know you, and so we have faith in you, O Jesus.**

Reader 1: Help us act with love toward one another.

Reader 2: Help us share the light of your love.

Reader 3: Give us the hope of living with you in heaven.

All: **Amen.**

Leader: Let us pray.

Bow your heads as the leader prays.

All: **Amen.**

Sing together.

This little light of mine I'm gonna let it shine,
This little light of mine I'm gonna let it shine;
This little light of mine I'm gonna let it shine,
Let it shine, let it shine, let it shine.

"This Little Light of Mine": African-American spiritual

Repasar y aplicar

A **Trabaja con palabras** Empareja cada descripción de la columna 2 con el término correcto de la columna 1.

Columna 1		Columna 2
______	1. fe	a. Te ayuda a tener confianza en Dios.
______	2. amor	b. Te ayuda a creer.
______	3. virtud	c. Te ayuda a desarrollar buenos hábitos.
______	4. práctica	d. Te ayuda a ser bondadoso.
______	5. esperanza	e. Es una buena cualidad o un buen hábito.

B **Relaciona** Escribe una manera en que muestras tu fe a los demás.

____

____

____

Actividad Vive tu fe

Recuerda a una persona de fe Piensa en alguna persona de fe que conozcas. Escribe una descripción de esa persona y dibújala en el espacio en blanco.

____

____

CHAPTER 14

Review and Apply

A Work with Words Match each description in Column 2 with the correct term in Column 1.

Column 1	Column 2
_____ **1.** faith	**a.** helps you trust in God
_____ **2.** love	**b.** helps you believe
_____ **3.** virtue	**c.** develops good habits
_____ **4.** practice	**d.** helps you show kindness
_____ **5.** hope	**e.** a good quality or good habit

B Make Connections Write one way that you show your faith to others.

____

____

____

Activity Live Your Faith

Remember a Person of Faith Think of someone you know who is a true person of faith. Write a description of the person, and sketch his or her picture next to your description in the space provided.

____

____

La fe en familia

Lo que creemos

- Los dones que has recibido de Dios de la fe, la esperanza y el amor te ayudan a vivir una vida buena y moral.
- Jesús llama a los cristianos a ser la luz del mundo.

LA SAGRADA ESCRITURA

Juan 9, 1–7 habla acerca de ver la luz de Cristo. ¿Cómo puedes ayudar a los demás a ver la luz de Jesús?

Visita **www.harcourtreligion.com** para encontrar recursos basados en el año litúrgico y lecturas semanales de la Sagrada Escritura.

Actividad
Vive tu fe

Hablen sobre la virtud ¿Qué momentos difíciles ha tenido tu familia? ¿Cómo superaron los malos momentos? Conversen sobre las virtudes de la fe, la esperanza y el amor. Cada miembro de la familia debe decir cómo lo ayudaron estas virtudes en los momentos difíciles.

Siervos de la fe

▲ Santa Genoveva c. 422–500

Siendo muy joven, **Genoveva** consagró su vida a Dios sirviendo a los demás. Fue a vivir a París, donde hizo buenas obras. Evitó que Atila el Huno y su ejército atacaran París organizando al pueblo para que ayunara y orara. Genoveva dio de comer a los hambrientos. También convenció al rey de que tuviera compasión hacia los prisioneros y de que construyera una iglesia. Su día se celebra el 3 de enero.

Una oración en familia

Santa Genoveva, ruega por nosotros para que vivamos nuestra fe con valentía y amor. Amén.

 CIC *Consulta el Catecismo de la Iglesia Católica, números 1813 y 2105, para obtener más información sobre el contenido del capítulo.*

CHAPTER 14

Family Faith

Catholics Believe

- God's gifts of faith, hope, and love help you live a good and moral life.
- Christians are called by Jesus to be the light of the world.

SCRIPTURE

John 9:1–7 is about seeing the light of Jesus. How can you help others see Jesus' light?

GO ONLINE **www.harcourtreligion.com** For weekly Scripture readings and seasonal resources

Activity

Live Your Faith

Talk About Virtue What difficult times has your family had? How did you get through the bad times? Talk about the virtues of faith, hope, and love. Have each family member say how these virtues help him or her in bad times.

People of Faith

▲ Saint Genevieve c. 422–500

At an early age, **Genevieve** gave her life to God by serving others. She moved to Paris, where she did good works. Attila the Hun and his army spared Paris because she led the people in fasting and prayer. Genevieve gave food to starving people. She persuaded the king to have mercy on prisoners and to build a church. Her feast day is January 3.

Family Prayer

Saint Genevieve, pray for us that we may live our faith with courage and love. Amen.

CCC *See Catechism of the Catholic Church 1813, 2105 for further reading on chapter content.*

Capítulo 15 La Iglesia nos guía

Oremos

Líder: Oh Dios, por favor ayúdame a seguirte.
"En tu verdad guía mis pasos, instrúyeme,
tú que eres mi Dios y mi Salvador".
Salmo 25, 5

Todos: Oh Dios, por favor ayúdame a seguirte. Amén.

Actividad Comencemos

Tomar decisiones Mira la fotografía. Mercedes y Lucía se están burlando de Mónica y diciendo cosas feas sobre ella. Mercedes y Lucía tomaron una decisión equivocada.

- ¿Qué decisiones equivocadas toman a veces los niños de tu edad?

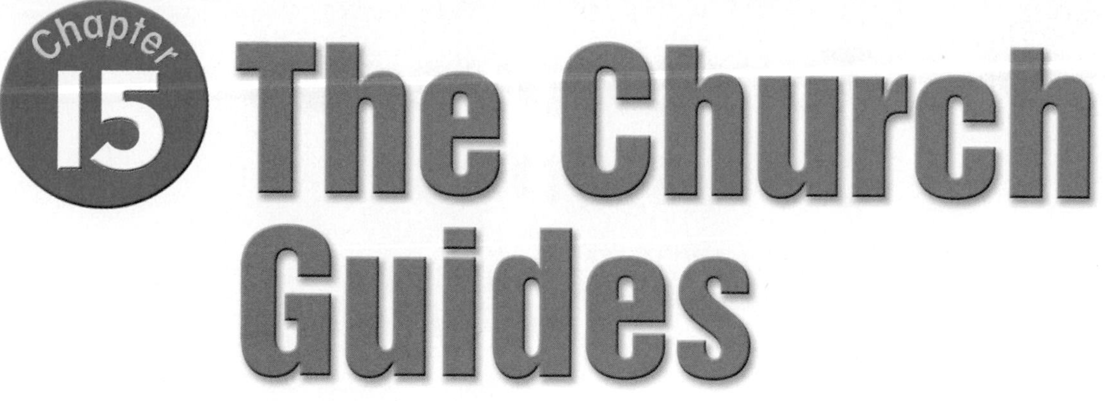

Chapter 15 The Church Guides

Let Us Pray

Leader: O God, please help me follow you.
"Guide me in your truth and teach me,
for you are God my savior."
Psalm 25:5

All: O God, please help me follow you. Amen.

Activity Let's Begin

Making Choices Look at the picture. Meredith and Lucinda are making fun of Chelsea and saying mean things about her. Meredith and Lucinda have made wrong choices.

- What wrong choices do young people your age sometimes make?

Tomar buenas decisiones

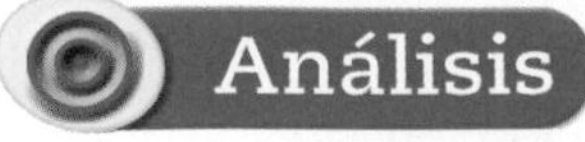

¿Cómo puede cambiar alguien que ha pecado?

Cada vez que tomas una decisión equivocada, debes hacer algo para reparar tu error. Este es un relato de alguien que tomó la decisión de pensar solamente en sí mismo.

UN RELATO

El gigante egoísta

Había una vez un gigante que vivía en un bello jardín. Como quería que el jardín fuera solamente para él, el gigante construyó un muro para que nadie pudiera entrar.

Un día, un niño entró por una grieta que había en la pared y se trepó a un árbol. El árbol se llenó de flores y los pájaros empezaron a anidar en él.

El canto de los pájaros despertó al gigante. "¿Quién eres y qué le has hecho a mi jardín?", le preguntó al niño que estaba en el árbol.

"Lo único que hice fue subirme al árbol. Después llegaron las flores y los pájaros. Disculpa si causé algún daño", respondió el niño.

¿Cuál sería un buen final para este relato?

Make Good Choices

How can someone who has sinned change?

Whenever you make a wrong choice, you must do something to make things right again. This is a story of someone who made a choice to think only of himself.

A STORY

The Selfish Giant

Once there was a giant who lived in a beautiful garden. The giant wanted the garden all to himself. He built a wall around it so that no one could get in.

One day, a child entered through a crack in the wall and climbed a tree. The tree burst into flowers, and birds came to nest in it.

The giant was awakened by the birds' song. "Who are you, and what have you done to my garden?" he called to the boy in the tree.

"I only climbed the tree. Then the flowers and birds came. I'm sorry if I hurt something," the boy said.

What would be a good ending for this story?

Cambiar tu vida

Este relato de la Biblia trata sobre una persona que cambió para bien.

LA SAGRADA ESCRITURA **Hechos 9, 1–30**

Saulo y Jesús

Poco después de su Resurrección, Jesús volvió a su Padre. Un hombre llamado Saulo comenzó a entregar a los discípulos de Jesús a las autoridades.

Un día, cuando Saulo viajaba de una ciudad a otra, lo envolvió una luz brillante y una voz le dijo: "Saulo, Saulo, ¿por qué me persigues?".

Saulo preguntó: "¿Quién eres tú?".

La voz respondió: "Yo soy Jesús. Entra en la ciudad y haz lo que se te diga".

Saulo hizo lo que Jesús le había pedido. Fue bautizado y se transformó en un importante predicador y escritor cristiano. Hoy en día, se le conoce como san Pablo, su otro nombre.

Basado en *Hechos 9, 1–30*

Actividad Comparte tu fe

Piensa: ¿Cómo crees que se sintió Saulo cuando le habló Jesús?

Comunica: Conversa con tu grupo sobre los sentimientos de Saulo.

Actúa: Con tu grupo, representa con mímica cómo cambiaron el rostro y el cuerpo de Saulo cuando lo envolvió la luz de Jesús.

Change Your Life

This scripture story is about someone who changed for the better.

SCRIPTURE Acts 9:1–30

Saul and Jesus

Shortly after his Resurrection, Jesus returned to his Father. A man named Saul began turning in followers of Jesus to the authorities.

One day Saul was traveling between towns. A bright light flashed around him. He heard a voice say, "Saul, Saul, why are you persecuting me?"

Saul asked, "Who are you?"

The voice answered, "I am Jesus. Go into the city and do what you are told to do."

Saul did as Jesus said. He was baptized and became a great Christian preacher and writer. He is now known as Saint Paul, his other name.

Based on *Acts 9:1–30*

Activity Share Your Faith

Think: How do you think Saul felt when Jesus was talking to him?

Share: Talk about Saul's feelings with your group.

Act: With your group, create a mime to show how Saul's face and body changed as he was touched by the light of Jesus.

Pautas para vivir

Análisis **¿Quién te puede ayudar a tomar buenas decisiones morales?**

A veces, todos necesitamos ayuda para tomar buenas decisiones. El Espíritu Santo te ayuda, y también la **gracia** de Dios que recibes en los sacramentos. Tus padres, los sacerdotes y los maestros pueden ayudarte a formar tu **conciencia**. La Iglesia también te ayuda a través de sus enseñanzas. Las normas básicas de la Iglesia se llaman **preceptos**.

Preceptos de la Iglesia

	Precepto	Cómo te guía cada precepto
1.	Participa en la Misa los domingos y fiestas de precepto. Santifica esos días y evita los trabajos innecesarios.	Te recuerda que debes dedicar tiempo a estar con Jesús y con tu comunidad parroquial, fortalece tu fe, te ayuda a descansar y te anima a disfrutar del mundo que Dios te dio.
2.	Celebra el sacramento de la Reconciliación al menos una vez al año si has cometido un pecado grave.	Te ayuda a hacer un repaso de tu vida para que pienses cuándo necesitas el perdón de Dios y qué acciones debes mejorar.
3.	Recibe la Sagrada Comunión al menos una vez al año durante la Pascua.	Fortalece tu fe y te hace uno con Jesús.
4.	Guarda ayuno y abstinencia en los días de penitencia.	Te ayuda a participar del sacrificio de Jesús, a ejercitarte espiritualmente y a experimentar el hambre que sufren los pobres.
5.	Da tu tiempo, dones y dinero para apoyar a la Iglesia.	Te anima a apoyar a la Iglesia y participar en sus obras.

Guides for Living

Who and what can help you make good moral choices?

At times, everyone needs help to make good choices. The Holy Spirit helps you. God's **grace** in the sacraments can help you. Parents, priests, and teachers can help you form your **conscience**. The Church, through its teachings, also helps. The **precepts** are the basic laws of the church.

Precepts of the Church

	Precept	How Each Precept Guides You
1.	Take part in Mass on Sundays and holy days. Keep these days holy, and avoid unnecessary work.	Makes sure that you take time to be with Jesus and your parish community, strengthens your faith, rests your body, and encourages you to enjoy the world God has given you
2.	Celebrate the Sacrament of Reconciliation at least once a year if there is serious sin.	Helps you look at your life to see how you need God's forgiveness and which actions you need to improve
3.	Receive Holy Communion at least once a year during Easter time.	Strengthens your faith and makes you one with Jesus
4.	Fast and abstain on days of penance.	Helps you share in the sacrifice of Jesus, train yourself spiritually, and experience the hunger of people who are poor
5.	Give your time, gifts, and money to support the Church.	Encourages you to support the Church and participate in its works

Decisiones

Al igual que el gigante y que Saulo, todos tomamos decisiones equivocadas alguna vez. La decisión deliberada de desobedecer a Dios se conoce como *pecado*. Cuando pecas, dañas tu relación con Dios y con los demás.

Puedes recibir el perdón de Dios en el sacramento de la Reconciliación, que también se conoce como Confesión o Penitencia. Mediante el sacramento de la Reconciliación, la Iglesia te da la oportunidad de hacer lo siguiente:

- Examinar lo que has hecho.
- Decir que estás arrepentido, pedir perdón y recibir la absolución.
- Reparar o compensar el mal que has causado y cambiar tu comportamiento.

¿Por qué es importante el sacramento de la Reconciliación?

Palabras de fe

La **gracia** es el don de amor que voluntariamente nos hace Dios al entregarnos su vida y su amistad.

Tu **conciencia** es un don de Dios que te ayuda a diferenciar entre el bien y el mal.

Los **preceptos de la Iglesia** son algunas de las normas básicas que deben cumplir los católicos.

Actividad Practica tu fe

Decidir entre todos Forma con varios compañeros un "Equipo de decisiones". Conversen sobre cuáles serían las mejores decisiones en la siguiente situación. Luego, escribe una lista de las decisiones que hayan tomado.

- Desde tu asiento alcanzas a ver el examen de tu mejor amiga, y sabes que ella es la que siempre obtiene la mejor calificación de toda la clase.

____

____

____

Choices

Like the giant and Saul, everyone makes wrong choices at times. The deliberate choice to disobey God is called *sin*. When you sin, you hurt your relationship with God and other people.

You can experience God's forgiveness in the Sacrament of Reconciliation, also called Confession or Penance. Through the Sacrament of Reconciliation, the Church gives you a chance to take these actions:

- Look at what you have done.
- Say you are sorry, seek forgiveness, and receive absolution.
- Repair or make up for the wrong you have done, and change your behavior.

Why is the Sacrament of Reconciliation important?

Words of Faith

Grace is God's free and loving gift to humans of his own life and friendship.

Your **conscience** is a gift from God that helps you know the difference between right and wrong.

The **precepts of the Church** are some of the basic laws that Catholics should follow.

Activity Connect Your Faith

Talk It Over Form a "Decision Team" with several of your classmates. Talk about making good choices in the following situation, and list your choices in the space below.

- You can see your best friend's test paper from where you are sitting, and you know that she always gets the highest grade.

____

____

____

Oración de perdón

Reúnanse y comiencen con la señal de la cruz.

Canten juntos.

Muéstrate bondadoso con nosotros,
puesto que en ti, Señor, hemos confiado.

Líder: Dios Padre nuestro, venimos ante ti a pedir perdón. Muchas veces no hemos obrado bien.

Líder: Si nos hemos peleado y nos hemos hablado mal,

Todos: **Canten el estribillo.**

Líder: Si hemos sido perezosos en casa y en la escuela,

Todos: **Canten el estribillo.**

Líder: Si hemos perdido muchas ocasiones de hacer el bien,

Todos: **Canten el estribillo.**

Líder: Oremos.

Inclinen la cabeza mientras el líder reza.

Todos: Amén.

Basado en el Ritual de la Penitencia

Prayer for Forgiveness

Gather and begin with the Sign of the Cross.

Sing together.

Lord, let your mercy be on us,
as we place our trust in you.

"Psalm 33: Lord, Let Your Mercy" © 1969, 1981, and 1997 ICEL.

Leader: God our Loving Father, we come to you to ask forgiveness. Sometimes we have not behaved as we should.

Leader: If we have quarreled and called each other names,

All: **Sing the refrain.**

Leader: If we are lazy at home and in school,

All: **Sing the refrain.**

Leader: If we have not done good for others when we had the chance,

All: **Sing the refrain.**

Leader: Let us pray.

Bow your heads as the leader prays.

All: Amen.

Based on the
Rite of Penance

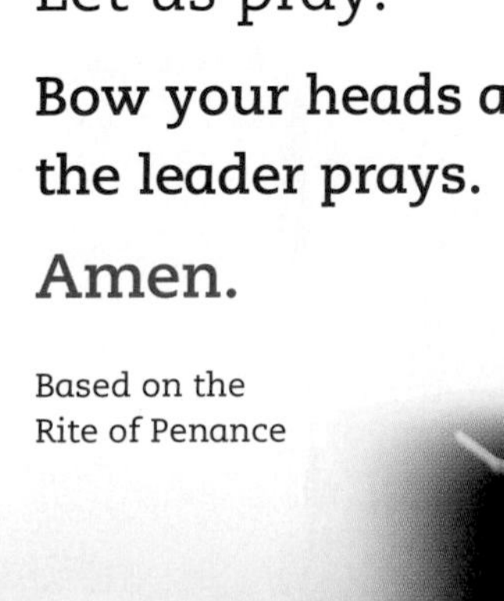

Repasar y aplicar

Comprueba lo que aprendiste Encierra en un círculo o escribe la respuesta correcta.

1. Tu conciencia es ______.
   a. una oración b. una guía c. un pecado
2. Un pecado es ______.
   a. una virtud b. un accidente c. la decisión deliberada de desobedecer a Dios
3. NO deberías guiarte por ______.
   a. el egoísmo b. la Iglesia c. el Espíritu Santo
4. Al participar de los sacramentos, creces en ____________.
5. Nombra dos de los preceptos de la Iglesia.

____

____

Actividad Vive tu fe

Haz señales de tránsito Imagina una carretera con señales. En cada señal, escribe algo que te ayude a tomar buenas decisiones morales.

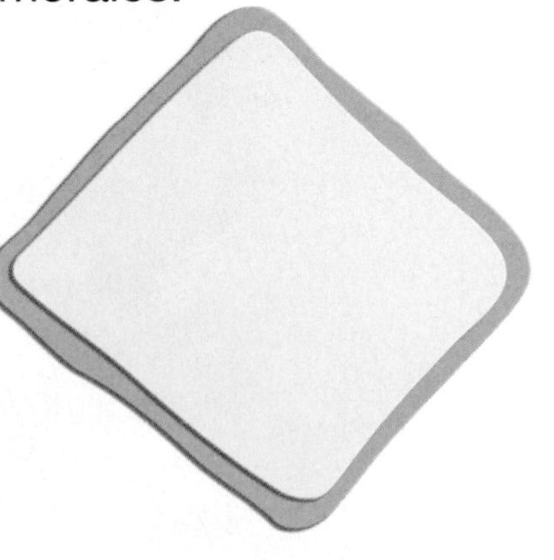

CHAPTER 15

Review and Apply

Check Understanding Circle or write the correct answer.

1. Your conscience is a _____.
   - a. prayer
   - b. guide
   - c. sin
2. A sin is _____.
   - a. a virtue
   - b. an accident
   - c. a deliberate choice to disobey God
3. You should NOT be guided by _____.
   - a. selfishness
   - b. the Church
   - c. the Holy Spirit
4. You grow in __________ by participating in the sacraments.
5. Name two of the precepts of the Church.

____

____

Activity Live Your Faith

Make Signs Imagine a road with signs along the way. On each sign, write one thing that helps you make good moral choices.

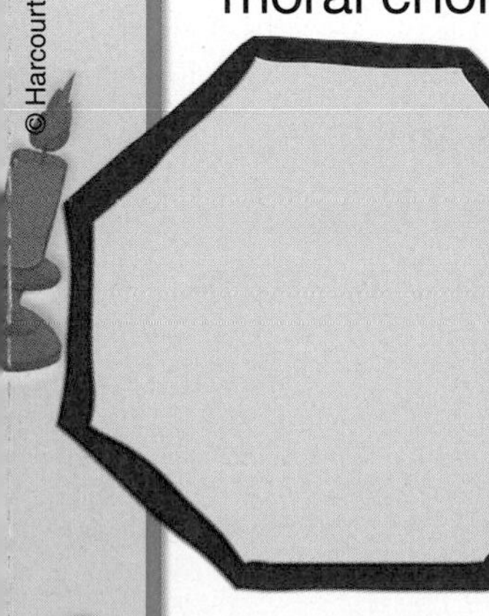

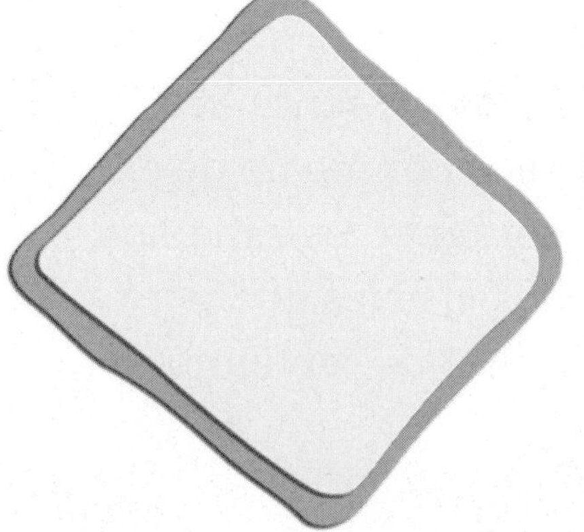

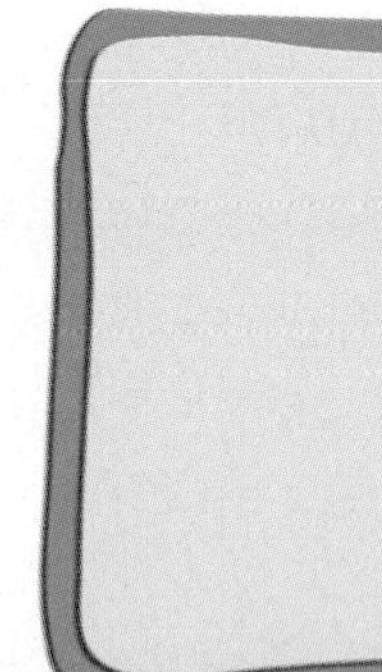

CAPÍTULO 15

La fe en familia

Lo que creemos

- El Espíritu Santo y las enseñanzas de la Iglesia te ayudan a tomar buenas decisiones.
- Tu conciencia y la gracia también te ayudan a serle fiel a Dios.

LA SAGRADA ESCRITURA

2 Corintios 6, 1–4 y 7–10 habla acerca de la importancia de trabajar unidos para Dios.

Visita **www.harcourtreligion.com** para encontrar recursos basados en el año litúrgico y lecturas semanales de la Sagrada Escritura.

Actividad

Vive tu fe

Cambiar para bien Lean el relato completo de la conversión de Saulo (ver *Hechos 9, 1–30*). Hablen sobre el relato. ¿Qué le pasó a Saulo? ¿Cómo cambió su vida la intervención de Dios? ¿Qué hizo Saulo para reparar el daño que había causado a los cristianos? Decidan en algo que les gustaría cambiar para bien en su familia, y pídanle ayuda a Dios para hacerlo realidad.

Siervos de la fe

Francesco Forgione nació en Italia y adoptó el nombre de **Pío** al hacerse fraile capuchino. El padre Pío oía las confesiones de cientos de personas que acudían de todas partes a confesar sus pecados y a sentir la misericordia de Dios por medio de él. Se hizo famoso por tener los estigmas, que son las heridas visibles de Cristo. Su día se celebra el 23 de septiembre.

▲ San Pío (Padre Pío) 1887–1968

Una oración en familia

San Pío, ruega por nosotros para que aprendamos a recurrir a Dios a menudo, para pedir perdón y misericordia. Amén.

 CIC *Consulta el Catecismo de la Iglesia Católica, números 1496 y 2041, para obtener más información sobre el contenido del capítulo.*

CHAPTER 15

Family Faith

Catholics Believe

- The Holy Spirit and the teachings of the Church help you make good choices.
- Your conscience and grace also help you follow God.

SCRIPTURE

2 Corinthians 6:1–4, 7–10 is about working together for God.

GO ONLINE **www.harcourtreligion.com** For weekly Scripture readings and seasonal resources

Activity

Live Your Faith

Change Your Family Read the complete story of Saul's conversion. (See *Acts 9:1–30.*) Talk about the story. What happened to Saul? How did God change his life? What did Saul do to repair the harm he had done to Christians? Decide on one good change your family could make, and ask God for help in making it.

People of Faith

▲ **Saint Pio (Padre Pio) 1887–1968**

Francesco Forgione was born in Italy. He took the name **Pio** when he became a Capuchin priest. Padre Pio heard the confessions of people who traveled from all over to confess their sins and to feel God's mercy through him. Padre Pio was known for having the *stigmata,* the visible wounds of Christ. His feast day is September 23.

Family Prayer

Saint Pio, pray for us that we may learn to turn to God often for forgiveness and mercy. Amen.

CCC *See Catechism of the Catholic Church 1496, 2041 for further reading on chapter content.*

Repaso de la Unidad 5

A **Trabaja con palabras** Empareja cada descripción de la columna I con el término correcto de la columna 2.

Columna I

_____ 1. Una voz interior que te dice la diferencia entre el bien y el mal.

_____ 2. Las enseñanzas de Jesús que muestran el camino a la verdadera felicidad.

_____ 3. Obligaciones básicas de los católicos.

_____ 4. Buenas cualidades, o hábitos de bondad.

_____ 5. Resume los Diez Mandamientos y las Bienaventuranzas.

Columna 2

a. Bienaventuranzas

b. ley del amor

c. preceptos de la Iglesia

d. virtudes

e. conciencia

B **Comprueba lo que aprendiste** Completa cada enunciado encerrando en un círculo la palabra o frase correcta.

6. Recibimos el perdón de Dios mediante el Sacramento (de la Reconciliación/del Bautismo).
7. Jesús dijo: "Ustedes son (la luz/los líderes) del mundo".
8. Cuando pecas, dañas tu relación (contigo mismo/con Dios).
9. (José/Pablo) fue vendido como esclavo por sus hermanos.
10. Dios le cambió el nombre a Saulo por el de (Pablo/Simón).

Unit 5 Review

A **Work with Words** Match each description in Column 1 with the correct term in Column 2.

Column 1

_____ **1.** an inner voice that tells you the difference between right and wrong

_____ **2.** Jesus' teachings that show the way to true happiness

_____ **3.** basic duties of Catholics

_____ **4.** good qualities, or habits of goodness

_____ **5.** sums up the Ten Commandments and the Beatitudes

Column 2

a. Beatitudes

b. law of love

c. precepts of the Church

d. virtues

e. conscience

B **Check Understanding** Complete each sentence by circling the correct word.

6. You can experience God's forgiveness in the Sacrament of (Reconciliation/Baptism).

7. Jesus said, "You are the (light/leader) of the world."

8. When you sin, you hurt your relationship with (yourself/God).

9. (Joseph/Paul) was sold by his brothers into slavery.

10. God changed Saul's name to (Paul/Simon).

UNIDAD 6

Los siete sacramentos

Capítulo 16

Sacramentos de Iniciación

¿Cómo entras a formar parte de la Iglesia Católica?

Capítulo 17

Sacramentos de Curación

¿Por qué son importantes el perdón y la curación?

Capítulo 18

Sacramentos de Servicio

¿Cómo puedes servir a Dios y a los demás?

¿Qué crees que vas a aprender en esta unidad acerca de los siete sacramentos?

UNIT 6

The Seven Sacraments

Sacraments of Initiation

How do you become a member of the Catholic Church?

Sacraments of Healing

Why are forgiveness and healing important?

Sacraments of Service

How can you serve God and others?

What do you think you will learn in this unit about the seven sacraments?

Capítulo 16 Sacramentos de Iniciación

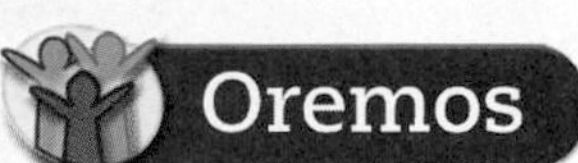

Líder: Dios de amor, ayúdanos a responder a tu llamado.
"Canten al Señor un canto nuevo:
su alabanza en la asamblea de los santos".
Salmo 149, 1

Todos: Dios de amor, ayúdanos a responder a tu llamado.
Amén.

Actividad Comencemos

La mariposa

Escondida en su capullo
Late en silencio una vida.
Y al fin dos alas bonitas
Se asoman con alegría y orgullo.
La oruga está muy cambiada
Y la Monarca radiante saluda al día.

- ¿Qué signos de vida has visto hoy?

Chapter 16 Sacraments of Initiation

Let Us Pray

Leader: Loving God, help us answer your call.
"Sing to the LORD a new song,
a hymn in the assembly of the faithful."
Psalm 149:1

All: Loving God, help us answer your call. Amen.

Activity Let's Begin

Butterfly

Unseen within its silent shell
A life is stirring there,
Till one day wings emerge to beat
And loft into the air.
Now Caterpillar's gone away
And Monarch brightly greets
the day.

- What signs of life have you seen today?

Una nueva vida

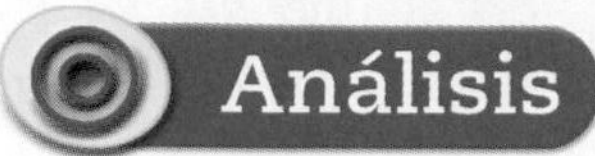

¿Cómo entras a formar parte de la Iglesia Católica?

La oruga emprende una nueva vida convirtiéndose en mariposa. La mayoría de las personas inician también una nueva vida en Dios al ser bautizadas poco después de nacer. Este relato trata sobre un adulto que encontró una nueva vida en Cristo.

UN RELATO

Comienza una nueva vida

La familia de Gonzalo miraba un vídeo de la celebración de la Vigilia Pascual.

La tía Estela y otros adultos celebraron tres sacramentos en una misma noche. Primero fueron bautizados. Luego, fueron ungidos con el óleo consagrado, conocido como **crisma** y, por último, recibieron la Sagrada Comunión.

Después de la Misa, todos reían y abrazaban a la tía Estela y a sus compañeros. Gonzalo disfrutó mucho aquel día, ¡y se le veía de lo más contento en el vídeo!

¿Cómo celebra tu familia el comienzo de algo nuevo?

New Life

Focus **How do you become a member of the Catholic Church?**

The caterpillar gains new life as a butterfly. Most people receive new life in God when they are baptized as babies. This story is about an adult who found new life in Christ.

A STORY

New Life Begins

Brad's family was watching a videotape of the Easter Vigil celebration.

Aunt Stella and the other adults celebrated three sacraments in one evening. First, they were baptized. Then, they were anointed with the blessed oil called **chrism**. Finally, they received Holy Communion.

After Mass, everyone was laughing and hugging Aunt Stella and the others. Brad enjoyed all the excitement, and he looked very happy on the videotape!

How does your family celebrate new beginnings?

La vida en la Iglesia

Después de ver el vídeo, la familia se sentó a mirar un álbum de fotos. "Mira, Gonzalo", dijo su hermana Cristina. "Estas fotos son de tu Bautismo y estas de tu Primera Comunión".

Notaron que había algunas diferencias entre las celebraciones. Gonzalo había sido bautizado cuando era un bebé en la pila bautismal, pero la tía Estela se había metido en la fuente bautismal. Gonzalo estaba vestido con un vestido bautismal blanco, pero la tía Estela usó una túnica blanca. Gonzalo hizo la Primera Comunión cuando estaba en segundo grado. Estela, en cambio, era una persona mayor y recibió la Eucaristía el mismo día en que fue bautizada.

Sin embargo, otras cosas eran iguales. Gonzalo y Estela tuvieron el mismo padrino y los dos fueron bautizados por el padre Aguirre.

La mamá de Gonzalo sonrió y dijo: "Ahora todos los miembros de la familia Fernández somos también miembros de la familia de la Iglesia".

Palabras de fe

El **crisma** es el óleo consagrado que se usa en los sacramentos del Bautismo, de la Confirmación y del Orden.

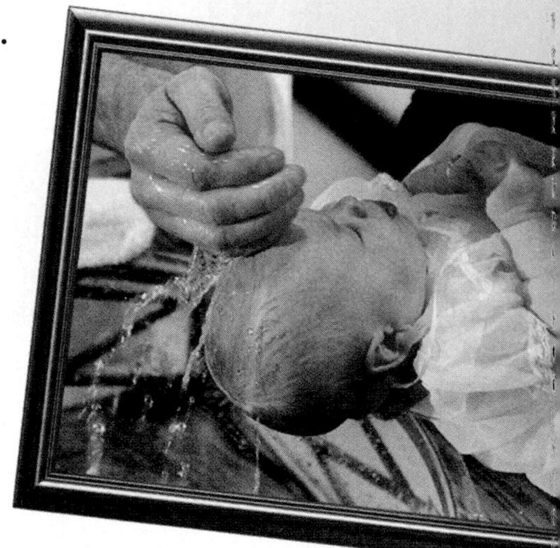

Actividad — Comparte tu fe

Piensa: Recuerda el día de tu Primera Comunión.

Comunica: Cuéntale a tu grupo cómo fue aquel día tan especial.

Actúa: Haz un dibujo de uno de los relatos de tus compañeros.

Life in the Church

After they saw the videotape, the family looked at a photo album. "Look, Brad," his sister Krista said. "Here are pictures of your Baptism. And here you are on your First Communion day."

The family noticed some differences between the celebrations. Brad had been baptized as a baby at the baptismal font, but Aunt Stella had stepped into the baptismal pool. Baby Brad had worn a white baptismal gown, but Aunt Stella wore a white robe. Brad received First Communion for the first time in second grade. Stella was an adult, and she received Eucharist on the same day she was baptized.

Still, some things were the same. Brad's godfather was Aunt Stella's sponsor, too. Father Russell had baptized both Brad and Aunt Stella.

Brad's mom smiled. "Now we're not only members of the Gordon family—we're all members of the same Church family, too."

Words of Faith

Chrism is the blessed oil used in the Sacraments of Baptism, Confirmation, and Holy Orders.

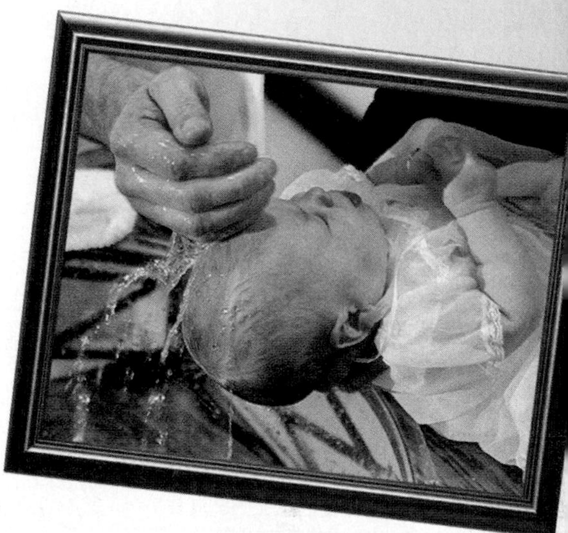

Activity: Share Your Faith

Think: Remember the day of your First Communion.

Share: Tell your small group about this special day.

Act: Draw a picture about one of the stories you heard in your group.

Dones de Dios

Análisis **¿Qué significan los sacramentos de Iniciación?**

La tía Estela celebró tres sacramentos en la Vigilia Pascual. Los **sacramentos** son signos que provienen de Jesús y que conceden la gracia, que es la vida de Dios en las personas. Mediante la fuerza del Espíritu Santo, Jesús actúa en los sacramentos y a través de ellos.

LA SAGRADA ESCRITURA — Hechos 2, 38–41

Muchos son bautizados

Después de que el Espíritu Santo descendiera sobre los discípulos de Jesús en Pentecostés, Pedro les dijo a los que se habían reunido lo que debían hacer.

Pedro dijo a la multitud: "Arrepiéntanse, y que cada uno de ustedes se haga bautizar en el nombre de Jesús, el Mesías, para que sus pecados sean perdonados. Entonces recibirán el don del Espíritu Santo".

Pedro le dijo a la gente que la promesa de Jesús era para todos. Muchos acogieron su mensaje. Aquel día se bautizaron unas 3,000 personas.

Basado en *Hechos 2, 38–41*

Los miembros de la comunidad de la Iglesia son transformados por medio de los sacramentos. El Bautismo, la Confirmación y la Eucaristía se conocen como los **sacramentos de Iniciación**.

Gifts from God

What do the Sacraments of Initiation mean?

Aunt Stella celebrated three sacraments at the Easter Vigil. **Sacraments** are signs that come from Jesus and give grace, God's life in people. Through the power of the Holy Spirit, Jesus works in and through the sacraments.

SCRIPTURE — Acts 2:38–41

Many Are Baptized

After the Holy Spirit came to Jesus' followers at Pentecost, Peter told those who were gathered what they should do.

Peter said to the crowd, "Repent and be baptized, every one of you, in the name of Jesus Christ for the forgiveness of your sins; and you will receive the gift of the holy Spirit."

Peter told the people that Jesus' promise was meant for everyone. Many of them accepted his message. About 3,000 people were baptized that day.

Based on *Acts 2:38–41*

Members of the Church community are changed through the sacraments. Baptism, Confirmation, and Eucharist are called the **Sacraments of Initiation**, or beginning.

Compartir el amor de Dios

En cada uno de los sacramentos de Iniciación ves las acciones y oyes las palabras del ministro, que actúa en nombre de la Santísima Trinidad. El Hijo, por el poder del Espíritu Santo, comparte contigo el amor del Padre.

Palabras de fe

Los **sacramentos** son signos que provienen de Jesús y que conceden la gracia.

Los **sacramentos de Iniciación** son el Bautismo, la Confirmación y la Eucaristía. Con estos tres sacramentos recibimos a los nuevos miembros de la Iglesia Católica.

Sacramentos de Iniciación

	Palabras y acciones	Efectos
Bautismo	El sacerdote o el diácono derrama agua en la cabeza de la persona o la sumerge diciendo: "Yo te bautizo en el nombre del Padre, y del Hijo, y del Espíritu Santo".	Quita el pecado original, perdona los pecados personales y da nueva vida en Cristo; marca a la persona como miembro del Cuerpo de Cristo, la Iglesia; une a todos los cristianos.
Confirmación	El obispo o el sacerdote impone sus manos sobre la cabeza de la persona y luego la unge con el crisma diciendo: "Recibe por esta señal el Don del Espíritu Santo".	Sella y completa el Bautismo; fortalece el vínculo de la persona con la Iglesia; reafirma la unión con Cristo; fortalece el espíritu para vivir la fe.
Eucaristía	El sacerdote reza la plegaria eucarística, consagrando el pan y el vino. Luego comparte el Cuerpo y la Sangre de Cristo con la comunidad de la Iglesia.	Perdona los pecados veniales y aumenta la gracia; une a todos los que comparten la Eucaristía en el Cuerpo de Cristo.

Actividad Practica tu fe

¡Bienvenido! Dibuja a continuación a tu familia de la Iglesia dando la bienvenida a un nuevo miembro.

Sharing God's Love

In each of the Sacraments of Initiation, you see the actions and hear the words of the minister, who acts in the name of the Holy Trinity. The Son, by the power of the Holy Spirit, shares with you the love of the Father.

Sacraments are signs that come from Jesus and give grace.

The **Sacraments of Initiation** are Baptism, Confirmation, and Eucharist. They celebrate membership in the Catholic Church.

Sacraments of Initiation

	Words and Actions	Effects
Baptism	The priest or deacon pours water on or immerses the person, saying, "I baptize you in the name of the Father, and of the Son, and of the Holy Spirit."	Removes original sin, forgives personal sin, and gives new life in Christ; marks the person as a member of Christ's Body, the Church; unites all Christians
Confirmation	The bishop or priest lays hands on the person's head and then anoints him or her with chrism, saying, "Be sealed with the Gift of the Holy Spirit."	Seals and completes Baptism; strengthens the person's bond with the Church; unites the person more fully with Christ; strengthens him or her in living the faith
Eucharist	The priest prays the Eucharistic Prayer, consecrating bread and wine; then he shares Christ's Body and Blood with the Church community.	Brings forgiveness of venial sins and an increase of grace; unites all who share the Eucharist into the one Body of Christ

Activity Connect Your Faith

Show Welcome In the space below, draw a picture of your Church family welcoming a new member.

Orar con la Palabra de Dios

Reúnanse y comiencen con la señal de la cruz.

Líder: Dios Padre nuestro, ayúdanos a vivir siempre las promesas de nuestro Bautismo, como hizo Jesús.

Lector 1: Lectura del santo Evangelio según san Marcos.

Lean Marcos 1, 9–11.

Lector 2: Jesús fue al río Jordán desde Nazaret.

Lector 3: Fue bautizado por Juan.

Lector 1: Cuando salió del agua, el Espíritu descendió sobre Él en forma de paloma.

Lector 2: Palabra del Señor.

Todos: **Gloria a ti, Señor Jesús.**

Líder: Oremos.

Inclinen la cabeza mientras el líder reza.

Todos: **Amén.**

Canten juntos.

¡Cristo es tu fortaleza!
¡Aprende a conocerlo y seguirlo hoy!

Pray with God's Word

Let Us Pray

Gather and begin with the Sign of the Cross.

Leader: God our Father, help us always live out the promises of our Baptism, just as Jesus did.

Reader 1: A reading from the Gospel according to Mark.

Read Mark 1:9–11.

Reader 2: Jesus went to the Jordan River from Nazareth.

Reader 3: He was baptized by John.

Reader 1: When he came out of the water, the Spirit came down from the sky in the form of a dove.

Reader 2: The Gospel of the Lord.

All: **Praise to you, Lord Jesus Christ.**

Leader: Let us pray.

Bow your head as the leader prays.

All: **Amen.**

Sing together.

Christ will be your strength!

Learn to know and follow him!

"Christ Will Be Your Strength" © 1988, GIA Publications, Inc.

Repasar y aplicar

Comprueba lo que aprendiste Encierra en un círculo la respuesta correcta. Corrige los enunciados falsos.

1. ¿Cuál de estos NO es un sacramento de Iniciación?
   - a. Bautismo
   - b. Eucaristía
   - c. Orden
   - d. Confirmación
2. ¿Qué es el crisma?
   - a. Óleo consagrado que se utiliza en algunos sacramentos.
   - b. Una hostia para la Comunión.
   - c. Una oración.
3. Los sacramentos son signos de la gracia.

   Verdadero Falso ____________________
4. Cantar himnos hace que se perdonen los pecados veniales y que crezcamos en gracia.

   Verdadero Falso ____________________
5. La Confirmación fortalece tu vínculo con tus padres.

   Verdadero Falso ____________________

Actividad Vive tu fe

Diseña Haz un folleto sobre los sacramentos que hayas celebrado. Incluye dibujos, fotografías o texto escrito por ti u otros miembros de tu familia.

CHAPTER 16

Review and Apply

Check Understanding Circle the correct answer. Correct any false statements.

1. Which of the following is NOT a Sacrament of Initiation?
   - a. Baptism
   - b. Eucharist
   - c. Holy Orders
   - d. Confirmation
2. What is chrism?
   - a. blessed oil used during certain sacraments
   - b. a Communion wafer
   - c. a prayer
3. Sacraments are signs of grace.

   True False ______________________
4. Singing hymns brings forgiveness of venial sins and an increase of grace.

   True False ______________________
5. Confirmation strengthens your bond with your parents.

   True False ______________________

Activity Live Your Faith

Create Make a booklet about the sacraments you have celebrated. Include drawings, photographs, or writing by you and other members of your family.

CAPÍTULO 16

La fe en familia

Lo que creemos

- Los sacramentos son signos que provienen de Jesús y que conceden la gracia.
- Los sacramentos de Iniciación son el Bautismo, la Confirmación y la Eucaristía.

LA SAGRADA ESCRITURA

Hechos 2, 17 habla acerca de los dones de Dios. Lee el versículo y habla sobre lo que significa para tu familia.

APRENDE en línea Visita **www.harcourtreligion.com** para encontrar recursos basados en el año litúrgico y lecturas semanales de la Sagrada Escritura.

Actividad

Vive tu fe

Dar la bienvenida a los nuevos miembros Pregunten quién se está preparando para los sacramentos de Iniciación en su parroquia. Piensen cómo pueden ayudar a uno de esos catecúmenos a sentirse bienvenido a la parroquia. Por ejemplo, podrían, junto con otras familias, invitar al catecúmeno y su familia a cenar en la casa de alguno de ustedes.

Siervos de la fe

▲ San Isaac Jogues 1607–1644

Isaac Jogues fue sacerdote y exploró América del Norte. Fue ordenado sacerdote en Francia y enviado a Canadá en 1636, donde predicó el Evangelio durante seis años. Isaac fue tomado prisionero por los indígenas en New York. Un grupo de colonizadores holandeses lo liberó, y él prosiguió con su misión en Canadá, pero lo mató un grupo hostil de indígenas. Su día se celebra el 19 de octubre.

Una oración en familia

San Isaac, ruega por nosotros para que entendamos y creamos en nuestro trabajo por la misión de la Iglesia. Ayúdanos a llevar el amor de Dios a los demás. Amén.

CIC *Consulta el Catecismo de la Iglesia Católica, números 1131–1132, 1212 y 1271, para obtener más información sobre el contenido del capítulo.*

CHAPTER 16

Family Faith

Catholics Believe

- Sacraments are signs that come from Jesus and give grace.
- The Sacraments of Initiation are Baptism, Confirmation, and Eucharist.

SCRIPTURE

Acts 2:17 is about gifts from God. Read the verse and talk about what it means for your family.

GO ONLINE **www.harcourtreligion.com**
For weekly Scripture readings and seasonal resources

Activity

Live Your Faith

Welcome New Members Find out who in your parish is preparing for the Sacraments of Initiation. Choose a way to help one of the catechumens feel more welcome in your parish. For example, you and other families could invite a catechumen and his or her family to a potluck dinner at one of your homes.

▲ Saint Isaac Jogues 1607–1644

People of Faith

Isaac Jogues was a priest and an explorer in North America. He became a priest in France and was sent to Canada in 1636. He spent six years preaching the gospel. Isaac was held captive by Native Americans in New York. He was freed by Dutch settlers but continued his mission in Canada. A hostile group of Native Americans killed him. His feast day is October 19.

Family Prayer

Saint Isaac, pray for us that we may understand and believe in our work for the Church's mission. Help us bring God's love to others. Amen.

CCC *See Catechism of the Catholic Church 1131–1132, 1212, 1271 for further reading on chapter content.*

Capítulo 17 Sacramentos de Curación

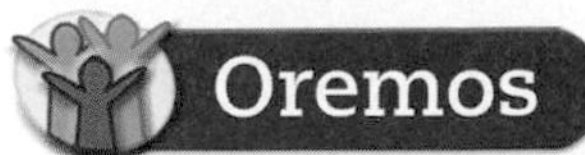

Oremos

Líder: Oh Dios, dame fortaleza.
"Señor, Dios mío,
clamé a ti y tú me sanaste".
Salmo 30, 3

Todos: Oh Dios, dame fortaleza. Amén.

Actividad Comencemos

Arreglar las cosas Ricardo y su tío Antonio estaban arreglando la bicicleta. "Hoy fue el peor día de mi vida", dijo Ricardo. "Le conté a Carlos que Amelia había dicho que su proyecto de arte era feo. Amelia se enteró y ahora los dos están enojados conmigo. ¿Cómo puedo arreglar las cosas?".

"No será tan fácil como engrasar esta cadena", contestó el tío Antonio.

- ¿Qué puede hacer Ricardo para solucionar su problema?

Chapter 17

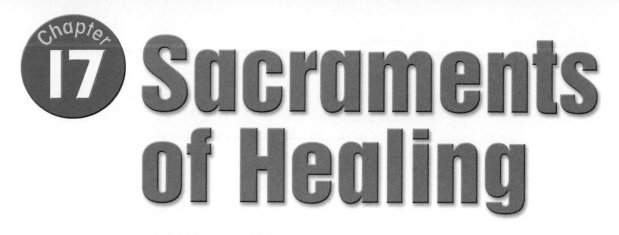

Sacraments of Healing

Let Us Pray

Leader: O God, give me strength.
"O LORD, my God,
I cried out to you and you healed me."
Psalm 30:3

All: O God, give me strength. Amen.

Activity Let's Begin

Making Things Right Russell and his Uncle Anton were working on his bike. "I had the worst day ever," Russell said. "I told Carlos that Amelia said his art project looked dumb. Amelia found out, and now they're both mad at me. How can I make things right?"

"It won't be as easy as oiling this chain," Uncle Anton replied.

- What can Russell do about his problem?

Jesús cura

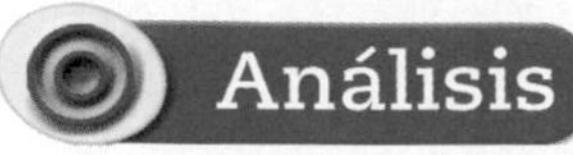

Análisis ¿Cómo puede curar la fe?

A lo largo de su vida, Jesús ayudó a muchas personas a solucionar sus problemas y curó a quienes tenían fe en Él. Lee este relato sobre cómo curó Jesús a la hija de un hombre. La escena comienza con Jesús predicando ante una multitud.

LA SAGRADA ESCRITURA Lucas 8, 40–42; 49–56

Jesús da nueva vida

Jairo: Por favor, déjenme pasar. Tengo que hablar con Jesús.

Mujer: Pareces preocupado. Apártense, dejen pasar a este hombre para que vea a Jesús.

Jairo: Jesús, por favor, te suplico que vengas a mi casa. Mi única hija se está muriendo.

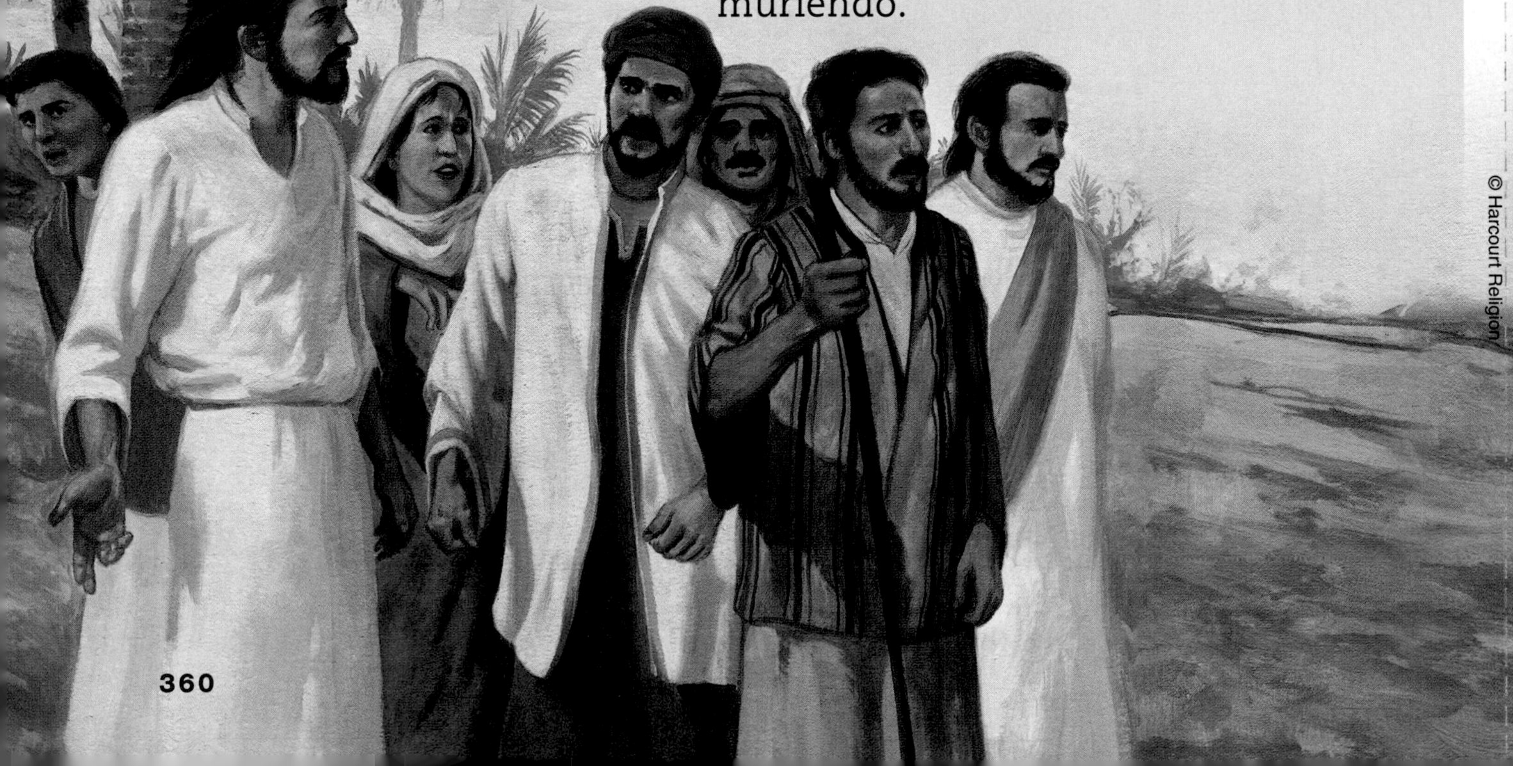

Jesus Heals

Focus How can faith lead to healing?

During his life, Jesus helped make things right for many people. He healed people who had faith in him. Read the story about Jesus healing a man's daughter. The scene begins with a crowd standing around Jesus as he teaches.

SCRIPTURE Luke 8:40–42, 49–56

Jesus Gives New Life

Jairus: Please let me through. I must talk to Jesus.

Woman: You look worried. Stand aside. Let this man through to see Jesus.

Jairus: Jesus, please. I beg you to come to my home. My only daughter is dying.

Sirviente de Jairo:	Jairo, tengo malas noticias. Tu hija ha muerto.
Jesús:	No temas: basta que creas, y tu hija se salvará.
Esposa de Jairo:	Jesús, gracias por venir a nuestra casa. Todos estamos tristes porque nuestra hija acaba de morir.
Jesús:	La niña no está muerta, sino dormida. Ahora salgan todos excepto sus padres y mis tres amigos.
Multitud:	No sabe lo que dice. ¡Esa niña está muerta!
Jesús:	[tocando a la niña] ¡Niña, despierta!

[La niña despierta; sus padres la abrazan.]

Jesús:	Por favor, les pido que no digan a nadie lo que sucedió hoy aquí.
Esposa de Jairo:	¡Muchas gracias, Jesús, por devolvernos a nuestra hija!

Basado en *Lucas 8, 40–42; 49–56*

Actividad Comparte tu fe

Piensa: Reflexiona sobre el relato de la curación de la hija de Jairo.

Comunica: ¿Cómo crees que se sintió Jairo cuando Jesús curó a su hija?

Actúa: Representa el relato con un grupo de compañeros. Cuenta cómo te sentiste al representar tu papel.

Jairus's servant: Jairus, I have sad news. Your daughter is dead.

Jesus: Jairus, don't be afraid. Have faith, and your daughter will be all right.

Jairus's wife: Jesus, thank you for coming to our home. Everyone is sad because our daughter just died.

Jesus: She isn't dead. She is sleeping. Now everyone except her parents and my three friends must leave.

Crowd: He doesn't know what he's talking about. She really is dead!

Jesus: [touching the girl] Child, wake up!

[The girl wakes up; her parents hug her.]

Jesus: Please don't tell anyone what I did here today.

Jairus's wife: Thank you so much, Jesus! You have given us back our daughter.

Based on *Luke 8:40–42, 49–56*

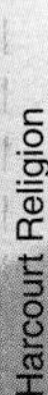

Activity Share Your Faith

Think: Reflect on the story of the healing of Jairus's daughter.

Share: How do you think Jairus felt after Jesus healed his daughter?

Act: With a group of classmates, act out the story. Tell how you felt when you played your part.

Sacramentos de Curación

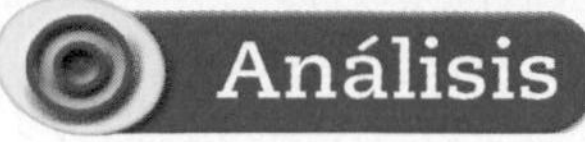

¿Cómo ayudan los sacramentos de Curación a los cristianos?

Los **sacramentos de Curación** son la Reconciliación, o Penitencia, y la Unción de los enfermos. Estos sacramentos ayudan a las personas que han pecado o que están enfermas.

En la Reconciliación confiesas tus pecados y te son perdonados. En la Unción de los enfermos, el sacerdote ora para que Dios envíe su amor curativo a la persona que es ungida. Este sacramento muestra que todas las personas son especiales y que la vida es sagrada.

Solamente el sacerdote puede oficiar los sacramentos de Curación. Como en todos los sacramentos, en estos sacramentos también se usan palabras y acciones para mostrar el amor de Dios.

¿Alguna vez presenciaste la Unción de los enfermos?

Signos de curación

Sacramento	Acción	Palabras
Reconciliación	El sacerdote extiende la mano y bendice.	"Yo te absuelvo de tus pecados en el nombre del Padre, y del Hijo, y del Espíritu Santo".
Unción de los enfermos	El sacerdote unge con el óleo de los enfermos la cabeza y las manos de la persona que está muy enferma o es anciana.	"Por esta santa Unción, y por su bondadosa misericordia te ayude el Señor con la gracia del Espíritu Santo. Para que, libre de tus pecados, te conceda la salvación y te conforte en tu enfermedad".

Sacraments of Healing

How do the Sacraments of Healing help Christians?

The **Sacraments of Healing** are Reconciliation, or Penance, and the Anointing of the Sick. These sacraments help people in times of sin or sickness.

During Reconciliation you confess your sins and are forgiven. In the Anointing of the Sick, the priest prays that God will send his healing love to the person who is being anointed. This sacrament shows that every person is special and that life is sacred.

Only a priest can preside at the Sacraments of Healing. Like all sacraments, these sacraments use words and actions to show God's love.

Have you ever been present at the Anointing of the Sick?

Signs of Healing

Sacrament	Action	Words
Reconciliation	The priest extends his hand in blessing.	"I absolve you from your sins in the name of the Father, and of the Son, and of the Holy Spirit."
Anointing of the Sick	The priest uses the oil of the sick to anoint the head and hands of the person who is very sick or aged.	"Through this holy anointing may the Lord in his love and mercy help you with the grace of the Holy Spirit. May the Lord who frees you from sin save you and raise you up."

El pecado y la enfermedad

Entre el pecado y la enfermedad hay una diferencia muy importante. La enfermedad puede separarte de los demás, pero tú no eliges estar enfermo. En cambio, cuando pecas, eliges alejarte de Dios y de los demás, y eres responsable de esa decisión.

Palabras de fe

Los **sacramentos de Curación** son la Reconciliación y la Unción de los enfermos. Con estos sacramentos se conceden el perdón de Dios y la curación a los que padecen enfermedades físicas o espirituales.

La Iglesia se preocupa por nosotros

Los efectos del pecado y de la enfermedad a veces son similares. Ambos pueden hacerte sentir apartado de Dios y de las personas que amas. Los sacramentos de Curación permiten a la comunidad compartir tus penas y tus alegrías. Estos sacramentos demuestran que la Iglesia se preocupa por las personas. La Iglesia ora para que Jesús cure a las personas, tanto espiritual como físicamente.

Actividad Practica tu fe

Usa palabras de curación A menudo, el pecado y la enfermedad te alejan de las personas que amas. Con estas letras, forma palabras o frases que digan cómo te ayuda la Iglesia.

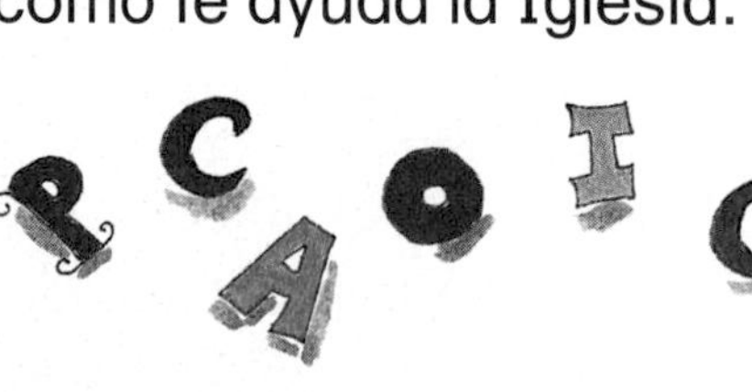

____

____

Sin and Sickness

Sin and sickness are different in a very important way. Sickness may separate you from others, but you do not choose to be sick. However, when you sin, you make a choice to turn away from God and others; and you are responsible for that decision.

Words of Faith

The **Sacraments of Healing** are Reconciliation and the Anointing of the Sick. In these sacraments God's forgiveness and healing are given to those suffering physical and spiritual sickness.

The Church Cares

The effects of sin and sickness can be similar. Both can make you feel separated from God and from people you love. The Sacraments of Healing allow the community a chance to share your sorrows and joys. These sacraments show that the Church cares about people. The Church prays for Jesus' spiritual and physical healing.

Activity Connect Your Faith

Use Healing Words Sin and sickness often separate you in some way from those you love. Using the letters below, create words or phrases that tell how the Church helps you.

____

____

Oración por la curación

Reúnanse y comiencen con la señal de la cruz.

Líder: Dios quiere que le pidamos todo lo que necesitemos por medio de nuestras oraciones. Oramos por todos aquellos que necesitan la curación de Dios.

Lector 1: Dios de amor, tú pones a cada familia bajo tu cuidado.

Lector 2: Tú conoces nuestras necesidades físicas y espirituales.

Todos: **Fortalécenos con tu gracia para que podamos crecer en la fe y en el amor.**

Lector 1: Te lo pedimos por nuestro Señor Jesucristo, tu Hijo,

Lector 2: Que, siendo Dios, vive y reina contigo en la unidad del Espíritu Santo.

Todos: **Por los siglos de los siglos. Amén.**

Basado en una oración del Rite of the Anointing of the Sick.

Canten juntos.

¡Sublime gracia, qué dulce fue,
a un infeliz salvó!
Perdido andaba y Él me encontró.
Ciego era y su luz me sanó.

"Amazing Grace" St. 1–4, John Newton; St. 5, atribuido a John Rees

Prayer for Healing

Gather and begin with the Sign of the Cross.

Leader: God wants us to ask for what we need in prayer. We pray now for those people we know who need God's healing.

Reader 1: Loving God, you take every family under your care.

Reader 2: You know our physical and spiritual needs.

All: **Strengthen us with your grace so that we may grow in faith and love.**

Reader 1: We ask this through our Lord Jesus Christ, your Son,

Reader 2: Who lives and reigns with you and the Holy Spirit.

All: **One God, for ever and ever. Amen.**

Based on a prayer from the Rite of the Anointing of the Sick

Sing together.

Amazing grace! how sweet the sound, That saved a wretch like me! I once was lost, but now am found, Was blind, but now I see.

"Amazing Grace" St. 1–4, John Newton; St. 5, attr. to John Rees

Repasar y aplicar

Comprueba lo que aprendiste Encierra en un círculo la palabra Verdadero si el enunciado es verdadero o la palabra Falso si el enunciado es falso. Corrige los enunciados falsos.

1. La fe en el poder de curación de Jesús fue importante en el relato de la hija de Jairo.

   Verdadero Falso ______________________

2. La Eucaristía es un sacramento de Curación.

   Verdadero Falso ______________________

3. Los sacramentos de Curación ayudan a las personas tanto en lo físico como en lo espiritual.

   Verdadero Falso ______________________

4. El óleo se utiliza para la Unción de los enfermos.

   Verdadero Falso ______________________

5. La enfermedad y el pecado te alejan de Dios.

   Verdadero Falso ______________________

Actividad Vive tu fe

Reza por los demás Haz una lista de personas que estén enfermas o que tengan otras necesidades. Elige a una de esas personas y pide a Dios por ella una vez al día, durante cinco días.

1 2 3 4 5

CHAPTER 17

Review and Apply

Check Understanding Circle True if a statement is true, and circle False if a statement is false. Correct any false statements.

1. Faith in Jesus' healing power was important in the story of Jairus's daughter.

   True False ______________________________

2. Eucharist is a Sacrament of Healing.

   True False ______________________________

3. The Sacraments of Healing help people physically and spiritually.

   True False ______________________________

4. Oil is used for the Anointing of the Sick.

   True False ______________________________

5. Both sickness and sin separate you from God.

   True False ______________________________

Activity Live Your Faith

Pray for Others Make a list of people who are ill or have other needs. Choose one of the people, and pray to God for that person once each day for five days.

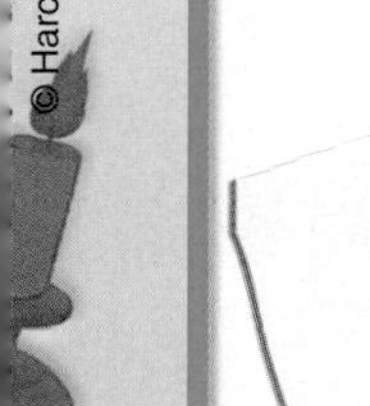

CAPÍTULO 17

La fe en familia

Lo que creemos

- Los sacramentos de Curación son la Reconciliación y la Unción de los enfermos.
- En estos sacramentos, la Iglesia ora por la curación espiritual y física.

LA SAGRADA ESCRITURA

La Carta de Santiago 5, 13–15 fue escrita sobre la Unción de los enfermos y el perdón de los pecados.

Visita **www.harcourtreligion.com** para encontrar recursos basados en el año litúrgico y lecturas semanales de la Sagrada Escritura.

Actividad

Vive tu fe

Muestren su amor En familia, visiten siempre que puedan a familiares, amigos y vecinos que estén enfermos o sean ancianos. Si no pueden visitar a las personas que necesitan su ayuda, llámenlas o muéstrenles su amor enviándoles tarjetas hechas por ustedes.

▲ Santa Isabel de Hungría 1207–1231

Siervos de la fe

Isabel de Hungría fue una princesa húngara que se casó con el príncipe Luis de Alemania. Se preocupaba por los pobres y por los que sufrían, y les daba de comer en la puerta del castillo en que vivía. Vendió sus joyas y usó el dinero para construir hospitales. Antes de morir, entregó todas sus pertenencias a los pobres. El día de Santa Isabel se celebra el 17 de noviembre.

Una oración en familia

Santa Isabel, ruega por nosotros para que seamos bondadosos con los pobres y los enfermos. Amén.

CHAPTER 17

Family Faith

Catholics Believe

- The Sacraments of Healing are Reconciliation and the Anointing of the Sick.
- In these sacraments the Church prays for spiritual and physical healing.

SCRIPTURE

James 5:13–15 was written about the Anointing of the Sick and the forgiveness of sin.

GO ONLINE **www.harcourtreligion.com** For weekly Scripture readings and seasonal resources

Activity

Live Your Faith

Show Your Love As a family, as often as possible, visit relatives, friends, and neighbors who are ill or aged. If you cannot visit the people who need your help, call the person or show your love by sending homemade cards.

People of Faith

▲ Saint Elizabeth of Hungary 1207–1231

Elizabeth was a princess of Hungary who married Prince Ludwig of Germany. She cared for people who were poor and suffering. At the castle gate, Elizabeth fed those who were poor. She sold her jewels and used the money to build hospitals. Before she died, she gave her belongings to people who were poor. Saint Elizabeth's feast day is November 17.

Family Prayer

Saint Elizabeth, pray for us that we may be kind to people who are poor and sick. Amen.

CCC *See Catechism of the Catholic Church 1420, 1421 for further reading on chapter content.*

Capítulo 18 Sacramentos de Servicio

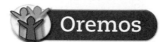

Oremos

Líder: Querido Dios, somos tus siervos para siempre.
"Pero el Señor libra el alma de sus siervos,
el que se ampara en él no tendrá
que pagar".

Salmo 34, 23

Todos: Querido Dios, somos tus siervos para siempre. Amén.

Actividad Comencemos

Un día especial "¡Feliz aniversario, mamá y papá! Sabemos que hoy es un día especial para ustedes, y por eso les preparamos el desayuno", dijo Jeremías.

"¡Mmm! ¡Qué rico!", exclamó el papá.

"Ustedes siempre hacen cosas especiales por nosotros. Ahora nos toca a nosotros hacer algo especial por ustedes", dijo Sandra.

- ¿Qué cosas especiales haces por tus padres?

Chapter 18 Sacraments of Service

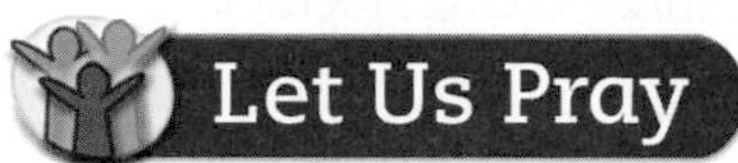

Let Us Pray

Leader: Dear God, we are your servants forever.
"The LORD redeems loyal servants;
no one is condemned whose refuge is God."

Psalm 34:23

All: Dear God, we are your servants forever. Amen.

Activity Let's Begin

A Special Day "Happy anniversary, Mom and Dad! We know today is special for you, so we made you breakfast," said Jeremy.

"Wow, what a feast!" Dad said.

"You always do special things for us. Now it's our turn to do something special for you," said Samantha.

- What special things do you do for your parents?

Recuerdos de familia

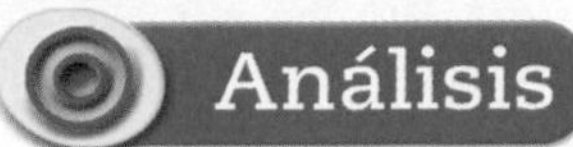

¿Cómo sirven a los demás las personas casadas y los ministros ordenados?

Un aniversario es una fecha en que se recuerda un día especial de amor y compromiso. Jeremías y Sandra aprendieron algo acerca del día en que se casaron sus padres.

UN RELATO

El relato de la boda

"Estabas muy linda, mamá", dijo Sandra.

"Es porque estaba muy contenta", contestó su mamá.

"Recuerdo que estaba feliz porque, a partir de ese día, tu mamá y yo íbamos a estar juntos para siempre y a compartir las alegrías y las tristezas", dijo su papá.

"Compartir las alegrías es lindo, pero, ¿las tristezas también?", preguntó Sandra.

"Mira, hija", dijo la mamá, "todos tenemos malos momentos, pero los míos serían peores si no tuviera a tu papá. Muchas veces, rezamos juntos para pedirle a Dios que nos ayude. Y los buenos momentos son incluso mejores, porque los comparto con alguien que amo".

¿Qué buenos recuerdos de su boda y de su vida matrimonial te han contado tus familiares?

Family Memories

How do married people and ordained men serve others?

An anniversary is a time to remember a special day of love and commitment. Jeremy and Samantha learn about their parents' wedding day.

A STORY

The Wedding Story

"Mom, you looked pretty," Samantha said.

"It's because I was so happy," said her mother.

"I remember being happy because your mom and I were promising to be with each other forever and to share good and bad times," Dad said.

"I know it's fun to share good times. But bad times?" asked Samantha.

"Well, Samantha," said Mom, "everyone has bad times, but mine would be worse if I didn't have your dad. We often ask God to help us. The good times are even better because I share them with someone I love."

What good memories of weddings and married life have family members shared with you?

EXPLORACIÓN Explore

Compartir los recuerdos de la boda

"Miren una foto del padre Vargas cuando fue testigo de nuestros **votos** matrimoniales", dijo la mamá de Sandra y Jeremías. "El padre también se reunió con nosotros antes de que nos casáramos y nos habló de la importancia del matrimonio. Nos pidió que fuéramos a unas clases especiales para aprender sobre el matrimonio. Los sacerdotes y los diáconos hacen muchas tareas que no siempre vemos".

"¿Qué clase de tareas?", preguntó Jeremías.

"Enseñan acerca de la fe y guían a las personas para que tomen buenas decisiones. Visitan a los enfermos y sirven en la parroquia de muchas otras maneras. Los sacerdotes celebran la Misa y otros sacramentos. Los diáconos bautizan y son testigos en las bodas. Los sacerdotes y los diáconos cumplen un papel importante", le explicó su papá.

"Igual que las personas casadas", dijo Sandra."Claro, igual que las personas casadas. Dios nos ayuda a todos a hacer nuestro trabajo", dijo su mamá.

Palabras de fe

Los **votos** son promesas sagradas que se hacen a Dios o ante Él. En el matrimonio, un hombre y una mujer prometen ante Dios amarse y ser fieles el uno al otro.

Actividad Comparte tu fe

Piensa: ¿Qué es el amor?

Comunica: Habla sobre los diferentes significados del amor y sobre cómo puedes mostrar amor a los demás.

Actúa: Diseña una tarjeta de aniversario sobre el amor y dásela a un amigo o pariente que esté celebrando un aniversario.

Sharing Wedding Memories

"Look, there's a picture of Father Schmidt, witnessing our wedding **vows**," said Mom. "He also met with us before we were married and talked to us about how important marriage is. He asked us to go to some special classes to learn more about marriage. Priests and deacons do a lot of work that you don't always see."

"What kind of work?" asked Jeremy.

"They teach people about the faith and guide them in making good decisions. They visit people who are sick and serve the parish in many other ways. Priests celebrate Mass and other sacraments. Deacons baptize and witness marriages. Priests and deacons have important roles," said Dad.

"Just like married people," said Samantha. "Yes, just like married people. God helps all of us do his work," said Mom.

Words of Faith

Vows are sacred promises that are made to or before God. In marriage a man and a woman make their promises to love each other and to be faithful before God.

Activity — Share Your Faith

Think: What is love?

Share: Talk about different meanings of love and how you can show love for others.

Act: Design an anniversary card about love, and give it to a friend or relative who is celebrating an anniversary.

Servir al pueblo de Dios

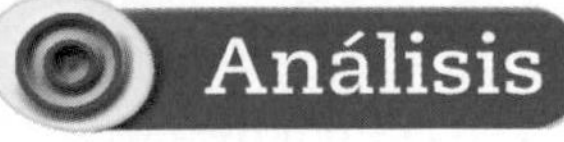

¿Cómo continúan la obra de Jesús los sacramentos al Servicio de la comunidad?

Los padres de Sandra y Jeremías tenían algo en común con el padre Vargas, el sacerdote del relato: habían celebrado un **sacramento al Servicio de la comunidad**. Los dos sacramentos de Servicio son el Orden (Orden sacerdotal) y el Matrimonio.

El Orden es el sacramento por el que los hombres se hacen diáconos, sacerdotes u obispos. Cuando un hombre recibe el Orden, es ordenado y pasa a compartir el ministerio de Jesús de una manera especial. San Pablo escribió acerca del trabajo de los primeros ministros de la Iglesia.

LA SAGRADA ESCRITURA

Vean, pues, en nosotros a servidores de Cristo y administradores de las obras misteriosas de Dios. Los administradores tienen que ser dignos de confianza.

Basado en *1 Corintios 4, 1–2*

Sacramentos al Servicio de la comunidad

	Palabras y acciones	Efectos
Matrimonio	En presencia de un sacerdote o diácono y de otros testigos, un hombre y una mujer prometen amarse y ser fieles el uno al otro.	La gracia de amarse como Cristo ama a su Iglesia y de permanecer fieles; la gracia de acoger y educar a los hijos.
Orden (ordenación para el sacerdocio)	El obispo impone las manos sobre la cabeza del hombre que va a ser ordenado y reza al Espíritu Santo.	La autoridad para ejercer el sacerdocio ministerial, con potestad para dirigir a la comunidad de la Iglesia, enseñar y gobernar.

Serving God's People

How do the Sacraments of Service continue Jesus' work?

The parents and the priest in the story had something in common. They had celebrated a **Sacrament of Service**. The two Sacraments of Service are Holy Orders and Matrimony.

Holy Orders is the sacrament in which men become deacons, priests, or bishops. When a man receives Holy Orders, he is ordained. He shares Jesus' ministry in a special way. Saint Paul wrote about the work of the Church's early ministers.

Think of us as servants of Christ and stewards of the mysteries of God. Stewards must be trustworthy.

Based on *I Corinthians* 4:1–2

Sacraments of Service

	Words and Actions	Effects
Matrimony	In front of a priest or deacon and other witnesses, a woman and a man promise to love each other and to be faithful.	The grace to love each other as Christ loves his Church and to remain faithful; the grace to welcome and raise children
Holy Orders (ordination to the priesthood)	A bishop lays his hands on the man to be ordained and prays to the Holy Spirit.	The authority to minister as a priest, with the authority to lead the Church community, to teach, and to govern

Servirse los unos a los otros

Las personas que contraen matrimonio también comparten el ministerio de Jesús. El sacramento del Matrimonio une a un hombre y a una mujer en el matrimonio cristiano. Las personas casadas sirven a Dios amándose y sirviéndose el uno al otro, y también amando y sirviendo a sus hijos.

A veces, los esposos se sirven el uno al otro trabajando ambos para que sus familias puedan tener casa y comida.

En algunos casos, el hombre y la mujer tienen que vivir separados. Sin embargo, deben hacer todo lo posible para ayudar a su familia. La Iglesia se preocupa por todas esas familias y las apoya.

Palabras de fe

Los **sacramentos al Servicio de la comunidad** son el Orden y el Matrimonio. Ambos celebran el compromiso de las personas de servir a Dios y a la comunidad.

Todos están llamados

A través del Bautismo y de la Confirmación, todos los miembros de la Iglesia están llamados a poner sus dones al servicio del pueblo de Dios. De cualquier manera que respondas a ese llamado, estarás sirviendo a Dios y fortaleciendo a la comunidad de la Iglesia.

Aprende sobre los sacramentos al Servicio de la comunidad En el espacio a continuación, escribe dos preguntas que te gustaría hacer a tu párroco y a una persona casada acerca de cómo sirven a Dios y a la comunidad.

____

____

Serving One Another

Married people share Jesus' ministry, too. The Sacrament of Matrimony joins a man and a woman in Christian marriage. They serve God by loving and serving each other and any children they may have.

Sometimes both husbands and wives serve each other by working at jobs so that their families will have food and shelter.

Sometimes a man and a woman have to live apart from each other. However, they must still do the best they can to help their families. The Church cares for and supports all of these families.

Words of Faith

The **Sacraments of Service** are Holy Orders and Matrimony. They celebrate people's commitment to serve God and the community.

All Are Called

Through Baptism and Confirmation, all members of the Church are called to use their gifts in service to God's people. No matter how you answer that call, you serve God and strengthen the Church community.

Activity Connect Your Faith

Learn About Sacraments of Service In this space, write two questions that you would like to ask your pastor and a married person about how they serve.

____

____

Oración de agradecimiento

Reúnanse y comiencen con la señal de la cruz.

Líder: Dios generoso, te damos gracias por los dones de servicio de los obispos, los sacerdotes, los diáconos y las personas casadas.

Lector 1: Por los sacerdotes que nos guían hacia ti,

Todos: Te damos gracias, Señor.

Lector 2: Por los diáconos que nos ayudan a buscarte,

Todos: Te damos gracias, Señor.

Lector 3: Por los obispos que guían a tu pueblo,

Todos: Te damos gracias, Señor.

Lector 4: Por las personas casadas que se guían una a otra hacia Dios,

Todos: Te damos gracias, Señor.

Lector 5: Por los padres que nos enseñan cómo amarte,

Todos: Te damos gracias, Señor.

Canten juntos.

Me permites ser tu siervo
como lo es Cristo Jesús,
gracia pide para mí
y mi siervo también serás.

Prayer of Thanks

Gather and begin with the Sign of the Cross.

Leader: Generous God, we thank you for the gifts of service of bishops, priests, deacons, and married people.

Reader 1: For priests who lead us to you,

All: **We thank you, God.**

Reader 2: For deacons who help us find you,

All: **We thank you, God.**

Reader 3: For bishops who guide your people,

All: **We thank you, God.**

Reader 4: For married people who lead each other to God,

All: **We thank you, God.**

Reader 5: For parents who show us how to love you,

All: **We thank you, God.**

Sing together.

Will you let me be
your servant,
Let me be as
Christ to you; Pray that I may have the grace
to Let you be my servant, too.

"The Servant Song" © 1977, Scripture in Song (a div. of Integrity Music, Inc.)

Repasar y aplicar

Comprueba lo que aprendiste Completa cada enunciado con el término correcto del vocabulario.

VOCABULARIO

votos
Orden
Matrimonio
ordenado
sacerdote

1. Un hombre debe ser ________________ para celebrar la Misa.
2. Los ________________ que se hacen en el sacramento del Matrimonio duran toda la vida.
3. Solamente los hombres están llamados a recibir el________________.
4. El Orden celebra el compromiso de un hombre con el ministerio de Jesús como ________________, diácono u obispo.
5. El ________________ une a un hombre y a una mujer.

Actividad Vive tu fe

Escribe una lista Escribe una lista de las cosas que puedes hacer para mostrar tu agradecimiento por todo lo que hacen por ti los adultos de tu familia. Elige una idea que los sorprenda totalmente y ponla en práctica esta semana.

____

____

____

____

____

____

Review and Apply

Check Understanding Complete each sentence with the correct term from the Word Bank.

WORD BANK

vows
Holy Orders
Matrimony
ordained
priest

1. A man must be ____________________ to celebrate the Mass.
2. The ____________________ made during the Sacrament of Matrimony last a lifetime.
3. Only men are called to receive ____________________.
4. Holy Orders celebrates a man's commitment to Jesus' ministry as a ____________________, deacon, or bishop.
5. ____________________ unites a man and a woman.

Activity Live Your Faith

Write a List Brainstorm a list of things you can do to show your thanks for what the adults in your family do for you. Choose an idea that would surprise them completely, and act on it this week.

____

____

____

____

____

____

CAPÍTULO 18

La fe en familia

Lo que creemos

- Los sacramentos al Servicio de la comunidad son el Orden y el Matrimonio.
- Estos sacramentos celebran el compromiso de las personas ante Dios y la comunidad.

LA SAGRADA ESCRITURA

I Corintios 13 habla acerca del significado del amor y de su importancia.

Visita **www.harcourtreligion.com** para encontrar recursos basados en el año litúrgico y lecturas semanales de la Sagrada Escritura.

Actividad

Vive tu fe

Apoya a los demás Ayuda a una familia que esté pasando por un momento difícil. Decide qué puedes hacer para ayudar a esa familia. Estas son algunas familias a las que podrías ayudar.

- Una familia con un bebé o con niños pequeños.
- Una familia que esté sufriendo debido a una muerte o una enfermedad.
- Una pareja de ancianos sin hijos que los cuiden.

Siervos de la fe

▲ Santa Margarita de Escocia 1045–1093

Margarita fue una princesa que naufragó con su familia en la costa escocesa. Al casarse con Malcolm, el rey de Escocia, llevó educación y compasión a la corte escocesa. Ayudó a los huérfanos y sirvió a los pobres satisfaciendo sus necesidades. También ayudó a reparar muchos templos de Escocia. El día de Santa Margarita se celebra el 16 de noviembre.

Una oración en familia

Santa Margarita, ruega por nosotros para que podamos llevar una vida de servicio a nuestras familias, a nuestro país y a nuestra Iglesia. Amén.

 CIC *Consulta el Catecismo de la Iglesia Católica, números 1534 y 1535, para obtener más información sobre el contenido del capítulo.*

CHAPTER 18

Family Faith

Catholics Believe

- The Sacraments of Service are Holy Orders and Matrimony.
- These sacraments celebrate people's commitment to God and the community.

SCRIPTURE

I Corinthians 13 tells you what love is and how important it is.

GO ONLINE **www.harcourtreligion.com** For weekly Scripture readings and seasonal resources

Activity
Live Your Faith

Support Others Reach out to a family who may be having difficulties at this time. Decide what you can do to support that family. Here are some families you might be able to help.

- A family with a new baby or very young children
- A family experiencing a death or an illness
- An elderly couple with no children to look after them

People of Faith

▲ Saint Margaret of Scotland 1045–1093

Margaret was a princess who was shipwrecked with her family near Scotland. She married Malcolm, the king of Scotland. She brought great learning and compassion to the Scottish court. She helped orphans and served the needs of those who were poor. Margaret helped repair many church buildings in Scotland. Saint Margaret's feast day is November 16.

Family Prayer

Saint Margaret, pray for us that we may lead lives of service to our families, our country, and our Church. Amen.

CCC *See Catechism of the Catholic Church 1534, 1535 for further reading on chapter content.*

Repaso de la Unidad 6

A **Trabaja con palabras** Completa cada enunciado.

1. Los ______________________ son promesas sagradas que se hacen a Dios o ante Él.
2. Los sacramentos ______________________ celebran el compromiso de las personas de servir a Dios y a la comunidad.
3. Los ______________________ son signos que provienen de Jesús y que conceden la gracia.
4. Los sacramentos de ______________________ celebran la pertenencia a la Iglesia católica.
5. El ______________________ es el óleo consagrado que se usa en algunos sacramentos.

B **Comprueba lo que aprendiste** Completa la tabla con los nombres de los sacramentos.

Sacramentos	
Iniciación	**Curación**
6.	9.
7.	10.
8.	

Unit 6 Review

A Work with Words Complete each statement.

1. ______________________ are sacred promises that are made to or before God.

2. Sacraments of ______________________ celebrate people's commitment to serve God and the community.

3. ______________________ are signs that come from Jesus and give grace.

4. Sacraments of ______________________ celebrate membership in the Catholic Church.

5. ______________________ is blessed oil used in some sacraments.

B Check Understanding Complete the chart below with the names of the sacraments.

Sacraments	
Initiation	**Healing**
6.	9.
7.	10.
8.	

UNIDAD 7

El Reino de Dios

Capítulo 19

Somos de Dios

¿Cuál es la alianza entre Dios y su pueblo?

Capítulo 20

La Iglesia hoy

¿Cómo trabaja hoy la Iglesia por el Reino de Dios?

Capítulo 21

¡Vida para siempre!

¿Qué pueden esperar los cristianos al final de la vida?

¿Qué crees que vas a aprender en esta unidad acerca del Reino de Dios?

UNIT 7

The Kingdom of God

Belonging to God

What is the covenant between God and his people?

The Church Today

How does the Church work for the kingdom of God?

Life Forever!

What can Christians look forward to at the end of their lives?

What do you think you will learn in this unit about the kingdom of God?

INVITACIÓN Invite

Capítulo 19 Somos de Dios

Líder: Dios fiel, ayúdanos a seguir por tu camino hacia el amor.
"Amor y lealtad son todos sus caminos,
para el que guarda su alianza y sus mandatos".
Salmo 25, 10

Todos: Dios fiel, ayúdanos a seguir por tu camino hacia el amor. Amén.

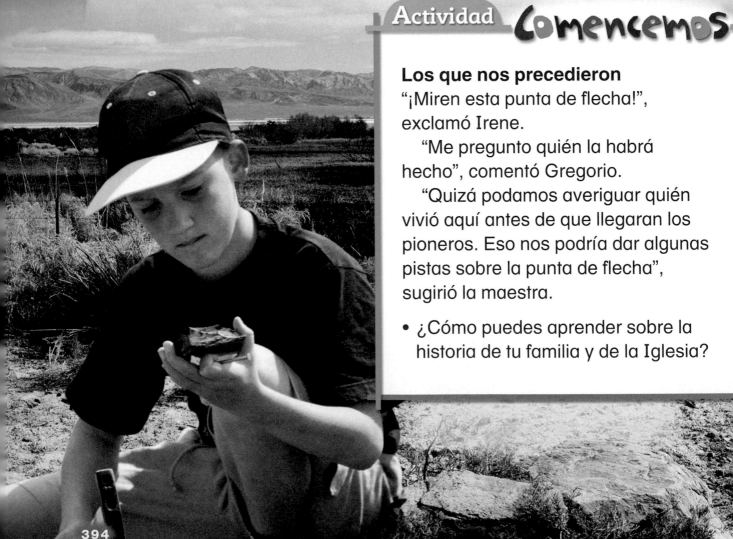

Actividad Comencemos

Los que nos precedieron

"¡Miren esta punta de flecha!", exclamó Irene.

"Me pregunto quién la habrá hecho", comentó Gregorio.

"Quizá podamos averiguar quién vivió aquí antes de que llegaran los pioneros. Eso nos podría dar algunas pistas sobre la punta de flecha", sugirió la maestra.

- ¿Cómo puedes aprender sobre la historia de tu familia y de la Iglesia?

Chapter 19 Belonging to God

Let Us Pray

Leader: Faithful God, help us follow your path to love.

"All the paths of the LORD are faithful love
toward those who honor the covenant
demands."

Psalm 25:10

All: Faithful God, help us follow your path to love. Amen.

Activity Let's Begin

Those Who Came Before

"Wow, look at this arrowhead!" LaNae said.

"I wonder who made it," said Greg.

"Maybe we can find out about who lived here before the pioneers. That might give us clues about the arrowhead," Ms. Ortiz suggested.

- What are some ways to learn about the past in your family and in the Church?

Historia familiar

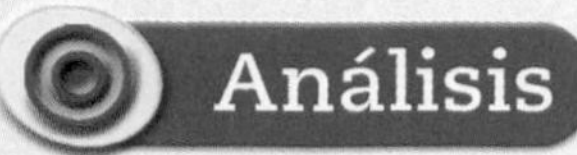

¿Cuál fue la alianza entre Dios y Abraham?

Los orígenes de la historia de la Iglesia se remontan a la antigüedad. Este es el relato de la primera vez que Dios llamó a su pueblo.

UN RELATO

Yo seré tu Dios

"Cuéntame cosas que pasaron antes de que yo naciera", dijo Isaac.

Sara sonrió y dijo: "Tu padre y yo estábamos tristes porque no teníamos hijos. Una noche, tu padre salió y volvió diciendo que había estado hablando con Dios".

"Tu padre le dijo a Dios: Tú sabes que confiamos en ti, pero no tenemos hijos".

La madre de Isaac continuó: "Dios le pidió a tu padre que mirara las estrellas y le dijo: Tu familia será más numerosa que las estrellas. Ellos serán mi pueblo y yo seré su Dios. Todas las naciones serán bendecidas a través de ti. Esta es mi **alianza** contigo, mi promesa".

Isaac terminó la historia: "Yo comparto esa promesa y lo mismo harán mis hijos".

¿Qué relatos familiares te gusta oír una y otra vez?

Family History

What was God's covenant with Abraham?

The beginnings of the Church's history go back to ancient times. Here is the story of the time when God first called his people.

A STORY

I Will Be Your God

"Tell me about before I was born," said Isaac.

Sarah smiled. "Your father and I were sad. We had no children. One night your father went outside. When he came back, he said that he and God had been speaking.

"Your father said to God, 'You know that we trust you, but we have no children.'"

Isaac's mother continued, "God told your father to look up at the stars. God said, 'Your family will outnumber the stars. They will be my people, and I will be their God. All nations will be blessed through you. This is my **covenant**, my promise to you.'"

Isaac finished the story, "I share that promise, and so will my children."

? What family stories do you enjoy hearing again and again?

Conexión con el pasado

Dios cumplió su promesa. La familia de Abraham creció hasta convertirse en el pueblo de Israel. Dios fue fiel a la alianza.

Un día, en una familia judía nació Jesús, el Hijo de Dios. Por medio de la muerte y Resurrección de Jesús, Dios extendió la alianza a todos los pueblos. La promesa de Dios se cumplió en Jesús y, a través de Jesús, todos los pueblos fueron salvados del poder del pecado y de la muerte eterna.

Los discípulos de Jesús y los miembros de la Iglesia siguen siendo un signo de la alianza de Dios al proclamar la Buena Nueva de Jesús y el Reino de Dios.

¿Cuál fue la alianza entre Dios y el pueblo de Israel?

Palabras de fe

Una **alianza** es una promesa o contrato sagrado entre Dios y los seres humanos.

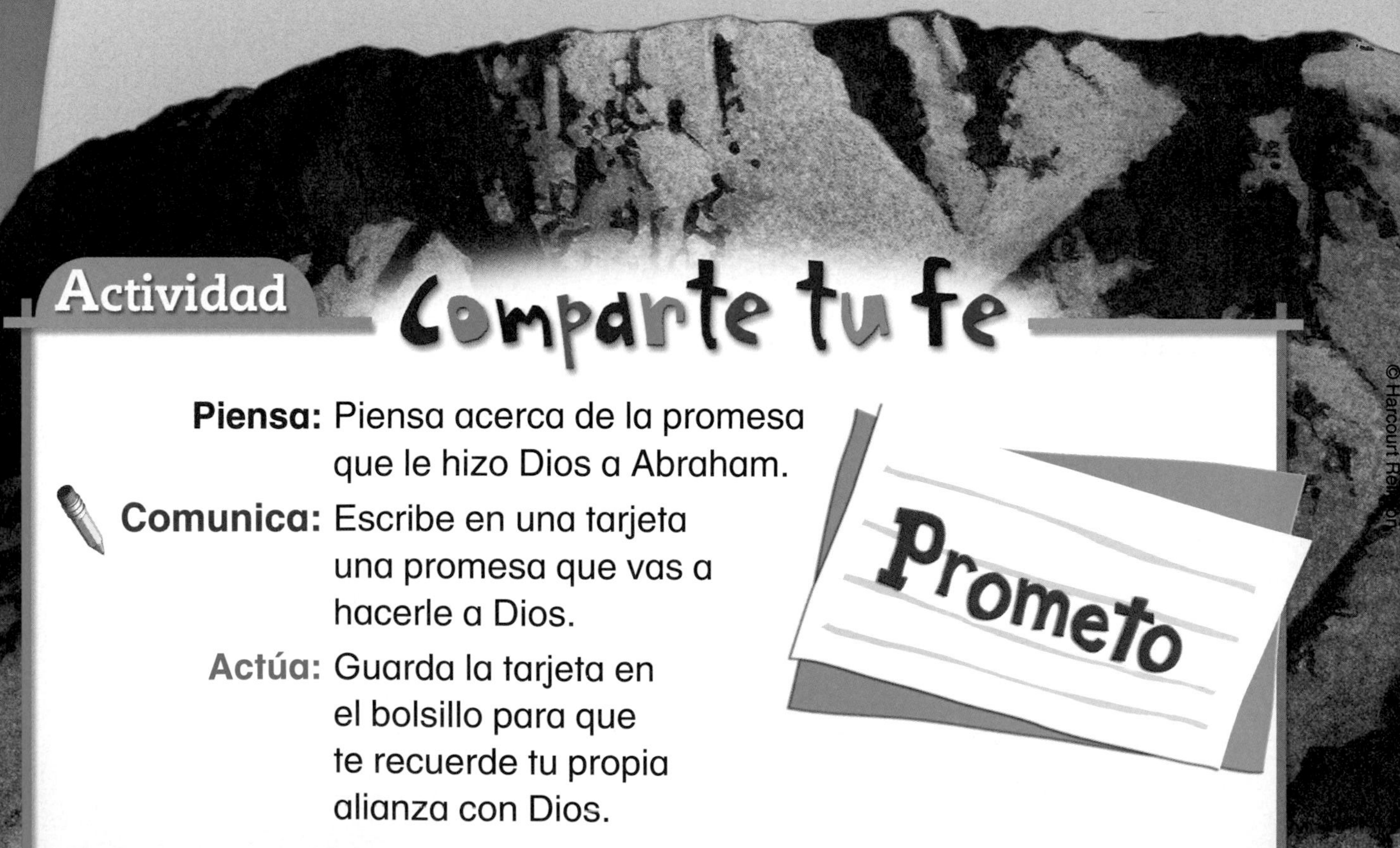

Actividad Comparte tu fe

Piensa: Piensa acerca de la promesa que le hizo Dios a Abraham.

Comunica: Escribe en una tarjeta una promesa que vas a hacerle a Dios.

Actúa: Guarda la tarjeta en el bolsillo para que te recuerde tu propia alianza con Dios.

Connected to the Past

God kept his promise. Abraham's family grew to be the people of Israel. God was faithful to the covenant.

Then Jesus, God's own Son, was born into a Jewish family. God extended the covenant to all people through Jesus' death and Resurrection. God's promise was fulfilled in Jesus. All people were saved from the power of sin and everlasting death through Jesus.

Followers of Jesus and members of the Church continue to be a sign of God's covenant. They do this as they proclaim the good news of Jesus and God's kingdom.

What was the covenant between God and the people of Israel?

Words of Faith

A **covenant** is a sacred promise or agreement between God and humans.

Activity Share Your Faith

Think: Think about God's promise to Abraham.

Share: Write on an index card a promise you will make with God.

Act: Keep the index card in your pocket to remind you of your own covenant with God.

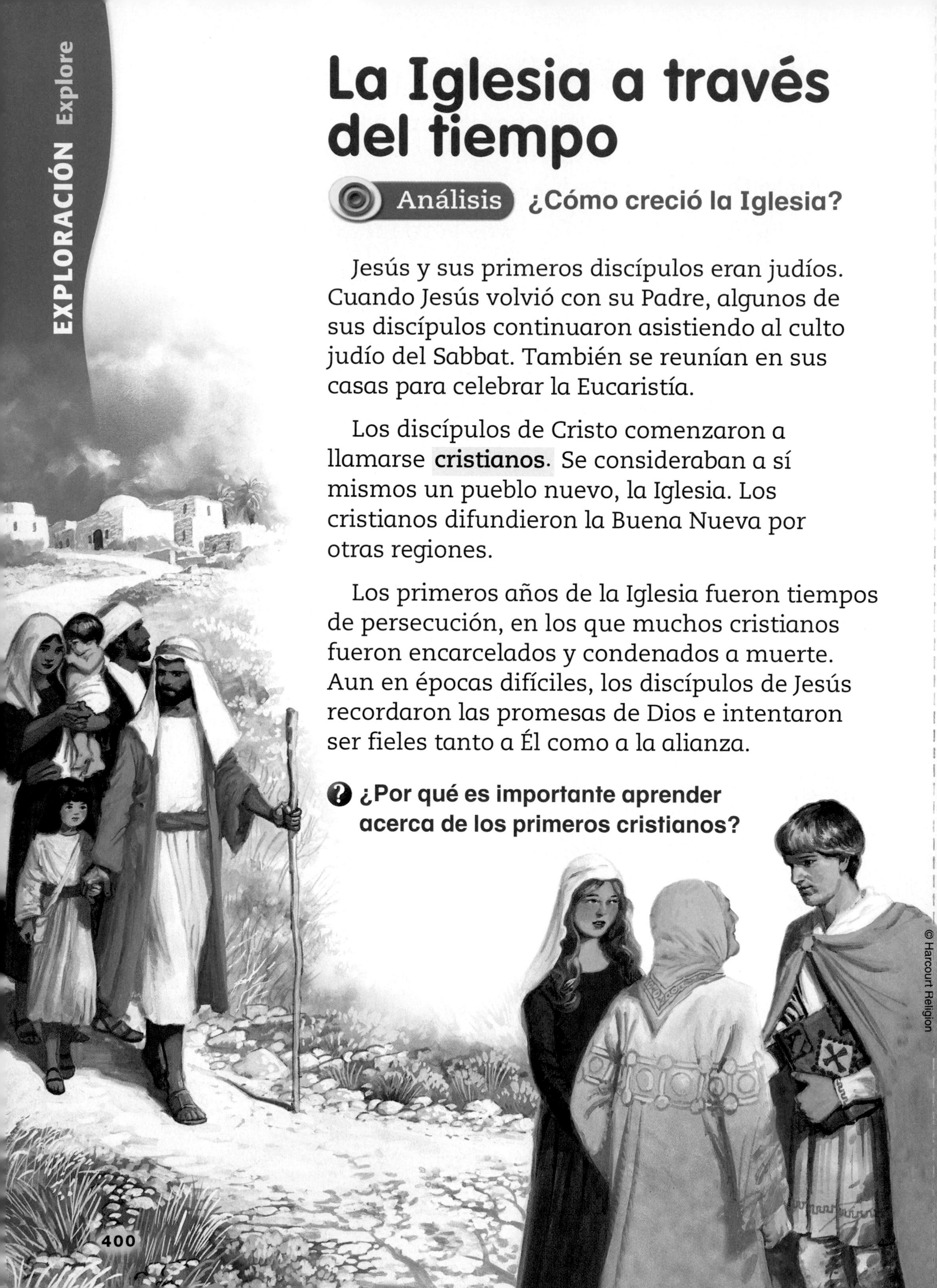

La Iglesia a través del tiempo

Análisis ¿Cómo creció la Iglesia?

Jesús y sus primeros discípulos eran judíos. Cuando Jesús volvió con su Padre, algunos de sus discípulos continuaron asistiendo al culto judío del Sabbat. También se reunían en sus casas para celebrar la Eucaristía.

Los discípulos de Cristo comenzaron a llamarse **cristianos**. Se consideraban a sí mismos un pueblo nuevo, la Iglesia. Los cristianos difundieron la Buena Nueva por otras regiones.

Los primeros años de la Iglesia fueron tiempos de persecución, en los que muchos cristianos fueron encarcelados y condenados a muerte. Aun en épocas difíciles, los discípulos de Jesús recordaron las promesas de Dios e intentaron ser fieles tanto a Él como a la alianza.

¿Por qué es importante aprender acerca de los primeros cristianos?

The Church Through Time

How did the Church grow?

Jesus and his first followers were Jews. After Jesus returned to the Father, some of his followers continued to attend Jewish services on the Sabbath. They also gathered to celebrate the Eucharist in their homes.

The followers of Christ became known as **Christians**. They saw themselves as a new people, as the Church. Christians spread the good news to other lands.

The early years of the Church were times of persecution, when many Christians were imprisoned or put to death. Even in difficult times, Jesus' followers remembered God's promises and tried to be faithful to him and to the covenant.

Why is it important to learn about the early Christians?

La Iglesia crece

Los cristianos mantienen viva a la Iglesia y la hacen crecer. Cuando los invasores del norte atacaron Roma, los cristianos de Irlanda y Escocia mantuvieron vivo el Evangelio en los monasterios. Los santos como Patricio, Brígida, Kevin y Columba continuaron la misión de la Iglesia.

Palabras de fe

Los **cristianos** son discípulos de Jesucristo. La palabra *cristiano* proviene de *Cristo.*

Hasta la actualidad

Muchos de los santos sobre los que has leído este año en Siervos de la fe llevaron la palabra de Dios a tierras lejanas con gran valentía. Gracias a ellos, la fe católica se extendió por África, Asia, Europa y las Américas.

La historia de la Iglesia sigue escribiéndose día a día. Tú y todas las personas que siguen a Jesús son también una parte importante de la fe.

Actividad Practica tu fe

Describe a los cristianos ¿Cómo saben los demás que eres cristiano?

Saben que soy discípulo de Jesús porque

___

La familia de mi parroquia muestra que sigue a Jesús cuando

___

Cuando pienso en los católicos, pienso en

___

The Church Grows

Christians kept the Church alive and growing. When invaders from the North attacked Rome, Christians in Ireland and Scotland kept the gospel alive in monasteries. Saints including Patrick, Brigid, Kevin, and Columba carried on the Church's mission.

Words of Faith

Christians are followers of Jesus Christ. The word *Christian* comes from *Christ*.

Into the Present

Many saints you have read about this year in People of Faith have bravely carried the word of God to distant lands. The Catholic faith has spread throughout Africa, Asia, Europe, and the Americas.

The Church's history is still being written today. You and all people who follow Jesus are an important part of the story of faith as well.

Activity — Connect Your Faith

Describe Christians How do people know that you are a Christian?

People know that I am a follower of Jesus because

____

My parish family shows that it follows Jesus by

____

When I think of Catholic Christians, I think of

____

Oración de fe

Reúnanse y comiencen con la señal de la cruz.

Líder: Dios Padre nuestro, recordamos hoy a nuestros antepasados, que caminaron contigo en la fe.

Lector 1: La fe es alcanzar lo que hemos esperado. Es nuestra esperanza en lo que no hemos visto.

Lector 2: Por la fe, creemos que Dios creó el mundo.

Lector 3: Por la fe, Noé construyó un arca cuando no veía agua.

Lector 1: Por la fe, Abraham obedeció a Dios cuando lo envió a un lugar lejano.

Lector 2: Por la fe, Moisés guió al pueblo de Dios a través del Mar Rojo como si fuera tierra seca.

Lector 3: Pero Dios tenía algo aun mejor para su pueblo.

Basado en Hebreos 11

Todos: **Demos gracias a Dios.**

Canten juntos.

¡Por la fe caminamos,
por la fe caminamos,
por la fe caminamos hacia el Reino!
¡Al orar escuchamos,
en sabiduría crecemos,
por la fe caminamos,
a la tierra prometida vamos!

Prayer of Faith

Gather and begin with the Sign of the Cross.

Leader: God our Father, we remember today our ancestors who have walked in faith with you.

Reader 1: Faith is getting what we have hoped for. It is our hope of what we have not seen.

Reader 2: By faith we believe that God created the world.

Reader 3: By faith Noah built an ark when he could see no water.

Reader 1: By faith Abraham obeyed when God sent him to a faraway place.

Reader 2: By faith Moses led God's people across the Red Sea as if it were dry land.

Reader 3: Yet God had something even better for his people.

Based on Hebrews 11

All: **Thanks be to God.**

Sing together.

We are walking by faith, we are walking by faith, we are walking by faith to the kingdom! In prayer we will listen, in your wisdom we will grow; we will walk by faith till we come to the promised land!

Repasar y aplicar

Trabaja con palabras Escribe o encierra en un círculo la respuesta correcta.

1. Dios (abandonó/fue fiel) al pueblo de Israel.
2. Los primeros cristianos se reunían a orar en el culto judío y en las (casas/iglesias católicas).
3. Los primeros cristianos (ocultaron/compartieron) su fe y a veces fueron perseguidos por ello.
4. ¿Qué es una alianza?

   ____

5. ¿Cuál fue la alianza de Dios con Abraham y Sara?

   ____

Actividad Vive tu fe

Honra a un santo Recuerda a un santo cristiano que haya colaborado en la difusión de la Palabra de Dios. Cuenta la historia del santo en tus propias palabras o con dibujos. Escribe una cosa que puedes hacer para seguir el ejemplo de ese santo.

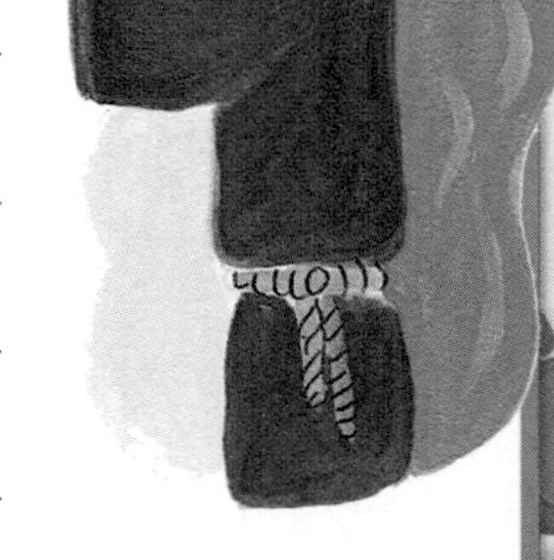

____

____

____

____

____

____

____

____

Review and Apply

Work with Words Write or circle the correct response.

1. God (abandoned/was faithful to) the people of Israel.
2. Early Christians met to pray at Jewish services and in (homes/Catholic churches).
3. Early Christians (hid/shared) their faith and were sometimes persecuted for doing so.
4. What is a covenant?

   ____

5. What was God's covenant with Abraham and Sarah?

   ____

Activity Live Your Faith

Praise a Saint Recall a Christian saint who helped spread the word of God. Tell the saint's story in your own words or in pictures. Name one thing you can do to follow the example of that saint.

____

____

____

____

____

____

____

____

CAPÍTULO 19

La fe en familia

Lo que creemos

- Dios cumplió su promesa de ser fiel para siempre enviándonos a su Hijo, Jesús.
- La Iglesia continúa siendo un signo de la alianza de Dios.

LA SAGRADA ESCRITURA

2 Corintios 3, 1–18 cuenta que los primeros cristianos se consideraban a sí mismos ministros.

Visita **www.harcourtreligion.com** para encontrar recursos basados en el año litúrgico y lecturas semanales de la Sagrada Escritura.

Actividad

Vive tu fe

Conversen sobre la vida cristiana Lean sobre cómo era la vida de los primeros cristianos en *Hechos 2, 42–47* y *Hechos 4, 32–35*. Conversen sobre cómo vivían y por qué creen ustedes que, para los primeros cristianos, era importante vivir de esa manera. Hagan una lista de las semejanzas que hay entre tu familia y tu comunidad parroquial y las primeras comunidades cristianas.

Siervos de la fe

▲ San Clemente de Roma murió c. 100 d.C.

Clemente fue uno de los primeros discípulos de Jesús. Fue obispo de Roma y uno de los primeros papas. Clemente trabajó mucho para ayudar a crecer a la Iglesia y enseñó a la gente por medio de cartas. Algunas veces su nombre se menciona en la Misa. El día de San Clemente se celebra el 23 de noviembre.

Una oración en familia

San Clemente, ruega por nosotros para que defendamos nuestra fe. Ayúdanos a enseñar a otros lo que es importante para nosotros como discípulos de Jesús. Amén.

 CIC *Consulta el Catecismo de la Iglesia Católica, números 781 y 1612, para obtener más información sobre el contenido del capítulo.*

CHAPTER 19

Family Faith

Catholics Believe

- God kept his promise to be forever faithful when he sent his Son, Jesus.
- The Church continues to be a sign of God's covenant.

SCRIPTURE

2 Corinthians 3:1–18 tells how the early Christians saw themselves as ministers.

www.harcourtreligion.com
For weekly Scripture readings and seasonal resources

Activity

Live Your Faith

Talk About Christian Living Read about the lives of the early Christians in *Acts 2:42–47* and *Acts 4:32–35*. Discuss how they lived and why you think it was important for the early Christians to live this way. List some ways in which your family and your parish community are like the early Christian community.

▲ Saint Clement of Rome died c. A.D. 100

People of Faith

Clement was one of Jesus' early followers. He became bishop of Rome and was one of the first popes. Clement worked hard to help the Church grow. He taught people by writing letters. Sometimes you hear his name during Mass. Saint Clement's feast day is November 23.

Family Prayer

Saint Clement, pray for us that we may stand up for our faith. Help us teach others about what is important to us as followers of Christ. Amen.

CCC *See Catechism of the Catholic Church 781, 1612 for further reading on chapter content.*

Capítulo 20

La Iglesia hoy

Oremos

Líder: Dios Creador nuestro, ayúdanos a construir tu Iglesia.
"La piedra rechazada por los maestros
pasó a ser la piedra principal".

Salmo 118, 22

Todos: Dios Creador nuestro, ayúdanos a construir tu Iglesia. Amén.

Actividad Comencemos

¿Qué harías tú? "Imaginen que tienen el poder para solucionar uno solo de los problemas que hay en el mundo", dijo la hermana Rosario. "¿Qué problema elegirían?".

Los niños se quedaron en silencio un momento. Entonces comenzaron a hacer sugerencias.

"Yo eliminaría las guerras", dijo Ernesto.

"Yo acabaría con la pobreza", respondió Ana.

"Yo, con la contaminación", dijo Josefina.

- ¿Qué problema tratarías de resolver? ¿Por qué?

Chapter 20 The Church Today

Let Us Pray

Leader: God our Creator, help us build up your Church.
"The stone the builders rejected
has become the cornerstone."
Psalm 118:22

All: God our Creator, help us build up your Church. Amen.

Activity Let's Begin

What Would You Do? "Imagine that you have the power to solve just one problem in the world," Sister Lorraine said. "Which problem would you choose?"

The children were silent for a moment. Then they started to make suggestions.

"I would end wars," Ernesto said.

"I would make sure that nobody was poor," Anna said.

"I would stop pollution," said Jen.

- Which problem would you choose to solve? Why?

La obra de la Iglesia

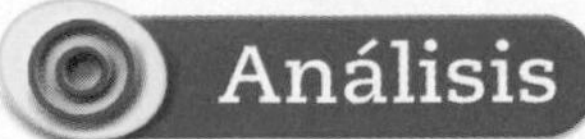

¿Cómo podemos cambiar el mundo cada uno de nosotros?

En el mundo hay muchos problemas que solucionar. La Iglesia trabaja para resolver esos problemas. Lee el siguiente relato sobre una niña que ayudó a los demás.

UN RELATO

El concierto de Colleen

Colleen dedicó sus vacaciones de verano a preparar un acontecimiento especial. Quería ayudar a los demás organizando un concierto. Invitó a músicos para que la ayudaran, eligió la música y buscó un director para la banda.

Colleen y su banda dieron el concierto en su barrio una tarde de verano.

"Yo quería que la gente disfrutara de la música, pero también quería recaudar dinero para la lucha contra una enfermedad que tiene un amigo mío. Recolectamos mucho dinero y además nos divertimos", dijo Colleen. "Y lo mejor de todo es que quizás el dinero ayude a los científicos a encontrar una cura para la enfermedad".

¿Cómo ayudó el concierto de Colleen a cambiar el mundo?

The Work of the Church

What difference can one person make?

The world has many problems that need to be solved. The Church is working to solve these problems. Read this story about a girl who helped others.

A STORY

Colleen's Concert

Colleen spent her summer vacation planning a special event. She wanted to help people by holding a concert. She invited musicians to help. She chose music and found a leader for the band.

Colleen's concert was held on a summer evening in her neighborhood.

"I wanted people to enjoy the music, but I also wanted to make money to help fight an illness one of my friends has. We earned a lot of money, and we had fun," Colleen said. "Best of all, maybe the money will help scientists find a cure for an illness."

How did Colleen's concert make a difference in the world?

Hacer la obra de Jesús

Colleen trabajó mucho para solucionar un problema que le preocupaba. Una vez Jesús envió a varios de sus discípulos a cambiar el mundo.

LA SAGRADA ESCRITURA Mateo 10, 5–14

Los discípulos son enviados

Jesús envió a sus discípulos en una misión: anunciar su Buena Nueva y curar a los enfermos. Estas son las instrucciones que les dio.

Vayan a visitar al pueblo de Israel. Díganles que el Reino de Dios está ahora cerca. Curen a los enfermos. No lleven provisiones, ni más ropa ni sandalias que las que lleven puestas. Cuando lleguen a un pueblo, busquen alguna persona buena y alójense en su casa. Al entrar en una casa, bendíganla. Si las personas no los quieren aceptar o escuchar, salgan de la casa o del pueblo y no se preocupen más por ello.

Basado en *Mateo 10, 5–14*

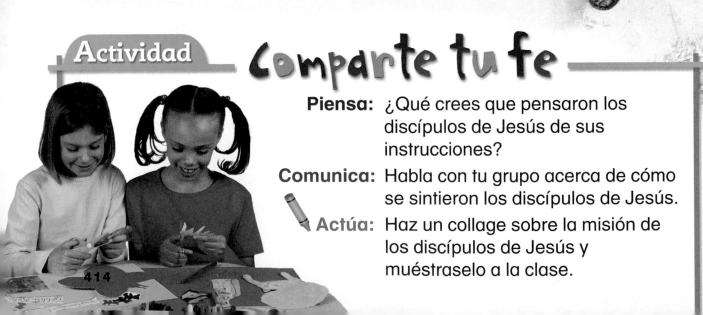

Actividad Comparte tu fe

Piensa: ¿Qué crees que pensaron los discípulos de Jesús de sus instrucciones?

Comunica: Habla con tu grupo acerca de cómo se sintieron los discípulos de Jesús.

Actúa: Haz un collage sobre la misión de los discípulos de Jesús y muéstraselo a la clase.

Doing Jesus' Work

Colleen worked hard to solve a problem. Jesus once sent out some of his followers to make a difference.

SCRIPTURE Matthew 10:5–14

Sending Out the Disciples

Jesus sent his followers on a mission to tell his good news and cure people who were sick. These are the instructions he gave them.

Travel to visit the people of Israel. Tell them that the kingdom of God is at hand. Cure people who are sick. Don't take supplies or extra clothes or sandals. Whenever you come to a town, find a good person's home, and stay there as long as you are in the town. When you go into a house, bless it. If people do not accept you or listen to you, leave the house or town and have nothing to do with it.

Based on *Matthew 10:5–14*

Activity Share Your Faith

Think: What do you think Jesus' followers thought about his instructions?

Share: Talk with your group about how Jesus' followers felt.

Act: Make a collage about their mission. Share it with your class.

Ayudar hoy

¿Cómo ayuda la Iglesia en el mundo actual?

Tú sabes que hay muchos problemas en el mundo. Algunos problemas son tan graves que quizá pienses que una persona de tu edad no puede hacer nada por solucionarlos. Quizá pienses que no tienes suficiente dinero o poder para cambiar las cosas. Piensa en los Apóstoles, que partieron a anunciar la Buena Nueva de Jesús. Luego, piensa en Colleen. El dinero que ella recaudó podría ayudar a los científicos a encontrar la cura para una enfermedad.

Cada vez que trabajas como los Apóstoles o como Colleen para mejorar el mundo, trabajas por el Reino de Dios. Cada vez que das de comer a alguien que tiene hambre, detienes una pelea o das esperanza a una persona, estás compartiendo la Buena Nueva de Jesús.

La fe católica no se refiere solo al pasado y al futuro. También es importante el presente. Aquí y ahora, tú eres la Iglesia.

¿Qué puedes hacer ahora mismo para mejorar el mundo?

Help Today

How does the Church help others in the world today?

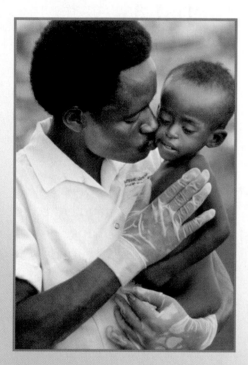

You know that there are many problems in the world. Some of the problems are so big that you may think someone your age can't help solve them. You may think that you don't have enough money or power to make a difference. Think about the Apostles who set out with Jesus' good news. Then think about Colleen. The money she raised might help scientists find a cure for a disease.

Every time you work as the Apostles or Colleen did to make the world better, you work for the kingdom of God. Every time you feed a person who is hungry, stop a fight, or give someone hope, you are sharing the good news of Jesus.

The Catholic faith is not only about the past and the future. It is about the present. Right here, right now, you are the Church.

? What can you do right now to make the world better?

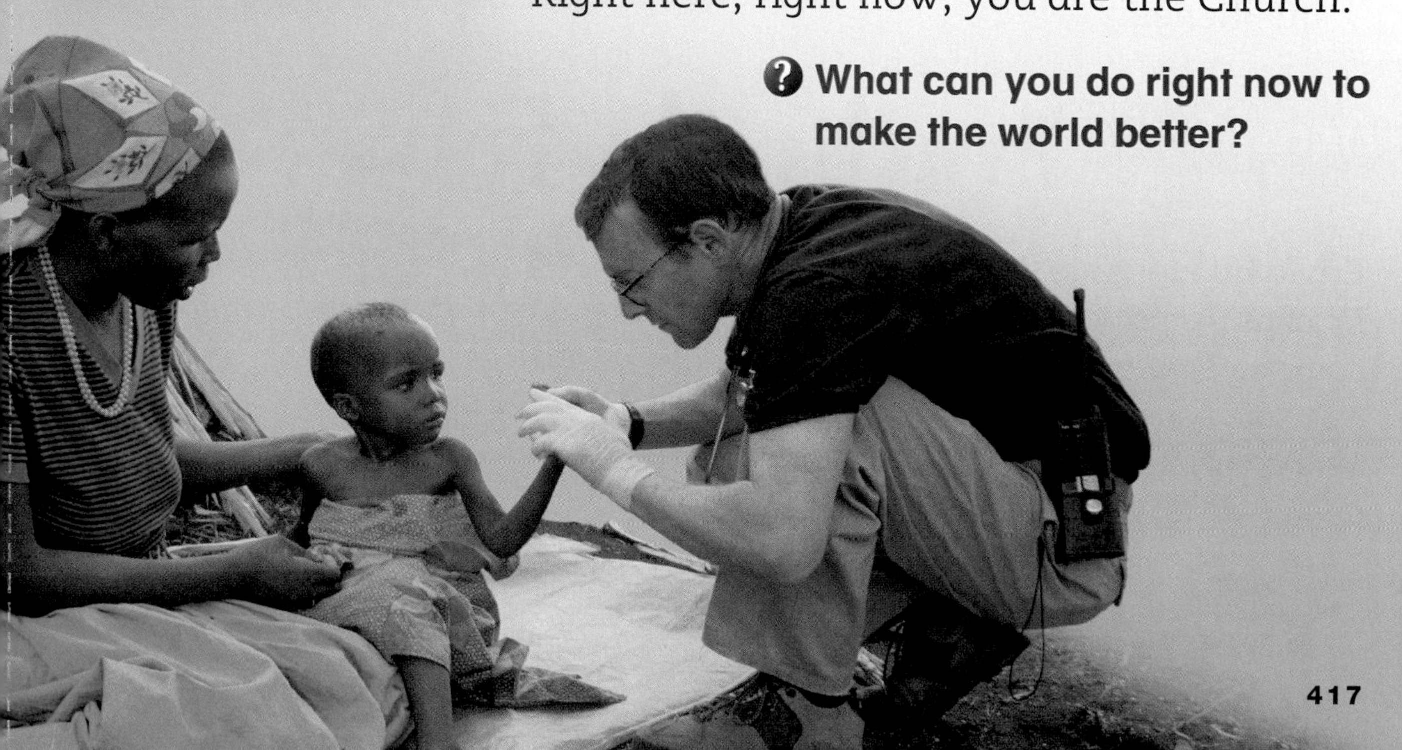

Compartir una misión

La misión de la Iglesia es anunciar la Buena Nueva, santificar al mundo y servir a Dios y a los demás. La Iglesia es un signo del Reino de Dios que ayuda a la gente a participar del amor de la Santísima Trinidad. Tú haces lo mismo cuando transmites la **justicia**, el amor y la **paz** de Dios con tus palabras y acciones. Cuando recibes el Bautismo se te pide que hagas todo esto.

Como miembro de la Iglesia, te unes a su obra. El Espíritu te fortalece para que hables de Jesús a los demás. Puedes trabajar por los derechos básicos de las personas, como el alimento, la ropa, la vivienda y la dignidad. También puedes atender a los pobres, a los enfermos o a los que están solos.

Palabras de fe

La **justicia** es la virtud de dar a Dios y a los demás lo que les corresponde.

La **paz** es la verdadera unión entre las personas, que las hace respetarse unas a otras y mantener el orden. Es el resultado del trabajo conjunto por la justicia.

¿Por qué ayudar a los demás?

Cuando colaboras con la misión de la Iglesia estás siguiendo el ejemplo de Jesús. Ayudas a los demás porque todos son tus hermanos y hermanas. Dios llama a todas las personas a que se unan en su familia y compartan lo que tienen.

Actividad Practica tu fe

Envía un mensaje
Muchas veces, la gente diseña camisetas para enviar algún mensaje especial. Escribe en esta camiseta un mensaje acerca de la misión de la Iglesia.

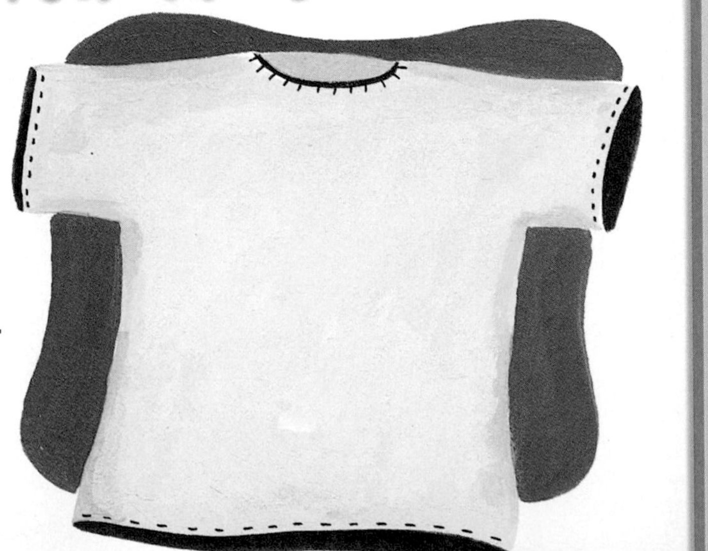

Sharing a Mission

The mission of the Church is to share the good news, to make the world holy, and to serve God and one another. The Church is a sign of God's kingdom. The Church helps people share in the love of the Holy Trinity. You do this when your words and actions show God's **justice**, love, and **peace**. You are asked to do this at your baptism.

As a member of the Church, you join in its work. The Spirit strengthens you to tell others about Jesus. You can work for everyone's basic rights, such as food, clothing, shelter, and dignity. You can care for people who are poor, ill, or lonely.

Words of Faith

Justice is the virtue of giving God and others what is their due.

Peace is the true unity among people that makes them want to respect one another and keep order. It is the good effect of working for justice.

Why Help Others?

When you help with the Church's mission, you follow the example of Jesus. You do this because all people are your sisters and brothers. God calls all people to be united in his family and to share what they have.

Activity Connect Your Faith

Send a Message People often create T-shirts to send a special message. On the T-shirt shown here, create a message about the Church's mission.

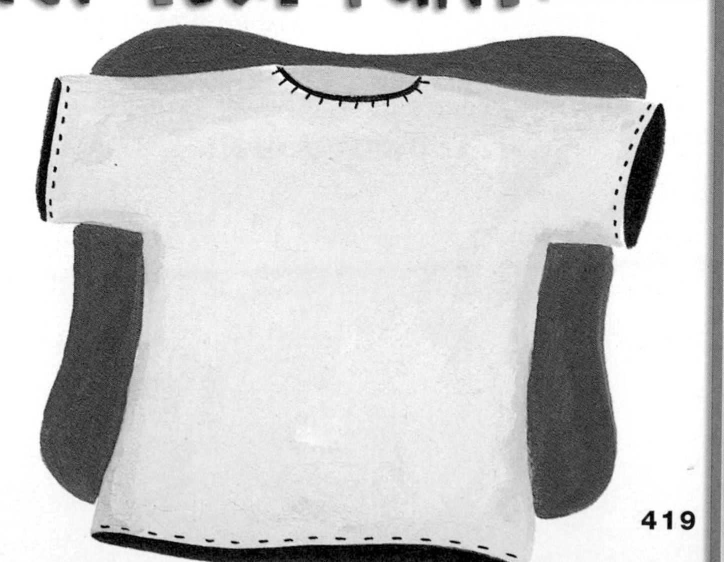

Oración por la paz

Reúnanse y comiencen con la señal de la cruz.

Canten juntos.

Un instrumento de tu paz
y de tu amor, hazme Señor.
En este mundo desesperado
de tu alegría una fuente seré.
Donde haya odio, lleve yo amor,
donde haya mal, alivio y perdón.
Donde haya duda, lleve la fe
y en las tinieblas, yo lleve tu luz.

Maestro, ayúdame a comprender
más que a pedir comprensión,
a consolar y llevar amor
más que a pedir a otros amor.
A poder ver que recibiré
todo de ti si todo lo doy,
que al perdonar me perdonarás,
y que al morir, nueva vida tendré.

Inclinen la cabeza mientras el líder reza.

Todos: Amén.

Prayer for Peace

Gather and begin with the Sign of the Cross.

Sing together.

Make me, Lord, a means of your peace;
make me, O Lord, a means of your love.
In this world, despairing and sad, make
me a source of courage and joy.
Where there is hatred, let me bring
love, where there is harm, your pardon
to soothe. Help me bring faith where
there is but doubt, and where it is
dark, the light of your truth.

Master, grant that I may not seek
so much consolation as to console,
Understanding as to understand,
so much to be loved as rather to
love. Help me to see in giving to all
how we in turn receive from your
hand, How we are pardoned as we
forgive, and how we, in death, are
born to new life.

Bow your heads as the leader prays.

All: Amen.

Repasar y aplicar

A Trabaja con palabras Escribe la letra de la respuesta correcta y luego encierra en un círculo la palabra Verdadero o Falso. Corrige los enunciados falsos.

	Columna 1	Columna 2
______	**1.** misión	**a.** Mostrar con palabras y acciones.
______	**2.** dar testimonio	**b.** Es un trabajo o tarea que eres enviado a realizar.
______	**3.** justicia	**c.** Dar a los demás lo que les corresponde.

4. Los discípulos de Jesús llevaron consigo mucho dinero y provisiones cuando salieron a ayudar a los demás.

Verdadero Falso ____________________________

5. Cuando ayudas a los demás, estás compartiendo el Reino de Dios en la tierra.

Verdadero Falso ____________________________

B Comprueba lo que aprendiste ¿Qué es la paz?

____

Actividad Vive tu fe

Haz un dibujo en el que estés trabajando por la justicia o la paz.

Review and Apply

A Work with Words Write the letter of the correct response, and then circle True or False. Correct any false statements.

Column 1		Column 2
_____	1. mission	a. to show by words or actions
_____	2. witness	b. a job or duty that you are sent to do
_____	3. justice	c. giving people what is their due

4. Jesus' followers carried lots of money and supplies when they went out to help others.

   True False ______________________

5. When you help others today, you share in God's kingdom on earth.

   True False ______________________

B Check Understanding What is peace?

____

Activity Live Your Faith

Draw a picture of yourself working for justice or peace.

La fe en familia

Lo que creemos

- Todos los miembros de la Iglesia comparten su misión de trabajar por la paz y la justicia.
- La Iglesia es un signo del Reino de Dios.

LA SAGRADA ESCRITURA

Gálatas 3, 27–28 nos cuenta que todos los cristianos somos de Cristo.

Visita **www.harcourtreligion.com** para encontrar recursos basados en el año litúrgico y lecturas semanales de la Sagrada Escritura.

Actividad

Vive tu fe

Preocuparse por los demás Los cristianos trabajan para que se respeten los derechos de todas las personas, especialmente los derechos de los pobres, de los enfermos y de los que están solos. Diseña una tarjeta que muestre cómo puedes ayudar a una persona pobre o a alguien que está enfermo o solo.

Siervos de la fe

Jean Donovan trabajaba como misionera laica en El Salvador. Compartía sus dones de la alegría, la música y el amor con los niños pobres para darles esperanza. Jean fue asesinada junto con tres hermanas religiosas por la Guardia Nacional de El Salvador. Los miembros de esa organización temían que las cuatro mujeres enseñaran al pueblo de El Salvador acerca de los derechos humanos.

▲ Jean Donovan 1953–1980

Una oración en familia

Querido Dios, ayúdanos a llevar alegría y esperanza a los que las necesitan. Amén.

 CIC *Consulta el Catecismo de la Iglesia Católica, números 2044 y 2046, para obtener más información sobre el contenido del capítulo.*

CHAPTER 20

Family Faith

Catholics Believe

- All members of the Church share in its mission to work for peace and justice.
- The Church is a sign of the kingdom of God.

SCRIPTURE

Galatians 3:27–28 tells us that all Christians belong to Christ.

www.harcourtreligion.com
For weekly Scripture readings and seasonal resources

Activity

Live Your Faith

Concern for Others Christians work to make sure that every person's human rights are protected, especially the rights of people who are poor, ill, or lonely. Create a note card that shows one way that you can help a person who is poor, ill, or lonely.

People of Faith

▲ Jean Donovan
1953–1980

Jean Donovan worked as a lay missionary in El Salvador. She shared her gifts of laughter, music, and love with children who were poor. She gave them hope. Jean was killed along with three religious sisters by the El Salvador national guard. Members of that organization feared that the four women would teach the people of El Salvador about human rights.

Family Prayer

Dear God, help us bring joy and hope to those in need. Amen.

CCC See Catechism of the Catholic Church 2044-2046 for further reading on chapter content.

Capítulo 21 ¡Vida para siempre!

Oremos

Líder: Padre de amor, alabamos tu nombre por siempre.
"Tu reino es reino por todos los siglos,
y tu imperio por todas las edades".
Salmo 145, 13

Todos: Padre de amor, alabamos tu nombre por siempre. Amén.

Actividad Comencemos

El regalo de la vida "Abuela, ¿qué está haciendo papá?", preguntó Tomás.

"Está trayendo todos los regalos para tu nueva hermanita", contestó la abuela.

El papá de Tomás entró con los brazos cargados de flores, globos y un gran oso de peluche. "Papá, ¿dónde está mamá?", le preguntó Tomás.

Su papá contestó: "Trae el regalo más importante de todos: ¡tu hermanita!".

"¿Dónde está? ¡Quiero verla!", dijo Tomás con una sonrisa.

- ¿Alguna vez le diste la bienvenida a alguien de tu familia? Cuenta tu experiencia.

Chapter 21 Live Forever!

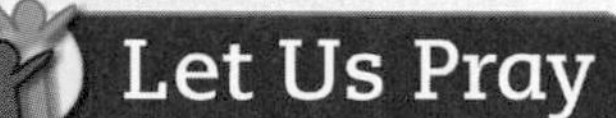

Let Us Pray

Leader: Loving Father, we praise your name forever.
"Your reign is a reign for all ages,
your dominion for all generations."
Psalm 145:13

All: Loving Father, we praise your name forever. Amen.

Activity Let's Begin

The Gift of Life "Grandma, what is Dad doing?" Tommy asked.

"He's bringing in all the gifts for your new baby sister," Grandma said.

Dad came in carrying flowers, balloons, and a large teddy bear. "Dad, where is Mom?" Tommy wondered.

Dad replied, "She is bringing in the most important gift, your baby sister!"

"Wow! I can't wait to see her," Tommy said, smiling.

- Have you ever welcomed a new family member? Tell about it.

El ciclo de la vida

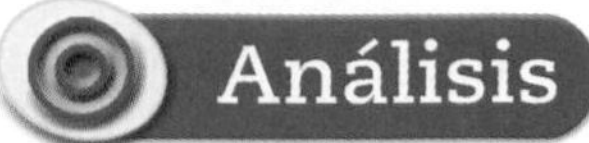

¿Qué sucede después de la muerte?

El ciclo de la vida comienza con el nacimiento y termina con la muerte. Lee el siguiente relato, que trata sobre el ciclo de la vida y cómo sobrellevar una pérdida.

UN RELATO

La pequeña margarita

Al comienzo de la primavera, de una semilla nació un capullito llamado Margarita. Margarita se hizo amiga de otro capullito que se llamaba Girasol.

Margarita creció y se transformó en una pequeña flor blanca con el centro amarillo. Girasol se hizo muy alta, y le salieron unos pétalos amarillos y un gran centro marrón. A las dos flores les gustaba el rocío fresco de la mañana y el sol cálido del verano.

Un día, soplaba un viento muy frío. Margarita vio que en sus hojas se había formado hielo.

"¿Qué está pasando?", preguntó.

Girasol le contestó: "Al final del verano, nos llega la hora de morir. Cuando mueras, tus semillas volverán al suelo. ¡Y de ellas nacerán flores nuevas!".

"Ahora me siento mucho mejor", dijo Margarita.

Agachó la cabeza y suspiró: "Tuve una vida muy linda".

¿Por qué se sintió mejor Margarita al saber que de sus semillas nacerían flores?

Cycles of Life

What happens after death?

The cycle of life begins with birth and ends in death. Read this story about the cycle of life and dealing with loss.

A STORY

The Little Daisy

Early one spring, a little bud named Daisy grew from a seed. She became friends with a bud named Sunflower.

Daisy grew into a small white flower with a little yellow head. Sunflower grew very tall with yellow petals and a large brown head. They both loved the fresh morning dew and the warm summer sun.

One day the wind got very cold. Daisy noticed that ice had formed on her leaves.

"What is happening?" she asked.

Sunflower said, "At the end of summer, it is time for us to die. When you die, your seeds will fall back into the ground. New flowers will bloom from your seeds!"

"I feel much better now," said Daisy.

She laid her head down and said, "I've had a beautiful life."

Why did Daisy feel better after learning that flowers would bloom from her seeds?

Una nueva vida

Cuando Jesús vino a la tierra, dijo a los pueblos que, si creían en Él, tendrían vida eterna. Su propia Resurrección es la prueba de que su promesa es verdadera. Sus discípulos lo vieron vivo después de haber muerto. Más tarde, Juan, uno de los discípulos de Jesús, tuvo una visión de lo que sucedería al fin de los tiempos. Esto es lo que dijo acerca de su visión.

LA SAGRADA ESCRITURA

Después vi un cielo nuevo y una tierra nueva. La antigua creación había desaparecido. Vi una ciudad santa que bajaba del cielo. Era como una nueva Jerusalén. Oí la voz de Dios que decía que ya no habría más llanto ni pena; ya no habría más sufrimiento ni muerte.

Basado en *Apocalipsis 21, 1–4*

Actividad Comparte tu fe

Piensa: Imagina cómo serían un cielo nuevo y una tierra nueva.

Comunica: ¿Qué aspecto tendrían? Haz un dibujo.

Actúa: Lleva el dibujo a tu casa y ponlo donde todos lo vean. Les recordará la esperanza que tenemos los cristianos gracias a Jesús.

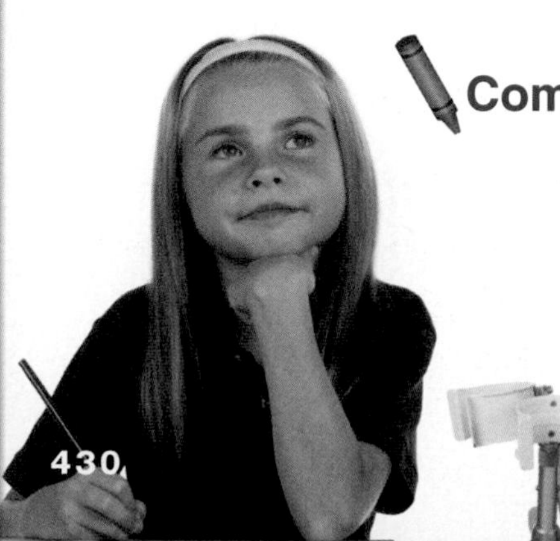

New Life

When Jesus came to earth, he told people that if they believed in him, they would have everlasting life. His own Resurrection is the proof that his promise is true. His followers saw him alive after he had died. Later, John, who was one of Jesus' followers, had a vision from God of what would come at the end of time. This is what John said about his vision.

SCRIPTURE

I saw a new heaven and a new earth. The old creation had passed away. I saw a holy city coming out of the sky. It was like a new Jerusalem. I heard God's voice saying that there would be no more tears or sadness, no more suffering or death.

Based on *Revelation 21:1–4*

Activity Share Your Faith

Think: Imagine what a new heaven and earth would be like.

Share: What will the new heaven and earth look like? Draw a picture.

Act: Take the picture home and hang it for all to see. This will remind you of the hope that Christians have because of Jesus.

El futuro de la Iglesia

Análisis ¿Qué creen los cristianos sobre el futuro?

La Iglesia espera con ilusión la reunión con Dios, sabiendo que, después de la muerte, el Reino de Dios alcanzará su plenitud.

Al morir seremos juzgados e iremos al **cielo**, al **infierno** o al **purgatorio**. Todas las personas serán juzgadas al fin de los tiempos, como dijo Jesús. Quienes amaron a Dios y a los demás vivirán con Dios para siempre.

Así como esperas con ilusión los buenos momentos en la tierra, también puedes esperar con ilusión la segunda venida de Cristo y el **juicio final**, que tendrá lugar al fin de los tiempos. Los católicos viven con la esperanza de que la gracia de Dios y sus actos de amor los guíen hacia la vida eterna con Dios.

? ¿Por qué esperan con ilusión los cristianos la segunda venida de Cristo?

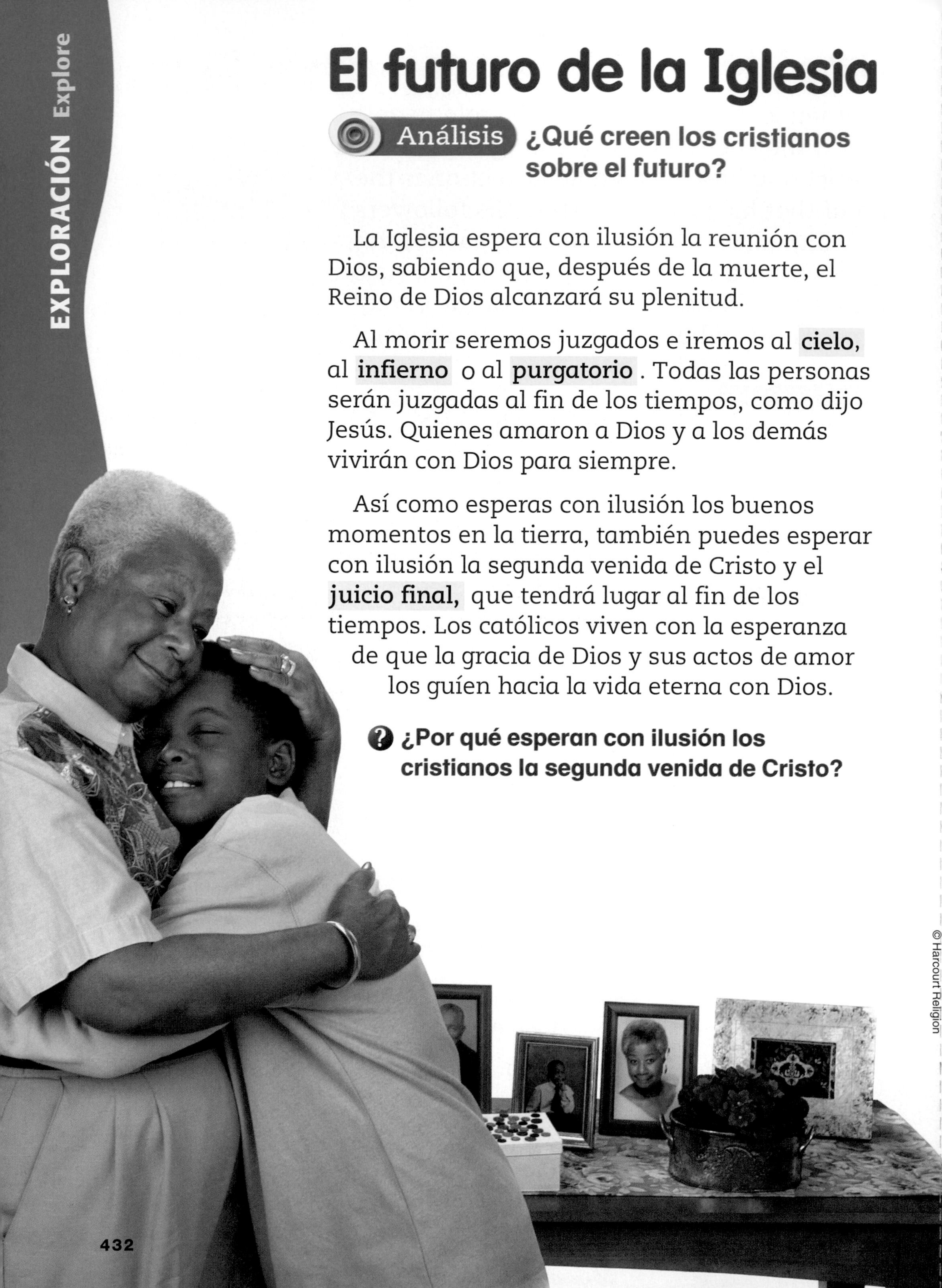

The Church's Future

Focus **What do Christians believe about the future?**

The Church looks forward to a reunion with God. The Church looks beyond death to the coming of God's kingdom in its fullness.

When we die we will be judged and go to **heaven**, **hell**, or **purgatory**. At the end of time all people will be judged, as Jesus said. Those who have loved God and have loved others will live with God forever.

Just as you look forward to good times on earth, you can look forward to Christ's second coming and the **last judgment** at the end of time. Catholics live in hope that God's grace and their loving actions will lead to everlasting life with God.

? Why do Christians look forward to the second coming of Christ?

El principio y el fin

La Biblia empieza y termina con relatos acerca de la creación. En el libro del Génesis, el primer libro de la Biblia, puedes leer cómo Dios creó todas las cosas por amor. El último libro, el libro del Apocalipsis, termina con la visión de Juan de una nueva creación, el Reino eterno de Dios. Cuenta que el mundo y la Iglesia serán perfectos, y todos los fieles resucitarán a una nueva vida.

El Hijo de Dios, la Palabra de Dios, estuvo presente en la creación y estará presente al fin de los tiempos. En la visión de Juan, Jesucristo dice:

LA SAGRADA ESCRITURA

"Yo soy el Alfa y la Omega, el Primero y el Último, el Principio y el Fin".

Apocalipsis 22, 13

Palabras de fe

El **cielo** es estar con Dios felices para siempre.

El **infierno** es estar apartados de Dios para siempre por haberlo rechazado totalmente.

El **purgatorio** es un estado de purificación final antes de entrar al cielo.

El **juicio final** será al fin de los tiempos. Jesús volverá a la tierra para juzgar a los vivos y a los muertos, y para llevar el Reino de Dios a su plenitud.

Actividad Practica tu fe

Haz una pegatina para el carro Todos los que amen a Dios y a los demás estarán con Dios para siempre. Piensa en un mensaje para compartir con los que no conocen el amor de Dios. Escribe en este recuadro el texto de una pegatina para el carro que comunique tu mensaje. Decora tu pegatina.

The Beginning and the End

The Bible begins and ends with stories of creation. In the Book of Genesis, the first book of the Bible, you read how God created all things out of love. The last book, the Book of Revelation, ends with John's vision of a new creation. This is God's everlasting kingdom. The world and the Church will then be perfect. All faithful people will be raised to new life.

The Son of God, the Word of God, was present at the creation, and he will be present at the end of time. In John's vision Jesus Christ says,

SCRIPTURE

"I am the Alpha and the Omega, the first and the last, the beginning and the end."

Revelation 22:13

Words of Faith

Heaven is being with God forever in happiness.

Hell is being separated forever from God because of a choice to turn away from him completely.

Purgatory is a state of final cleansing before entrance into heaven.

Last judgment is at the end of time. Jesus will come again to judge the living and the dead and to bring the kingdom of God to its fullness.

Activity Connect Your Faith

Make a Bumper Sticker All people who love God and others will be with God forever. Think about a message to share with those who do not know God's love. In the box below, write a bumper sticker to share your message. Decorate your bumper sticker.

Oración por el Reino

Reúnanse y comiencen con la señal de la cruz.

Líder: Nos encontramos reunidos para orar por la venida del Reino.

Lector 1: Señor, hemos aprendido mucho acerca de ti este año.

Lector 2: Nos hemos enseñado los unos a los otros acerca de tu amor.

Lector 3: Ayúdanos a aprender aun más sobre ti en la escuela, en nuestra casa y cuando jugamos.

Lector 1: Ayúdanos a crecer para que seamos más bondadosos y mostremos tu amor a todos los que nos conocen.

Lector 2: Al fin de nuestra vida terrenal, júzganos por nuestros actos de amor.

Lector 3: Esperamos reunirnos con tus santos y gozar por siempre en tu presencia.

Todos: **¡Ven, Señor Jesús! Amén.**

Canten juntos.

¡Ven! ¡Vive en la luz! ¡Brilla en el gozo
y en su amor!
¡Dios nos llama a ser luz en el mundo
y a vivir y ser libres en el Reino de Dios!

Prayer for the Kingdom

Gather and begin with the Sign of the Cross.

Leader: We gather and share a prayer for the coming of the kingdom.

Reader 1: God, we have learned so much about you this year.

Reader 2: We have taught one another about your love.

Reader 3: Help us learn even more about you in school, at home, and at play.

Reader 1: Help us grow to be more caring people, who will show your love to all who know us.

Reader 2: When our earthly lives end, judge us by our loving deeds.

Reader 3: We hope to join your saints and rejoice in your presence forever.

All: **Come, Lord Jesus! Amen.**

Sing together.

Come! Live in the
light! Shine with
the joy and the love
of the Lord! We are
called to be light for the
kingdom, to live in the
freedom of the city of God!

Repasar y aplicar

A Comprueba lo que aprendiste Completa cada enunciado con el término correcto del vocabulario.

1. Nuestra vida terrenal terminará con la ______________.
2. Todos seremos ______________ y enviados al ______________, al ______________, o al ______________.
3. Al fin de los tiempos, ______________ volverá a la tierra.
4. Eso será el ______________ y la segunda ______________.
5. Si has vivido con ______________, tendrás un lugar en el ______________ para siempre.

VOCABULARIO

cielo
muerte
Jesús
amor
juicio final
Reino de Dios
infierno
purgatorio
juzgados
venida

B Relaciona Imagina que tuvieras que explicarle qué es el cielo a un niño pequeño. ¿Qué le dirías?

____

____

Actividad Vive tu fe

Recuerda Tomar decisiones que muestren amor y seguir a Jesús puede ayudarte a formar parte del Reino de Dios para siempre. Haz un cartel que ayude a recordarte hacer estas cosas durante el verano.

CHAPTER 21

Review and Apply

A Check Understanding Complete each sentence with the correct term from the Word Bank.

1. Our earthly life will end in ____________.
2. Each peron will be ____________ and sent to ____________, ____________, or ____________.
3. At the end of time, ____________ will come again.
4. This is the ____________ and the second ____________.
5. If you have lived with ____________, you will have a place in ____________ forever.

WORD BANK

heaven
death
Jesus
love
last judgment
God's kingdom
hell
purgatory
judged
coming

B Make Connections Imagine that you must explain heaven to a younger child. What will you say?

____

____

Activity Live Your Faith

Remind Yourself Making loving choices and following Jesus are things you can do so that you will be part of God's kingdom forever. Make a sign that will remind you to do this over the summer.

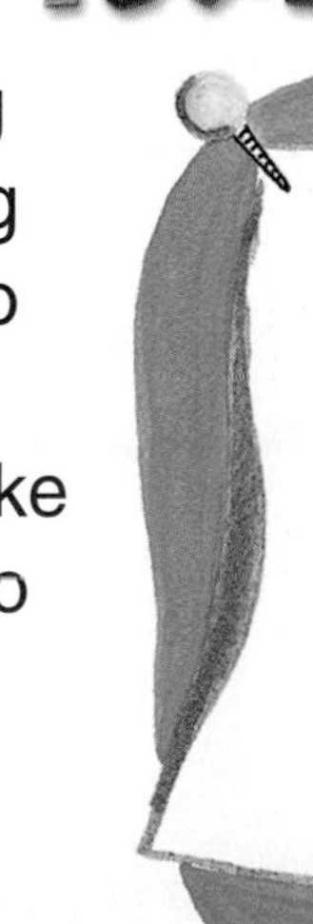

La fe en familia

Lo que creemos

- Las personas que mueren en amistad con Dios viven para siempre en su presencia.
- Al fin del mundo, Cristo nos juzgará por la forma en que hayamos vivido.

LA SAGRADA ESCRITURA

Juan 14, 1–4 habla acerca del lugar que te prepara Jesús. Lee los versículos y habla sobre ellos con tu familia.

Visita **www.harcourtreligion.com** para encontrar recursos basados en el año litúrgico y lecturas semanales de la Sagrada Escritura.

Actividad

Vive tu fe

Proyecto en familia Organicen una reunión familiar especial para recordar a los seres queridos que murieron. Cuenten historias sobre cómo mostraron amor esas personas. Oren para que encuentren gozo y paz en el Reino de Dios.

Siervos de la fe

▲ San Dimas murió c. 33 d.C.

Dimas fue uno de los dos delincuentes que fueron crucificados junto a Jesús. Antes de morir, admitió su culpa y dijo que merecía ser castigado por sus acciones. Después dijo: "Jesús, acuérdate de mí cuando entres en tu Reino" *(Lucas 23, 42)*. Jesús le contestó que estaría con él en el paraíso aquel mismo día.

Una oración en familia

San Dimas, ruega por nosotros para que veamos las cosas con la claridad con la que tú las viste. Ayúdanos a estar cerca de Jesús ahora y en la hora de nuestra muerte. Amén.

 CIC *Consulta el Catecismo de la Iglesia Católica, números 1023–1029 y 1039, para obtener más información sobre el contenido del capítulo.*

Family Faith

Catholics Believe

- People who die in God's friendship live forever in God's presence.
- At the end of the world, Christ will judge all people on the way they chose to live their lives.

SCRIPTURE

John 14:1–4 is about Jesus' preparing a place for you. Read the verses and talk about them with your family.

GO ONLINE **www.harcourtreligion.com** For weekly Scripture readings and seasonal resources

Activity

Live Your Faith

Family Project Have a special family gathering for remembering loved ones who have died. Tell stories about how those people showed love. Pray that they find joy and peace in God's kingdom.

▲ Saint Dismas died c. A.D. 33

People of Faith

Dismas was one of the two criminals who were crucified at the same time as Jesus. Dismas admitted his own guilt and said that he deserved punishment for his actions. Then Dismas said, "Jesus, remember me when you come into your kingdom" *(Luke 23:42)*. Jesus replied that Dismas would be in paradise with him that same day.

Family Prayer

Saint Dismas, pray for us that we may see things as clearly as you did. Help us be close to Jesus now and at the hour of our death. Amen.

CCC *See Catechism of the Catholic Church 1023–1029, 1039 for further reading on chapter content.*

Repaso de la Unidad 7

A Trabaja con palabras Encierra en un círculo la letra de la opción que mejor completa cada enunciado.

1. Una ______ es una promesa sagrada entre Dios y los seres humanos.

   a. voto b. alianza c. compromiso

2. El ______ es un estado de purificación final antes de entrar al cielo.

   a. purificación b. infierno c. purgatorio

3. El ______ es estar apartados de Dios para siempre.

   a. purgatorio b. infierno c. tinieblas

4. La ______ es la virtud de dar a Dios y a los demás lo que les corresponde.

   a. paz b. caridad c. justicia

5. El ______ es estar con Dios para siempre.

   a. paz b. justicia c. cielo

B Comprueba lo que aprendiste Completa cada enunciado con el término correcto del vocabulario.

VOCABULARIO

juicio final
Israel
dar testimonio
muerte
paz

6. La familia de Abraham creció hasta convertirse en el pueblo de ______________.
7. ______________ es mostrar con palabras y acciones.
8. La ______________ hace que las personas se respeten entre sí.
9. Nuestra vida terrenal terminará con la ______________.
10. En el ______________________________, Jesús vendrá a juzgar a los vivos y a los muertos.

Unit 7 Review

A Work with Words Circle the letter of the choice that best completes each sentence.

1. A _____ is a sacred promise between God and humans.
   a. vow b. covenant c. commitment
2. _____ is the state of preparation before heaven.
   a. purification b. hell c. purgatory
3. _____ is being separated from God forever.
   a. purgatory b. hell c. darkness
4. _____ is the virtue that moves people to give God and their neighbors what is their due.
   a. peace b. charity c. justice
5. _____ is being with God forever.
   a. peace b. justice c. heaven

B Check Understanding Complete each sentence with the correct word(s) from the Word Bank.

WORD BANK

last judgment
Israel
witness
death
peace

6. Abraham's family grew to become the people of __________.
7. To show by words or action is to __________.
8. __________ makes people want to respect one another.
9. Our earthly lives will end in __________.
10. At the __________, Jesus will come to judge the living and the dead.

Recursos católicos

Sagrada Escritura

La Biblia

La **Biblia** es un libro sagrado. También se le conoce como la Sagrada Escritura. Contiene la Palabra de Dios escrita por personas. La Biblia está dividida en dos partes: el Antiguo Testamento y el Nuevo Testamento. Cada una de esas partes consta de varios libros.

Datos de fe

Los judíos llaman *Torá* a los primeros cinco libros de su Biblia.

El Antiguo Testamento

El Antiguo Testamento también se conoce como la Sagrada Escritura hebrea. Cuenta la historia del pueblo hebreo y de su alianza con Dios. La Iglesia utiliza lecturas del Antiguo Testamento en casi todas las Misas. En el Antiguo Testamento hay relatos de la Biblia que tú conoces. Por ejemplo, los relatos de Adán y Eva, Noé, Abraham y Sara, Moisés, José y sus hermanos, y el rey David están en el Antiguo Testamento. Todos estos relatos te hablan de tus antepasados en la fe.

El Nuevo Testamento

El Nuevo Testamento cuenta la historia de nuestra fe desde el nacimiento de Jesús. Los primeros cuatro libros se conocen como los evangelios. Hablan de la vida de Jesús en la tierra y de cómo murió y resucitó

Catholic Source Book

Scripture

The Bible

The **Bible** is a holy book. The Bible is also called Scripture. It contains God's word written down by humans. The Bible is made up of two parts, the Old Testament and the New Testament. Many different books are included in the Bible.

Faith Fact

Jewish people call the first five books of their Bible the *Torah*.

Old Testament

The Old Testament is also called the Hebrew Scriptures. It tells the story of the Hebrew people and their covenant with God. The Church reads from the Old Testament at most Masses. The Old Testament includes Bible stories that you know. The stories of Adam and Eve, Noah, Abraham and Sarah, Moses, Joseph and his brothers, and King David are in the Old Testament. These stories tell you about your ancestors in faith.

New Testament

The New Testament tells the story of our faith since Jesus was born. The first four books are called the Gospels. They tell about Jesus' life on

para salvarnos. El libro llamado *Hechos de los Apóstoles* cuenta cómo creció la Iglesia después de que Jesús regresó al Padre. Las cartas de san Pablo y de otros líderes de la Iglesia explican a los discípulos de Jesús cómo vivir la fe. Por último, el libro del Apocalipsis animó a los cristianos que estaban siendo perseguidos, y en cierto modo describe lo que sucederá al fin de los tiempos, cuando Jesús vuelva a la tierra en gloria.

Los evangelios

La palabra *Evangelio* significa "buena nueva". El mensaje del Evangelio es la Buena Nueva del Reino de Dios y de su amor salvador. La Iglesia da el nombre de *evangelios* a los primeros cuatro libros del Nuevo Testamento, que hablan de la vida y las enseñanzas de Jesús. En todas las Misas se lee un pasaje de uno de los cuatro evangelios.

Las parábolas

Las parábolas son relatos que se usan para enseñar. Jesús contaba parábolas para hablar del Reino de Dios. Las parábolas también cuentan de cómo se llega al Reino. El relato del fariseo y el publicano es una parábola que nos enseña cómo debemos rezar.

earth and how he died and rose to save us. A book called the *Acts of the Apostles* tells how the Church grew after Jesus returned to his Father. Letters from Saint Paul and other Church leaders tell Jesus' followers how to live their faith. Finally, the Book of Revelation encouraged Christians who were being persecuted, and, in some ways, tells what will happen at the end of time, when Jesus comes again in glory.

Gospels

The word *gospel* means "good news." The gospel message is the good news of God's kingdom and saving love. The Church gives the name *Gospels* to the first four books of the New Testament that tell about Jesus' life and teachings. Every Mass includes a reading from one of the four Gospels.

Parables

Parables are teaching stories. Jesus used parables to tell about the kingdom of God. Parables also tell how to live in the kingdom. The story of the Pharisee and the tax collector is a parable. It teaches about the right way to pray.

El Reino de Dios

El Reino de Dios tiene dos significados. El Reino de Dios está aquí y ahora en la tierra. Está presente cuando los discípulos de Jesús anuncian la Buena Nueva y muestran el amor y la bondad de Dios a los demás. El Reino de Dios llegará a su plenitud al fin de los tiempos. Entonces, los discípulos de Jesús vivirán con Dios para siempre en paz total y alegría.

Las cartas

San Pablo visitó iglesias de lugares lejanos para ayudarlas a crecer y a difundir la Buena Nueva. También escribió cartas a las comunidades que había visitado. En sus cartas, les daba consejos para resolver problemas y trabajar unidos como discípulos de Jesús. Esas cartas forman parte del Nuevo Testamento. Una de las lecturas que se hacen en la Misa se toma de las cartas de san Pablo o de otro fundador de la Iglesia.

Los versículos de la Biblia

Para aprender a leer las citas bíblicas, usa el ejemplo de *Mateo* 8, 23–27.

Mateo es el nombre de un libro de la Biblia. El número del capítulo siempre aparece después del nombre del libro. Por lo tanto, 8 es el número del capítulo y los números 23–27 se refieren a los versículos.

The Kingdom of God

The kingdom of God means two things. The kingdom of God is here on earth right now. It happens when Jesus' followers share the good news and show God's love and care to others. The kingdom of God will come in fullness at the end of time. Then Jesus' followers will live forever with God in perfect peace and joy.

Letters

Saint Paul made visits to churches in distant places. He helped the churches grow and spread the good news. He also wrote letters to the churches he visited. He gave advice on how to solve problems and how to work together as Jesus' followers. These letters are part of the New Testament. One reading at Mass comes from a letter of Saint Paul or another early Church leader.

Bible Verses

To learn how to read Bible citations, use the example of *Matthew 8:23–27*.

Matthew is the name of a book in the Bible. The chapter number always comes after the name of the book, so 8 is the chapter number. The numbers 23–27 are line numbers.

Dios

Hay tres Personas en un solo Dios: Dios Padre, Dios Hijo y Dios Espíritu Santo. El término que usamos para referirnos a las tres Personas en un solo Dios es la **Santísima Trinidad.**

Dios Padre

Los cristianos honramos a Dios Padre como creador de todo cuanto existe. La Iglesia ora a Dios Padre. Jesús enseñó a sus discípulos que Dios es el Padre de todos. Les dijo que oraran usando las palabras "Padre nuestro, que estás en el cielo".

Dios Hijo

Los cristianos honramos a Jesús, Dios Hijo, como Salvador de todos. Jesús es Dios pero también se hizo humano.

Los cristianos creemos que Jesús es el Mesías, el elegido de Dios. *Mesías* es una palabra hebrea que significa "el ungido" o "el elegido de Dios". Jesús fue elegido para salvar a la humanidad del pecado y de la muerte.

Dios Espíritu Santo

Los cristianos honramos a Dios Espíritu Santo como la persona que nos cuida y nos guía. El Espíritu Santo nos sostiene, nos da consuelo y nos ayuda a llevar una vida más santa. La Iglesia usa símbolos para representar al Espíritu Santo. La paloma, la llama y el viento son símbolos del Espíritu Santo.

Datos de fe

Nombres del Nuevo Testamento

A algunas personas nunca se les llama por su nombre en el Nuevo Testamento. Con el tiempo, la Iglesia les fue dando un nombre a cada una de esas personas. Entre los nombres tradicionales se encuentran Melchor, Gaspar y Baltasar, los tres Reyes Magos que llevaron regalos al Niño Jesús.

Creed

God

There are three Persons in one God—God the Father, God the Son, and God the Holy Spirit. The word for three Persons in one God is **Trinity**.

God the Father

Christians honor God the Father as the creator of all that exists. The Church prays to God the Father. Jesus taught his followers that God was his Father and their Father, too. Jesus said to pray using the words, "Our Father, who art in heaven."

God the Son

Christians honor Jesus, God the Son, as the Savior of all people. Jesus is God, and he also became human.

Christians believe that Jesus is the Messiah, God's chosen one. *Messiah* is a Hebrew word that means "the anointed one" or "the one chosen by God." Jesus was chosen to save humans from sin and death.

God the Holy Spirit

Christians honor God the Holy Spirit as the person who helps and guides us. The Holy Spirit supports and comforts us and helps us live holier lives. The Church uses symbols to describe the Holy Spirit. A dove, a flame, and the wind are all symbols of the Holy Spirit.

Faith Fact

New Testament Names

Some people are never called by name in the New Testament. Over time, the Church has given them names. Among these traditional names are Casper, Melchior, and Balthasar for the three wise men who brought gifts to the Christ Child.

La Iglesia

La Iglesia es la comunidad de todos los bautizados que creen en Dios y siguen a Jesús. El término *iglesia* proviene de dos palabras diferentes. Una significa "pueblo convocado", y la otra "que pertenece al Señor". La Iglesia también se conoce como el "Pueblo de Dios".

Otro nombre de la Iglesia es "el Cuerpo de Cristo". Este nombre indica que estás muy unido con los demás y con Jesús. Los miembros de la Iglesia trabajan unidos, así como las partes del cuerpo trabajan unidas. La misión de la Iglesia es anunciar la Buena Nueva del Reino de Dios.

La comunión de los santos

Todos los vivos y los muertos que creen en Jesús y siguen su camino forman parte de la comunión de los santos. Esto incluye a los vivos, que están en la tierra, y los muertos que están en el purgatorio o en el cielo. Las personas que están en la tierra se unen en la comunión de los santos cuando celebran la Eucaristía.

Los líderes de la Iglesia

El Papa, los cardenales, los obispos y arzobispos, los párrocos y otros sacerdotes dirigen y guían a los discípulos de Jesús. Este diagrama representa cómo están organizados los líderes de la Iglesia.

Datos de fe

Los nombres de los papas

Cada papa escoge su nombre al ser elegido. Normalmente, el nombre honra a un santo al que el nuevo papa admira. Por respeto, ningún papa ha elegido el nombre de Pedro II.

Papa
Cardenales
Arzobispos
Obispos
Sacerdotes

The Church

The Church is the community of all baptized people who believe in God and follow Jesus. The word *church* comes from two different words. One means "a community called together." The other means "belonging to the Lord." The Church is also sometimes called the "People of God."

Another name for the Church is "The Body of Christ." This name shows that you are closely joined with others and with Jesus. Church members work together just as parts of the body work together. The Church's mission is to tell the good news of God's kingdom.

Faith Fact

Popes' Names

Each newly elected pope chooses a name for himself. The chosen name usually honors a holy person the new pope admires. But out of respect, no new pope has called himself Peter II.

The Communion of Saints

All people living and dead who believe in Jesus and follow his way are part of the communion of saints. This includes people now alive on earth and people who have died and are now in purgatory or heaven. People on earth join in the communion of saints when they celebrate the Eucharist.

Church Leaders

The pope, cardinals, bishops and archbishops, pastors, and other priests lead and guide Jesus' followers. This chart shows how the Church's leaders are organized.

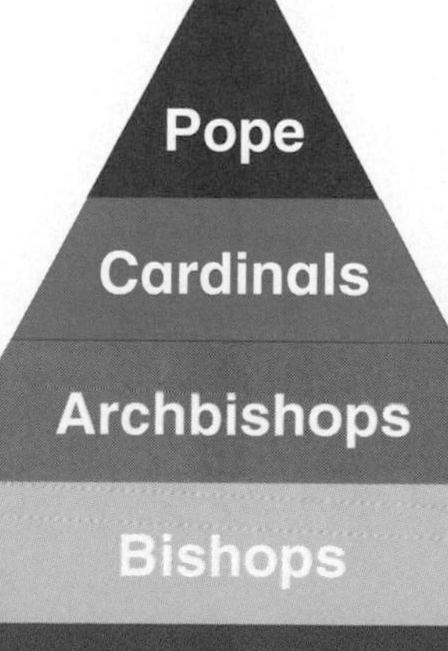

Los atributos de la Iglesia

La Iglesia tiene cuatro atributos. Decimos que la Iglesia es una, santa, católica y apostólica.

1. La Iglesia es **una** porque el poder del Espíritu Santo une a todos los miembros en una sola fe.
2. La Iglesia es **santa** porque refleja la santidad de Dios.
3. La Iglesia es **católica** porque Jesús la envió a anunciar la Buena Nueva al mundo entero.
4. La Iglesia es **apostólica** porque los Apóstoles trabajaron con Jesús para fundarla. Hoy en día, la Iglesia enseña lo que enseñaron los Apóstoles, y los obispos nos dirigen como lo hicieron los Apóstoles.

Los doce Apóstoles

Pedro
Santiago
Juan
Andrés
Felipe
Tomás
Bartolomé
Mateo
Santiago, hijo de Alfeo
Simón el cananeo
Judas
Tadeo

Marks of the Church

There are four marks of the Church. We say the Church is one, holy, catholic, and apostolic.

1. The Church is **one** because the power of the Holy Spirit unites all the members in one faith.
2. The Church is **holy** because it shows God's holiness.
3. The Church is **catholic** because Jesus sent the Church out to tell the good news to the whole world.
4. The Church is **apostolic** because the Apostles worked with Jesus to begin the Church. The Church today teaches what the Apostles taught, and the bishops lead in the place of the Apostles.

The Twelve Apostles

Peter
James
John
Andrew
Philip
Thomas
Bartholomew
Matthew
James, son of Alphaeus
Simon the Zealot
Judas
Matthias

La vida después de la muerte

La Iglesia espera la venida del Reino de Dios. Cuando una persona cristiana muere, confía en la promesa de la vida eterna con Dios.

Cielo, infierno y purgatorio

Cuando las personas mueren, van al cielo, al infierno o al purgatorio. El cielo es estar con Dios felices para siempre. El infierno es estar apartados de Dios para siempre. El purgatorio es la preparación para entrar en el cielo después de la muerte. La palabra *purgatorio* significa "purificar". El purgatorio prepara a las personas para que puedan estar con Dios en el cielo.

El juicio final

Todos los cristianos esperan la llegada de una época de paz y felicidad al fin de los tiempos. En ese momento, Jesús volverá a juzgar a los vivos y a los muertos. Entonces el Reino de Dios alcanzará su plenitud. La Iglesia llama a estos acontecimientos la segunda venida y el juicio final. Estos son tiempos de esperanza y alegría para los cristianos. Los discípulos de Jesús creemos en la promesa del eterno Reino de Dios.

Datos de fe

¿Hacia dónde?

Normalmente, las iglesias europeas se construían orientadas hacia el este, de manera que el sol iluminara el altar por la mañana. Las iglesias orientadas hacia el este también están orientadas hacia la ciudad santa de Jerusalén.

Life After Death

The Church looks forward to the coming of God's kingdom. When a Christian dies, he or she looks forward to the promise of life forever with God.

Faith Fact

Which Way?

Churches in Europe were usually built facing east, so that the morning sun would shine on the altar. A church that faced east would also be pointing toward the holy city of Jerusalem.

Heaven, Hell, and Purgatory

After people die, they will be in heaven, hell, or purgatory. Heaven is being happy with God forever. Hell is being separated from God forever. Purgatory is a preparation for heaven after death. The word *purgatory* means "making pure." Purgatory makes a person ready to be with God in heaven.

Judgment

At the end of time, all Christians look forward to a time of happiness and peace. At that time Jesus will come again to judge the living and the dead. Then the kingdom of God will come in fullness. The Church calls these events the second coming and the last judgment. These are times of hope and joy for Christians. Jesus' followers believe in the promise of God's everlasting kingdom.

María

María es la madre de Jesús, y por eso se le llama Madre de Dios. La Iglesia honra a María porque estuvo dispuesta a hacer lo que Dios le pidió. María es un modelo para los cristianos de todas las épocas y lugares.

Los títulos de María

La Iglesia honra a María con muchos títulos. Cada uno de esos títulos dice algo sobre ella y expresa por qué es tan amada. A María se le conoce como la Inmaculada Concepción, la Santísima Virgen, la Señora, Nuestra Señora del Perpetuo Socorro, la Reina de los Cielos, el Auxilio de los Cristianos, la Estrella de la mañana y la Reina de los Ángeles.

Los nombres de María

Muchos cristianos honran a María poniéndoles su nombre a sus hijas. María, Mary y Marie son formas del nombre que seguramente conoces. Marilyn, Maureen, Moira, Marianne y Marita son nombres que significan "María" en diferentes idiomas. El nombre *Madonna* significa "señora" en italiano. *Regina* significa "reina" en latín. Virginia es un nombre que se refiere a la virginidad de María. En los países de habla hispana, las niñas también se llaman Lupe (por Nuestra Señora de Guadalupe), Concepción (por la Inmaculada Concepción), Dolores (por Nuestra Señora de los Dolores) o Gracia (por Nuestra Señora de Gracia). Fátima y Lourdes, lugares en los que se apareció María, también se usan como nombres para honrar a la Madre de Dios.

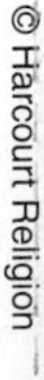

Mary

Mary is Jesus' mother. For this reason she is called the Mother of God. The Church honors Mary because she was willing to do what God asked. Mary is a model for Christians of all times and places.

Titles of Mary

The Church honors Mary with many titles. Each tells something about her and why she is so loved. Mary is called the Immaculate Conception, the Blessed Virgin, the Madonna, Our Lady of Perpetual Help, Queen of Heaven, Help of Christians, the Morning Star, and Queen of Angels.

Mary Names

Many Christians honor Mary by naming their children after her. Mary, Marie, and Maria are forms of the name you may know. Marilyn, Maureen, Moira, Marianne, and Marita are names that mean "Mary" in other languages. The name *Madonna* means "my lady" in Italian. *Regina* means "queen" in Latin. And Virginia is a name that refers to Mary's virginity. In Spanish-speaking countries children are also named Lupe (for Our Lady of Guadalupe), Concepción (for the Immaculate Conception), Dolores (for Our Lady of Sorrows), or Gracia (for Our Lady of Grace). Fatima and Lourdes, places where Mary has appeared, have also been used as names to honor the Mother of God.

Liturgia

La Misa

La Misa tiene dos partes principales: la Liturgia de la Palabra y la Liturgia Eucarística. Durante la Liturgia de la Palabra, escuchas la Palabra de Dios. Hay lecturas de la Sagrada Escritura. El sacerdote pronuncia una homilía, explica las lecturas y les dice a los cristianos cómo llevar a cabo la misión de la Iglesia.

La Liturgia Eucarística incluye oraciones y cánticos de acción de gracias y de alabanza a Dios. En ella se hacen las ofrendas del pan y del vino. Después de que el sacerdote las bendice, estas ofrendas se convierten en el Cuerpo y la Sangre de Cristo. Los miembros de la Iglesia se dan la paz unos a otros. Esto muestra que están listos para acercarse a la mesa del Señor. Los fieles participan en el sacrificio de Jesús cuando reciben la Comunión.

Cuando termina la Misa, los miembros de la Iglesia son enviados a "predicar el amor y servir al Señor" en su propia comunidad.

Datos de fe

Las Misas de los indígenas

La Misa se ha traducido a dos lenguas indígenas: navajo y choctaw.

▲ ***La Virgen y el Niño choctaw*, por el padre John Giuliani**

Liturgy

Faith Fact

Native American Masses

The Mass has been translated into two Native American languages, Navajo and Choctaw.

▲ ***Choctaw Virgin and Child*, Father John Giuliani**

The Mass

The Mass includes two main parts: the Liturgy of the Word and the Liturgy of the Eucharist. At the Liturgy of the Word you listen to the word of God. There are readings from Scripture. The priest gives a homily. He explains the readings and tells Christians how to carry out the Church's mission.

The Liturgy of the Eucharist includes prayers and songs thanking and praising God, and offering the gifts of bread and wine. Then the priest blesses the bread and wine, which become the Body and Blood of Christ. Church members give one another a sign of peace. This shows they are ready to come to the Lord's table. The people share in Jesus' sacrifice when they receive Communion.

When the Mass ends, Church members are sent to "go forth to love and serve the Lord" in their own community.

Ordinario de la Misa

Ritos iniciales

- Señal de la cruz y saludo
- Rito de la bendición y aspersión del agua bendita o acto penitencial
- Señor, ten piedad (Kyrie)
- Gloria
- Oración colecta

Liturgia de la Palabra

- Primera Lectura
- Salmo Responsorial
- Segunda Lectura
- Aclamación del Evangelio
- Proclamación del Evangelio
- Homilía
- Profesión de fe
- Oración de los fieles

Liturgia Eucarística

- Preparación del altar y presentación de los dones
- Plegaria eucarística
- Prefacio
- Acción de gracias y alabanza por las grandes obras de Dios
- Santo, Santo, Santo (Sanctus)
- Invocación al Espíritu Santo
- Consagración del pan y el vino
- Aclamación memorial
- Ofrecimiento del sacrificio eucarístico a Dios
- Plegaria por los vivos y los difuntos
- Doxología y Gran Amén

Rito de la comunión

- La Oración del Señor
- La paz
- Fracción del pan
- Invitación a la comunión
- Comunión y canto de comunión
- Período de silencio o cántico de alabanza
- Oración después de la comunión

Rito de conclusión

- Saludo
- Bendición
- Despedida

Order of the Mass

Introductory Rites

- Sign of the Cross and Greeting
- Rite of Blessing and Sprinkling Rite *or* Penitential Rite
- Lord, Have Mercy (Kyrie)
- Gloria
- Opening Prayer

Liturgy of the Word

- First Reading
- Responsorial Psalm
- Second Reading
- Gospel Acclamation
- Proclamation of the Gospel
- Homily
- Profession of Faith
- General Intercessions

Liturgy of the Eucharist

- Preparation of the Altar and the Gifts
- Eucharistic Prayer
- Preface
- Thanks and praise for the great works of God
- Holy, Holy, Holy (Sanctus)
- Calling on the Holy Spirit
- Consecration of bread and wine
- Memorial Acclamation
- Offering the Eucharistic sacrifice to God
- Prayers for the living and the dead
- Doxology and Great Amen

Communion Rite

- Lord's Prayer
- Sign of Peace
- Breaking of the Bread
- Invitation to Communion
- Communion and Communion Song
- Period of Silence or Song of Praise
- Prayer After Communion

Concluding Rite

- Greeting
- Blessing
- Dismissal

Liturgia

Los sacramentos

Sacramentos de Iniciación

Bautismo
Confirmación
Eucaristía

Sacramentos de Curación

Reconciliación
Unción de los enfermos

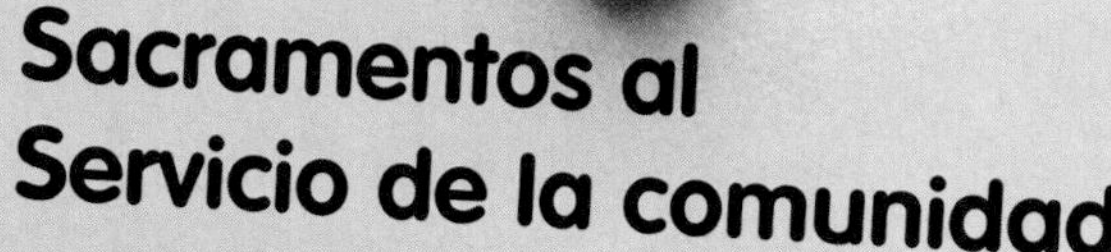

Sacramentos al Servicio de la comunidad

Matrimonio
Orden (Orden sacerdotal)

Sacramentales

Los sacramentales te recuerdan a Dios. Suelen constar de alguna acción, como la señal de la cruz. Los crucifijos, las estampas y las medallas te recuerdan a Jesús, a la Virgen María o a los santos. Los ramos te recuerdan la entrada de Jesús en Jerusalén. Después de la Misa del Domingo de Ramos, puedes quedarte con el ramo y ponerlo en tu casa en un lugar visible. Todos estos son sacramentales populares.

Bendiciones

La bendición es un signo especial y una oración. Las bendiciones alaban a Dios y le piden que proteja a una persona, un lugar, una cosa o una acción. En muchas iglesias, los sacerdotes bendicen mascotas o animales de granja el día que se conmemora a san Francisco de Asís (4 de octubre).

The Sacraments

Sacraments of Initiation

Baptism
Confirmation
Eucharist

Sacraments of Healing

Reconciliation
Anointing of the Sick

Sacraments of Service

Matrimony
Holy Orders

Sacramentals

Sacramentals remind you of God. Sacramentals often include an action like the Sign of the Cross. Crucifixes, holy cards, and medals remind you of Jesus, the Blessed Mother, or the saints. Palm branches remind you of Jesus' entry into Jerusalem. After the Palm Sunday service, you can keep and display the palm branches in your home. These are all popular sacramentals.

Blessings

A blessing is a special sign and prayer. Blessings praise God. They ask for God's care for a person, a place, a thing, or an action. In many churches on the feast day of Saint Francis of Assisi (October 4), the priest blesses pets or farm animals.

Datos de fe

Colores litúrgicos

Hay ciertos colores que se utilizan en determinados tiempos del año litúrgico. Estos colores se utilizan en algunas partes de los ornamentos del sacerdote.

Verde: Domingos del Tiempo Ordinario

Rojo: Domingo de Ramos, Viernes Santo, Pentecostés

Rosado: Tercer domingo de Adviento y cuarto domingo de Cuaresma

Morado o violeta: Adviento y Cuaresma

Blanco: Navidad, Pascua, fiestas del Señor, de María y fiestas de los santos que no son mártires, o funerales

Devociones

Las devociones son oraciones especiales que honran a Dios, a María o a los santos. Las visitas al Santísimo Sacramento son una devoción popular para honrar a Jesús. El rosario es una devoción para honrar a María. Las devociones nos recuerdan que debemos rezar fuera de la Misa.

Lugares sagrados

Una *catedral* es la iglesia que es la sede de una diócesis. Se encuentra en la ciudad desde la que el obispo o arzobispo guía a su pueblo. Una *basílica* es una iglesia a la que el papa ha otorgado especial importancia. Los católicos hacen peregrinaciones, o visitas especiales, a las basílicas.

Objetos de la Iglesia

- **altar** El altar es la mesa central que se encuentra en el frente de la iglesia. El sacerdote celebra la Misa en el altar.

- **ambón** El lugar en que se lee la Sagrada Escritura y se predican las homilías. El ambón también se conoce como púlpito o facistol.

- **pila o fuente bautismal** El recipiente que contiene el agua para el Bautismo.

- **cirio pascual** Un cirio grande y adornado que se enciende con el fuego nuevo en la Vigilia Pascual. Este cirio se enciende en todas las Misas durante el Tiempo Pascual. También se enciende en los bautizos y en los funerales.

- **sagrario o tabernáculo** El lugar en que se guarda el Santísimo Sacramento y se le rinde culto.

- **ornamentos** La ropa especial que usa el sacerdote cuando celebra los sacramentos.

Devotions

Devotions are special prayers that honor God, Mary, or the saints. Visits to the Blessed Sacrament are a popular devotion to honor Jesus. The Rosary is a devotion to honor Mary. Devotions help people remember to pray outside of the Mass.

Sacred Places

A *cathedral* is the home church of a diocese. It is in the city where the bishop or archbishop leads his people. A *basilica* is a church given special importance by the pope. Catholics make pilgrimages, or special visits, to basilicas.

Objects in the Church Building

- **altar** The altar is the central table in the front of the church. The priest celebrates Mass at the altar.
- **ambo** A place where Scripture is read and homilies are preached. The ambo is also called the pulpit or lectern.

- **baptismal font or pool** The container that holds the water for Baptism.
- **Paschal candle** A large, decorated candle lit from the new fire at the Easter Vigil. This candle is lit at all the Masses during the Easter Season. It is also lit at baptisms and funerals.

- **tabernacle** A place to keep and worship the Blessed Sacrament.
- **vestments** Special clothing that the priest wears while celebrating the sacraments.

Faith Fact

Liturgical Colors

Certain colors are used during certain seasons of the Church year. These colors are used for parts of the priest's vestments.

Green: Sundays in Ordinary Time

Red: Palm Sunday, Good Friday, Pentecost

Rose: Third Sunday of Advent and Fourth Sunday of Lent

Purple or **Violet:** Advent and Lent

White: Christmas, Easter, Feasts of the Lord, Mary, and the saints not martyred, or funerals

Moral

Los Diez Mandamientos

Los Diez Mandamientos	Su Significado
1. Amarás a Dios sobre todas las cosas.	Da a Dios el primer lugar en tu vida.
2. No tomarás el nombre de Dios en vano.	Usa siempre el nombre de Dios de manera reverente.
3. Santificarás las fiestas.	Los domingos asiste a Misa y descansa.
4. Honrarás a tu padre y a tu madre.	Obedece a tus padres y a los que te cuidan.
5. No matarás.	Cuida de ti mismo y de los demás.
6. No cometerás actos impuros.	Sé respetuoso con todas las personas.
7. No robarás.	Respeta a las personas y respeta sus pertenencias.
8. No dirás falso testimonio ni mentirás.	Respeta a los demás diciendo siempre la verdad.
9. No desearás la mujer de tu prójimo.	No sientas celos por las amistades de los demás.
10. No codiciarás los bienes ajenos.	No envidies lo que tienen los demás.

El gran mandamiento

[Jesús] contestó: "Amarás al Señor tu Dios con todo tu corazón, con toda tu alma, con todas tus fuerzas y con toda tu mente; y amarás a tu prójimo como a ti mismo".

Lucas 10, 27

Morality

The Ten Commandments

The Ten Commandments	Their Meaning
1. I am the LORD your God: You shall not have strange Gods before me.	Keep God first in your life.
2. You shall not take the name of the LORD your God in vain.	Always use God's name in a reverent way.
3. Remember to keep holy the LORD's day.	Attend Mass and rest on Sunday.
4. Honor your father and your mother.	Obey your parents and guardians.
5. You shall not kill.	Care for yourself and others.
6. You shall not commit adultery.	Be respectful of every person.
7. You shall not steal.	Respect other people and their property.
8. You shall not bear false witness against your neighbor.	Respect others by always telling the truth.
9. You shall not covet your neighbor's wife.	Don't be jealous of other people's friendships.
10. You shall not covet your neighbor's goods.	Don't be jealous of what other people have.

The Great Commandment

[Jesus] said in reply, "You shall love the Lord your God with all your heart, with all your soul, with all your strength, with all your mind; and your neighbor as yourself."

Luke 10:27

Moral

Datos de fe

La señora Sabiduría

Hay partes del Antiguo Testamento que hablan de la sabiduría como si fuera una persona, normalmente una mujer. El nombre Sofía viene de la palabra griega que significa sabiduría.

Las Bienaventuranzas

Felices los que tienen el espíritu del pobre,
porque de ellos es el Reino de los Cielos.
Felices los que lloran,
porque recibirán consuelo.
Felices los pacientes,
porque recibirán la tierra en herencia.
Felices los que tienen hambre y sed de justicia,
porque serán saciados.
Felices los compasivos,
porque obtendrán misericordia.
Felices los de corazón limpio,
porque verán a Dios.
Felices los que trabajan por la paz,
porque serán reconocidos como hijos de Dios.
Felices los que son perseguidos por causa
del bien,
porque de ellos es el Reino de los Cielos.

Mateo 5, 3–10

The Beatitudes

Blessed are the poor in spirit,
for theirs is the kingdom of heaven.
Blessed are they who mourn,
for they will be comforted.
Blessed are the meek,
for they will inherit the land.
Blessed are they who hunger and thirst for
righteousness,
for they will be satisfied.
Blessed are the merciful,
for they will be shown mercy.
Blessed are the clean of heart,
for they will see God.
Blessed are the peacemakers,
for they will be called children of God.
Blessed are they who are persecuted for the
sake of righteousness,
for theirs is the kingdom of heaven.

Matthew 5:3–10

Faith Fact

Lady Wisdom

Parts of the Old Testament speak of wisdom as a person, usually a woman. The name Sophia comes from the Greek word for wisdom.

Examen de conciencia

1. Ora al Espíritu Santo para que te ayude a examinar tu conciencia.

2. Lee las Bienaventuranzas, los Diez Mandamientos, el gran mandamiento y los preceptos de la Iglesia.

3. Hazte estas preguntas:

   ¿Cuándo no hice lo que Dios quería?
   ¿A quién ofendí?
   ¿Qué cosas hice sabiendo que estaban mal?
   ¿Qué cosas debería haber hecho, pero no hice?
   ¿Hice penitencia e intenté cambiar?
   ¿En qué áreas todavía tengo dificultades?
   ¿Estoy arrepentido de todos mis pecados?

La gracia

La gracia es la vida de Dios en ti. No es algo físico, sino un don que recibes de una manera especial con el Bautismo. Creces en la gracia de Dios cuando celebras los sacramentos.

La solidaridad

Todas las personas, especialmente quienes sufren necesidades, son tus hermanas y hermanos. Cuando las personas están unidas en la familia de Dios, y cuando comparten alegrías y tristezas con los demás, muestran su solidaridad unos con otros.

Examination of Conscience

1. Pray to the Holy Spirit to help you examine your conscience.
2. Read the Beatitudes, the Ten Commandments, the Great Commandment, and the precepts of the Church.
3. Ask yourself these questions:

   When have I not done what God wants me to do?
   Whom have I hurt?
   What have I done that I knew was wrong?
   What have I not done that I should have done?
   Have I done penance and tried to change?
   With what am I still having trouble?
   Am I sorry for all my sins?

Grace

Grace is God's life in you. Grace is not something physical. You receive the gift of grace in a special way at Baptism. You grow in God's grace through celebrating the sacraments.

Solidarity

All people, especially those in need, are your sisters and brothers. When people are united in God's family, and when they share joys and sorrows with others, they are in solidarity with one another.

Datos de fe

Nombres y títulos de Jesús

Se han dado muchos nombres y títulos a Jesús. Cada uno de ellos dice algo especial acerca de Jesús, o es una manera de honrarlo. Estos son algunos de esos nombres y títulos: Cristo, Salvador, Señor, Cordero de Dios, Hijo de Dios, Hijo del Hombre, la Palabra, y el Siervo Sufriente.

La virtud

Tomar buenas decisiones basadas en el amor te ayuda a desarrollar hábitos de bondad, que se conocen como virtudes. La palabra *virtud* significa "fortaleza". La práctica de estos hábitos de bondad te ayuda a tomar decisiones aun más marcadas por el amor. Las *virtudes teologales* de la fe, la esperanza y el amor son dones de Dios.

Fe: La fe es creer en Dios y en todo lo que Dios te ha enseñado. Tú crees porque Jesús te enseñó el camino que debes seguir en la vida.

Esperanza: La esperanza es la virtud que te ayuda a confiar en lo que Dios te mostró. Es el don de esperar la felicidad de la vida eterna con Dios y la venida del Reino de Dios.

Amor: Tú muestras tu amor a Dios alabándolo y siendo bueno con los demás. Ayudas a los demás y escuchas a tus amigos cuando tienen problemas. Haces obras de caridad. La Iglesia te pide que muestres tu amor a Dios tratando a todos con bondad y con respeto.

Virtue

Making good and loving choices helps you develop habits of goodness, called virtues. The word *virtue* means "strength." Practicing these habits of goodness helps you to make even more loving choices. The *theological virtues* of faith, hope, and love are gifts from God.

Faith—Faith is believing in God and all that God has shown you. You believe because Jesus taught you how to live.

Hope—Hope is the virtue that helps you trust in what God has shown you. It is the gift of looking forward to the happiness of life forever with God and the coming of God's kingdom.

Love—You show your love for God by praising God and loving other people. You help people. You listen to friends who have problems. You do kind things. The Church wants you to show love for God by treating everyone with kindness and respect.

Faith Fact

Names and Titles for Jesus

Jesus has been given many names and titles. Each tells something special about Jesus or is a way to honor him. These names and titles include Christ, Savior, Lord, Lamb of God, Son of God, Son of Man, the Word, and the Suffering Servant.

La señal de la cruz

En el nombre del Padre, y del Hijo, y del
Espíritu Santo.
Amén.

La Oración del Señor

Padre nuestro, que estás en el cielo,
santificado sea tu Nombre;
venga a nosotros tu reino;
hágase tu voluntad en la tierra como en el cielo.
Danos hoy nuestro pan de cada día;
perdona nuestras ofensas,
como también nosotros perdonamos
a los que nos ofenden;
no nos dejes caer en la tentación,
y líbranos del mal.
Amén.

Ave María

Dios te salve, María, llena eres de gracia;
el Señor es contigo;
bendita tú eres entre todas las mujeres,
y bendito es el fruto de tu vientre, Jesús.
Santa María, Madre de Dios,
ruega por nosotros pecadores,
ahora y en la hora de nuestra muerte.
Amén.

Prayer

The Sign of the Cross

In the name of the Father, and of the Son,
and of the Holy Spirit.
Amen.

The Lord's Prayer

Our Father,
who art in heaven,
hallowed be thy name;
thy kingdom come;
thy will be done on earth
as it is in heaven.
Give us this day our daily bread;
and forgive us our trespasses
as we forgive those who
trespass against us;
and lead us not into temptation,
but deliver us from evil.
Amen.

Hail Mary

Hail, Mary, full of grace,
the Lord is with you!
Blessed are you among women,
and blessed is the fruit of your womb, Jesus.
Holy Mary, Mother of God,
pray for us sinners,
now and at the hour of our death.
Amen.

Gloria al Padre (Doxología)

Gloria al Padre, al Hijo, al Espíritu Santo. Como era en el principio, ahora y siempre, por los siglos de los siglos.
Amén.

Bendición de los alimentos

Bendícenos, Señor, y bendice estos alimentos
que por tu bondad vamos a tomar.
Por Jesucristo nuestro Señor.
Amén.

Datos de fe

Versión más larga de la Oración del Señor

Muchos cristianos añaden un verso al final de la Oración del Señor: "Tuyo es el reino, tuyo el poder y la gloria, por siempre, Señor".

Acto de fe, esperanza y amor

Mi Dios, en ti creo,
en ti confío,
a ti te amo sobre todas las cosas,
con todo mi corazón, con toda mi mente,
con todas mis fuerzas.
Te amo porque eres infinitamente bueno
y digno de ser amado;
Y, porque te amo,
estoy arrepentido con toda mi alma de haberte ofendido.
Señor, ten piedad de mí, pecador.
Amén.

Glory to the Father (Doxology)

Glory to the Father, and to the Son, and to the Holy Spirit:
as it was in the beginning, is now, and will be for ever.
Amen.

Blessing Before Meals

Bless us, O Lord, and these your gifts
which we are about to receive from your goodness.
Through Christ our Lord.
Amen.

Act of Faith, Hope, and Love

My God, I believe in you,
I trust in you,
I love you above all things,
with all my heart and mind and strength.
I love you because you are supremely good and worth loving;
and because I love you,
I am sorry with all my heart for offending you.
Lord, have mercy on me, a sinner.
Amen.

Faith Fact

A Longer Lord's Prayer

Many Christians include an extra line at the end of the Lord's Prayer: "The kingdom, and the power, and the glory are yours, now and forever."

Oración al Espíritu Santo

Ven, Espíritu Santo, llena los corazones de los
fieles y enciende en ellos el fuego de Tu amor.
Envía Tu Espíritu, y serán creados.
Y renovarás la faz de la tierra.

El Credo de los Apóstoles

Creo en Dios, Padre todopoderoso,
Creador del cielo y de la tierra.
Creo en Jesucristo, su único Hijo, nuestro Señor,
que fue concebido por obra y gracia del
Espíritu Santo,
nació de santa María Virgen,
padeció bajo el poder de Poncio Pilato,
fue crucificado, muerto y sepultado,
descendió a los infiernos,
al tercer día resucitó de entre los muertos,
subió a los cielos
y está sentado a la derecha de Dios,
Padre todopoderoso.
Desde allí ha de venir a juzgar a vivos y muertos.
Creo en el Espíritu Santo,
la santa Iglesia católica,
la comunión de los santos,
el perdón de los pecados,
la resurrección de la carne
y la vida eterna. Amén.

Prayer to the Holy Spirit

Come, Holy Spirit, fill the hearts of your faithful.
And kindle in them the fire of your love.
Send forth your Spirit and they shall be created.
And you will renew the face of the earth.

The Apostles' Creed

I believe in God, the Father almighty,
creator of heaven and earth.
I believe in Jesus Christ, his only Son,
our Lord.
He was conceived by the power of the Holy Spirit
and born of the Virgin Mary.
He suffered under Pontius Pilate,
was crucified, died, and was buried.
He descended to the dead.
On the third day, he rose again.
He ascended into heaven,
and is seated at the right hand of the Father.
He will come again to judge the living and the dead.
I believe in the Holy Spirit,
the holy catholic Church,
the communion of saints,
the forgiveness of sins,
the resurrection of the body,
and the life everlasting. Amen.

Acto de contrición

Dios mío, con todo mi corazón
me arrepiento de todo el mal
que he hecho y de todo lo
bueno que he dejado de hacer.
Al pecar, te he ofendido a ti,
que eres el Supremo Bien
y digno de ser amado
sobre todas las cosas.
Propongo firmemente,
con la ayuda de tu gracia,
hacer penitencia,
no volver a pecar y huir
de las ocasiones de pecado.
Señor: Por los méritos de la pasión
de nuestro Salvador Jesucristo,
apiádate de mí.

Datos de fe

Amén

"Amén" es una palabra hebrea que expresa aprobación. Dices "Amén" al final de la mayoría de las oraciones para expresar que crees que las palabras de la oración son verdaderas.

Act of Contrition

My God,
I am sorry for my sins with all my heart.
In choosing to do wrong
and failing to do good,
I have sinned against you
whom I should love above all things.
I firmly intend, with your help,
to do penance,
to sin no more,
and to avoid whatever leads me to sin.
Our Savior Jesus Christ
suffered and died for us.
In his name, my God, have mercy.

Faith Fact

Amen

"Amen" is a Hebrew word that shows agreement. You say "Amen" at the end of most prayers to show that you believe the words of the prayer are true.

Palabras de fe

alabanza Acción de honrar a alguien que es bueno y santo. (174)

alianza Promesa o contrato sagrado entre Dios y los seres humanos. (398)

Apóstoles Los primeros doce líderes que eligió Jesús. (246)

autoridad Tener autoridad significa estar a cargo de algo y tener el poder para tomar decisiones. (122)

B

Biblia La Palabra de Dios escrita en palabras humanas. La Biblia es el libro sagrado de la Iglesia. (102)

Bienaventuranzas Enseñanzas de Jesús que muestran el camino de la verdadera felicidad y te dicen cómo vivir en el Reino de Dios. (298)

católica Palabra que significa "universal" o "por todas partes". La Iglesia es católica porque es para todas las personas de todas las épocas y lugares. (276)

cielo Estar con Dios felices para siempre. (434)

comunidad Un grupo de personas que trabajan unidas por una razón especial. (104)

comunión de los santos Todos los que han sido redimidos por Jesús: personas que están en la tierra, personas que han muerto y están en el purgatorio, y los santos, que están en el cielo. (262)

conciencia Un don de Dios que te ayuda a diferenciar entre el bien y el mal. (330)

crear Hacer algo completamente nuevo. Solamente Dios puede crear algo donde antes no existía nada. (86)

credo Proclamación que contiene las creencias esenciales acerca de Dios Padre, Dios Hijo y Dios Espíritu Santo, y acerca de otras enseñanzas de la Iglesia. (142)

crisma El óleo consagrado que se usa en los sacramentos del Bautismo, de la Confirmación y del Orden. (346)

cristianos Discípulos de Jesucristo. La palabra "cristiano" proviene de "Cristo". (402)

Cuerpo de Cristo La Iglesia se conoce también como el Cuerpo de Cristo, y Cristo es su cabeza. Todos los bautizados son miembros del Cuerpo de Cristo. (222)

culto Acción de adorar y alabar a Dios. (158)

diócesis Un área de la Iglesia formada por muchas parroquias y dirigida por un obispo. (246)

esperanza La virtud que te ayuda a confiar en lo que Dios te ha revelado. (312)

Evangelio Una palabra que significa "buena nueva". El mensaje del Evangelio es la Buena Nueva del Reino de Dios y su amor salvador. (190)

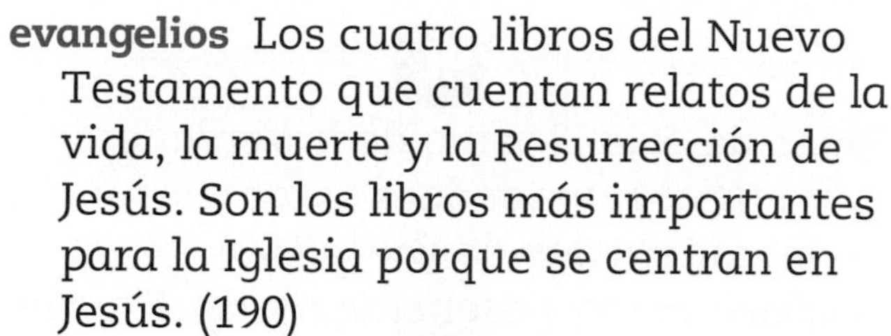

evangelios Los cuatro libros del Nuevo Testamento que cuentan relatos de la vida, la muerte y la Resurrección de Jesús. Son los libros más importantes para la Iglesia porque se centran en Jesús. (190)

fe La virtud de creer y confiar en Dios. Por la fe crees en todo lo que Dios te enseña a través de la Iglesia. (312)

gracia El don de amor que voluntariamente nos hace Dios al entregarnos su vida y su amistad. (330)

Iglesia La comunidad del Pueblo de Dios reunida en el nombre de Jesucristo. (106)

infierno Estar apartados de Dios para siempre por haberlo rechazado totalmente. (434)

juicio final Al fin de los tiempos, Jesús volverá a la tierra para juzgar a los vivos y a los muertos, y para llevar el Reino de Dios a su plenitud. (434)

justicia La virtud de dar a Dios y a los demás lo que les corresponde. (418)

ley del amor La ley del amor de Jesús resume los Diez Mandamientos y las Bienaventuranzas en un solo enunciado: "Que se amen los unos a los otros. Ustedes deben amarse unos a otros como yo los he amado". (Juan 13, 34). (298)

liturgia La comunidad rinde culto y adora a Dios en la Misa y los demás sacramentos. (156)

Liturgia de la Vigilia Pascual Se celebra la noche del Sábado Santo. En la Vigilia Pascual se da la bienvenida a los nuevos miembros de la Iglesia. (344)

Matrimonio El sacramento que une a un hombre y a una mujer cristianamente. (380)

mesías Palabra hebrea que significa "ungido". Los cristianos creen que Jesús es el Mesías, el que ha sido ungido o elegido. (194)

misión Un trabajo o tarea de la que una persona se hace responsable. La misión de la Iglesia es anunciar la Buena Nueva del Reino de Dios. (278)

misioneros Personas que viajan para comunicar la Buena Nueva de Jesús. (278)

Misterio Pascual El misterio del sufrimiento, la muerte, la Resurrección y la Ascensión de Jesús. (210)

obispos Hombres ordenados para trabajar con el papa, enseñando y guiando a la Iglesia. Son los sucesores de los Apóstoles. (246)

oración Acto de hablar con Dios y escucharlo. Es elevar tu mente y tu corazón a Dios. (170)

oración de los fieles Oración en la que pides a Dios que ayude a otras personas. (174)

Orden El sacramento en el que un hombre es ordenado para servir a Jesús y a la Iglesia como diácono, sacerdote u obispo. (380)

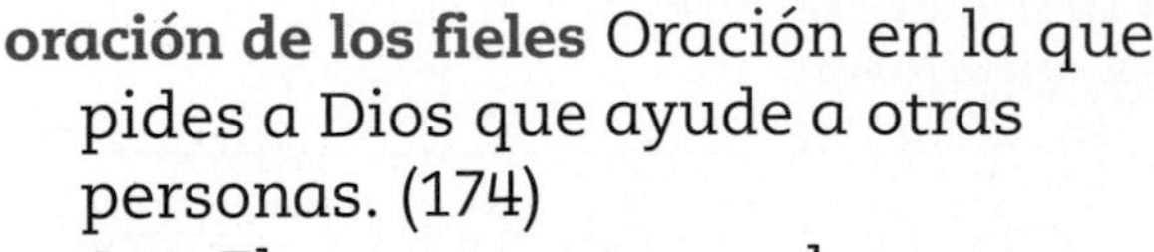

Papa El sucesor de san Pedro y obispo de Roma. El Papa es el máximo maestro y guía de la Iglesia. (244)

parábolas Relatos que contaba Jesús para enseñar y para describir el Reino de Dios. (194)

Pascua judía Fiesta judía que recuerda y celebra que Dios liberó a los israelitas de la esclavitud en Egipto. (210)

paz La verdadera unión entre las personas, que las hace respetarse unas a otras y mantener el orden. Es el resultado del trabajo conjunto por la justicia. (418)

pecado La decisión deliberada de desobedecer a Dios. Cuando pecas, dañas tu relación con Dios y con los demás. (330)

Pentecostés Fiesta que celebra la venida del Espíritu Santo cincuenta días después de la Pascua. (262)

petición Solicitud de algo que quieres o necesitas. (174)

preceptos de la Iglesia Algunas de las normas básicas que deben cumplir los católicos. (330)

purgatorio Estado de purificación final antes de entrar al cielo. (434)

Reino de Dios El reino de la verdadera justicia, el verdadero amor y la verdadera paz de Dios. (194)

respetar Prestar atención a lo que dicen las personas y tratarlas como te gustaría que te trataran a ti. (90)

responsabilidad Un deber o una tarea que se te ha confiado. Dios da a los seres humanos la responsabilidad de cuidar de su creación. (90)

Resurrección El acontecimiento en el que Dios Padre hizo que Jesús pasara de la muerte a la nueva vida, mediante la fuerza del Espíritu Santo. (210)

sacramentos Signos que provienen de Jesús y que conceden la gracia. (350)

sacramentos al Servicio de la comunidad El Orden y el Matrimonio. Celebran el compromiso de las personas de servir a Dios y a la comunidad. (382)

sacramentos de Curación La Reconciliación y la Unción de los enfermos. Con estos sacramentos se conceden el perdón de Dios y la curación a los que padecen enfermedades físicas o espirituales. (366)

sacramentos de Iniciación El Bautismo, la Confirmación y la Eucaristía. Con estos tres sacramentos recibimos a los nuevos miembros de la Iglesia Católica. (350)

sacrificio Renunciar a algo por un bien mayor. (206)

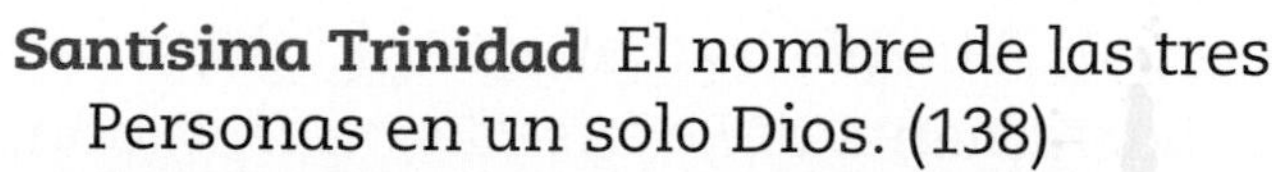

Santísima Trinidad El nombre de las tres Personas en un solo Dios. (138)

Santísimo Sacramento La Sagrada Eucaristía. Este término se refiere especialmente al pan consagrado que se guarda en el tabernáculo. (158)

segunda venida Jesús volverá a la tierra a juzgar a los vivos y a los muertos y el Reino de Dios alcanzará su plenitud. (432)

Unción de los enfermos Este sacramento concede el perdón de Dios y la curación a los que padecen enfermedades físicas o espirituales. (364)

virtudes Buenas cualidades, o hábitos de bondad. Las virtudes teologales de la fe, la esperanza y el amor son dones de Dios. (314)

virtudes teologales La fe, la esperanza y el amor, que son dones de Dios. (314)

Visitación El nombre con que se conoce la visita de María a Isabel. (118)

votos Promesas sagradas que se hacen a Dios o ante Él. En el matrimonio, un hombre y una mujer prometen ante Dios amarse y ser fieles el uno al otro. (378)

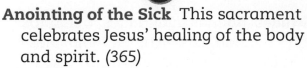

Words of Faith

Anointing of the Sick This sacrament celebrates Jesus' healing of the body and spirit. *(365)*

Apostles The first twelve leaders called by Jesus. *(247)*

authority To have authority is to be in charge of something and have the power to make decisions. *(123)*

Beatitudes Teachings of Jesus that show the way to true happiness and tell how to live in God's kingdom. *(299)*

Bible God's word written in human words. The Bible is the holy book of the Church. *(103)*

bishops Ordained men who work with the pope in teaching and guiding the Church. The bishops are the successors of the Apostles. *(247)*

Blessed Sacrament The Holy Eucharist, especially the blessed Bread that is kept in the tabernacle. *(159)*

Body of Christ A name for the Church of which Christ is the head. All the baptized are members of the body. *(223)*

catholic A word that means "universal" or "everywhere." The Church is meant for all people in all times and all places. *(277)*

chrism The blessed oil used in the Sacraments of Baptism, Confirmation, and Holy Orders. *(347)*

Christians Followers of Jesus Christ. The word "Christian" comes from "Christ." *(403)*

Church The community of the People of God gathered in the name of Jesus Christ. *(107)*

communion of saints Everyone who has been redeemed by Jesus—people on earth, people who have died and are in purgatory, and the saints in heaven. *(263)*

community A group of people who work together for a special reason. *(105)*

conscience A gift from God that helps you know the difference between right and wrong. *(331)*

covenant A sacred promise or agreement between God and humans. *(399)*

create To make something completely new. Only God can create something where nothing existed before. *(87)*

Creed A statement of the basic beliefs about God the Father, God the Son, and God the Holy Spirit, and about other teachings of the Church. *(143)*

diocese An area of the Church made up of many parishes and led by a bishop. *(247)*

Easter Vigil Liturgy Celebrated on Holy Saturday evening. New members are welcomed into the Church at the Easter Vigil. *(345)*

faith Belief and trust in God. By faith you believe all that God teaches you through the Church. *(313)*

gospel A word that means "good news." The gospel message is the good news of God's kingdom and saving love. *(191)*

Gospels The four books in the New Testament that tell the stories of Jesus' life, death, and Resurrection. They are the most important books for the Church because they focus on Jesus. *(191)*

Grace God's free and loving gift to humans of his own life and friendship. *(331)*

heaven Being with God forever in happiness. *(435)*

hell Being separated from God forever because of a choice to turn away from him. *(435)*

Holy Orders The sacrament in which a man is ordained to serve Jesus and the Church as a deacon, priest, or bishop. *(381)*

Holy Trinity The name for the three Persons in one God. *(139)*

hope The virtue that helps you trust in what God has shown you. *(313)*

intercession Asking for God's help for others. *(175)*

justice The virtue of giving God and others what is their due. *(419)*

kingdom of God God's rule of justice, love, and peace. *(195)*

last judgment When Jesus will come again at the end of time to judge the living and the dead and bring the kingdom of God to its fullness. *(435)*

law of love Jesus' law of love sums up the Ten Commandments and the Beatitudes in one statement: "Love one another. As I have loved you, so you also should love one another" (John 13:34). *(299)*

liturgy The community worships and praises God in the Mass and the other sacraments. *(157)*

Matrimony The sacrament that joins a man and a woman in Christian marriage. *(381)*

messiah A Hebrew word that means "anointed." Christians believe that Jesus is the Messiah—the one who has been anointed, or chosen. *(195)*

mission A job or duty that someone takes responsibility for. The Church's mission is to announce the good news of God's kingdom. *(279)*

missionaries People who travel to share Jesus' good news. *(279)*

parables Teaching stories that Jesus used to describe the kingdom of God. *(195)*

Paschal mystery The mystery of Jesus' suffering, death, Resurrection, and Ascension. *(211)*

Passover Jewish feast that recalls and celebrates how God led the Israelites out of slavery in Egypt. *(211)*

peace True unity among people that makes them want to respect one another and keep order. It is the good effect of working for justice. *(419)*

Pentecost The feast that celebrates the coming of the Holy Spirit fifty days after Easter. (263)

petition A request for something you want or need. *(175)*

pope The successor of Saint Peter and bishop of Rome. The pope is the highest teacher and guide in the Church. *(245)*

praise To give honor. You praise someone who is good and holy. *(175)*

prayer Talking and listening to God. It is raising your mind and heart to God. *(171)*

precepts of the Church Some of the basic laws Catholics should follow. *(331)*

purgatory A state of final cleansing before entrance into heaven. *(435)*

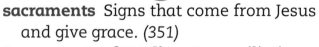

respect Paying attention to what people say and treating them the way you would like to be treated. *(91)*

responsibility A duty or a job that you are trusted to do. God gives humans the responsibility of caring for his creation. *(91)*

Resurrection The event of Jesus' being raised from death to new life by God the Father through the power of the Holy Spirit. *(211)*

sacraments Signs that come from Jesus and give grace. *(351)*

Sacraments of Healing Reconciliation and the Anointing of the Sick. In these sacraments God's forgiveness and healing are given to those suffering physical and spiritual sickness. *(367)*

Sacraments of Initiation Baptism, Confirmation, and Eucharist. They celebrate membership in the Catholic Church. *(351)*

Sacraments of Service Holy Orders and Matrimony. They celebrate people's commitment to serve God and the community. *(383)*

sacrifice To give up something for a greater good. *(207)*

second coming When Jesus will come again to judge the living and the dead. This will bring the kingdom of God to its fullness. *(433)*

sin The deliberate choice to disobey God. When you sin, you hurt your relationship with God and other people. *(331)*

theological virtues Faith, hope, and love, which are gifts from God. *(315)*

virtues Good qualities, or habits of goodness. The theological virtues of faith, hope, and love are gifts from God. *(315)*

Visitation The name of the visit of Mary to Elizabeth. *(119)*

vows Sacred promises that are made to or before God. In marriage a man and a woman make their promises to love each other and to be faithful before God. *(379)*

worship To adore and honor God. *(159)*

Los números en negrita indican las páginas con la definición de los términos.

Abraham, 396–398
acción de gracias, 174
Acto de contrición, 482
Acto de fe, esperanza y amor, 478
Adviento, 24–27, 466
agua bendita, 64–65, 67
alabanza, **174**, **484**
alianza, 396–**398**, **484**
altar, 466
ambón, 466
amor, 314, 418, 474
a los enemigos, 296–298
a los demás, 104, 116–122
como virtud, 314, 474
Antiguo Testamento, 292–294, 444
Apocalipsis, libro del, 446
Apóstoles, 102–104, 244–**246**, 260, 274, 416, 454, **484**
atributos de la Iglesia, 454
autoridad, **122**, **484**
Ave María, 476

Bartolomé Osypiuk, Beato, 304
basílica, 466
Bautismo, 59, 64, 67, 344–350, 382, 418, 464
bendición, 174, 464
Biblia, **102**, 190, 444–448
Bienaventuranzas, **298**, 470, **484**
Bowman, Thea, 164
Brígida, Santa, 402
Buena Nueva, 72, 188–194

cartas, 446–448
catedral, 466
católica, **276**, 454, **484**
celebraciones, 152–154
Ver también días de fiesta de la Iglesia
Cena, Última, 56
Ver también Eucaristía
Chardin, Pierre Teilhard de, 96
ciclo de la vida, el, 428
cielo, **432–434**, 456, **484**
Cirilo, San, 40
cirio pascual, 466
Clemente de Roma, San, 408
Columba, San, 402
comunidad, 90, **104**–106, 156, 256–258, 452, **484**
comunión de los santos, **262**, 452, 484
conciencia, 328–**330**, 472, **484**
confesión, 330, 364–366
Confirmación, sacramento de la, 348–350, 382, 464
crear, **86**–90, **484**
credos, **142**, 450–458, 480, **484**
Credo de los Apóstoles, 142, 480
crisma, 344–**346**, **484**
cristianos, 102–104, 222–226, 310, 400–**402**, **484**
cruz, 51
Cuaresma, 48–51, 466
Cuerpo de Cristo, **222**, 226, 452, **484**
Ver también Iglesia
culto, 156–**158**, 174, 484
Curación, sacramentos de, 360–**366**, 464, **486**

decisiones, 204–206, 324–334
devociones, 466
día del Señor, 64, 158
diáconos, 246, 378–380
días de fiesta de la Iglesia
de Beatos, 128, 284
de Navidad, 32–35
durante el Tiempo Ordinario, 16–19, 40
de Pentecostés, 72–75
de Santos, 112, 148, 200, 216, 232, 252, 268, 320, 336, 356, 372, 388, 408
Diez Mandamientos, 468
Dimas, San, 440
diócesis, 246, **484**
Dios
creación de, 86–90
imagen de, 90
Reino de, 72, 192–194, 416–418, 432, 448, 456
tres Personas en un solo, 136–142, 450, **485**
Ver también Santísima Trinidad
discípulos, 72, 414
domingo, 64, 178
dones, 84, 226
Donovan, Jean, 424
Doxología (Gloria al Padre), 478

enfermedad, 366
esperanza, **312**–314, 474, **484**
Espíritu Santo
venida del, 72–75, 260
como Dios, 450
como guía, 104, 262, 328
como parte de la Santísima Trinidad, 138–142
oración al, 480
obra del, 222, 348–350
Eucaristía, 156–158, 210, 348–350, 460–464
Evangelio, 446, **484**
evangelios, **190**, 444–446, **485**

familia, 116–122
fariseo y publicano, 168
fe, 262, **312**–314, 474, **485**
Felícitas, Santa, 268
Francisco de Asís, San, 112
fuente bautismal, 466

Génesis, 86
Genoveva, Santa, 320
Gloria al Padre (Doxología), 142, 478
gracia, 328–**330**, 348, **485**
gran mandamiento, 468
Gregorio, San, 252

Hechos de los Apóstoles, 446

Iglesia, 104–**106**, 452, 466, **485**
historia de la, 396–402
líderes de la, 240–246, 378–380, 452
atributos de la, 454
misión de la, 190, 272–278, 412–418
preceptos de la, 328–**330**
unidad de la, 222–226, 256–262, 472
obra de la, 412–418
culto de la, 156
Iglesia doméstica, 120–122
infierno, **432–434**, 456, **485**
Iniciación, sacramentos de, 342–350, 464, **486**
Isaac, 396
Isaac Jogues, San, 356
Isabel, Santa, 118
Isabel de Hungría, Santa, 372

Jairo, hija de, 360–362
Jesucristo
Nacimiento de, 32–35
elección de Pedro, 240–242
en la conversión de Pablo, 326
discípulos de, 102, 400–402, 414
Buena Nueva de, 188–192
como curador, 360–362
Última Cena, 154
como Mesías, 194
nombres y títulos de, 24, 27, 474
nueva vida en, 64, 67, 344–346, 430
como parte de la Santísima Trinidad, 138–142
oración de, 172
Resurrección y Ascensión de, 56–59, 64–67, 208–210, 222, 430
sacrificio de, 206
segunda venida de, 432, 456
como Hijo de Dios, 450
en la sinagoga, 192
enseñanzas de, 72, 104, 138, 168–170, 194, 296–298, 310
obra de, 220–226, 398
José, hijo de Jacob, 292–294
José Vaz, Beato, 284
Juan Bautista, San, 27
Juan, Evangelio según, 190
Juan de Mata, San, 148
Juan, San, 430
Juanito Manzano, 272–274
Jueves Santo, 56
judío, pueblo, 154, 210, 396–400
juicio, 432, 456
juicio final, **434**, 456, **485**
justicia, **418**, **485**

Kevin, San, 402

ley del amor, **298, 485**
líderes, 240–246
liturgia, **156**, 460–466, **485**
Liturgia de la Palabra, 460–462
litúrgicos, tiempos y colores, 466
llamado, 382
Lucas, Evangelio según, 190
lugares sagrados, 466
Luis, Beato, 128
luz, 24–27, 308–310

Mandamientos, 468
Marcos, Evangelio según, 190
Margarita de Escocia, Santa, 388
María, Beata, 128
Mariana de Jesús, Santa, 232
María, Madre de Dios, 16–19, 118–120, 262, 458
María Magdalena, Santa, 208, 216
mártir, 304
Mateo, Evangelio según, 190
matrimonio, 376–382, 464
Matrimonio, sacramento del, 376–**382,** 464, **485**
Merton, Thomas, 180
Metodio, San, 40
Mesías, 192–**194,** 450, **485**
Ver también Jesucristo
Misa, 32, 152, 156–158, 190–192, 210, 460–462
misión, 272–**278,** 414, 452, **486**
misioneros, 40, 43, 276–**278,** 424, **485**
misterio, 136, **140**
Misterio Pascual, 208–**210, 485**
moral, 468–474
muerte, 428–430, 456

Navidad, tiempo de, 32–35
nueva tierra, 430
nueva vida, 344–346, 430
nuevo cielo, 430
Nuevo Testamento, 190, 444–450

obispos, 244–**246,** 380, **485**
oración, 120, 168–**170, 485**
Ver también oraciones individuales en las páginas 476–482 y al comienzo y final de cada capítulo
oración de los fieles, **174, 486**
Oración del Señor, 170–172, 476–478
Orden, **380**–382, 464, **486**
Ordinario, Tiempo, 16–19, 40–43, 466
ornamentos, **466**

P

Pablo, San , 274–276, 326, 380, 446–448
Padrenuestro , 170–172
Papa, **244,** 452, **486**
parábolas, 446, **486**
Pascua judía, 154, **210, 486**
pascual, cirio, 466
Pascua, tiempo de, 64–67, 158, 466
párroco, 246
parroquias, 246
Patricio, San, 136–138, 402
paz, **418, 486**
pecado, 90, **330,** 366, **486**
Pedro Canisio, San, 200
Pedro, San, 240–244, 348
Penitencia, 330, 364–366
Pentecostés, 72–75, **262, 486**
perdón, 292–294, 330–332
Perpetua, Santa, 268
persecución, 400–402
petición, **174, 486**
Pío, San, 336
preceptos de la Iglesia, 328–**330, 486**
promesas, 204–206
purgatorio, 262, **432–434,** 456, **486**

Reconciliación, sacramento de la , 328–330, 364–366, 464
Reino de Dios, 72, 192–**194,** 418, 432, 448, 456, **486**
responsabilidad, **90, 486**
Resurrección, 56, 64–67, 208–**210,** 430, **486**

Sabbat, 400
Sábado Santo, 56
sabiduría, 470
sacerdotes, 364, 378–380
sacramentales, 464
sacramentos, 156, 210, 246, 328, 348–**350, 486**
de Curación, 360–**366,** 464, **486**
de Iniciación, 342–**350,** 464, **486**
al Servicio de la comunidad, 376–**382,** 464, **486**
sacrificio, 204–**206, 486**
Sagrada Comunión, 158, 344–346, 460–462
Ver también Misa
Sagrada Escritura, **192,** 444–448
salvador, 192
Ver también Biblia
santidad, 260–262
Santísima Trinidad, 88, 122, **136**–142, **138,** 156–350, 450, **487**
Santísimo Sacramento, **158, 487**
Ver también Eucaristía
santo, 64
santos, 16, 262, 402
Ver también nombres individuales de los santos
Sara, 396
Saulo, 326
Ver también Pablo, San
segunda venida de Cristo, 456, **487**
señal de la cruz, 51, 142, 462, 476
Servicio de la comunidad, sacramentos al, 376–**382,** 464, **486**
sinagoga, 192
solidaridad, 472

tabernáculo, 158, **466**
talento, **226**
Torá, 444
Triduo Pascual, 56–59

Última Cena, 154, 158
Ver también Misa
Unción de los enfermos, sacramento de la, 364–366, 464, **487**
unidad , **90,** 222, 256–262, 268, 362

vela, 308
Viernes Santo, 56
vigilia, 56
Vigilia Pascual, 56, 59, 344, **485**
virtudes, 312–**314,** 474, **487**
virtudes teologales, **474, 487**
Visitación, **118, 487**
votos, **378, 487**

Boldfaced numbers refer to pages on which the terms are defined.

Abraham (Abram), 397–399
Act of Contrition, 483
Act of Faith, Hope, and Love, 479
Acts of the Apostles, 447
Advent, 28–31, 467
altar, 467
ambo, 467
Anointing of the Sick, Sacrament of, **365**–367, 465, **488**
Apostles, 103–105, 245–**247**, 261, 275, 415–417, 455, **488**
Apostle's Creed, 143, 481
authority, **123**, **488**

Baptism, 63, 68, 71, 345–351, 383, 419, 465
baptismal font, 467
Bartholomew Osypiuk, Blessed, 305
basilica, 467
Beatitudes, **299**, 471, **488**
Bible, **103**, 191, 445–449
bishops, 245–**247**, 381, **488**
Blessed Sacrament, **159**, **488**
See also Eucharist
blessing, 175, 465
Body of Christ, **223**, 227, 453, **488**
See also Church
Browman, Thea, 165
Brigid, Saint, 403

C

calling, 383
candles, 309, 467
cathedrals, 467
catholic, **277**, 455, **488**
celebrations, 153–155
See also feast days
Chardin, Pierre Teilhard de, 97
choices, 205–207, 325–335
chrism, 345–**347**, **488**
Christians, 103–105, 223–227, 311, 401–**403**, **488**
Christmas Season, 36–39
Church, 105–**107**, 453, **488**
- history of, 397–403
- leaders of, 241–247, 379–381, 453
- marks of, 455
- mission of, 191, 273–279, 413–419
- precepts of, 329–**331**
- unity of, 223–227, 257–263, 473
- work of, 412–**418**
- worship of, 157

Clement of Rome, Saint, 409
Columba, Saint, 403
Commandments, 469
communion of the saints, **263**, 453, 483
community, 91, **105**–107, 157, 257–259, 453, **488**
Confession, 331, 365–367
Confirmation, Sacrament of, 349–351, 383, 465
conscience, 329–**331**, 473, **488**
covenant, 397–**399**, **488**
create, **87**–91, **488**
Creeds, **143**, 451–459, 481, **488**
cross, 55
cycle of life, 429
Cyril, Saint, 44

deacons, 247, 379–381
death, 429–431, 457
devotions, 467
diocese, 247, **488**
disciples, 76
Dismas, Saint, 441
domestic Church, 121–123
Donovan, Jean, 425
Doxology (Glory to the Father), 479

Easter Season, 68–71, 159, 467
Easter Vigil, 60, 63, 345, **489**
Elizabeth, Saint, 119
Elizabeth of Hungary, Saint, 373
Eucharist, 157–159, 211, 349–351, 461, 465

faith, 263, **313**–315, 475, **489**
family, 117–123
feast days
- of Blessed, 129, 285
- Christmas, 36–39
- during Ordinary Time, 20, 44
- of Pentecost, 76–79
- of Saints, 113, 149, 201, 217, 233, 253, 269, 321, 337, 357, 373, 389, 409

Felicity, Saint, 269
forgiveness, 293–295, 331–333
Francis of Assisi, Saint, 113

Genesis, 87
Genevieve, Saint, 321
gifts, 85, 227
Glory to the Father (Doxology), 143, 479
God
- creation of, 87–91
- image of, 91
- kingdom of, 76, 193–195, 417–419, 433, 449, 457
- three persons in one, 137–143, 451, 489

See also Holy Trinity
Good Friday, 60
good news, 76, 189–195
gospel, 447, **489**
Gospels, **191**, 445–447, **489**
grace, 329–**331**, 349, **489**
Great Commandment, 469
Gregory, Saint, 253

Hail Mary, 477
Healing, Sacraments of, 361–**367**, 465, **490**
heaven, **433**–435, 457, **489**
hell, **433**–435, 457, **489**
holiness, 261–263
holy, 68
Holy Communion, 159, 345–347, 461–463
See also Mass
Holy Orders, **381**–383, 465, **489**
Holy Saturday, 60
Holy Spirit
- coming of, 76–79, 261
- as God, 451
- as guide, 105, 263, 329
- part of Holy Trinity, 139–143
- prayer to, 481
- work of, 223, 349–351

Holy Thursday, 60
Holy Trinity, 89, 123, 137–143, 139, 157, 451, **489**
holy water, 68, 71
hope, **313**–315, 475, **489**

Initiation, Sacraments of, 343–351, 465, 491
intercession, **175**, **489**
Isaac, 397
Isaac Jogues, Saint, 357

Jairus's daughter, 361–363
Jesus Christ
- birth of, 36–39
- choosing of Peter, 241–243
- at conversion of Paul, 327
- followers of, 103, 401–403, 415
- good news of, 189–193
- as healer, 361–363
- Last Supper, 155
- as Messiah, 195
- names and titles of, 28, 31, 475
- new life in, 68, 71, 345–347, 431
- part of the Holy Trinity, 139–143
- prayer of, 173
- Resurrection and Ascension of, 60–63, 68–71, 211, 223, 431
- sacrifice of, 207
- second coming of, 433, 457
- as Son of God, 451
- in Synagogue, 193
- teachings of, 76, 105, 139, 169–171, 195, 297–299, 311
- work of, 221–227, 399

Jewish people, 155, 211, 397–401
John, Gospel of, 191
John, Saint, 431
Johnny Appleseed, 273–275
John of Matha, Saint, 149
John the Baptist, Saint, 28
Joseph, son of Jacob, 293–295
Joseph Vaz, Blessed, 285
judgment, 433, 457
justice, **419**, **489**

K

Kevin, Saint, 403
kingdom of God, 76, 193–195, 419, 433, 449, 457, **489**

L

last judgment, **435**, 457, **489**
Last Supper, 155, 159
See also Mass
law of love, **299**, **489**
leaders, 241–247
Lent, 52–55, 467
letters, 447–449
light, 28–31, 309–311
liturgical seasons and colors, 467
liturgy, **157**, 461–467, **489**
Liturgy of the Word, 461–463
Lord's Day, 68, 159
Lord's Prayer, 171–173, 477–479
Lord's Supper, 60
See also Eucharist
love, 419
  of enemies, 297–299
  of others, 105, 117–123
  as virtue, 315, 475
Luigi, Blessed, 129
Luke, Gospel of, 191

M

Margaret of Scotland, Saint, 389
Maria, Blessed, 129
Mark, Gospel of, 191
Marks of the Church, 455
marriage, 377–383, 465
martyr, 305
Mary, Mother of God, 20–23, 119–121, 263, 459
Mary Ann of Quito, Saint, 233
Mary Magdalene, Saint, 209, 217
Mass, 36, 153, 157–159, 191–193, 211, 461–463
Matrimony, Sacrament of, 377–**383**, 465, **489**
Matthew, Gospel of, 191
Merton, Thomas, 181
messiah, 193–**195**, 451, **490**
See also Jesus Christ
Methodius, Saint, 44
mission, 273–279, 415, 453, **490**
missionaries, 44, 47, 277–**279**, 425, **490**
morality, 469–475
mystery, 137, **141**

N

new earth, 431
new heaven, 431
new life, 345–347, 431
New Testament, 191, 445–449, 451

O

Old Testament, 293–295, 445
Ordinary Time, 20–23, 44–47, 467
Our Father, 171–173

parables, 447, **490**
parishes, 247
Paschal candle, 467
Paschal mystery, 209–**211**, **490**
Passover, 155, **211**, **490**
pastor, 247
Patrick, Saint, 137–139, 403
Paul, Saint, 275–277, 327, 381, 447–449
peace, **419**, **490**
Penance, 331, 365–367
Pentecost, 76–79, **263**, **490**
Perpetua, Saint, 269
persecution, 401–403
Peter, Saint, 241–245, 349
Peter Canisius, Saint, 201
petition, **175**, **490**
Pharisee and the Tax Collector, 169
Pio, Saint, 337
pope, **245**, 453, **490**
praise, **175**, **490**
prayer, 169–**171**, **490**
See also individual prayers on pages 477–483 and at beginning and end of each chapter
precepts of the Church, 329–**331**, **490**
priests, 365, 379–381
promises, 205–207
purgatory, 263, 433–**435**, 457, **490**

Reconciliation, Sacrament of, 329–331, 365–367, 465, 490
responsibility, **91**
Resurrection, 60, 68–71, 209–**211**, 431, **490**
Revelation, Book of, 447

Sabbath, 401
sacramentals, 465
sacraments, 157, 211, 247, 329, 349–**351**, **490**
  of Healing, 361–**367**, 465, **490**
  of Initiation, 343–**351**, 465, **491**
  of Service, 377–**383**, 465, **491**
sacred places, 467
sacrifice, 205–**207**, **491**
saints, 20, 263, 403
See also names of individual Saints
Sarah, 397
Saul, 327
See also Paul, Saint
savior, 193
Scripture, **193**, 445–449
See also Bible
second coming of Christ, 457, **491**
Service, Sacraments of, 377–**383**, 465, **491**
sickness, 367
Sign of the Cross, 55, 143, 463, 477
sin, 91, **331**, 367, **491**
solidarity, 473
Sunday, 68, 179
synagogue, 193

tabernacle, 159, **467**
talent, **227**
Ten Commandments, 469
thanksgiving, 175
theological virtues, **475**, **491**
Torah, 445
Triduum, 60–63

unity, 91, 223, 257–269, 363

vestments, **467**
vigil, 60
virtues, 313–**315**, 475, **491**
Visitation, **119**, **491**
vows, **379**, **491**

wisdom, 471
worship, 157–**159**, 175, 491

Illustration Credits
86, 87 (cr) Gray Glover; 86, 87 (cr) Lori Lohstoeter; 96, 97 (bl) Lois Woolley; 100, 101 (b) Jean Hirashima; 102, 103 (cr) Adam Hook; 106, 107 (br) Judy Stead; 112, 113 (bl) Lois Woolley; 118, 119 (cr) Phil Howe; 128, 129 (bl) Lois Woolley; 134, 135 (b) Gray Glover; 136, 137 (b) Paul Bachem; 138, 139 (b) Paul Bachem; 148, 149 (bl) Lois Woolley
154, 155 (cr) Robert Sauber; 164, 165 (bl) Lois Woolley; 168, 169 (b) Kevin Beilfuss; 178, 179 (br) Judy Stead; 180, 181 (bl) Lois Woolley; 188, 189 (bl) Peter Fiore; 190, 191 (br) Judy Stead; 192, 193 (b) Bill Maughan; 200, 201 (bl) Lois Woolley; 208, 209 (b) Kevin Bielfuss; 210, 211 (br) Judy Stead; 216, 217 (bl) Lois Woolley; 224, 225 (bl) Adam Hook; 230, 231 (br) Judy Stead; 232, 233 (bl) Lois Woolley; 240, 241 (br) Micheal Jaroszko; 242, 243 (tr) Michael Jaroszko; 242, 243 (cr) Michael Jaroszko; 246, 247 (br) Judy Stead; 252, 253 (bl) Lois Woolley; 258, 259 (br) Judy Stead; 260, 261 (b) Jeff Preston; 262, 263 (cr) Jeff Preston; 268, 269 (bl) Lois Woolley; 270, 271 (b) Phil Howe; 272, 273 (bl) Frank Riccio; 274, 275 Judy Stead; 276, 277 (b) Kevin Bielfuss; 284, 285 (bl) Lois Woolley; 292, 293 (cl) Bill Maughan; 292, 293 (bl) Bill Maughan; 294, 295 (cr) Bill Maughan; 296, 297 (b) Michael Jaroszko; 304, 305 (bl) Lois Woolley; 308, 309 (b) Corey Wolfe; 310, 311 (cr) Corey Wolfe; 318, 319 (br) Judy Stead; 320, 321 (bl) Lois Woolley; 324, 325 (bl) Philip Howe; 326, 327 (tr) Mario Capaldi; 328, 329 (c) Judy Stead; 336, 337 (bl) Lois Woolley; 342, 343 (bl) Lori Lohstoeter; 348, 349 (bl) Robert Rodriguez; 350, 351 (br) Judy Stead; 356, 357 (bl) Lois Woolley; 360, 361 (b) Dave Henderson; 362, 363 (tr) Dave Henderson; 366, 367 (b) Judy Stead; 372, 373 (bl) Lois Woolley; 386, 387 (cr) Judy Stead; 388, 389 (bl) Lois Woolley; 396, 397 (b) Jeff Preston; 400, 401 (b) Tom Newsom; 402, 403 (br) Judy Stead; 406, 407 (cr) Judy Stead; 408, 409 (bl) Lois Woolley; 414, 415 (tr) Adam Hook; 418, 419 (br) Judy Stead; 424, 425 (bl) Lois Woolley; 428, 429 (bl) Lori Lohstoeter; 428, 429 (bkgd) Lori Lohstoeter; 438, 439 (bl) Judy Stead; 440, 441 (bl) Lois Woolley.

Photo Credits
82, 83 (b) Tom Stack & Associates; 84, 85 (bl) Ed McDonald; 88, 89 (bc) Rob Gage/Taxi/Getty Images; 88, 89 (r) Ed McDonald; 90, 91 (cr) David Young-Wolff/PhotoEdit; 92, 93 (cr) Jim Cummins/Taxi/Getty Images; 98, 99 (bl) Eric Camden; 98, 99 Eric Camden; 102, 103 (bl) Ed McDonald; 104, 105 (cl) Tom & Dee Ann McCarthy/CORBIS; 104, 105 (bl) LWA-Dann Tardif/CORBIS; 106, 107 (c) Brand X Pictures/Getty Images; 108, 109 (cl) Myrleen Ferguson Kate/PhotoEdit; 112, 113 (cr) Eric Camden; 114, 115 Walter Hodges/Corbis; 116, 117 (bl) Eric Camden; 120, 121 Sonny Senser; 122, 123 (tr) Adam Smith/Taxi/Getty Images; 124, 125 (br) Myrleen Ferguson Cate/PhotoEdit; 140, 141 (bl) Ken Chernus/The Image Bank/Getty Images; 140, 141 (cl) Thinkstock/Royalty-Free/Getty Images; 142, 143 (cr) James L. Shaffer/Shaffer Photography; 144, 145 (br) Myrleen Ferguson Kate/PhotoEdit; 148, 149 (cr) Ed McDonald; 150, 151 (bl) Jose Carrillo/PhotoEdit; 150, 151 (br) Harcourt/Corel Stock Photo Library; 152, 153 (bl) FK Photo/Corbis; 154, 155 (br) Sonny Senser; 156, 157 (cl) Jim Whitmer; 156, 157 (b) Gene Plastaid/The Crosiers; 158, 159 (cr) Bill Wittman; 160, 161 (cr) James L. Shaffer/Shaffer Photography; 164, 165 (cr) Tom Stewart/ Corbis; 166, 167 (bl) Cleo Photography; 170, 171 (br) Ed McDonald; 172-175 (b) Eric Camden; 176, 177 (br) Myrleen Ferguson Cate/ PhotoEdit; 180, 181 (cr) Ed McDonald; 186, 187 (b) Ed McDonald; 196, 197 (br) Myrleen Ferguson Cate/ PhotoEdit; 202, 203 (bl) Eric Camden; 202, 203 (bkgd) Photowood Inc./CORBIS; 204, 205 (bl) Ed McDonald; 206, 207 (tr) Ed McDonald; 212, 213 (br) Jim Whitmer; 216, 217 (cr) David Young-Wolff/Stone/Getty Image; 218, 219 (b) Kevin Cozad/O'Brien Productions/CORBIS; 220, 221 (bl) Eric Camden; 222, 223 (cr) Bill Wittman; 226, 227 (cr) AFP PHOTO/Stan Honda/Corbis; 228, 229 (cr) Rubberball Productions; 232, 233 (cr) Bill Wittman; 238, 239 (b) Eric Camden; 242, 243 (br) Ed McDonald; 244, 245 (bl) Vittoriano Rastelli/Corbis; 246, 247 (cr) Bill Wittman; 248, 249 (br) Gene Plastaid/The Crosiers; 254, 255 (b) Robert Harding World Imagery/Robert Harding Picture Library Ltd/Alamy.com; 256, 257 (bl) Mary Kate Denny/PhotoEdit; 258, 259 (tr) Patrick Robert/Corbis Sygma; 258, 259 (b) Digital Vision/Getty Images; 264, 265 (br) Novastock/PhotoEdit; 264, 265 (br) getty/taxi/Walter Wick; 268, 269 (cr) Ariel Skelley/ Corbis; 280, 281 (br) Jim Whitmer; 290, 291 (b) Eric Camden; 294, 295 (br) Ed McDonald; 298, 299 (cr) Photodisc Red/Getty Images; 300, 301 (r) Ed McDonald; 306, 307 (b) Adam Woolfitt/ Corbis; 312, 313 (b) Sonny Senser; 316, 317 (cr) David Toase/PhotoDisc; 320, 321 (cr) Eric Camden; 322,

323 (b) LWA Dan Tardif/Corbis; 324, 325 (bkgd) Ed McDonald; 330, 331 (br) Ed McDonald; 332, 333 (br) Myrleen Ferguson Cate/PhotoEdit; 336, 337 (cr) Warren Morgan/Corbis; 344, 345 Jack Holtel/Photographik Company; 346, 347 (cr) Ed McDonald; 346, 347 (cr) Gene Plastaid/The Crosiers; 350, 351 (cl) OSF/Leach/Animals Animals; 350, 351 (bkgd) Sonny Senser; 352, 353 (br) Eric Camden; 358, 359 (b) Ed McDonald; 362, 363 (br) Ed McDonald; 364, 365 (cl) Jack Holtel/Photographik Company; 364, 365 (bkgd) Sonny Senser; 366, 367 (cr) Jim Whitmer; 368, 369 (cr) Myrleen Cate/Stone/Getty Images; 372, 373 (cr) Ronnie Kaufman/ Corbis/ Stock Market; 374, 375 (b) Ed McDonald; 376, 377 (cl) Ed McDonald; 376, 377 (bl) Ed McDonald; 378, 379 (cr) Bill Wittman; 380, 381 (cl) Comstock Images/Royalty-Free; 380, 381 (bkgd) Sonny Senser; 382, 383 (cr) Paul Barton/Corbis; 384, 385 (cr) Gene Plastaid/The Crosiers; 388, 389 (cr) Brad Martin/Image Bank/Getty Images; 394, 395 (b) plainpicture/Kucher, W./Alamy.com; 394, 395 (bkgd) Gordon Whitten/Corbis; 402, 403 (cr) Bill Wittman; 404, 405 (cr) David Keaton/Corbis; 408, 409 (cr) Ed McDonald; 410, 411 (b) Steven Ruben/The Image Works, Inc.; 412, 413 (bl) Charles Mistral/Alamy.com; 414, 415 (bl) Sonny Senser; 416, 417 (tl) David Turnley/Corbis; 416, 417 (bl) Stephen Epstein/Ponka Wonka; 418, 419 (tr) Jayanata Shaw/Reuters New Media, Inc.; 420, 421 (bl) Bill Wittman; 426, 427 (bl) Ed McDonald; 430, 431 (bl) Ed McDonald; 432, 433 (bl) Eric Camden; 434, 435 (c) Gene Plastaid/The Crosiers; 436, 437 (br) Natural Selection; 440, 441 (cr) Ronnie Kaufman/Corbis.

Acknowledgments

For permission to translate/reprint copyrighted material, grateful acknowledgment is made to the following sources:

Carolrhoda Books, Inc., a division of Lerner Publishing Group: Adapted from *Keep the Lights Burning, Abbie* (Retitled: "Abbie's Light") by Peter and Connie Roop. Text copyright 1985 by Carolrhoda Books, Inc., a division of Lerner Publishing Group.

GRM Associates, Inc., on behalf of the Estate of Ida M. Cullen: From "The Wakeupworld" (Retitled: "Song of the Wake-Up-World") in *On These I Stand* by Countee Cullen. Text copyright © 1940 by Harper & Brothers; text copyright renewed © 1968 by Ida M. Cullen.

Hope Publishing Co., Carol Stream, IL 60188: Lyrics from "We Are the Church" by Richard Avery and Donald Marsh. Lyrics copyright © 1972 by Hope Publishing Co. Lyrics from "Spirit-Friend" by Tom Colvin. Lyrics © 1969 by Hope Publishing Co.

Integrity Media, Inc., 1000 Cody Road, Mobile, AL 36695: Lyrics from "The Servant Song" by Richard Gillard. Lyrics © 1977 by Scripture In Song (c/o Integrity Music) /ASCAP.

International Commission on English in the Liturgy, Inc.: From the English translation of "Psalm 33: Lord, Let Your Mercy" and "Psalm 19: Their Message Goes Out" in *Lectionary for Mass*. Translation © 1969, 1981, 1997 by International Committee on English in the Liturgy, Inc. (ICEL).

Obra Nacional de la Buena Prensa, A.C.: From "Salmo 32" in *Leccionario I* by Conferencia Episcopal Mexicana. Text copyright © by Obra Nacional de la Buena Prensa, A.C. From "Salmo 18" in *Leccionario III* by Conferencia Episcopal Mexicana. Text copyright © 1998 by Obra Nacional de la Buena Prensa, A.C.

OCP Publications 5536 NE Hassalo, Portland, OR 97213: Lyrics from "Veni, Sancte, Spiritus" by Christopher Walker. Lyrics © 1981, 1982 by Christopher Walker.

Patricia Joyce Shelly: Lyrics from "All Grownups, All Children" by Patricia Joyce Shelly. Lyrics © 1977 by Patricia Joyce Shelly.